Modern CMake for C++

Discover a better approach to building, testing, and packaging your software

Rafał Świdziński

BIRMINGHAM—MUMBAI

Modern CMake for C++

Copyright © 2022 Packt Publishing

All rights reserved. No part of this book may be reproduced, stored in a retrieval system, or transmitted in any form or by any means, without the prior written permission of the publisher, except in the case of brief quotations embedded in critical articles or reviews.

Every effort has been made in the preparation of this book to ensure the accuracy of the information presented. However, the information contained in this book is sold without warranty, either express or implied. Neither the author, nor Packt Publishing or its dealers and distributors, will be held liable for any damages caused or alleged to have been caused directly or indirectly by this book.

Packt Publishing has endeavored to provide trademark information about all of the companies and products mentioned in this book by the appropriate use of capitals. However, Packt Publishing cannot guarantee the accuracy of this information.

Associate Group Product Manager: Richa Tripathi
Publishing Product Manager: Rohit Rajkumar
Senior Editor: Mark Dsouza
Content Development Editor: Divya Vijayan
Technical Editor: Joseph Aloocaran
Copy Editor: Safis Editing
Project Coordinator: Rashika Ba
Proofreader: Safis Editing
Indexer: Tejal Daruwale Soni
Production Designer: Jyoti Chauhan
Marketing Coordinator: Elizabeth Varghese

First published: February 2022

Production reference: 2120422

Published by Packt Publishing Ltd.
Livery Place
35 Livery Street
Birmingham
B3 2PB, UK.

ISBN 978-1-80107-005-8

www.packt.com

To my family: my parents, Bożena and Bogdan, my sisters, Ewelina and Justyna, and my wife, Katarzyna, for their ongoing support and advice.

– Rafał Świdziński

Contributors

About the author

Rafał Świdziński works as a staff engineer at Google. With over 10 years of professional experience as a full stack developer, he has been able to experiment with a vast multitude of programming languages and technologies. During this time, he has been building software under his own company and for corporations including Cisco Meraki, Amazon, and Ericsson.

Originally from Łódź, Poland, he now lives in London, UK, from where he runs a YouTube channel, "Smok," discussing topics related to software development. He tackles technical problems, including real-life and work-related challenges encountered by many people in the field. Throughout his work, he explains the technical concepts in detail and demystifies the art and science behind the role of software engineer. His primary focus is on high-quality code and the craftsmanship of programming.

About the reviewers

Sergio Guidi Tabosa Pessoa is a software engineer with more than 30 years of experience in software development and maintenance, from complex enterprise software projects to modern mobile applications. In the early days, he worked primarily with the Microsoft stack, but soon discovered the power of the UNIX and Linux operating systems. Even though he has worked with many languages over the years, C and C++ remain his favorite languages for their power and speed.

He has a bachelor's degree in computer science and an MBA in IT management and is always hungry to learn new technologies, break code, and learn from his mistakes. He currently lives in Brazil with his wife, two Yorkshire Terriers, and two cockatiels.

> *First and foremost, I would like to thank all the people involved in this project, including the author for crafting such a great piece of work, and Packt Publishing for giving me this opportunity. I also would like to thank my beautiful wife, Lucia, as well as Touché and Lion, for their patience and for allowing me the time needed to help with this book.*

Holding an engineering degree from ENSEEIHT and a Ph.D. in computer science from UVSQ in France, **Eric Noulard** has been writing and compiling source code in a variety of languages for 20 years. A user of CMake since 2006, he has also been an active contributor to the project for several years. During his career, Eric has worked for private companies and government agencies. He is now employed by Antidot, a software vendor responsible for developing and marketing high-end information retrieval technology and solutions.

Mohammed Alqumairi is a software engineer at Cisco Meraki with experience in developing critical and performant backend services using a variety of languages and frameworks, with a particular focus on modern C++, CMake, and the Poco libraries. Mohammed graduated with honors from City, University of London, with a B.Sc. in Computer Science.

Table of Contents

Preface

Section 1: Introducing CMake

1
First Steps with CMake

Technical requirements	4
Understanding the basics	5
What is CMake?	5
How does it work?	7
Installing CMake on different platforms	10
Docker	11
Windows	12
Linux	13
macOS	13
Building from the source	14
Mastering the command line	14
CMake	15
CTest	26
CPack	27
The CMake GUI	28
CCMake	29
Navigating the project files	30
The source tree	30
The build tree	30
Listfiles	31
CMakeLists.txt	32
CMakeCache.txt	33
The Config-files for packages	34
The cmake_install.cmake, CTestTestfile.cmake, and CPackConfig.cmake files	35
CMakePresets.json and CMakeUserPresets.json	35
Ignoring files in Git	39
Discovering scripts and modules	40
Scripts	40
Utility modules	41
Find-modules	41
Summary	42
Further reading	42

2
The CMake Language

Technical requirements	44	**Understanding control structures in CMake**	**63**
The basics of the CMake Language syntax	**45**	Conditional blocks	63
Comments	45	Loops	68
Command invocations	47	Command definitions	70
Command arguments	49	**Useful commands**	**76**
Working with variables	**53**	The message() command	76
Variable references	54	The include() command	78
Using the environment variables	55	The include_guard() command	79
Using the cache variables	57	The file() command	79
How to correctly use the variable scope in CMake	59	The execute_process() command	79
		Summary	**80**
Using lists	**61**	**Further reading**	**81**

3
Setting Up Your First CMake Project

Technical requirements	84	Cross-compilation – what are host and target systems?	100
Basic directives and commands	**85**	Abbreviated variables	100
Specifying the minimum CMake version – cmake_minimum_required()	85	Host system information	101
Defining languages and metadata – project()	86	Does the platform have 32-bit or 64-bit architecture?	102
		What is the endianness of the system?	103
Partitioning your project	**87**	**Configuring the toolchain**	**103**
Scoped subdirectories	90	Setting the C++ standard	103
Nested projects	92	Insisting on standard support	104
External projects	92	Vendor-specific extensions	105
Thinking about the project structure	**93**	Interprocedural optimization	105
Scoping the environment	**99**	Checking for supported compiler features	106
Discovering the operating system	99	Compiling a test file	106

Disabling in-source builds	108	Further reading	111
Summary	110		

Section 2: Building With CMake

4
Working with Targets

Technical requirements	116	Using a custom command as a generator	132
The concept of a target	116	Using a custom command as a target hook	134
Dependency graph	118		
Visualizing dependencies	121	**Understanding generator expressions**	135
Target properties	122		
What are transitive usage requirements?	123	General syntax	136
Dealing with conflicting propagated properties	126	Types of evaluation	137
		Examples to try out	144
Meet the pseudo targets	128	**Summary**	148
Build targets	130	Further reading	148
Writing custom commands	131		

5
Compiling C++ Sources with CMake

Technical requirements	152	General level	165
The basics of compilation	152	Function inlining	167
How compilation works	153	Loop unrolling	168
Initial configuration	155	Loop vectorization	170
Managing sources for targets	156	**Managing the process of compilation**	171
Preprocessor configuration	158	Reducing compilation time	171
Providing paths to included files	158	Finding mistakes	176
Preprocessor definitions	159		
Configuring the headers	162	**Summary**	182
Configuring the optimizer	164	Further reading	183

6
Linking with CMake

Technical requirements	186	Dynamically linked duplicated symbols	197
Getting the basics of linking right	186	Use namespaces – don't count on a linker	199
Building different library types	191	The order of linking and unresolved symbols	200
Static libraries	191	Separating main() for testing	202
Shared libraries	192	Summary	205
Shared modules	193	Further reading	206
Position-independent code	193		
Solving problems with the One Definition Rule	194		

7
Managing Dependencies with CMake

Technical requirements	208	Git-cloning dependencies for projects that don't use Git	228
How to find installed packages	209		
Discovering legacy packages with FindPkgConfig	215	Using ExternalProject and FetchContent modules	229
Writing your own find-modules	219	ExternalProject	230
Working with Git repositories	224	FetchContent	236
Providing external libraries through Git submodules	224	Summary	240
		Further reading	241

Section 3: Automating With CMake

8
Testing Frameworks

Technical requirements	246	Using CTest to standardize testing in CMake	248
Why are automated tests worth the trouble?	246	Build-and-test mode	250

Test mode	251	GMock	274
Creating the most basic unit test for CTest	257	Generating test coverage reports	281
Structuring our projects for testing	263	Avoiding the SEGFAULT gotcha	287
Unit-testing frameworks	267	Summary	287
Catch2	268	Further reading	288
GTest	271		

9
Program Analysis Tools

Technical requirements	292	Link what you use	302
Enforcing the formatting	292	Dynamic analysis with Valgrind	303
Using static checkers	297	Memcheck	303
Clang-Tidy	301	Memcheck-Cover	308
Cpplint	301	Summary	310
Cppcheck	301	Further reading	311
include-what-you-use	302		

10
Generating Documentation

Technical requirements	314	Summary	323
Adding Doxygen to your project	314	Further reading	324
Generating documentation with a modern look	321	Other documentation generation utilities	324

11
Installing and Packaging

Technical requirements	326	Installing logical targets	332
Exporting without installation	326	Low-level installation	336
Installing projects on the system	330	Invoking scripts during installation	344
		Creating reusable packages	346

Understanding the issues with relocatable targets	346	How to use components in find_package()	359
Installing target export files	348	How to use components in the install() command	360
Writing basic config-files	350		
Creating advanced config-files	353	**Packaging with CPack**	**362**
Generating package version files	357	**Summary**	**366**
Defining components	**359**	**Further reading**	**367**

12
Creating Your Professional Project

Technical requirements	**370**	Applying testing scenarios	393
Planning our work	**371**	Adding static analysis tools	396
Project layout	**375**	**Installing and packaging**	**398**
Object libraries	376	Installation of the library	399
Shared libraries versus static libraries	376	Installation of the executable	400
Project file structure	377	Packaging with CPack	401
Building and managing dependencies	**379**	**Providing the documentation**	**401**
Building the Calc library	381	Automatic documentation generation	402
Building the Calc Console executable	383	Not-so-technical documents of professional project	404
Testing and program analysis	**388**	**Summary**	**407**
Preparing the coverage module	390	**Further reading**	**408**
Preparing the Memcheck module	392		

Appendix
Miscellaneous Commands

The string() command	**412**	**The list() command**	**416**
Search and replace	412	Reading	416
Manipulation	413	Searching	416
Comparison	414	Modification	417
Hashing	414	Ordering	418
Generation	414	**The file() command**	**418**
JSON	415	Reading	418

Writing	419	Locking	420
Filesystem	419	Archiving	421
Path conversion	420		
Transfer	420	**The math() command**	**421**

Index

Other Books You May Enjoy

Preface

Creating top-notch software isn't an easy task. Developers researching this subject online frequently have problems determining which advice is up to date and which approaches have already been superseded by fresher, better practices. At the same time, most resources explain this process chaotically, without the proper background, context, and structure.

Modern CMake for C++ is an end-to-end guide offering a simpler experience, as it treats building C++ solutions in a comprehensive manner. It teaches you how to use CMake in your CMake projects, and also shows you what makes them maintainable, elegant, and clean. It guides you through the automation of complex tasks appearing in many projects, including building, testing, and packaging.

The book instructs you on how to form the source directories, as well as build targets and packages. As you progress, you will learn how to compile and link executables and libraries, how these processes work in detail, and how to optimize all steps to achieve the best results. You'll also understand how to add external dependencies to the project: third-party libraries, testing frameworks, program analysis tools, and documentation generators. Finally, you'll explore how to export, install, and package your solution for internal and external purposes.

After completing this book, you'll be able to use CMake confidently on a professional level.

Who this book is for

Learning the C++ language often isn't enough to prepare you for delivering projects to the highest standards. If you're interested in becoming a professional build engineer, a better software developer, or simply want to become proficient with CMake, if you'd like to understand how projects come together and why, if you're transitioning from a different build environment, or if you're interested in learning modern CMake from the ground up, then this book is for you.

What this book covers

Chapter 1, *First Steps with CMake*, covers how to install and use CMake's command line, along with what files make up the project.

Chapter 2, *The CMake Language*, provides key code information: comments, command invocations and arguments, variables, lists, and control structures.

Chapter 3, *Setting Up Your First CMake Project*, introduces the basic configuration of a project, the required CMake version, project metadata, and file structure, as well as the toolchain setup.

Chapter 4, *Working with Targets*, introduces the logical build targets that produce artifacts for executables and libraries.

Chapter 5, *Compiling C++ Sources with CMake*, explains how the details of compilation process works and how it can be controlled in a CMake project.

Chapter 6, *Linking with CMake*, provides general information on linking, static, and shared libraries. This chapter also explains how to structure a project so that it can be tested.

Chapter 7, *Managing Dependencies with CMake*, explains the dependency management methods available in modern CMake.

Chapter 8, *Testing Frameworks*, describes how to add the most popular testing frameworks to your project, as well as how to use the CTest utility available in the CMake toolset.

Chapter 9, *Program Analysis Tools*, covers how to perform automatic formatting, as well as static and dynamic analyses, in your project.

Chapter 10, *Generating Documentation*, explains how to use Doxygen to generate manuals for users straight from the C++ source code.

Chapter 11, *Installing and Packaging*, shows how to prepare your project to be used in other projects or installed on the system. We'll also see an explanation of the CPack utility.

Chapter 12, *Creating Your Professional Project*, sets out how to put together all the knowledge you have acquired hitherto in to a fully formed project.

Appendix: *Miscellaneous Commands*, provides a quick reference of the most popular commands: `string()`, `list()`, `file()`, and `math()`.

To get the most out of this book

Basic familiarity with C++ and Unix-like systems is assumed throughout the book. Although this isn't a strict requirement, it will prove helpful in fully understanding the examples given in this book.

This book targets CMake 3.20, but most of the techniques described should work from CMake 3.15 (features that were added after are usually highlighted).

All examples have been tested on Debian with the following packages installed:

```
clang-format clang-tidy cppcheck doxygen g++ gawk git
graphviz lcov libpqxx-dev libprotobuf-dev make pkg-config
protobuf-compiler tree valgrind vim wget
```

To experience the same environment, it is recommended to use the Docker images, as explained in *Chapter 1*.

If you are using the digital version of this book, we advise you to type the code yourself or access the code from the book's GitHub repository (a link is available in the next section). Doing so will help you avoid any potential errors related to the copying and pasting of code.

Download the example code files

You can download the example code files for this book from GitHub at `https://github.com/PacktPublishing/Modern-CMake-for-Cpp`. If there's an update to the code, it will be updated in the GitHub repository.

We also have other code bundles from our rich catalog of books and videos available at `https://github.com/PacktPublishing/`. Check them out!

Download the color images

We also provide a PDF file that has color images of the screenshots and diagrams used in this book. You can download it here: `https://static.packt-cdn.com/downloads/9781801070058_ColorImages.pdf`.

Conventions used

There are a number of text conventions used throughout this book.

`Code in text`: Indicates code words in the text, database table names, folder names, filenames, file extensions, pathnames, dummy URLs, user input, and Twitter handles. Here is an example: "Select `Debug`, `Release`, `MinSizeRel`, or `RelWithDebInfo` and specify it as follows."

A block of code is set as follows:

```
cmake_minimum_required(VERSION 3.20)
project(Hello)
add_executable(Hello hello.cpp)
```

When we wish to draw your attention to a particular part of a code block, the relevant lines or items are set in bold:

```
cmake_minimum_required(VERSION 3.20)
project(app)
message("Top level CMakeLists.txt")
add_subdirectory(api)
```

Any command-line input or output is written as follows:

```
cmake --build <dir> --parallel [<number-of-jobs>]
cmake --build <dir> -j [<number-of-jobs>]
```

Bold: Indicates a new term, an important word, or words that you see on screen. For instance, words in menus or dialog boxes appear in **bold**. Here is an example: "If all else fails and we need to use the big guns there is always **trace mode**."

> **Tips or Important Notes**
> Appear like this.

Get in touch

Feedback from our readers is always welcome.

General feedback: If you have questions about any aspect of this book, email us at customercare@packtpub.com and mention the book title in the subject of your message.

Errata: Although we have taken every care to ensure the accuracy of our content, mistakes do happen. If you have found a mistake in this book, we would be grateful if you would report this to us. Please visit www.packtpub.com/support/errata and fill in the form.

Piracy: If you come across any illegal copies of our works in any form on the internet, we would be grateful if you would provide us with the location address or website name. Please contact us at copyright@packt.com with a link to the material.

If you are interested in becoming an author: If there is a topic that you have expertise in and you are interested in either writing or contributing to a book, please visit authors.packtpub.com.

Share Your Thoughts

Once you've read *Modern CMake for C++*, we'd love to hear your thoughts! Scan the QR code below to go straight to the Amazon review page for this book and share your feedback.

https://packt.link/r/1801070059

Your review is important to us and the tech community and will help us make sure we're delivering excellent quality content.

Section 1: Introducing CMake

Getting the basics right is critical to understanding the more advanced subjects and avoiding silly mistakes. This is where the majority of CMake users get in trouble: without a proper foundation, it's difficult to achieve the right outcome. No wonder. It's tempting to skip the introductory material and jump right in where the action is and get things done quickly. We address both points in this section by explaining the core topics of CMake and by hacking together a few lines of code to show what the simplest project looks like.

To build an appropriate mental context, we'll explain what CMake is exactly and how it does its job, along with what the command line is like. We'll talk about the different build stages and learn the language used to generate build systems. We'll also discuss CMake projects: what files they contain, how to approach their directory structure, and we'll explore their primary configuration.

This section comprises the following chapters:

- *Chapter 1, First Steps with CMake*
- *Chapter 2, The CMake Language*
- *Chapter 3, Setting Up Your First CMake Project*

1
First Steps with CMake

There is something magical about turning source code into a working application. It is not only the effect itself, that is, a working mechanism that we devise and bring to life, but the very process or act of exercising the idea into existence.

As programmers, we work in the following loop: design, code, and test. We invent changes, we phrase them in a language that the compiler understands, and we check whether they work as intended. To create a proper, high-quality application from our source code, we need to meticulously execute repetitive, error-prone tasks: invoking the correct commands, checking the syntax, linking binary files, running tests, reporting issues, and more.

It takes great effort to remember each step every single time. Instead, we want to stay focused on the actual coding and delegate everything else to automated tooling. Ideally, this process would start with a single button, right after we have changed our code. It would be smart, fast, extensible, and work in the same way across different OSs and environments. It would be supported by multiple **Integrated Development Environments (IDEs)** but also by **Continuous Integration (CI)** pipelines that test our software after a change is submitted to a shared repository.

CMake is the answer to many such needs; however, it requires a bit of work to configure and use correctly. This is not because CMake is unnecessarily complex but because the subject that we're dealing with here is. Don't worry. We'll undergo this whole learning process very methodically; before you know it, you will have become a building guru.

I know you're eager to rush off to start writing your own CMake projects, and I applaud your attitude. Since your projects will be primarily for users (yourself included), it's important for you to understand that perspective as well.

So, let's start with just that: becoming a CMake power user. We'll go through a few basics: what this tool is, how it works in principle, and how to install it. Then, we'll do a deep dive on the command line and modes of operation. Finally, we'll wrap up with the purposes of different files in a project, and we'll explain how to use CMake without creating a project at all.

In this chapter, we're going to cover the following main topics:

- Understanding the basics
- Installing CMake on different platforms
- Mastering the command line
- Navigating the project files
- Discovering scripts and modules

Technical requirements

You can find the code files that are present in this chapter on GitHub at https://github.com/PacktPublishing/Modern-CMake-for-Cpp/tree/main/examples/chapter01.

To build examples provided in this book always use recommended commands:

```
cmake -B <build tree> -S <source tree>
cmake --build <build tree>
```

Be sure to replace placeholders `<build tree>` and `<source tree>` with appropriate paths. As a reminder: **build tree** is the path to target/output directory, **source tree** is the path at which your source code is located.

Understanding the basics

The compilation of C++ source code appears to be a fairly straightforward process. Let's take a small program, such as a classic `hello.cpp` application, as follows:

chapter-01/01-hello/hello.cpp

```cpp
#include <iostream>

int main() {
    std::cout << "Hello World!" << std::endl;
    return 0;
}
```

Now, all we need to do to get an executable is to run a single command. We call the compiler with the filename as an argument:

```
$ g++ hello.cpp -o a.out
```

Our code is correct, so the compiler will silently produce an executable binary file that our machine can understand. We can run it by calling its name:

```
$ ./a.out
Hello World!
$
```

However, as our projects grow, you will quickly understand that keeping everything in a single file is simply not possible. Clean code practices recommend that files should be kept small and in well-organized structures. The manual compilation of every file can be a tiresome and fragile process. There must be a better way.

What is CMake?

Let's say we automate building by writing a script that goes through our project tree and compiles everything. To avoid any unnecessary compilations, our script will detect whether the source has been modified since the last time we ran it (the script). Now, we'd like a convenient way to manage arguments that are passed to the compiler for each file – preferably, we'd like to do that based on configurable criteria. Additionally, our script should know how to link all of the compiled files in a binary or, even better, build whole solutions that can be reused and incorporated as modules in bigger projects.

The more features we will add the higher the chance that we will get to a full-fledged solution. Building software is a very versatile process and can span multiple different aspects:

- Compiling executables and libraries
- Managing dependencies
- Testing
- Installing
- Packaging
- Producing documentation
- Testing some more

It would take a very long time to come up with a truly modular and powerful C++ building application that is fit for every purpose. And it did. Bill Hoffman at Kitware implemented the first versions of CMake over 20 years ago. As you might have already guessed, it was very successful. It now has a lot of features and support from the community. Today, CMake is being actively developed and has become the industry standard for C and C++ programmers.

The problem of building code in an automated way is much older than CMake, so naturally, there are plenty of options out there: Make, Autotools, SCons, Ninja, Premake, and more. But why does CMake have the upper hand?

There are a couple of things about CMake that I find (granted, subjectively) important:

- It stays focused on supporting modern compilers and toolchains.
- CMake is truly cross-platform – it supports building for Windows, Linux, macOS, and Cygwin.
- It generates project files for popular IDEs: Microsoft Visual Studio, Xcode, and Eclipse CDT. Additionally, it is a project model for others such as CLion.
- CMake operates on just the right level of abstraction – it allows you to group files in reusable targets and projects.
- There are tons of projects that are built with CMake and offer an easy way to include them in your project.
- CMake views testing, packaging, and installing as an inherent part of the build process.
- Old, unused features get deprecated to keep CMake lean.

CMake provides a unified, streamlined experience across the board. It doesn't matter if you're building your software in an IDE or directly from the command line; what's really important is it takes care of post-build stages as well. Your **Continous Integration/ Continous Deployment (CI/CD)** pipeline can easily use the same CMake configuration and build projects using a single standard even if all of the preceding environments differ.

How does it work?

You might be under the impression that CMake is a tool that reads source code on one end and produces binaries on the other – while that's true in principle, it's not the full picture.

CMake can't build anything on its own – it relies on other tools in the system to perform the actual compilation, linking, and other tasks. You can think of it as the orchestrator of your building process: it knows what steps need to be done, what the end goal is, and how to find the right workers and materials for the job.

This process has three stages:

- Configuration
- Generation
- Building

The configuration stage

This stage is about reading project details stored in a directory, called the **source tree**, and preparing an output directory or **build tree** for the generation stage.

CMake starts by creating an empty build tree and collecting all of the details about the environment it is working in, for example, the architecture, the available compilers, the linkers, and the archivers. Additionally, it checks whether a simple test program can be compiled correctly.

Next, the `CMakeLists.txt` project configuration file is parsed and executed (yes, CMake projects are configured with CMake's coding language). This file is the bare minimum of a CMake project (source files can be added later). It tells CMake about the project structure, its targets, and its dependencies (libraries and other CMake packages). During this process, CMake stores collected information in the build tree such as system details, project configurations, logs, and temp files, which are used for the next step. Specifically, a `CMakeCache.txt` file is created to store more stable variables (such as paths to compilers and other tools) and save time during the next configuration.

The generation stage

After reading the project configuration, CMake will generate a **buildsystem** for the exact environment it is working in. Buildsystems are simply cut-to-size configuration files for other build tools (for example, Makefiles for GNU Make or Ninja and IDE project files for Visual Studio). During this stage, CMake can still apply some final touches to the build configuration by evaluating **generator expressions**.

> **Note**
> The generation stage is executed automatically after the configuration stage. For this reason, this book and other resources often refer to both of these stages when mentioning "configuration" or "generation" of a buildsystem. To explicitly run just the configuration stage, you can use the cmake-gui utility.

The building stage

To produce the final artifacts specified in our project, we have to run the appropriate **build tool**. This can be invoked directly, through an IDE, or using the CMake command. In turn, these build tools will execute steps to produce **targets** with compilers, linkers, static and dynamic analysis tools, test frameworks, reporting tools, and anything else you can think of.

The beauty of this solution lies in the ability to produce buildsystems on demand for every platform with a single configuration (that is, the same project files):

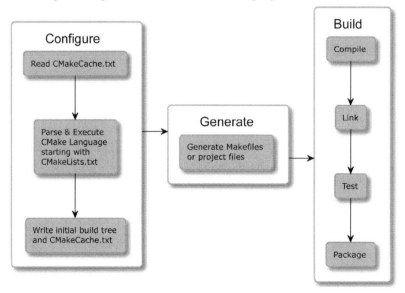

Figure 1.1 – The stages of CMake

Do you remember our hello.cpp application from the *Understanding the basics* section? CMake makes it really easy for you to build it. All we need is the following CMakeLists.txt file next to our source and two simple commands, cmake -B buildtree and cmake --build buildtree, as follows:

chapter01/01-hello/CMakeLists.txt: Hello world in the CMake language

```
cmake_minimum_required(VERSION 3.20)
project(Hello)
add_executable(Hello hello.cpp)
```

Here is the output from the Dockerized Linux system (note that we'll discuss Docker in the *Installing CMake on different platforms* section):

```
root@5f81fe44c9bd:/root/examples/chapter01/01-hello# cmake -B buildtree.
-- The C compiler identification is GNU 9.3.0
-- The CXX compiler identification is GNU 9.3.0
-- Check for working C compiler: /usr/bin/cc
-- Check for working C compiler: /usr/bin/cc -- works
-- Detecting C compiler ABI info
-- Detecting C compiler ABI info - done
-- Detecting C compile features
-- Detecting C compile features - done
-- Check for working CXX compiler: /usr/bin/c++
-- Check for working CXX compiler: /usr/bin/c++ -- works
-- Detecting CXX compiler ABI info
-- Detecting CXX compiler ABI info - done
-- Detecting CXX compile features
-- Detecting CXX compile features - done
-- Configuring done
-- Generating done
-- Build files have been written to: /root/examples/chapter01/01-hello/buildtree
root@5f81fe44c9bd:/root/examples/chapter01/01-hello# cmake --build buildtree/
Scanning dependencies of target Hello
```

```
[ 50%] Building CXX object CMakeFiles/Hello.dir/hello.cpp.o
[100%] Linking CXX executable Hello
[100%] Built target Hello
```

All that's left is to run it:

```
root@68c249f65ce2:~# ./buildtree/Hello
Hello World!
```

Here, we have generated a buildsystem that is stored in the `buildtree` directory. Following this, we executed the build stage and produced a final binary that we were able to run.

Now you know what the end result looks like, I'm sure you will be full of questions: what are the prerequisites to this process? What do these commands mean? Why do we need two of them? How do I write my own project files? Do not worry – these questions will be answered in the following sections.

> **Getting Help**
>
> This book will provide you with the most important information that is relevant to the current version of CMake (at the time of writing, this is 3.20). To provide you with the best advice, I have explicitly avoided any deprecated and no longer recommended features. I highly recommend using, at the very least, version 3.15, which is considered "the Modern CMake." If you require more information, you can find the latest, complete documentation online at `https://cmake.org/cmake/help/`.

Installing CMake on different platforms

CMake is a cross-platform, open-source software written in C++. That means you can, of course, compile it yourself; however, the most likely scenario is that you won't have to. This is because precompiled binaries are available for you to download from the official web page at `https://cmake.org/download/`.

Unix-based systems provide ready-to-install packages directly from the command line.

> **Note**
>
> Remember that CMake doesn't come with compilers. If your system doesn't have them installed yet, you'll need to provide them before using CMake. Make sure to add the paths to their executables to the PATH environment variable so that CMake can find them.
>
> To avoid solving tooling and dependency problems while learning from this book, I recommend choosing the first installation method: Docker.

Let's go through different environments on which CMake can be used.

Docker

Docker (https://www.docker.com/) is a cross-platform tool that provides OS-level virtualization, allowing applications to be shipped in complete packages, called containers. These are self-sufficient bundles that contain a piece of software with all of its libraries, dependencies, and tools required to run it. Docker executes its containers in lightweight environments that are isolated one from another.

This concept makes it extremely convenient to share whole toolchains, which are necessary for a given process, configured and ready to go. I can't stress enough how easy things become when you don't need to worry about minuscule environmental differences.

The Docker platform has a public repository of container images, https://registry.hub.docker.com/, that provides millions of ready-to-use images.

For your convenience, I have published two Docker repositories:

- `swidzinski/cmake:toolchain`: This contains the curated tools and dependencies that are necessary to build with CMake.
- `swidzinski/cmake:examples`: This contains the preceding toolchain and all of the projects and examples from this book.

The first option is for readers who simply want a clean-slate image ready to build their own projects, and the second option is for hands-on practice with examples as we go through the chapters.

You can install Docker by following the instructions from its official documentation (please refer to `docs.docker.com/get-docker`). Then, execute the following commands in your Terminal to download the image and start the container:

```
$ docker pull swidzinski/cmake:examples
$ docker run -it swidzinski/cmake:examples
root@b55e271a85b2:root@b55e271a85b2:#
```

Note that all of the examples are available in the directories matching this format: `/root/examples/examples/chapter-<N>/<M>-<title>`.

Windows

Installing in Windows is straightforward – simply download the version for 32 or 64 bits. You can pick a portable ZIP or MSI package for Windows Installer.

With the ZIP package, you will have to add the CMake bin directory to the `PATH` environment variable so that you can use it in any directory without any such errors:

```
'cmake' is not recognized as an internal or external command,
operable program or batch file.
```

If you prefer convenience, simply use the MSI installer:

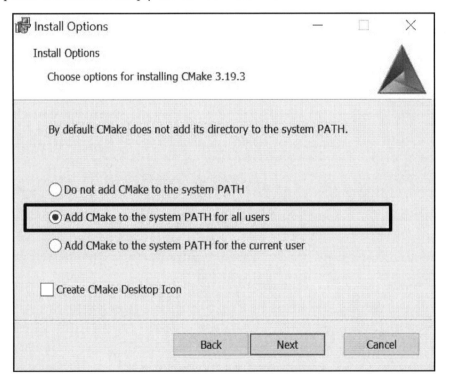

Figure 1.2 – The installation wizard can set up the PATH environment variable for you

As I mentioned earlier, this is open-source software, so it is possible to build CMake yourself. However, first, you will have to get a binary copy of CMake on your system. So, why use other build tools if you have your own, right? This scenario is used by CMake contributors to generate newer versions.

On Windows, we also require a build tool that can finalize the build process started by CMake. A popular choice here is Visual Studio, for which the Community Edition is available for free from Microsoft's website: `https://visualstudio.microsoft.com/downloads/`.

Linux

Getting CMake on Linux is the same as getting any other popular package. Simply use your package manager from the command line. Packages are usually kept up to date with fairly recent versions. However, if you are after the latest version, you can download the installation script from the website:

The script for Linux x86_64

```
$ wget -O - https://github.com/Kitware/CMake/releases/download/v3.20.0/cmake-3.20.0-linux-x86_64.sh | bash
```

The script for Linux aarch64

```
$ wget -O - https://github.com/Kitware/CMake/releases/download/v3.20.0/cmake-3.20.0-Linux-aarch64.sh | bash
```

The package for Debian/Ubuntu

```
$ sudo apt-get install cmake
```

The package for Red Hat

```
$ yum install cmake
```

macOS

This platform is also strongly supported by CMake developers. The most popular choice of installation is through MacPorts:

```
$ sudo port install cmake
```

Alternatively, you can use Homebrew:

```
$ brew install cmake
```

Building from the source

If all else fails – or if you're on a special platform – download the source from the official website and compile it yourself:

```
$ wget https://github.com/Kitware/CMake/releases/download/v3.20.0/cmake-3.20.0.tar.gz
$ tar xzf cmake-3.20.0.tar.gz
$ cd cmake-3.20.0
$ ./bootstrap
$ make
$ make install
```

Building from source is relatively slow and requires more steps. However, by doing it this way, you're guaranteed to use the latest version of CMake. This is especially apparent when compared to packages that are available for Linux: the older the version of the system, the fewer updates it gets.

Now that we have our CMake readily installed, let's learn how to use it!

Mastering the command line

The majority of this book will teach you how to prepare CMake projects for your users. To cater to their needs, we need to thoroughly understand how users interact with CMake in different scenarios. This will allow you to test your project files and ensure they're working correctly.

CMake is a family of tools and consists of five executables:

- `cmake`: This is the main executable that configures, generates, and builds projects.
- `ctest`: This is the test driver program used to run and report test results.
- `cpack`: This is the packaging program used to generate installers and source packages.
- `cmake-gui`: This is the graphical wrapper around `cmake`.
- `ccmake`: This is the console-based GUI wrapper around `cmake`.

CMake

This binary provides a few modes of operation (also called actions):

- Generating a project buildsystem
- Building a project
- Installing a project
- Running a script
- Running a command-line tool
- Getting help

Generating a project buildsystem

This is the first step required to build our project. Here are a few options in terms of how the CMake build action can be executed:

The syntax of the generation mode

```
cmake [<options>] -S <path-to-source> -B <path-to-build>
```
```
cmake [<options>] <path-to-source>
```
```
cmake [<options>] <path-to-existing-build>
```

We'll discuss these options in the upcoming sections. Right now, let's focus on choosing the right form of command. One important feature of CMake is the support for out-of-source builds or the production of artifacts in a separate directory. In contrast to tools such as GNU Make, this ensures the source directory is kept clean from any build-related files and avoids polluting our **Version Control Systems** (**VCS**) with unnecessary files or ignore directives. This is why it's best to use the first form of command of generation mode: specify the path to source tree with `-S` option followed by path to the directory of the produced buildsystem specified with `-B`:

```
cmake -S ./project -B ./build
```

The preceding command will generate a buildsystem in the `./build` directory (or create it if it's missing) from the source in the `./project` directory.

We can skip one of the arguments and `cmake` will "guess" that we intended to use the current directory for it. However, watch out. Skipping both will get you an in-source build, and that is messy.

> **Not Recommended**
>
> Do not use the second or third form of the `cmake <directory>` command. This is because it can produce a messy in-source build (we'll learn how to block that in *Chapter 3, Setting Up Your First CMake Project*). As hinted in the syntax snippet, the same command behaves differently if a previous build already exists in `<directory>`: it will use the cached path to the sources and rebuild from there. Since we often invoke the same commands from the Terminal command history, we might get into trouble here: before using this form, always check whether your shell is currently working in the right directory.

Examples

Build in the current directory, but take the source from one directory up (note that `-S` is optional):

```
cmake -S ..
```

Build in the `./build` directory, and use a source from the current directory:

```
cmake -B build
```

Options for generators

As discussed earlier, you can specify a few options during the generation stage. Selecting and configuring a generator decides which build tool from our system will be used for building, what build files will look like, and what the structure of the build tree will be.

So, should you care? Luckily, the answer is often "no." CMake does support multiple native buildsystems on many platforms; however, unless you have a few of them installed at the same time, CMake will correctly select it for you. This can be overridden by the `CMAKE_GENERATOR` environment variable or by specifying the generator directly on the command line, such as in the following:

```
cmake -G <generator-name> <path-to-source>
```

Some generators (such as Visual Studio) support a more in-depth specification of a toolset (compiler) and platform (compiler or SDK). Additionally, these have respective environment variables that override the default values: `CMAKE_GENERATOR_TOOLSET` and `CMAKE_GENERATOR_PLATFORM`. We can specify them directly, as follows:

```
cmake -G <generator-name>
      -T <toolset-spec> -A <platform-name>
      <path-to-source>
```

Windows users usually want to generate a buildsystem for their favorite IDE. On Linux and macOS, it's very common to use Unix Makefiles or Ninja generators.

To check which generators are available on your system, use the following command:

```
cmake --help
```

At the end of the `help` printout, you should observe a full list like this one:

There are plenty of generators available on Windows 10

```
The following generators are available on this platform:
Visual Studio 16 2019
Visual Studio 15 2017 [arch]
Visual Studio 14 2015 [arch]
Visual Studio 12 2013 [arch]
Visual Studio 11 2012 [arch]
Visual Studio 10 2010 [arch]
Visual Studio 9 2008 [arch]
Borland Makefiles
NMake Makefiles
NMake Makefiles JOM
MSYS Makefiles
MinGW Makefiles
Green Hills MULTI
Unix Makefiles
Ninja
Ninja Multi-Config
Watcom Wmake
CodeBlocks - MinGW Makefiles
CodeBlocks - NMake Makefiles
CodeBlocks - NMake Makefiles JOM
CodeBlocks - Ninja
CodeBlocks - Unix Makefiles
CodeLite - MinGW Makefiles
CodeLite - NMake Makefiles
CodeLite - Ninja
CodeLite - Unix Makefiles
```

```
Eclipse CDT4 - NMake Makefiles
Eclipse CDT4 - MinGW Makefiles
Eclipse CDT4 - Ninja
Eclipse CDT4 - Unix Makefiles
Kate - MinGW Makefiles
Kate - NMake Makefiles
Kate - Ninja
Kate - Unix Makefiles
Sublime Text 2 - MinGW Makefiles
Sublime Text 2 - NMake Makefiles
Sublime Text 2 - Ninja
Sublime Text 2 - Unix Makefiles
```

Options for caching

CMake queries the system for all kinds of information during the configuration stage. This information is cached in CMakeCache.txt in the build tree directory. There are a few options that allow you to manage that file more conveniently.

The first thing that is at our disposal is the ability to *prepopulate cached information*:

```
cmake -C <initial-cache-script> <path-to-source>
```

We can provide a path to the CMake script, which (only) contains a list of set() commands to specify variables that will be used to initialize an empty build tree.

The **initialization and modification** of existing cache variables can be done in another way (for instance, when creating a file is a bit much to only set a few variables). You can simply set them in a command line, as follows:

```
cmake -D <var>[:<type>]=<value> <path-to-source>
```

The :<type> section is optional (it is used by GUIs); you can use BOOL, FILEPATH, PATH, STRING, or INTERNAL. If you omit the type, it will be set to the type of an already existing variable; otherwise, it will be set to UNINITIALIZED.

One particularly important variable contains the type of the build: for example, debug and release. Many CMake projects will read it on numerous occasions to decide things such as the verbosity of messages, the presence of debugging information, and the level of optimization for created artifacts.

For single-configuration generators (such as Make and Ninja), you'll need to specify it during the configuration phase with the `CMAKE_BUILD_TYPE` variable and generate a separate build tree for each type of config: `Debug`, `Release`, `MinSizeRel`, or `RelWithDebInfo`.

Here's an example:

```
cmake -S . -B build -D CMAKE_BUILD_TYPE=Release
```

Note that multi-configuration generators are configured during the build stage.

We can **list cache** variables with the `-L` option:

```
cmake -L[A][H] <path-to-source>
```

Such a list will contain cache variables that aren't marked as `ADVANCED`. We can change that by adding the `A` modifier. To print help messages with variables - add the `H` modifier.

Surprisingly, custom variables that are added manually with the `-D` option won't be visible unless you specify one of the supported types.

The **removal** of one or more variables can be done with the following option:

```
cmake -U <globbing_expr> <path-to-source>
```

Here, the globbing expression supports the `*` wildcard and any `?` character symbols. Be careful when using these, as you might break things.

Both of the `-U` and `-D` options can be repeated multiple times.

Options for debugging and tracing

CMake can be run with a multitude of options that allow you to peek under the hood. To get general information about variables, commands, macros, and other settings, run the following:

```
cmake --system-information [file]
```

The optional file argument allows you to store the output in a file. Running it in the build tree directory will print additional information about the cache variables and build messages from the log files.

In our projects, we'll be using `message()` commands to report details of the build process. CMake filters the log output of these based on the current log level (by default, this is `STATUS`). The following line specifies the log level that we're interested in:

```
cmake --log-level=<level>
```

Here, `level` can be any of the following: `ERROR`, `WARNING`, `NOTICE`, `STATUS`, `VERBOSE`, `DEBUG`, or `TRACE`. You can specify this setting permanently in the `CMAKE_MESSAGE_LOG_LEVEL` cache variable.

Another interesting option allows you to **display log context** with each `message()` call. To debug very complex projects, the `CMAKE_MESSAGE_CONTEXT` variable can be used like a stack. Whenever your code enters a specific context, you can add a descriptive name to the stack and remove it when leaving. By doing this, our messages will be decorated with the current `CMAKE_MESSAGE_CONTEXT` variable like so:

```
[some.context.example] Debug message.
```

The option to enable this kind of log output is as follows:

```
cmake --log-context <path-to-source>
```

We'll discuss logging in more detail in *Chapter 2, The CMake Language*.

If all else fails – and we need to use the big guns – there is always **trace mode**. This will print every command with the filename and exact line number it is called from alongside its arguments. You can enable it as follows:

```
cmake --trace
```

Options for presets

As you might have gathered, there are many, many options that users can specify to generate a build tree from your project. When dealing with the build tree path, generator, cache, and environmental variable, it's easy to get confused or miss something. Developers can simplify how users interact with their projects and provide a `CMakePresets.json` file that specifies some defaults. To learn more, please refer to the *Navigating the project files* section.

To list all of the available presets, execute the following:

```
cmake --list-presets
```

You can use one of the available presets as follows:

```
cmake --preset=<preset>
```

These values override the system defaults and the environment. However, at the same time, they can be overridden with any arguments that are explicitly passed on the command line:

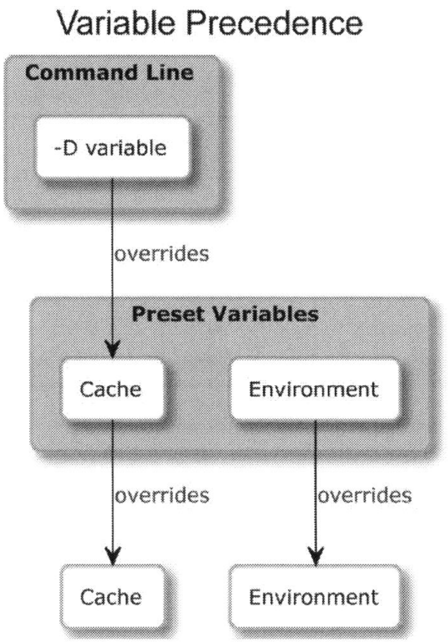

Figure 1.3 – How presets override CMakeCache.txt and the system environment variables

Building a project

After generating our build tree, we're ready for the next stage: *running the builder tool*. Not only does CMake know how to generate input files for many different builders, but it can also run them for you with arguments that are specific to our project.

> **Not Recommended**
>
> Many online sources recommend running GNU Make directly after the generation stage: `make`. This is a default generator for Linux and macOS, and it usually works. However, we prefer the method described in this section, as it is generator-independent and is supported across all platforms. As a result, we don't need to worry about the exact environment of every user of our application.

The syntax of the build mode

```
cmake --build <dir> [<options>] [-- <build-tool-options>]
```

In the majority of these cases, it is enough to simply provide the bare minimum to get a successful build:

```
cmake --build <dir>
```

CMake needs to know where the build tree is that we generated. This is the same path that we passed with the -B argument in the generation stage.

By providing a few options, CMake allows you to specify key build parameters that work for every builder. If you need to provide special arguments to your chosen, native builder, pass them at the end of the command after the -- token:

```
cmake --build <dir> -- <build-tool-options>
```

Options for parallel builds

By default, many build tools will use multiple concurrent processes to leverage modern processors and compile your sources in parallel. Builders know the structure of project dependencies, so they can simultaneously process steps that have their dependencies met to save users' time.

You might want to override that setting if you're building on a powerful machine (or to force a single-threaded build for debugging). Simply specify the number of jobs with either of the following options:

```
cmake --build <dir> --parallel [<number-of-jobs>]
cmake --build <dir> -j [<number-of-jobs>]
```

The alternative is to set it with the CMAKE_BUILD_PARALLEL_LEVEL environment variable. As usual, we can always use the preceding option to override the variable.

Options for target

We'll discuss targets in the second part of the book. For now, let's just say that every project is made up of one or more parts, called targets. Usually, we'll want to build all of them; however, on occasion, we might be interested in skipping some or explicitly building a target that was deliberately excluded from normal builds. We can do this as follows:

```
cmake --build <dir> --target <target1> -t <target2> ...
```

As you will observe, we can specify multiple targets by repeating the `-t` argument.

One target that isn't normally built is `clean`. This will remove all artifacts from the build directory. You can call it like this:

```
cmake --build <dir> -t clean
```

Additionally, CMake offers a convenient alias if you'd like to clean first and then implement a normal build:

```
cmake --build <dir> --clean-first
```

Options for multi-configuration generators

So, we already know a bit about generators: they come in different shapes and sizes. Some of them offer more features than others, and one of these features is the ability to build both `Debug` and `Release` build types in a single build tree.

Generators that support this feature include Ninja Multi-Config, Xcode, and Visual Studio. Every other generator is a single-configuration generator, and they require a separate build tree for that purpose.

Select `Debug`, `Release`, `MinSizeRel`, or `RelWithDebInfo` and specify it as follows:

```
cmake --build <dir> --config <cfg>
```

Otherwise, CMake will use `Debug` as the default.

Options for debugging

When things go bad, the first thing we should do is check the output messages. However, veteran developers know that printing all the details all of the time is confusing, so they often hide them by default. When we need to peek under the hood, we can ask for far more detailed logs by telling CMake to be verbose:

```
cmake --build <dir> --verbose
cmake --build <dir> -v
```

The same effect can be achieved by setting the `CMAKE_VERBOSE_MAKEFILE` cached variable.

Installing a project

When artifacts are built, users can install them on the system. Usually, this means copying files into the correct directories, installing libraries, or running some custom installation logic from a CMake script.

The syntax of the installation mode

```
cmake --install <dir> [<options>]
```

As with other modes of operation, CMake requires a path to a generated build tree:

```
cmake --install <dir>
```

Options for multi-configuration generators

Just like in the build stage, we can specify which build type we want to use for our installation (for more details, please refer to the *Building a project* section). The available types include `Debug`, `Release`, `MinSizeRel`, and `RelWithDebInfo`. The signature is as follows:

```
cmake --install <dir> --config <cfg>
```

Options for components

As a developer, you might choose to split your project into components that can be installed independently. We'll discuss the concept of components in further detail in *Chapter 11, Installing and Packaging*. For now, let's just assume they represent different parts of the solution. This might be something like `application`, `docs`, and `extra-tools`.

To install a single component, use the following option:

```
cmake --install <dir> --component <comp>
```

Options for permissions

If installation is carried on a Unix-like platform, you can specify default permissions for the installed directories, with the following option, using the format of `u=rwx,g=rx,o=rx`:

```
cmake --install <dir>
       --default-directory-permissions <permissions>
```

Options for the installation directory

We can prepend the installation path specified in the project configuration with a prefix of our choice (for example, when we have limited write access to some directories). The /usr/local path that is prefixed with /home/user becomes /home/user/usr/local. The signature for this option is as follows:

```
cmake --install <dir> --prefix <prefix>
```

Note that this won't work on Windows, as paths on this platform usually start with the drive letter.

Options for debugging

Similarly, to the build stage, we can also choose to view a detailed output of the installation stage. To do this, use any of the following:

```
cmake --build <dir> --verbose
cmake --build <dir> -v
```

The same effect can be achieved if the VERBOSE environment variable is set.

Running a script

CMake projects are configured using CMake's custom language. It's cross-platform, quite powerful, and already present. So, why not make it available for other tasks? Sure enough, you can write standalone scripts (we'll get to that at the end of this chapter).

CMake can run these scripts like so:

Syntax of the script mode

```
cmake [{-D <var>=<value>}...] -P <cmake-script-file>
      [-- <unparsed-options>...]
```

Running such a script won't run any configurations or generate stages. Additionally, it won't affect the cache. There are two ways you can pass values to this script:

- Through variables defined with the -D option.
- Through arguments that can be passed after a -- token. CMake will create CMAKE_ARGV<n> variables for all arguments passed to the script (including the -- token).

Running a command-line tool

On rare occasions, we might need to run a single command in a platform-independent way – perhaps copy a file or compute a checksum. Not all platforms were created equal, so not all commands are available in every system, or they have a different name.

CMake offers a mode in which to execute the most common ones in the same way across platforms:

The syntax of the command-line tool mode

```
cmake -E <command> [<options>]
```

As the use of this particular mode is fairly limited, we won't cover it in depth. However, if you're interested in the details, I recommend calling `cmake -E` to list all the available commands. To simply get a glimpse of what's on offer, CMake 3.20 supports the following commands:

`capabilities`, `cat`, `chdir`, `compare_files`, `copy`, `copy_directory`, `copy_if_different`, `echo`, `echo_append`, `env`, `environment`, `make_directory`, `md5sum`, `sha1sum`, `sha224sum`, `sha256sum`, `sha384sum`, `sha512sum`, `remove`, `remove_directory`, `rename`, `rm`, `server`, `sleep`, `tar`, `time`, `touch`, `touch_nocreate`, `create_symlink`, `create_hardlink`, `true`, and `false`.

If a command you'd like to use is missing, or you need a more complex behavior, consider wrapping it in a script and running it in `-P` mode.

Getting help

It comes without surprise that CMake offers extensive help that is accessible through its command line.

The syntax of the help mode

```
cmake --help[-<topic>]
```

CTest

Automated testing is very important in order to produce and maintain high-quality code. That's why we devoted an entire chapter to this subject (please refer to *Chapter 8*, *Testing Frameworks*), where we do a deep dive into the usage of CTest. It is one of the available command-line tools, so let's briefly introduce it now.

CTest is about wrapping CMake in a higher layer of abstraction, where the building stage becomes just one of the stepping stones in the process of developing our software. Other tasks that CMake can do for us include updating, running all kinds of tests, reporting the state of the project to external dashboards, and running scripts written in the CMake language.

More importantly, CTest standardizes running tests and reporting for solutions built with CMake. This means that as a user, you don't need to know which testing framework the project is using or how to run it. CTest provides a convenient façade to list, filter, shuffle, retry, and timebox test runs. Additionally, it can call CMake for you if a build is required.

The simplest way to run tests for a built project is to call `ctest` in the generated build tree:

```
$ ctest
Test project C:/Users/rapha/Desktop/CMake/build
Guessing configuration Debug
    Start 1: SystemInformationNew
1/1 Test #1: SystemInformationNew .........   Passed    3.19 sec

100% tests passed, 0 tests failed out of 1
Total Test time (real) =   3.24 sec
```

CPack

After we have built and tested our amazing software, we are ready to share it with the world. In a rare few instances, power users are completely fine with the source code, and that's what they want. However, the vast majority of the world is using precompiled binaries because of convenience and to save time.

CMake doesn't leave you stranded here; it comes with batteries included. CPack is built for the exact purpose of creating packages for different platforms: compressed archives, executable installers, wizards, NuGet packages, macOS bundles, DMG packages, RPMs, and more.

CPack works in a very similar way to CMake: it is configured with the CMake language and has many package generators to pick from (just don't confuse them with CMake buildsystem generators). We'll go through all the specific details in *Chapter 11, Installing and Packaging*, as this is quite a hefty tool that is meant for the final stages of CMake projects.

The CMake GUI

CMake for Windows comes with a GUI version to configure the building process of previously prepared projects. For Unix-like platforms, there is a version built with QT libraries. Ubuntu offers it in the `cmake-qt-gui` package.

To access the CMake GUI, run the `cmake-gui` executable:

Figure 1.4 – The CMake GUI – the configuring stage for a buildsystem using a generator for Visual Studio 2019

The GUI application is a convenient tool for users of your application, as the options found there are rather limited. It can be useful for those who aren't familiar with the command line and would prefer a window-based interface.

> **Not Recommended**
>
> I would definitely recommend GUI to end users craving convenience; however, as a programmer, I avoid introducing any manual, blocking steps that would require clicking on forms every time I build my programs. This is especially important for build automation in CI pipelines. These tools require headless applications so that the build can be fully executed without any user interaction.

CCMake

The `ccmake` executable is the CMake `curses` interface for Unix-like platforms (it's unavailable for Windows). It's not available as part of the CMake package, so users have to install it separately.

The command for Debian/Ubuntu systems is as follows:

```
$ sudo apt-get install cmake-curses-gui
```

Note that the project configuration settings can be specified interactively through this GUI. Brief instructions are provided at the bottom of the Terminal when the program is running:

The syntax of the CCMake command

```
ccmake [<options>]
ccmake {<path-to-source> | <path-to-existing-build>}
```

CCMake uses the same set of options as `cmake`:

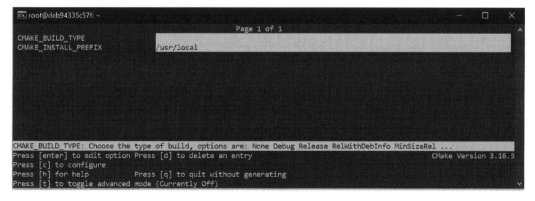

Figure 1.5 – The configuring stage in ccmake

As with **Graphical User Interfaces (GUIs)**, this mode is fairly limited and is intended to be used by less experienced users. If you're using a Unix machine, I recommend that you take a quick look and move on even quicker.

This concludes the basic introduction to command line of CMake. It's time to discover what is the structure of a typical CMake project.

Navigating the project files

CMake uses quite a few files to manage its projects. Let's attempt to get a general idea of what each file does before tinkering with the contents. It's important to realize, that even though a file contains CMake language commands, it's not certain that it's meant for developers to edit. Some files are generated to be used by subsequent tools, and any changes made to those files will be written over at some stage. Other files are meant for advanced users to adjust your project to their individual needs. Finally, there are some temporary files that provide valuable information in specific contexts. This section will also specify which of them should be in the *ignore file* of your version control system.

The source tree

This is the directory where your project will live (it is also called the **project root**). It contains all of the C++ sources and CMake project files.

Here are the key takeaways of this directory:

- It is required that you provide a `CMakeLists.txt` configuration file in its top directory.
- It should be managed with a VCS such as `git`.
- The path to this directory is given by the user with a `-S` argument of the `cmake` command.
- Avoid hardcoding any absolute paths to the source tree in your CMake code – users of your software can store the project under a different path.

The build tree

CMake uses this directory to store everything that gets generated during the build: the artifacts of the project, the transient configuration, the cache, the build logs, and anything that your native build tool will create. Alternative names for this directory include **build root** and **binary tree**.

Here are the key takeaways of this directory:

- Your binary files will be created here, such as executables and libraries, along with *object files* and archives used for final linking.
- Don't add this directory to your VCS – it's specific to your system. If you decide to put it inside the source tree, make sure to add it to the VCS ignore file.
- CMake recommends **out-of-source builds** or builds that produce artifacts in a directory that is separate from all source files. This way, we can avoid polluting our project's source tree with temporary, system-specific files (or **in-source builds**).
- It is specified with `-B` or as a last argument to the `cmake` command if you have provided a path to the source, for example, `cmake -S ../project ./`.
- It's recommended that your projects include an installation stage that allows you to put the final artifacts in the correct place in the system, so all temporary files used for building can be removed.

Listfiles

Files that contain the CMake language are called listfiles and can be included one in another, by calling `include()` and `find_package()`, or indirectly with `add_subdirectory()`:

- CMake doesn't enforce consistent naming for these files, but usually, they have a `.cmake` extension.
- A very important naming exception is a file called `CMakeLists.txt`, which is the first file to be executed in the configuration stage. It is required at the top of the source tree.
- As CMake walks the source tree and includes different listfiles, the following variables are set: `CMAKE_CURRENT_LIST_DIR`, `CMAKE_CURRENT_LIST_FILE`, `CMAKE_PARENT_LIST_FILE`, and `CMAKE_CURRENT_LIST_LINE`.

CMakeLists.txt

CMake projects are configured with `CMakeLists.txt` listfiles. You are required to provide at least one in the root of the source tree. Such a top-level file is the first to be executed in the configuration stage, and it should contain at least two commands:

- `cmake_minimum_required(VERSION <x.xx>)`: Sets an expected version of CMake (and implicitly tells CMake what policies to apply with regard to legacy behaviors).
- `project(<name> <OPTIONS>)`: This is used to name the project (the provided name will be stored in the `PROJECT_NAME` variable) and specify the options to configure it (we'll discuss this further in the *Chapter 2, The CMake Language*).

As your software grows, you might want to partition it into smaller units that can be configured and reasoned about separately. CMake supports this through the notion of subdirectories and their own `CMakeLists.txt` files. Your project structure might look similar to the following example:

```
CMakeLists.txt
api/CMakeLists.txt
api/api.h
api/api.cpp
```

A very simple `CMakeLists.txt` file can then be used to bring it all together:

CMakeLists.txt

```
cmake_minimum_required(VERSION 3.20)
project(app)
message("Top level CMakeLists.txt")
add_subdirectory(api)
```

The main aspects of the project are covered in the top-level file: managing the dependencies, stating the requirements, and detecting the environment. In this file, we also have an `add_subdirectory(api)` command to include another `CMakeListst.txt` file from the `api` directory to perform steps that are specific to the API part of our application.

CMakeCache.txt

Cache variables will be generated from `listfiles` and stored in `CMakeCache.txt` when the configure stage is run for the first time. This file resides in the root of the build tree and has a fairly simple format:

```
# This is the CMakeCache file.
# For build in directory:
  c:/Users/rapha/Desktop/CMake/empty_project/build
# It was generated by CMake: C:/Program
  Files/CMake/bin/cmake.exe
# You can edit this file to change values found and used by
  cmake.
# If you do want to change a value, simply edit, save, and
  exit the editor.
# The syntax for the file is as follows:
# KEY:TYPE=VALUE
# KEY is the name of a variable in the cache.
# TYPE is a hint to GUIs for the type of VALUE, DO NOT EDIT
  TYPE!.
# VALUE is the current value for the KEY.
########################
# EXTERNAL cache entries
########################
//Flags used by the CXX compiler during DEBUG builds.
CMAKE_CXX_FLAGS_DEBUG:STRING=/MDd /Zi /Ob0 /Od /RTC1
// ... more variables here ...
########################
# INTERNAL cache entries
########################
//Minor version of cmake used to create the current loaded
  cache
CMAKE_CACHE_MINOR_VERSION:INTERNAL=19
// ... more variables here ...
```

As you can observe from comments in the heading, this format is pretty self-explanatory. Cache entries in the `EXTERNAL` section are meant for users to modify, while the `INTERNAL` section is managed by CMake. Note that it's not recommended that you change them manually.

Here are several key takeaways to bear in mind:

- You can manage this file manually, by calling `cmake` (please refer to *Options for caching* in the *Mastering the command line* section), or through `ccmake`/`cmake-gui`.
- You can reset the project to its default configuration by deleting this file; it will be regenerated from the listfiles.
- Cache variables can be read and written from the listfiles. Sometimes, variable reference evaluation is a bit complicated; however, we will cover that in more detail in *Chapter 2, The CMake Language*.

The Config-files for packages

A big part of the CMake ecosystem includes the external packages that projects can depend on. They allow developers to use libraries and tools in a seamless, cross-platform way. Packages that support CMake should provide a configuration file so that CMake understands how to use them.

We'll learn how to write those files in *Chapter 11, Installing and Packaging*. Meanwhile, here's a few interesting details to bear in mind:

- **Config-files** (original spelling) contain information regarding how to use the library binaries, headers, and helper tools. Sometimes, they expose CMake macros to use in your project.
- Use the `find_package()` command to include packages.
- CMake files describing packages are named `<PackageName>-config.cmake` and `<PackageName>Config.cmake`.
- When using packages, you can specify which version of the package you need. CMake will check this in the associated `<Config>Version.cmake` file.
- Config-files are provided by package vendors supporting the CMake ecosystem. If a vendor doesn't provide such a config-file, it can be replaced with a **Find-module** (original spelling).
- CMake provides a package registry to store packages system-wide and for each user.

The cmake_install.cmake, CTestTestfile.cmake, and CPackConfig.cmake files

These files are generated in the build tree by the `cmake` executable in the generation stage. As such, they shouldn't be edited manually. CMake uses them as a configuration for the `cmake` install action, CTest, and CPack. If you're implementing an in-source build (not recommended), it's probably a good idea to add them to the VCS ignore file.

CMakePresets.json and CMakeUserPresets.json

The configuration of the projects can become a relatively busy task when we need to be specific about things such as cache variables, chosen generators, the path of the build tree, and more – especially when we have more than one way of building our project. This is where the presets come in.

Users can choose presets through the GUI or use the command line to `--list-presets` and select a preset for the buildsystem with the `--preset=<preset>` option. You'll find more details in the *Mastering the command line* section of this chapter.

Presets are stored in the same JSON format in two files:

- `CMakePresets.json`: This is meant for project authors to provide official presets.
- `CMakeUserPresets.json`: This is dedicated to users who want to customize the project configuration to their liking (you can add it to your VCS ignore file).

Presets are project files, so their explanation belongs here. However, they are not required in projects, and they only become useful when we have completed the initial setup. So, feel free to skip to the next section and return here later, if needed:

chapter-01/02-presets/CMakePresets.json

```json
{
  "version": 1,
  "cmakeMinimumRequired": {
    "major": 3, "minor": 19, "patch": 3
  },
  "configurePresets": [ ],
  "vendor": {
    "vendor-one.com/ExampleIDE/1.0": {
      "buildQuickly": false
```

```
      }
    }
}
```

`CMakePresets.json` specifies the following root fields:

- `Version`: This is required, and it is always `1`.
- `cmakeMinimumRequired`: This is optional. It specifies the CMake version in form of a hash with three fields: `major`, `minor`, and `patch`.
- `vendor`: An IDE can use this optional field to store its metadata. It's a map keyed with a vendor domain and slash-separated path. CMake virtually ignores this field.
- `configurePresets`: This is an optional array of available presets.

Let's add two presets to our `configurePresets` array:

chapter-01/02-presets/CMakePresets.json : my-preset

```
{
    "name": "my-preset",
    "displayName": "Custom Preset",
    "description": "Custom build - Ninja",
    "generator": "Ninja",
    "binaryDir": "${sourceDir}/build/ninja",
    "cacheVariables": {
      "FIRST_CACHE_VARIABLE": {
         "type": "BOOL", "value": "OFF"
      },
      "SECOND_CACHE_VARIABLE": "Ninjas rock"
    },
    "environment": {
      "MY_ENVIRONMENT_VARIABLE": "Test",
      "PATH": "$env{HOME}/ninja/bin:$penv{PATH}"
    },
    "vendor": {
      "vendor-one.com/ExampleIDE/1.0": {
         "buildQuickly": true
      }
```

```
    }
},
```

This file supports a tree-like structure, where children presets inherit properties from multiple parent presets. This means that we can create a copy of the preceding preset and only override the fields we need. Here's an example of what a child preset might look like:

chapter-01/02-presets/CMakePresets.json : my-preset-multi

```
{
    "name": "my-preset-multi",
    "inherits": "my-preset",
    "displayName": "Custom Ninja Multi-Config",
    "description": "Custom build - Ninja Multi",
    "generator": "Ninja Multi-Config"
}
```

> **Note**
> The CMake documentation only labels a few fields as explicitly required. However, there are some other fields that are labeled as optional, which must be provided either in the preset or inherited from its parent.

Presets are defined as maps with the following fields:

- `name`: This is a required string that identifies the preset. It has to be machine-friendly and unique across both files.
- `Hidden`: This is an optional Boolean hiding the preset from the GUI and command-line list. Such a preset can be a parent of another and isn't required to provide anything but its name.
- `displayName`: This is an optional string with a human-friendly name.
- `description`: This is an optional string describing the preset.
- `Inherits`: This is an optional string or array of preset names to inherit from. Values from earlier presets will be preferred in the case of conflicts, and every preset is free to override any inherited field. Additionally, `CMakeUserPresets.json` can inherit from project presets but not the other way around.
- `Vendor`: This is an optional map of vendor-specific values. It follows the same convention as a root-level `vendor` field.

- `Generator`: This is a *required or inherited* string that specifies a generator to use for the preset.
- `architecture` and `toolset`: These are optional fields for configuring generators that support these options (mentioned in the *Generating a project buildsystem* section). Each field can simply be a string or a hash with `value` and `strategy` fields, where `strategy` is either `set` or `external`. The `strategy` field, configured to `set`, will set the value and produce an error if the generator doesn't support this field. Configuring `external` means that the field value is set for an external IDE, and CMake should ignore it.
- `binaryDir`: This is a *required or inherited* string that provides a path to the build tree directory (which is absolute or relative to the source tree). It supports macro expansion.
- `cacheVariables`: This is an optional map of cache variables where keys denote variable names. Accepted values include `null`, `"TRUE"`, `"FALSE"`, a string value, or a hash with an optional `type` field and a required `value` field. `value` can be a string value of either `"TRUE"` or `"FALSE"`. Cache variables are inherited with a union operation unless the value is specified as `null` – then, it remains unset. String values support macro expansion.
- `Environment`: This is an optional map of environment variables where keys denote variable names. Accepted values include `null` or string values. Environment variables are inherited with a union operation unless the value is specified as `null` – then, it remains unset. String values support macro expansion, and variables might reference each other in any order, as long as there is no cyclic reference.

The following macros are recognized and evaluated:

- `${sourceDir}`: This is the path to the source tree.
- `${sourceParentDir}`: This is the path to the source tree's parent directory.
- `${sourceDirName}`: This is the last filename component of `${sourceDir}`. For example, for `/home/rafal/project`, it would be `project`.
- `${presetName}`: This is the value of the preset's name field.
- `${generator}`: This is the value of the preset's generator field.
- `${dollar}`: This is a literal dollar sign ($).
- `$env{<variable-name>}`: This is an environment variable macro. It will return the value of the variable from the preset if defined; otherwise, it will return the value from the parent environment. Remember that variable names in presets are case-sensitive (unlike in Windows environments).

- `$penv{<variable-name>}`: This option is just like `$env` but always returns values from the parent environment. This allows you to resolve issues with circular references that are not allowed in the environment variables of the preset.
- `$vendor{<macro-name>}`: This enables vendors to insert their own macros.

Ignoring files in Git

There are many VCSs; one of the most popular types out there is Git. Whenever we start a new project, it is good to make sure that we only check in to the repository files that need to be there. Project hygiene is easier to maintain if we just add generated, user, or temporary files to the `.gitignore` file. In this way, Git knows to automatically skip them when building new commits. Here's the file that I use in my projects:

chapter-01/01-hello/.gitignore

```
# If you put build tree in the source tree add it like so:
build_debug/
build_release/

# Generated and user files
**/CMakeCache.txt
**/CMakeUserPresets.json
**/CTestTestfile.cmake
**/CPackConfig.cmake
**/cmake_install.cmake
**/install_manifest.txt
**/compile_commands.json
```

Using the preceding file in your projects will allow for more flexibility for you and other contributors and users.

The unknown territory of project files has now been charted. With this map, you'll soon be able to write your own listfiles, configure the cache, prepare presets, and more. Before you sail on the open sea of project writing, let's take a look at what other kinds of self-contained units you can create with CMake.

Discovering scripts and modules

Work with CMake is primarily focused on projects that get built and the production of artifacts that get consumed by other systems, such as CI/CD pipelines and test platforms, or deployed to machines or artifact repositories. However, there are two other concepts of CMake that enable you to create with its language: scripts and modules. Let's take a closer look.

Scripts

To configure project building, CMake offers a platform-agnostic programming language. This comes with many useful commands. You can use this tool to write scripts that come with your project or are completely independent.

Think of it as a consistent way to do cross-platform work: instead of using bash scripts on Linux and batch or PowerShell scripts on Windows, you can have one version. Sure, you could bring in external tools such as Python, Perl, or Ruby scripts, but this is yet another dependency and will increase the complexity of your C/C++ projects. Yes, sometimes, this will be the only thing that can get the job done, but more often than not, we can get away with something far simpler.

We have already learned from the *Mastering the command line* section that we can execute scripts using the `-P` option: `cmake -P script.cmake`. But what are the actual requirements for the script file provided? Not that many: a script can be as complex as you like or an empty file. However, it is recommended that you call the `cmake_minimum_required()` command at the beginning of the script. This command tells CMake which policies should be applied to subsequent commands in this project (more details in *Chapter 3, Setting Up Your First CMake Project*).

---

chapter-01/03-script/script.cmake

```
# An example of a script
cmake_minimum_required(VERSION 3.20.0)
message("Hello world")
file(WRITE Hello.txt "I am writing to a file")
```

When running scripts, CMake won't execute any of the usual stages (such as configuration or generation), and it won't use the cache. Since there is no concept of a source/build tree in scripts, variables that usually hold references to these paths will contain the current working directory instead: `CMAKE_BINARY_DIR`, `CMAKE_SOURCE_DIR`, `CMAKE_CURRENT_BINARY_DIR`, and `CMAKE_CURRENT_SOURCE_DIR`.

Happy scripting!

Utility modules

CMake projects can use external modules to enhance their functionality. Modules are written in the CMake language and contain macro definitions, variables, and commands that perform all kinds of functions. They range from quite complex scripts (`CPack` and `CTest` also provide modules!) to fairly simple ones, such as `AddFileDependencies` or `TestBigEndian`.

The CMake distribution comes packed with almost 90 different utility modules. If that's not enough, you can download more from the internet by browsing curated lists, such as the one found at `https://github.com/onqtam/awesome-cmake`, or write a module from scratch.

To use a utility module, we need to call an `include(<MODULE>)` command. Here's a simple project showing this in action:

chapter-01/04-module/CMakeLists.txt

```
cmake_minimum_required(VERSION 3.20.0)
project(ModuleExample)
include (TestBigEndian)
test_big_endian(IS_BIG_ENDIAN)
if(IS_BIG_ENDIAN)
  message("BIG_ENDIAN")
else()
  message("LITTLE_ENDIAN")
endif()
```

We'll learn what modules are available as they become relevant to the subject at hand. If you're curious, a full list of bundled modules can be found at `https://cmake.org/cmake/help/latest/manual/cmake-modules.7.html`.

Find-modules

In the *The Config-files for packages* section, I mentioned that CMake has a mechanism that allows it to find files belonging to external dependencies that don't support CMake and don't provide a CMake config-file (or haven't). That's what find-modules are for. CMake provides over 150 modules that are able to locate different packages in the system. As was the case with utility modules, there are plenty more find-modules available online and another option is to write your own as a last resort.

You can use them by calling the `find_package()` command and providing the name of the package in question. Such a find-module will then play a little game of hide and seek and check all known locations of the software it is looking for. Following this, it defines variables (as specified in that module's manual) that allow you to build against that dependency.

For example, the `FindCURL` module searches for a popular *Client URL* library and defines the following variables: `CURL_FOUND`, `CURL_INCLUDE_DIRS`, `CURL_LIBRARIES`, and `CURL_VERSION_STRING`.

We will cover find-modules in more depth in *Chapter 7, Managing Dependencies with CMake*.

Summary

Now you understand what CMake is and how it works; you learned the key components of the CMake tool family and how to install them on a variety of systems. Like a true power user, you know all the ways in which to run CMake through the command line: buildsystem generation, building a project, installing, running scripts, command-line tools, and printing help. You are aware of the CTest, CPack, and GUI applications. This will help you to create projects, with the right perspective, for users and other developers. Additionally, you learned what makes up a project: directories, listfiles, configs, presets, and helper files, along with what to ignore in your VCS. Finally, you took a sneak peek at other non-project files: standalone scripts and modules.

In the next chapter, we will take a deep dive into CMake's programming language. This will allow you to write your own listfiles and open the door to your first script, project, and module.

Further reading

For more information, you can refer to the following resources:

- The official CMake web page and documentation: `https://cmake.org/`
- Single-configuration generators: `https://cgold.readthedocs.io/en/latest/glossary/single-config.html`
- The separation of stages in the CMake GUI: `https://stackoverflow.com/questions/39401003/why-there-are-two-buttons-in-gui-configure-and-generate-when-cli-does-all-in-one`

2
The CMake Language

Writing in the **CMake Language** is a bit tricky. When you read a CMake listfile for the first time, you may be under the impression that the language in it is so simple that it doesn't require any special training or preparation. What follows is very often a practical attempt to introduce changes and experiment with the code without a thorough understanding of how it works. We programmers are usually very busy and are overly keen to tackle any build-related issues with little investment. We tend to make gut-based changes hoping they just might do the trick. This approach to solving technical problems is called *voodoo programming*.

The CMake Language appears simple: after we have completed our small addition, fix, or hack, or added a one-liner, we realize that something isn't working. The time spent on debugging is often longer than that spent on actually studying the subject. Luckily, this won't be our fate – because this chapter covers the vast majority of the critical knowledge needed to use the CMake Language in practice.

In this chapter, we'll not only learn about the building blocks of the CMake Language – **comments**, **commands**, **variables**, and **control structures** – but we'll also give the necessary background and try them out in a clean and modern CMake example. CMake puts you in a bit of a unique position. On one hand, you perform a role of a build engineer; you need to understand all the intricacies of the compilers, the platforms, and everything else in-between. On the other hand, you're a developer; you're writing code that generates a buildsystem. Writing good code is hard and requires thinking on many levels at the same time – it should work and be easy to read, but it should also be easy to analyze, extend, and maintain. This is exactly what we're going to talk about here.

Lastly, we'll introduce some of the most useful and common commands in CMake. Commands that aren't used that often will be placed in the *Appendix* section (this will include a complete reference guide for the string, list, and file manipulation commands).

In this chapter, we're going to cover the following main topics:

- The basics of the CMake Language syntax
- Working with variables
- Using lists
- Understanding control structures in CMake
- Useful commands

Technical requirements

You can find the code files that are present in this chapter on GitHub at `https://github.com/PacktPublishing/Modern-CMake-for-Cpp/tree/main/examples/chapter02`.

To build examples provided in this book always use recommended commands:

```
cmake -B <build tree> -S <source tree>
cmake --build <build tree>
```

Be sure to replace placeholders `<build tree>` and `<source tree>` with appropriate paths. As a reminder: **build tree** is the path to target/output directory, **source tree** is the path at which your source code is located.

The basics of the CMake Language syntax

Composing CMake code is very much like writing in any other imperative language: lines are executed from top to bottom and from left to right, occasionally stepping into an included file or a called function. Depending on the mode (see the *Mastering the command line* section in *Chapter 1, First Steps with CMake*), the execution begins from the root file of the source tree (`CMakeLists.txt`) or a `.cmake` script file that was passed as an argument to `cmake`.

As we discussed in the previous chapter, scripts support the majority of the CMake Language (with the exclusion of any project-related functionality). As a result, they're a great way to start practicing the CMake syntax itself, and that's why we'll be using them here. After becoming comfortable writing basic listfiles, we'll start preparing actual project files in the next chapter. If you remember, scripts can be run with the following command:

```
cmake -P script.cmake
```

> **Note**
> CMake supports **7-bit ASCII** text files for portability across all platforms. You can use both `\n` or `\r\n` line endings. **UTF-8** with optional **Byte Order Markers (BOMs)** is supported in CMake versions above 3.0, and **UTF-16** is supported in CMake versions above 3.2.

Everything in a CMake listfile is either a *command invocation* or a *comment*.

Comments

Just like in **C++**, there are two kinds of comments – *single-line* comments and *bracket* (*multiline*) comments. But unlike in C++, bracket comments can be nested. Let me show you the syntax:

```
# single-line comments start with a hash sign "#"
# they can be placed on an empty line
message("Hi"); # or after a command like here.

#[=[
bracket comment
  #[[
    nested bracket comment
  #]]
#]=]
```

Multiline comments get their name from their symbol – they start with an opening square bracket ([ ), any number of equal (=) signs, and another square bracket: [= [. To close a bracket comment, use the same number of equal signs and reverse the brackets like so:] =].

Prepending opening bracket tokens with # is optional, and allows you to quickly disable a multiline comment by adding another # to the first line of the bracket comment like so:

```
##[=[ this is a single-line comment now
no longer commented
  #[[
     still, a nested comment
  #]]
#]=] this is a single-line comment now
```

That's a nifty trick, but when and how should we use comments in our CMake file? Since writing listfiles is essentially programming, it is a good idea to bring our best coding practices to them as well. Code that follows such practices is often called *clean* – a term used over the years by software development gurus like Robert C. Martin, Martin Fowler, and many other authors. What's considered helpful and harmful is often heavily disputed and, as you might guess, comments have not been left out of these debates.

Everything should be judged on a case-by-case basis, but generally agreed-upon guidelines say that good comments provide at least one of the following:

- **Information**: They can untangle complexities such as regex patterns or formatting strings.
- **Intent**: They can explain the intent of the code when it is unobvious from the implementation or interface.
- **Clarification**: They can explain concepts that can't be easily refactored or changed.
- **Warnings of consequences**: They can provide warnings, especially around code that can break other things.
- **Amplification**: They can underline the importance of an idea that is hard to express in code.
- **Legal clauses**: They can add this necessary evil, which is usually not the domain of a programmer.

If you can, avoid adding comments and adopt better naming practices, or refactor or correct your code. If you can, avoid adding comments of the following types:

- **Mandated**: These are added for completeness, but they are not really important.
- **Redundant**: These repeat what is already clearly written in the code.
- **Misleading**: These could be outdated or incorrect if they don't follow code changes.
- **Journal**: These note what has been changed and when (use **VCS** for this instead).
- **Dividers**: These mark sections.

Writing elegant code without comments is hard, but it improves the experience of the reader. Since we spend more time reading code than writing it, we should always try to *write readable code*, instead of just trying to write it quickly. I recommend checking out the *Further reading* section at the end of this chapter for some good references on *clean code*. If you're interested in comments in particular, you'll find a link to one of my many YouTube videos touching on this subject in depth.

Command invocations

Time for some action! Invoking commands is the bread and butter of CMake listfiles. To execute a command, you must provide its name, followed by parentheses, in which you may enclose a whitespace-separated list of **command arguments**.

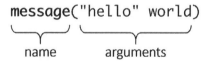

Figure 2.1 – An example of a command

Command names aren't case-sensitive, but there is a convention in the CMake community to use snake_case in command names (that is, lower-case words joined with underscores). You can also define your own commands, which we'll cover in the *Understanding control structures in CMake* section of this chapter.

What's especially striking in comparison to C++ is the fact that command invocations in CMake are not expressions. You can't provide another command as an argument to a called command, as *everything* between the parentheses is interpreted as an argument for that command.

C++ enthusiasts will find it surprising that CMake commands don't require semicolons at the end of an invocation. This is likely because each line of source can contain up to one command invocation, followed by an optional single-line comment. Alternatively, an entire line has to be part of a bracket comment. So, these are the only allowed formats:

```
command(argument1 "argument2" argument3)  # comment
# [[ multiline comment ]]
```

Putting a command after a bracket comment is not allowed:

```
# [[ bracket
]] command()
```

After removing any comments, whitespace, and empty lines, we get a list of command invocations. This creates an interesting perspective – CMake syntax is really simple, but is that a good thing? How do we even work with variables? Or, how do we direct the flow of the execution?

CMake provides commands for these actions and much more. To make things easier, we'll be introducing the relevant commands as we move through different examples, and they can be grouped into three categories:

- **Scripting commands**: These are always available, and they change the state of the command processor, access variables, and affect other commands and the environment.
- **Project commands**: These are available in projects, and they manipulate the project state and build targets.
- **CTest commands**: These are available in CTest scripts. They manage testing.

We'll cover the most useful scripting commands in this chapter (as they are also useful in projects). Project and CTest commands will be discussed in the following chapters as we introduce the concepts relating to build targets (*Chapter 3*, *Setting Up Your First CMake Project*) and testing frameworks (*Chapter 8*, *Testing Frameworks*).

Virtually every command relies on other elements of the language in order to function: variables, conditional statements, and first and foremost, command-line arguments. Let's see how we should use these.

Command arguments

Many commands require whitespace-separated arguments to parametrize how they behave. As you saw in *Figure 2.1*, there's something weird happening with the quotes around the arguments. Some arguments have quotes and others don't – what's up with that?

Under the hood, the only data type recognized by CMake is a *string*. This is why every command expects zero or more strings for its arguments. But plain, static strings aren't very useful, especially when we can't nest command invocations. Here's where arguments come into play – CMake will evaluate every argument to a static string and then pass them into the command. *Evaluating* means *string interpolation*, or substituting parts of a string with another value. This can mean replacing the *escape sequences*, expanding the *variable references* (also called *variable interpolation*), and unpacking *lists*.

Depending on the context, we might want to enable such evaluation as needed. And for that reason, CMake offers three types of arguments:

- **Bracket arguments**
- **Quoted arguments**
- **Unquoted arguments**

Each argument type offers a different level of evaluation and has a few small quirks to it.

Bracket arguments

Bracket arguments aren't evaluated because they are used to pass multiline strings, verbatim, as a single argument to commands. This means it will include whitespace in the form of tabs and newlines.

These arguments are structured exactly like comments – that is, they are opened with `[=[` and closed with `]=]`, where the number of the equal signs in the opening and closing tokens has to match (skipping the equal signs is fine too, but they still have to match). The only difference from comments is that you can't nest bracket arguments.

Here's an example of the use of such an argument with the `message()` command, which prints all passed arguments to the screen:

chapter02/01-arguments/bracket.cmake

```
message([[multiline
    bracket
    argument
```

```
]])

message([==[
  because we used two equal-signs "=="
  following is still a single argument:
  { "petsArray" = [["mouse","cat"],["dog"]] }
]==])
```

In the above example, we can see different forms of bracket arguments. The first one skips the equal sign. Note how putting closing tags on a separate line is visible as an empty line in the output:

```
$ cmake -P chapter02/01-arguments/bracket.cmake
multiline
bracket
argument

  because we used two equal-signs "=="
  following is still a single argument:
  { "petsArray" = [["mouse","cat"],["dog"]] }
```

The second form is useful when we're passing text that contains double brackets (]]) (highlighted in the code snippet), as they won't be interpreted as marking the end of the argument.

These kinds of bracket arguments have limited use – typically, to contain longer blocks of text. In most cases, we'll need something more dynamic, such as quoted arguments.

Quoted arguments

Quoted arguments resemble a regular C++ string – these arguments group together multiple characters, including whitespace, and they will expand *escape sequences*. Like C++ strings, they are opened and closed with a double quote character ("), so to include a quote character within the output string, you have to escape it with a backslash (\"). Other well-known escape sequences are supported as well: \\ denotes a literal backslash, \t is a tab character, \n is a newline, and \r is a carriage return.

This is where the similarities with C++ strings end. Quoted arguments can span multiple lines, and they will interpolate variable references. Think of them as having a built-in `sprintf` function from **C** or a `std::format` function from **C++20**. To insert a variable reference to your argument, wrap the name of the variable in a token like so: `${name}`. We'll talk more about variable references in the *Working with variables* section.

Let's try these arguments in action:

chapter02/01-arguments/quoted.cmake

```
message("1. escape sequence: \" \n in a quoted argument")
message("2. multi...
   line")
message("3. and a variable reference: ${CMAKE_VERSION}")
```

Can you guess how many lines will be in the output of the preceding script?

```
$ cmake -P chapter02/01-arguments/quoted.cmake
1. escape sequence: "
 in a quoted argument
2. multi...
line
3. and a variable reference: 3.16.3
```

That's right – we have one escaped quote character, one escaped newline, and a literal newline. All of them will be printed in the output. We also accessed a built-in `CMAKE_VERSION` variable, which we can see correctly interpolated on the last line.

Unquoted arguments

The last type of argument is definitely a bit rare in the programming world. We got used to the fact that strings have to be delimited in one way or another, for example, by using single quotes, double quotes, or a backslash. CMake deviates from this convention and introduces unquoted arguments. We might argue that dropping delimiters makes the code easier to read, just like skipping semicolons. Is that true? I'll let you form your own opinion.

Unquoted arguments evaluate both *escape sequences* and *variable references*. However, be careful with semicolons (`;`), as in CMake, this is treated as a delimiter. CMake will split the argument containing it into multiple arguments. If you need to use it, escape it with a backslash (`\;`). This is how CMake manages lists. I'll explain that in detail in the *Using lists* section.

You may find that these arguments are the most perplexing to work with, so here's an illustration to help clarify how these arguments are partitioned:

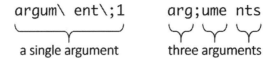

Figure 2.2 – Escape sequences cause separate tokens to be interpreted as a single argument

> **Question**
>
> Why does it matter if a value is passed as a single argument or many arguments? Some CMake commands require a specific number of arguments and ignore any overhead. If your arguments accidentally become separated, you'll get hard-to-debug errors.

Unquoted arguments cannot contain unescaped quotes (`"`), hashes (`#`), and backslashes (`\`). And if that's not enough rules to remember, parentheses (`( )`) are allowed only if they form correct, matching pairs. That is, you'll start with an opening parenthesis and close it before closing the command argument list.

Let's look at some examples of all of the above rules:

chapter02/01-arguments/unquoted.cmake

```
message(a\ single\ argument)
message(two arguments)
message(three;separated;arguments)
message(${CMAKE_VERSION})     # a variable reference
message(() () ())             # matching parentheses
```

What will be the output of the above? Let's have a look:

```
$ cmake -P chapter02/01-arguments/unquoted.cmake
a single argument
twoarguments
threeseparatedarguments
3.16.3
() () ()
```

Even a simple command such as `message()` is very particular about separated unquoted arguments:

- The space in `a single argument` was correctly printed when it was explicitly escaped.
- However, `twoarguments` and `threeseparatearguments` were *glued* together, since `message()` doesn't add any spaces on its own.

Now that we understand how to deal with the complexities and quirks of CMake arguments, we are ready to tackle the next interesting subject – working with all kinds of *variables* in CMake.

Working with variables

Variables in CMake are a surprisingly complex subject. Not only are there three categories of variables – normal, cache, and environment – but they also reside in different scopes, with specific rules on how one scope affects the other. Very often, a poor understanding of all these rules becomes a source of bugs and headaches. I recommend you study this section with care and make sure you understand all of concepts before moving on.

Let's start with some key facts about variables in CMake:

- Variable names are case-sensitive and can include almost any character.
- All variables are stored internally as strings, even if some commands can interpret them as values of other data types (even lists!).
- The basic variable manipulation commands are `set()` and `unset()`, but there are other commands that can affect variables, such as `string()` and `list()`.

To set a variable, we simply call `set()`, providing its name and the value:

chapter02/02-variables/set.cmake

```
set(MyString1 "Text1")
set([[My String2]] "Text2")
set("My String 3" "Text3")
message(${MyString1})
message(${My\ String2})
message(${My\ String\ 3})
```

As you can see, the use of brackets and quoted arguments allows for spaces to be included in the variable name. However, when referencing it later, we have to escape the whitespace with a backslash (\). For that reason, it is recommended to use only alphanumeric characters, dashes (-), and underscores (_) in variable names.

Also avoid reserved names (in upper, lower, or mixed case) that begin with any of the following: `CMAKE_`, `_CMAKE_`, or underscore (_), followed by the name of any CMake command.

> **Note**
>
> The `set()` command accepts a plain text variable name as its first argument, but the `message()` command uses a variable reference wrapped in the `${}` syntax. What would happen if we were to provide a variable wrapped in the `${}` syntax to the `set()` command? To answer that, we'll need to understand variable references better.

To unset a variable, we can use `unset()` in the following way: `unset(MyString1)`.

Variable references

I already mentioned references briefly in the *Command arguments* section, as they're evaluated for quoted and unquoted arguments. And we learned that to create a reference to a defined variable, we need to use the `${}` syntax, like so: `message(${MyString1})`.

On evaluation, CMake will traverse the scope stack (I'll explain that in a second) and replace `${MyString1}` with a value, or an empty string if no variable is found (CMake won't generate any error messages). This process is called *variable evaluation*, *expansion*, or *interpolation*.

Such interpolation is performed in an inside-out fashion. This means two things:

- If the following reference is encountered – `${MyOuter${MyInner}}` – CMake will try to evaluate `MyInner` first, rather than searching for a variable named `MyOuter${MyInner}`.
- If the `MyInner` variable is successfully expanded, CMake will repeat the expansion process until no further expansion is possible.

Let's consider an example with the following variables:

- `MyInner` with a `Hello` value
- `MyOuter` with a `${My` value

If we call the `message("${MyOuter}Inner} World")` command, the output we'll receive will be `Hello World`, and that is because `${MyOuter}` was replaced with a literal value, `${My`, which, when combined with the top-level value, `Inner}`, creates another variable reference – `${MyInner}`.

CMake will perform this expansion to the full extent, and only then will it pass the resulting values as arguments to the command. This is why when we call `set(${MyInner} "Hi")`, we won't actually be changing the `MyInner` variable, but instead, we'll change the `Hello` variable. CMake expands `${MyInner}` to `Hello` and passes that string as the first argument to the `set()` command, along with a new value, `Hi`. Very often, this is not what we want.

Variable references are a bit peculiar in how they work when it comes to variable categories, but in general, the following applies:

- The `${}` syntax is used to reference *normal* or *cache* variables.
- The `$ENV{}` syntax is used to reference *environment* variables.
- The `$CACHE{}` syntax is used to reference *cache* variables.

That's right, with `${}`, you might get a value from one category or the other. I'll explain that in the *How to correctly use the variable scope in CMake* section, but first, let's introduce some other categories of variables so that we understand clearly what they are.

> **Note**
> Remember that you can pass arguments to scripts through the command line after a `--` token. Values will be stored in the `CMAKE_ARGV<n>` variable and the count of the passed arguments will be in the `CMAKE_ARGC` variable.

Using the environment variables

This is the least complicated kind of variable. CMake makes a copy of the variables that were in the environment used to start the `cmake` process and makes them available in a single, global scope. To reference these variables, use the `$ENV{<name>}` syntax.

CMake also allows you to set (`set()`) and unset (`unset()`) these variables, but changes will only be made to a local copy in the running `cmake` process and not the actual system environment; moreover, these changes won't be visible to subsequent runs of builds or tests.

To modify or create a variable, use the `set(ENV{<variable>} <value>)` command, like so:

```
set(ENV{CXX} "clang++")
```

To clear an environment variable, use `unset(ENV{<variable>})`, like so:

```
unset(ENV{VERBOSE})
```

Be aware that there are a few environment variables that affect different aspects of CMake behavior. The `CXX` variable is one of them – it specifies what executable will be used for compiling C++ files. We'll cover other environmental variables, as they will become relevant for this book. A full list is available in the documentation:

https://cmake.org/cmake/help/latest/manual/cmake-env-variables.7.html

If you use `ENV` variables as arguments to your commands, the values will be interpolated during the generation of the buildsystem. This means that they will get baked into the build tree, and changing the environment for the build stage won't have any effect.

For example, take the following project file:

chapter02/03-environment/CMakeLists.txt

```
cmake_minimum_required(VERSION 3.20.0)
project(Environment)

message("generated with " $ENV{myenv})
add_custom_target(EchoEnv ALL COMMAND echo "myenv in build
   is" $ENV{myenv})
```

The preceding example has two steps: it will print the `myenv` environment variable during the configuration, and it will add a build stage through `add_custom_target()`, which echoes the same variable as part of the build process. We can test what happens with a bash script that uses one value for the configuration stage and another for the build stage:

chapter02/03-environment/build.sh

```
#!/bin/bash
export myenv=first
echo myenv is now $myenv
```

```
cmake -B build .
cd build
export myenv=second
echo myenv is now $myenv
cmake --build .
```

Running the preceding code clearly shows that the value set during the configuration is persisted to the generated buildsystem:

```
$ ./build.sh | grep -v "\-\-"
myenv is now first
generated with first
myenv is now second
Scanning dependencies of target EchoEnv
myenv in build is first
Built target EchoEnv
```

Using the cache variables

We first mentioned cache variables when discussing command-line options for cmake in *Chapter 1, First Steps with CMake*. Essentially, they're persistent variables stored in a CMakeCache.txt file in your build tree. They contain information gathered during the project configuration stage, both from the system (path to compilers, linkers, tools, and others) and from the user through the **GUI**. Cache variables are not available in *scripts* (since there's no CMakeCache.txt file) – they only exist in *projects*.

Cache variables can be referenced with the $CACHE{<name>} syntax.

To set a cache variable, use set() with the following syntax:

set(<variable> <value> CACHE <type> <docstring> [FORCE])

As you can see, there are some new required arguments (in comparison to the set() command for normal variables), and it also introduces first keywords: CACHE and FORCE.

Specifying `CACHE` as a `set()` argument means that we intend to change what was provided during the configuration stage, and it imposes a requirement to provide the variable `<type>` and `<docstring>` values. This is because these variables are configurable by the user and the GUI needs to know how to display it. The following types are accepted:

- `BOOL`: A Boolean on/off value. The GUI will show a checkbox.
- `FILEPATH`: A path to a file on a disk. The GUI will open a file dialog.
- `PATH`: A path to a directory on a disk. The GUI will open a directory dialog.
- `STRING`: A line of text. The GUI offers a text field to be filled. It can be replaced by a drop-down control by calling `set_property(CACHE <variable> STRINGS <values>)`.
- `INTERNAL`: A line of text. The GUI skips internal entries. The internal entries may be used to store variables persistently across runs. Use of this type implicitly adds the `FORCE` keyword.

The `<doctring>` value is simply a label that will be displayed by the GUI next to the field to provide more detail about this setting to the user. It is required even for an `INTERNAL` type.

Setting cache variables follows the same rules as environmental variables to some extent – values are overwritten only for the current execution of CMake. Take a look at this example:

```
set(FOO "BAR" CACHE STRING "interesting value")
```

The above call has no permanent effect if the variable exists in the cache. However, if the value doesn't exist in cache or an optional `FORCE` argument is specified, the value will be persisted:

```
set(FOO "BAR" CACHE STRING "interesting value" FORCE)
```

Setting the cache variables has some unobvious implications. That is, any normal variable with the same name will be removed. We'll find out why in the next section.

As a reminder, cache variables can be managed from the command line as well (check the appropriate section in *Chapter 1, First Steps with CMake*).

How to correctly use the variable scope in CMake

Variable scope is probably the hardest part of the whole concept of the CMake Language. This is maybe because we're so accustomed to how things are done in more advanced languages that support namespaces and scope operators. CMake doesn't have those mechanisms, so it deals with this issue in its own, somewhat unusual way.

Just to clarify, variable scopes as a general concept are meant to separate different layers of abstraction so that when a user-defined function is called, variables set in that function are local to it. These *local* variables aren't affecting the *global* scope, even if the names of the local variables are exactly the same as the global ones. If explicitly needed, functions should have read/write access to global variables as well. This separation of variables (or scopes) has to work on many levels – when one function calls another, the same separation rules apply.

CMake has two scopes:

- **Function scope**: For when custom functions defined with `function()` are executed
- **Directory scope**: For when a `CMakeLists.txt` listfile in a nested directory is executed from the `add_subdirectory()` command

We'll cover the preceding commands later in this book, but first, we need to know how the concept of variable scope is implemented. When a nested scope is created, CMake simply fills it with copies of all the variables from the current scope. Subsequent commands will affect these copies. But as soon as the execution of the nested scope is completed, all copies are deleted and the original, parent scope is restored.

Let's consider the following scenario:

1. The parent scope sets the `VAR` variable to `ONE`.
2. The nested scope starts and `VAR` is printed to console.
3. The `VAR` variable is set to `TWO`, and `VAR` is printed to the console.
4. The nested scope ends, and `VAR` is printed to the console.

The console's output will look like this: `ONE`, `TWO`, `ONE`. This is because the copied `VAR` variable is discarded after the nested scope ends.

How the concept of scope works in CMake has interesting implications that aren't that common in other languages. If you unset (`unset()`) a variable created in the parent scope while executing in a nested scope, it will disappear, but only in the nested scope. When the nested scope is completed, the variable is restored to its previous value.

This brings us to the behavior of variable referencing and the `${}` syntax. Whenever we try to access the normal variable, CMake will search for the variables from the current scope, and if the variable with such a name is defined, it will return its value. So far, so good. However, when CMake can't find a variable with that name (for example, if it didn't exist or was unset (`unset()`)), it will search through the cache variables and return a value from there if a match is found.

That's a possible gotcha if we have a nested scope calling `unset()`. Depending on where we reference that variable – in the inner or the outer scope – we'll be accessing the cache or the original value.

But what can we do if we really need to change the variable in the calling (parent) scope? CMake has a `PARENT_SCOPE` flag you can add at the end of the `set()` and `unset()` commands:

```
set(MyVariable "New Value" PARENT_SCOPE)
unset(MyVariable PARENT_SCOPE)
```

That workaround is a bit limited, as it doesn't allow accessing variables more than one level up. Another thing worth noting is the fact that using `PARENT_SCOPE` doesn't change variables in the current scope.

Let's see how variable scope works in practice and consider the following example:

chapter02/04-scope/CMakeLists.txt

```
function(Inner)
    message("   > Inner: ${V}")
    set(V 3)
    message("   < Inner: ${V}")
endfunction()

function(Outer)
    message(" > Outer: ${V}")
    set(V 2)
    Inner()
    message(" < Outer: ${V}")
endfunction()

set(V 1)
message("> Global: ${V}")
```

```
Outer()
message("< Global: ${V}")
```

We set the global variable, V, to 1, and then we call the Outer function; then set V to 2 and call the Inner function, and then set V to 3. After every step, we print the variable to the console:

```
> Global: 1
 > Outer: 1
  > Inner: 2
  < Inner: 3
 < Outer: 2
< Global: 1
```

As we explained previously, as we go deeper into the functions, the variable values are copied to the nested scope, but as we exit the scope, their original value is restored.

What would the output be if we changed the set() command of the Inner function to operate in the parent scope: set(V 3 PARENT_SCOPE)?

```
> Global: 1
 > Outer: 1
  > Inner: 2
  < Inner: 2
 < Outer: 3
< Global: 1
```

We affected the scope of the Outer function, but not the scope of the Inner function or the global scope!

The CMake documentation also mentions that CMake scripts bind variables in one directory scope (which is a bit redundant, as the only command that effectively creates a directory scope, add_subdirectory(), isn't allowed in scripts).

Since all variables are stored as strings, CMake has to take a more creative approach to more complex data structures such as *lists*.

Using lists

To store a **list**, CMake concatenates all elements into a string, using a semicolon (;) as a delimiter: a;list;of;5;elements. You can escape a semicolon in an element with a backslash, like so: a\;single\;element.

To create a list, we can use the `set()` command: `set(myList a list of five elements)`. Because of how lists are stored, the following commands will have exactly the same effect:

- `set(myList "a;list;of;five;elements")`
- `set(myList a list "of;five;elements")`

CMake automatically unpacks lists in unquoted arguments. By passing an unquoted `myList` reference, we effectively send more arguments to the command:

```
message("the list is:" ${myList})
```

The `message()` command will receive here six arguments: `"the list is:"`, `"a"`, `"list"`, `"of"`, `"five"`, `"elements"`. This may have unintended consequences, as the output will be printed without any additional spaces between the arguments:

```
the list is:alistoffiveelements
```

As you can see, this is a very simple mechanism, and it should be used carefully.

CMake offers a `list()` command that provides a multitude of subcommands to read, search, modify, and order lists. Here's a short summary:

```
list(LENGTH <list> <out-var>)
list(GET <list> <element index> [<index> ...] <out-var>)
list(JOIN <list> <glue> <out-var>)
list(SUBLIST <list> <begin> <length> <out-var>)
list(FIND <list> <value> <out-var>)
list(APPEND <list> [<element>...])
list(FILTER <list> {INCLUDE | EXCLUDE} REGEX <regex>)
list(INSERT <list> <index> [<element>...])
list(POP_BACK <list> [<out-var>...])
list(POP_FRONT <list> [<out-var>...])
list(PREPEND <list> [<element>...])
list(REMOVE_ITEM <list> <value>...)
list(REMOVE_AT <list> <index>...)
list(REMOVE_DUPLICATES <list>)
list(TRANSFORM <list> <ACTION> [...])
list(REVERSE <list>)
list(SORT <list> [...])
```

Most of the time, we don't really need to use lists in our projects. However, if you find yourself in that rare case where this concept would be convenient, you'll find a more in-depth reference of the `list()` command in the *Appendix* section.

Now that we know how to work with lists and variables of all kinds, let's shift our focus to controlling the execution flow and learn about control structures available in CMake.

Understanding control structures in CMake

The CMake Language wouldn't be complete without **control structures**! Like everything else, they are provided in the form of a command, and they come in three categories: **conditional blocks**, **loops**, and **command definitions**. Control structures are executed in scripts and during buildsystem generation for projects.

Conditional blocks

The only conditional block supported in CMake is the humble `if()` command. All conditional blocks have to be closed with an `endif()` command, and they may have any number of `elseif()` commands and one optional `else()` command in this order:

```
if(<condition>)
    <commands>
elseif(<condition>)  # optional block, can be repeated
    <commands>
else()               # optional block
    <commands>
endif()
```

As in many other imperative languages, the `if()`-`endif()` block controls which sets of commands will be executed:

- If the `<condition>` expression specified in the `if()` command is met, the first section will be executed.
- Otherwise, CMake will execute commands in the section belonging to the first `elseif()` command in this block that has met its condition.
- If there are no such commands, CMake will check if the `else()` command is provided and execute any commands in that section of the code.
- If none of the above conditions are met, the execution continues after the `endif()` command.

The provided <condition> expression is evaluated according to a very simple syntax.

The syntax for conditional commands

The same syntax is valid for if(), elseif(), and while() commands.

Logical operators

The if() conditions support the NOT, AND, and OR logical operators:

- NOT <condition>
- <condition> AND <condition>
- <condition> OR <condition>

Also, the nesting of conditions is possible with matching pairs of parentheses (()). As in all decent languages, the CMake Language respects the order of evaluation and starts from the innermost parenthesis:

- (<condition>) AND (<condition> OR (<condition>))

The evaluation of a string and a variable

For legacy reasons (because the variable reference (${}) syntax wasn't always around), CMake will try to evaluate *unquoted arguments* as if they are *variable references*. In other words, using a plain variable name (for example, VAR) inside a condition is equal to writing ${VAR}. Here's an example for you to consider, and a *gotcha*:

```
set(VAR1 FALSE)
set(VAR2 "VAR1")
if(${VAR2})
```

The if() condition works in a bit of a convoluted way here – first, it will evaluate ${VAR2} to VAR1, which is a recognized variable, and this in turn is evaluated to the FALSE string. Strings are considered Boolean true only if they equal any of the following constants (these comparisons are case insensitive):

- ON, Y, YES, or TRUE
- A non-zero number

This brings us to the conclusion that the condition in the preceding example will evaluate to false.

However, here's another catch – what would be the evaluation of a condition with an unquoted argument with a name of a variable containing a value such as BAR? Consider the following code example:

```
set(FOO BAR)
if(FOO)
```

According to what we have said so far, it would be `false`, as the BAR string doesn't meet the criteria to evaluate to a Boolean `true` value. That's unfortunately not the case, because CMake makes an exception when it comes to unquoted variable references. Unlike with quoted arguments, FOO won't be evaluated to BAR to produce an `if("BAR")` statement (which would be `false`). Instead, CMake will only evaluate `if(FOO)` to `false` if it is any of the following constants (these comparisons are case insensitive):

- OFF, NO, FALSE, N, IGNORE, NOTFOUND
- A string ending with -NOTFOUND
- An empty string
- Zero

So, simply asking for an undefined variable will be evaluated to `false`:

```
if (FOO)
```

However, defining a variable beforehand changes the situation, and the condition is evaluated to `true`:

```
set(FOO "FOO")
if (FOO)
```

> **Note**
> If you think that the behavior of unquoted arguments is confusing, wrap variable references in quoted arguments: `if ("${FOO}")`. This will result in argument evaluation before the provided argument is passed into the `if()` command, and the behavior will be consistent with the evaluation of strings.

In other words, CMake assumes that the user is asking if the variable is defined (and is not explicitly `false`). Luckily, we can explicitly check that fact (and not worry about the value inside):

```
if(DEFINED <name>)
if(DEFINED CACHE{<name>})
if(DEFINED ENV{<name>})
```

Comparing values

Comparison operations are supported with the following operators:

EQUAL, LESS, LESS_EQUAL, GREATER, and GREATER_EQUAL

They can be used to compare numeric values, like so:

```
if (1 LESS 2)
```

> **Note**
> The CMake documentation states that if one of the operands is not a number, the value will be `false`. But practical experiments show that the comparison of strings starting with a number works correctly: `if (20 EQUALS "20 GB")`.

You can compare software versions following the `major[.minor[.patch[.tweak]]]` format by adding a `VERSION_` prefix to any of the operators:

```
if (1.3.4 VERSION_LESS_EQUAL 1.4)
```

Omitted components are treated as zero, and non-integer version components truncate the compared string at that point.

For *lexicographic* string comparisons, we need to prepend an operator with the `STR` prefix (note the lack of an underscore):

```
if ("A" STREQUAL "${B}")
```

We often need more advanced mechanisms than simple equality comparisons. Fortunately, CMake also supports **POSIX regex** matching (the CMake documentation hints at an ERE flavor, but no support for specific regex character classes is mentioned). We can use the MATCHES operator as follows:

<VARIABLE|STRING> MATCHES <regex>

Any matched groups are captured in CMAKE_MATCH_<n> variables.

Simple checks

We already mentioned one simple check, DEFINED, but there are others that simply return true if a condition is met.

We can check the following:

- If a value is in a list: <VARIABLE|STRING> IN_LIST <VARIABLE>
- If a command is available for invocation: COMMAND <command-name>
- If a CMake policy exists: POLICY <policy-id> (this is covered in *Chapter 3, Setting Up Your First CMake Project*)
- If a CTest test was added with add_test(): TEST <test-name>
- If a build target is defined: TARGET <target-name>

We'll explore build targets in *Chapter 4, Working with Targets*, but for now, let's just say that targets are logical units of a build process in a project created with a add_executable(), add_library(), or add_custom_target() command that has already been invoked.

Examining the filesystem

CMake provides many ways of working with files. We rarely need to manipulate them directly, and normally we'd rather use a high-level approach. For reference, this book will provide a short list of the file-related commands in the *Appendix* section. But most often, only the following operators will be needed (behavior is well defined only for absolute paths):

- EXISTS <path-to-file-or-directory>: Checks if a file or directory exists

  This resolves symbolic links (it returns true if the target of the symbolic link exists).

- <file1> IS_NEWER_THAN <file2>: Checks which file is newer

This returns `true` if `file1` is newer than (or equal to) `file2` or if one of the two files doesn't exist.
- `IS_DIRECTORY path-to-directory`: Checks if a path is a directory
- `IS_SYMLINK file-name`: Checks if a path is a symbolic link
- `IS_ABSOLUTE path`: Checks if a path is absolute

Loops

Loops in CMake are fairly straightforward – we can use either `while()` or `foreach()` to repeatedly execute the same set of commands. Both of these commands support loop control mechanisms:

- The `break()` loop stops the execution of the remaining block and breaks from the enclosing loop.
- The `continue()` loop stops the execution of the current iteration and starts at the top of the next one.

While

The loop block is opened with a `while()` command and closed with an `endwhile()` command. Any enclosed commands will be executed as long as the `<condition>` expression provided in `while()` is `true`. The syntax for phrasing the condition is the same as for the `if()` command:

```
while(<condition>)
    <commands>
endwhile()
```

You probably guessed that – with some additional variables – the `while` loop can replace a `for` loop. Actually, it's way easier to use a `foreach()` loop for that – let's take a look.

Foreach loops

A foreach block comes in a few variants that execute enclosed commands for each value. Like other blocks, it has opening and closing commands: `foreach()` and `endforeach()`.

The simplest form of `foreach()` is meant to provide a C++-style `for` loop:

```
foreach(<loop_var> RANGE <max>)
   <commands>
endforeach()
```

CMake will iterate from `0` to `<max>` (inclusive). If we need more control, we can use the second variant, providing `<min>`, `<max>`, and, optionally, `<step>`. All arguments must be nonnegative integers. Also, `<min>` has to be smaller than `<max>`:

```
foreach(<loop_var> RANGE <min> <max> [<step>])
```

However, `foreach()` shows its true colors when it is working with lists:

```
foreach(<loop_variable> IN [LISTS <lists>] [ITEMS <items>])
```

CMake will take elements from all of the provided `<lists>` list variables, followed by all of the explicitly stated `<items>` values, and store them in `<loop variable>`, executing `<commands>` for every item, one by one. You can choose to provide only lists, only values, or both:

chapter02/06-loops/foreach.cmake

```
set(MY_LIST 1 2 3)
foreach(VAR IN LISTS MY_LIST ITEMS e f)
   message(${VAR})
endforeach()
```

The preceding code will print the following:

```
1
2
3
e
f
```

Or, we can use a short version (skipping the `IN` keyword) for the same result:

```
foreach(VAR 1 2 3 e f)
```

Since version 3.17, `foreach()` has learned how to zip lists (`ZIP_LISTS`):

```
foreach(<loop_var>... IN ZIP_LISTS <lists>)
```

Zipping lists means simply iterating through multiple lists and working on respective items with the same index. Let's look at an example:

chapter02/06-loops/foreach.cmake

```
set(L1 "one;two;three;four")
set(L2 "1;2;3;4;5")
foreach(num IN ZIP_LISTS L1 L2)
    message("num_0=${num_0}, num_1=${num_1}")
endforeach()
```

CMake will create a num_<N> variable for each list provided, which it will fill with items from each list. You can pass multiple `<loop_var>` variable names (one for every list) and each list will use a separate variable to store its items:

```
foreach(word num IN ZIP_LISTS L1 L2)
    message("word=${word}, num=${num}")
```

If the count of items differs between lists, CMake won't define variables for shorter ones.

So, that's everything covered with regard to *loops*.

Command definitions

There are two ways to define your own command: you can use the `macro()` command or the `function()` command. The easiest way to explain the differences between these commands is by comparing them to C-style preprocessor macros and actual C++ functions:

- A `macro()` command works more like a find-and-replace instruction than an actual subroutine call such as `function()`. Contrary to functions, macros don't create a separate entry on a call stack. This means that calling `return()` in a macro will return to the calling statement one level higher than it would for a function (possibly terminating the execution if we're already in the top scope).

- The `function()` command creates a separate scope for local variables, unlike the `macro()` command, which works in the variable scope of a caller. This may lead to confusing results. Let's talk about these details in the next section.

Both methods accept arguments that you can name and reference inside of a command block. Additionally, CMake allows you to access arguments passed in command calls with the following references:

- `${ARGC}`: The count of arguments
- `${ARGV}`: A list of all arguments
- `${ARG0}`, `${ARG1}`, `${ARG2}`: The value of an argument at a specific index
- `${ARGN}`: A list of anonymous arguments that were passed by a caller after the last expected argument

Accessing a numeric argument with an index outside of the `ARGC` bounds is undefined behavior.

If you decide to define a command with named arguments, every call has to pass all of them or it will be invalid.

Macros

Defining a macro is similar to any other block:

```
macro(<name> [<argument>...])
    <commands>
endmacro()
```

After this declaration, we may execute our macro by calling its name (function calls are case-insensitive).

The following example highlights all of the problems relating to variable scopes in macros:

chapter02/08-definitions/macro.cmake

```
macro(MyMacro myVar)
    set(myVar "new value")
    message("argument: ${myVar}")
endmacro()

set(myVar "first value")
message("myVar is now: ${myVar}")
MyMacro("called value")
message("myVar is now: ${myVar}")
```

Here's the output from this script:

```
$ cmake -P chapter02/08-definitions/macro.cmake
myVar is now: first value
argument: called value
myVar is now: new value
```

What happened? Despite explicitly setting `myVar` to `new value`, it didn't affect the output for `message("argument: ${myVar}")`! This is because arguments passed to macros aren't treated as real variables but rather as constant find-and-replace instructions.

On the other hand, the `myVar` variable in the global scope got changed from `first value` to `new value`. This behavior is called a *side effect* and is considered a bad practice, as it's hard to tell which variables might be affected by such a macro without reading it.

I recommend using functions whenever you can, as it will probably save you a lot of headaches.

Functions

To declare a command as a function, follow this syntax:

```
function(<name> [<argument>...])
    <commands>
endfunction()
```

A function requires a name and optionally accepts a list of names of expected arguments. If a function call passes more arguments than were declared, the excess arguments will be interpreted as anonymous arguments and stored in the `ARGN` variable.

As mentioned before, functions open their own scope. You can call `set()`, providing one of the named arguments of the function, and any change will be local to the function (unless `PARENT_SCOPE` is specified, as we discussed in the *How to correctly use the variable scope in CMake* section).

Functions follow the rules of the call stack, enabling returning to the calling scope with the `return()` command.

CMake sets the following variables for each function (these have been available since version 3.17):

- CMAKE_CURRENT_FUNCTION
- CMAKE_CURRENT_FUNCTION_LIST_DIR
- CMAKE_CURRENT_FUNCTION_LIST_FILE
- CMAKE_CURRENT_FUNCTION_LIST_LINE

Let's take a look at these function variables in practice:

chapter02/08-definitions/function.cmake

```
function(MyFunction FirstArg)
  message("Function: ${CMAKE_CURRENT_FUNCTION}")
  message("File: ${CMAKE_CURRENT_FUNCTION_LIST_FILE}")
  message("FirstArg: ${FirstArg}")
  set(FirstArg "new value")
  message("FirstArg again: ${FirstArg}")
  message("ARGV0: ${ARGV0} ARGV1: ${ARGV1} ARGC: ${ARGC}")
endfunction()

set(FirstArg "first value")
MyFunction("Value1" "Value2")
message("FirstArg in global scope: ${FirstArg}")
```

This prints the following output:

```
Function: MyFunction
File: /root/examples/chapter02/08-definitions/function.cmake
FirstArg: Value1
FirstArg again: new value
ARGV0: Value1 ARGV1: Value2 ARGC: 2
FirstArg in global scope: first value
```

As you can see, the general syntax and concept of the functions is very similar to macros, but this time – it actually works.

The procedural paradigm in CMake

Let's imagine for a second that we want to write some CMake code in the same way we would write a program in C++. We'll make a `CMakeLists.txt` listfile that will call three defined commands that may call defined commands of their own:

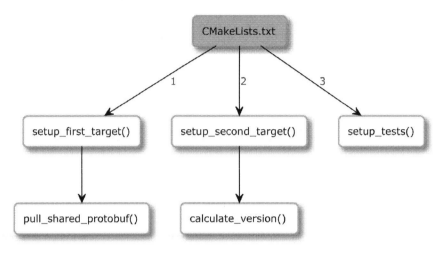

Figure 2.3 – A procedural call graph

Writing in this procedural style is a bit of a problem in CMake – you are required to provide command definitions you're planning to use ahead of time. The CMake parser will not have it any other way. Your code would look something like this:

```
cmake_minimum_required(...)
project(Procedural)
function(pull_shared_protobuf)
function(setup_first_target)
function(calculate_version)
function(setup_second_target)
function(setup_tests)

setup_first_target()
setup_second_target()
setup_tests()
```

What a nightmare! Everything is reversed! This code is very difficult to read as the most minuscule details are at the top of the file. A correctly structured piece of code lists the most general steps in the first subroutine, after which it provides the slightly more detailed subroutines, and pushes the most detailed steps to the very end of the file.

There are solutions to this problem: moving command definitions to other files and partitioning scopes across directories (scoped directories will be explained in detail in *Chapter 3*, *Setting Up Your First CMake Project*). But there is also a solution that is simple and elegant: declaring an entry-point macro at the top of the file and calling it at the very end of the file:

```
macro(main)
function(...) # key steps
function(...) # details
function(...) # fine details
main()
```

With this approach, our code is written with gradually narrowing scope, and because we're not actually calling the `main()` macro until the very end, CMake won't complain about the execution of undefined commands!

One last question remains – why use a macro over a recommended function? In this case, it's good to have unrestricted access to global variables, and since we're not passing any arguments to `main()`, we don't need to worry about the usual caveats.

You'll find a simple example of this concept in the `chapter-02/09-procedural/CMakeLists.txt` listfile in the GitHub repository for this book.

A word on naming conventions

Naming is famously hard in software development, but nevertheless, it's very important to maintain a solution that is easy to read and understand. When it comes to CMake scripts and projects, we should follow the rules of the *clean code* approach, as we would with any software development solution:

- Follow a consistent naming style (`snake_case` is an accepted standard in the CMake community).
- Use short but meaningful names (for example, avoid `func()`, `f()`, and suchlike).
- Avoid puns and cleverness in your naming.
- Use pronounceable, searchable names that don't require mental mapping.

Now that we know how to properly invoke the commands with the correct syntax, let's explore which commands will be the most beneficial to us to begin with.

Useful commands

CMake offers many, many scripting commands that allow you to work with variables and the environment. Some of them are covered extensively in the *Appendix* section, for example, `list()`, `string()`, and `file()` (we'll leave these explanations there and concentrate on projects in the main chapters). Others, such as `find_...()`, fit better in chapters that talk about managing dependencies. In this section, we'll briefly cover the most useful commands for scripts.

The message() command

We already know and love our trusty `message()` command, which prints text to standard output. However, there's a lot more to it than meets the eye. By providing a MODE argument, you can customize the style of the output, and in the case of an error, you can stop the execution of the code: `message(<MODE> "text")`.

The recognized modes are as follows:

- `FATAL_ERROR`: This stops processing and generation.
- `SEND_ERROR`: This continues processing, but skips generation.
- `WARNING`: This continues processing.
- `AUTHOR_WARNING`: A CMake warning. This continues processing.
- `DEPRECATION`: This works accordingly if either of the `CMAKE_ERROR_DEPRECATED` or `CMAKE_WARN_DEPRECATED` variables are enabled.
- `NOTICE` or omitted mode (default): This prints a message to `stderr` to attract the user's attention.
- `STATUS`: This continues processing and is recommended for main messages for users.
- `VERBOSE`: This continues processing and should be used for more detailed information that usually isn't very necessary.
- `DEBUG`: This continues processing and should contain any fine details that might be helpful when there's an issue with a project.
- `TRACE`: This continues processing and is recommended to print messages during the project development. Usually, these sorts of messages would be removed before publishing the project.

The following example stops execution after the first message:

chapter02/10-useful/message_error.cmake

```
message(FATAL_ERROR "Stop processing")
message("Won't print this.")
```

This means messages will be printed depending on the current log level (which is STATUS by default). We discussed how to change this in the previous chapter in the *Options for debugging and tracing* section. At that point, I promised to talk about debugging with CMAKE_MESSAGE_CONTEXT, so let's get to it. Since then, we have acquired an understanding of three important pieces to this puzzle: lists, scopes, and functions.

When we enable a command-line flag, cmake --log-context, our messages will be decorated with dot-separated context and stored in the CMAKE_MESSAGE_CONTEXT list. Consider the following example:

chapter02/10-useful/message_context.cmake

```
function(foo)
    list(APPEND CMAKE_MESSAGE_CONTEXT "foo")
    message("foo message")
endfunction()

list(APPEND CMAKE_MESSAGE_CONTEXT "top")
message("Before `foo`")
foo()
message("After `foo`")
```

The output of the preceding script will look like this:

```
$ cmake -P message_context.cmake --log-context
[top] Before `foo`
[top.foo] foo message
[top] After `foo`
```

The initial scope of the function is copied from the parent scope (which already has one item in the list: top). The first command in foo adds a new item with the foo function name to CMAKE_MESSAGE_CONTEXT. The message is printed, and the function scope ends, discarding the local, copied variables, and the previous scope (without foo) is restored.

This approach is useful with many nested functions in very complex projects. Hopefully, you won't ever need it, but I thought it is a really good example of how a function scope works in practice.

Another cool trick with `message()` is to add indentation to the `CMAKE_MESSAGE_INDENT` list (in exactly the same way as with `CMAKE_MESSAGE_CONTEXT`):

```
list(APPEND CMAKE_MESSAGE_INDENT "  ")
```

The output from our scripts can then look a bit cleaner:

```
Before `foo`
  foo message
After `foo`
```

Since CMake doesn't offer any real debugger with breakpoints or other tools, the ability to produce clean log messages comes in very handy when things don't go exactly as planned.

The include() command

We can partition our CMake code into separate files to keep things ordered and, well, *separate*. Then, we can reference them from our parent listfile by calling `include()`, as shown in the following example:

```
include(<file|module> [OPTIONAL] [RESULT_VARIABLE <var>])
```

If we provide a filename (a path with a `.cmake` extension), CMake will try to open and execute it. Note that no nested, separate scope will be created, so any changes to variables done in that file will affect the calling scope.

CMake will raise an error if a file doesn't exist unless we specify that it is optional with the `OPTIONAL` keyword. If we need to know if `include()` was successful, we can provide a `RESULT_VARIABLE` keyword with the name of the variable. It will be filled with a full path to the included file on success or not found (`NOTFOUND`) on failure.

When running in script mode, any relative paths will be resolved from the current working directory. To force searching in relation to the script itself, provide an absolute path:

```
include("${CMAKE_CURRENT_LIST_DIR}/<filename>.cmake")
```

If we don't provide a path but do provide the name of a module (without .cmake or otherwise), CMake will try to find a module and include it. CMake will search for a file with the name of `<module>.cmake` in `CMAKE_MODULE_PATH` and then in the CMake module directory.

The include_guard() command

When we include files that have side effects, we might want to restrict them so that they're only included once. This is where `include_guard([DIRECTORY|GLOBAL])` comes in.

Put `include_guard()` at the top of the included file. When CMake encounters it for the first time, it will make a note of this fact in the current scope. If the file gets included again (maybe because we don't control all of the files in our project), it won't be processed any further.

If we want to protect against inclusion in unrelated function scopes that won't share variables with each other, we should provide `DIRECTORY` or `GLOBAL` arguments. As the names suggest, the `DIRECTORY` keyword will apply the protection within the current directory and below, and the `GLOBAL` keyword applies the protection to the whole build.

The file() command

To give you an idea of what you can do with CMake scripts, let's take a quick glance at the most useful variants of the file manipulation command:

```
file(READ <filename> <out-var> [...])
file({WRITE | APPEND} <filename> <content>...)
file(DOWNLOAD <url> [<file>] [...])
```

In short, the `file()` command will let you read, write, and transfer files, and work with the filesystem, file locks, paths, and archives, all in a system-independent manner. Please see the *Appendix* section for more details.

The execute_process() command

Every now and then, you'll need to resort to using tools available in the system (after all, CMake is primarily a buildsystem generator). CMake offers a command for this purpose: you can use `execute_process()` to run other processes and collect their output. This command is a great fit for scripts, and it can also be used in projects during the configuration stage. Here's the general form of the command:

```
execute_process(COMMAND <cmd1> [<arguments>]... [OPTIONS])
```

CMake will use the API of the operating system to create a child process (so, shell operators such as `&&`, `||`, and `>` won't work). However, you can still chain commands and pass the output of one to another simply by providing the `COMMAND <cmd> <arguments>` arguments more than once.

Optionally, you may use a `TIMEOUT <seconds>` argument to terminate the process if it hasn't finished the task within the required limit, and you can set the `WORKING_DIRECTORY <directory>` as you need.

The exit codes of all tasks can be collected in a list by providing `RESULTS_VARIABLE <variable>` arguments. If you're only interested in the result of the last executed command, use the singular form: `RESULT_VARIABLE <variable>`.

To collect the output, CMake provides two arguments: `OUTPUT_VARIABLE` and `ERROR_VARIABLE` (which are used in a similar fashion). If you would like to merge both `stdout` and `stderr`, use the same variable for both arguments.

Remember that when writing projects for other users, you should make sure that the command you're planning to use is available on the platforms you claim to support.

Summary

This chapter opened the door to actual programming with CMake – you're now able to write great, informative comments and invoke built-in commands, and you understand how to correctly provide all kinds of arguments to them. This knowledge alone will help you understand the unusual syntax of CMake listfiles that you may have seen in other projects.

Next, we covered variables in CMake – specifically, how to reference, set, and unset normal, cache, and environment variables. We took a deep dive into how directory and function scopes work, and we discussed the issues (and their workarounds) relating to nested scopes.

We also covered lists and control structures. We discussed the syntax of conditions, their logical operations, the evaluation of unquoted arguments, and strings and variables. We learned how to compare values, do simple checks, and examine the state of the files in the system. This allows us to write conditional blocks and while loops. And while we were talking about loops, we also grasped the syntax of foreach loops.

I'm sure that knowing how to define your own commands with macro and function statements will help you write cleaner code in a more procedural style. We also shared a few ideas about how to structure our code better and come up with more readable names.

Finally, we were formally introduced to the `message()` command and its multiple log levels. We also studied how to partition and include listfiles, and we discovered a few other useful commands. I feel confident that with this material, we are ready to tackle the next chapter and write our first project in CMake.

Further reading

For more information on the topics covered in this chapter, you can refer to the following:

- *Clean Code: A Handbook of Agile Software Craftsmanship* (Robert C. Martin): `https://amzn.to/3cm69DD`

- *Refactoring: Improving the Design of Existing Code* (Martin Fowler): `https://amzn.to/3cmWk8o`

- *Which comments in your code ARE GOOD?* (Rafał Świdzinski): `https://youtu.be/4t9bpo0THb8`

- *What's the CMake syntax to set and use variables?* (StackOverflow): `https://stackoverflow.com/questions/31037882/whats-the-cmake-syntax-to-set-and-use-variables`

3
Setting Up Your First CMake Project

We have now gathered enough information to start talking about the core function of CMake: *building projects*. In CMake, a **project** contains all the source files and configuration necessary to manage the process of bringing our solutions to life. Configuration starts by performing all the checks: whether the target platform is supported, whether it has all the necessary dependencies and tools, and whether the provided compiler works and supports required features.

When that's done, CMake will generate a buildsystem for the build tool of our choice and run it. Source files will be compiled and linked with each other and their dependencies to produce output artifacts.

Projects can be used internally by a group of developers to produce packages that users can install on their systems through package managers or they can be used to provide single-executable installers. Projects can also be shared in an open-source repository so that users can use CMake to compile projects on their machines and install them directly.

Using CMake projects to their full potential will improve the developing experience and the quality of the produced code because we can automate many dull tasks, such as running tests after the build, checking code coverage, formatting the code, and checking source code with linters and other tools.

To unlock the power of CMake projects, we'll go over some key decisions first – these are how to correctly configure the project as a whole and how to partition it and set up the source tree so that all files are neatly organized in the right directories.

We'll then learn how to query the environment the project is built on – for example, what architecture it is? What tools are available? What features do they support? And what standard of the language is in use? Finally, we'll learn how to compile a test **C++** file to verify if the chosen compiler meets the standard requirements set in our project.

In this chapter, we're going to cover the following main topics:

- Basic directives and commands
- How to partition your project
- Thinking about the project structure
- Scoping the environment
- Configuring the toolchain
- Disabling in-source builds

Technical requirements

You can find the code files that are present in this chapter on GitHub at `https://github.com/PacktPublishing/Modern-CMake-for-Cpp/tree/main/examples/chapter03`.

To build examples provided in this book always use recommended commands:

```
cmake -B <build tree> -S <source tree>
cmake --build <build tree>
```

Be sure to replace placeholders `<build tree>` and `<source tree>` with appropriate paths. As a reminder: **build tree** is the path to target/output directory, **source tree** is the path at which your source code is located.

Basic directives and commands

In *Chapter 1, First Steps with CMake*, we already looked at a simple project definition. Let's revisit it. It is a directory with a `CMakeLists.txt` file that contains a few commands configuring the language processor:

chapter01/01-hello/CMakeLists.txt: Hello world in CMake language

```
cmake_minimum_required(VERSION 3.20)
project(Hello)
add_executable(Hello hello.cpp)
```

In the same chapter, in the *Project files* section, we learned about a few basic commands. Let's explain them in depth.

Specifying the minimum CMake version – cmake_minimum_required()

This isn't strictly a project-specific command, as it should be used with scripts as well, but it is so important that we repeat it here. As you know, `cmake_minimum_required()` will check whether the system has the right CMake version, but implicitly, it will also call another command, `cmake_policy(VERSION)`, which will tell CMake what the right policies are to use for this project. What are these policies?

Over the last 20 years of CMake's development, there have been many changes to how commands behave as CMake and the languages it supports have evolved. To keep the syntax clean and simple, CMake's team decided to introduce policies to reflect these changes. Whenever a backward-incompatible change was introduced, it came with a policy that enabled the new behavior.

By calling `cmake_minimum_required()`, we tell CMake that it needs to apply the policies up to the version provided in the argument. When CMake gets upgraded with new policies, we don't need to worry about them breaking our project, as the new policies won't be enabled. If we test the project with the newest version and if we're happy with the outcome, we can send the updated project to our users.

Policies can affect every single aspect of CMake, including other important commands like `project()`. For that reason, it is important to start your `CMakeLists.txt` file by setting the version you're working with. Otherwise, you will get warnings and errors.

Every version introduces quite a few policies – there isn't any real value in describing them unless you're having issues with upgrading legacy projects to the latest CMake version. In that case, refer to the official documentation on policies: `https://cmake.org/cmake/help/latest/manual/cmake-policies.7.html`.

Defining languages and metadata – project()

Technically, CMake doesn't need the `project()` command. Any directory containing the `CMakeLists.txt` file will be parsed in project mode. CMake implicitly adds that command to the top of the file. But we already know that we need to start by specifying the minimum version, so it's best not to forget about calling `project()`. We can use one of its two forms:

```
project(<PROJECT-NAME> [<language-name>...])
project(<PROJECT-NAME>
        [VERSION <major>[.<minor>[.<patch>[.<tweak>]]]]
        [DESCRIPTION <project-description-string>]
        [HOMEPAGE_URL <url-string>]
        [LANGUAGES <language-name>...])
```

We need to specify `<PROJECT-NAME>`, but the other arguments are optional. Calling this command will implicitly set the following variables:

- `PROJECT_NAME`
- `CMAKE_PROJECT_NAME` (only in the top-level `CMakeLists.txt`)
- `PROJECT_SOURCE_DIR`, `<PROJECT-NAME>_SOURCE_DIR`
- `PROJECT_BINARY_DIR`, `<PROJECT-NAME>_BINARY_DIR`

What languages are supported? Quite a few. Here's a list of language keywords you can use to configure your project: `C`, `CXX` (C++), `CUDA`, `OBJC` (Objective-C), `OBJCXX` (Objective C++), `Fortran`, `ISPC`, `ASM`, as well as `CSharp` (C#) and `Java`.

CMake enables C and C++ by default, so you may want to explicitly specify only `CXX` for your C++ projects. Why? The `project()` command will detect and test the available compilers for your chosen language, so choosing the correct ones will allow you to save time during the configuration stage by skipping any checks for unused languages.

Specifying `VERSION` will make the following variables available:

- `PROJECT_VERSION`, `<PROJECT-NAME>_VERSION`
- `CMAKE_PROJECT_VERSION` (only in the top-level `CMakeLists.txt`)
- `PROJECT_VERSION_MAJOR`, `<PROJECT-NAME>_VERSION_MAJOR`
- `PROJECT_VERSION_MINOR`, `<PROJECT-NAME>_VERSION_MINOR`
- `PROJECT_VERSION_PATCH`, `<PROJECT-NAME>_VERSION_PATCH`
- `PROJECT_VERSION_TWEAK`, `<PROJECT-NAME>_VERSION_TWEAK`

The preceding variables will be useful for configuring packages or for passing to compiled files to make the version available in the final executable.

Following this principle, we can set `DESCRIPTION` and `HOMEPAGE_URL`, which will set the variables in the same way.

CMake also allows specification of the used languages with `enable_language(<lang>)`, which will not create any metadata variables.

The preceding commands will allow us to create a basic listfile and initialize an empty project. Now, we can start adding things to build. Structure doesn't really matter for the tiny, single-file projects we have used in our examples so far. But what happens when there's more code?

Partitioning your project

As our solutions grow in the number of lines and files they have, we slowly understand that the inevitable is coming: either we start partitioning the project or we drown in lines of code and a multitude of files. We can approach this problem in two ways: by portioning the CMake code and by moving the source files to subdirectories. In both cases, we aim to follow the design principle called **separation of concerns**. Put simply, break your code into chunks, grouping code with closely related functionality while decoupling other pieces of code to create strong boundaries.

We talked a bit about partitioning CMake code when discussing listfiles in *Chapter 1, First Steps with CMake*. We spoke about the `include()` command, which allows CMake to execute the code from an external file. Calling `include()` doesn't introduce any scopes or isolations that are not defined within the file (if the included file contains functions, their scope will be handled correctly upon calling).

This method helps with separation of concerns, but only a little – specialized code is extracted to separate files and can even be shared across unrelated projects, but it can still pollute the global variable scope with its internal logic if the author is not careful. An old truth in programming is that *even the worst mechanism is better than the best intentions*. We'll learn how to deal with this problem in a second, but for now, let's shift our focus to source code.

Let's consider an example of software that supports a small car rental company – it will have many source files defining different aspects of the software: managing customers, cars, parking spots, long-term contracts, maintenance records, employee records, and so on. If we were to put all of these files in a single directory, finding anything would be a nightmare. Therefore, we create a number of directories in the main directory of our project and move the related files inside it. Our `CMakeLists.txt` file might look similar to this:

chapter03/01-partition/CMakeLists.txt

```
cmake_minimum_required(VERSION 3.20.0)
project(Rental CXX)
add_executable(Rental
               main.cpp
               cars/car.cpp
               # more files in other directories
)
```

That's all great, but as you can see, we still have the list of source files from the nested directory in a top-level file! To increase the separation of concerns, we could put the list of sources in another listfile and use the aforementioned `include()` command with a `cars_sources` variable, like so:

chapter03/02-include/CMakeLists.txt

```
cmake_minimum_required(VERSION 3.20.0)
project(Rental CXX)
include(cars/cars.cmake)
add_executable(Rental
               main.cpp
               ${cars_sources}
               # ${more variables}
)
```

The new nested listfile would contain the sources:

chapter03/02-include/cars/cars.cmake

```
set(cars_sources
    cars/car.cpp
#   cars/car_maintenance.cpp
)
```

CMake would effectively set `cars_sources` in the same scope as `add_executable`, filling the variable with all of the files. This solution works, but it has a few flaws:

- **The variables from the nested directory will pollute the top-level scope (and vice versa)**:

  While it's not an issue in a simple example, in more complex, multi-level trees with multiple variables used in the process, it can quickly become a hard-to-debug problem.

- **All of the directories will share the same configuration**:

  This issue shows its true colors as projects mature over the years. Without any granularity, we have to treat every translation unit the same, and we cannot specify different compilation flags, choose a newer language version for some parts of the code, and silence warnings in chosen areas of the code. Everything is global, meaning that we need to introduce changes to all of the source files at the same time.

- **There are shared compilation triggers**:

  Any changes to the configuration will mean that all of the files will have to be recompiled, even if the change is meaningless for some of them.

- **All of the paths are relative to the top-level**:

  Note that in `cars.cmake`, we had to provide a full path to the `cars/car.cpp` file. This results in a lot of repeated text ruining the readability and going against the **Don't Repeat Yourself** (**DRY**) principle of clean coding. Renaming a directory would be a struggle.

The alternative is to use the `add_subdirectory()` command, which introduces a variable scope and more. Let's take a look.

Scoped subdirectories

It's a common practice to structure your project following the natural structure of the filesystem, where nested directories represent the discrete elements of the application: the business logic, GUI, API, and reporting, and finally, separate directories with tests, external dependencies, scripts, and documentation. To support this concept, CMake offers the following command:

```
add_subdirectory(source_dir [binary_dir]
  [EXCLUDE_FROM_ALL])
```

As already established, this adds a source directory to our build. Optionally, we may provide a path in which built files will be written (`binary_dir`). The `EXCLUDE_FROM_ALL` keyword will disable the default building of targets defined in the subdirectory (we'll cover *targets* in the next chapter). This may be useful for separating parts of the project that aren't needed for the core functionality (for example, *examples* and *extensions*).

This command will look for a `CMakeLists.txt` file in the `source_dir` path (evaluated relative to the current directory). This file will then be parsed in the directory scope, meaning that all the flaws mentioned in the previous method aren't present:

- Variable changes are isolated to the nested scope.
- You're free to configure the nested artifacts however you like.
- Changing the nested `CMakeLists.txt` file doesn't require building unrelated targets.
- Paths are local to the directory, and they can even be added to the parent *include path* if desired.

Let's take a look at a project with `add_subdirectory()`:

```
chapter03/03-add_subdirectory# tree -A
.
├── CMakeLists.txt
├── cars
│   ├── CMakeLists.txt
│   ├── car.cpp
│   └── car.h
└── main.cpp
```

Here, we have two `CMakeLists.txt` files. The top-level file will use the nested directory, `cars`:

chapter03/02-add_subdirectory/CMakeLists.txt

```
cmake_minimum_required(VERSION 3.20.0)
project(Rental CXX)

add_executable(Rental main.cpp)

add_subdirectory(cars)
target_link_libraries(Rental PRIVATE cars)
```

The last line is used to link the artifacts from the `cars` directory to the `Rental` executable. It is a target-specific command, which we'll discuss in depth in the next chapter. Let's see what the nested listfile looks like:

chapter03/02-add_subdirectory/cars/CMakeLists.txt

```
add_library(cars OBJECT
    car.cpp
#   car_maintenance.cpp
)
target_include_directories(cars PUBLIC .)
```

As you can see, I have used `add_library()` to produce a globally visible target, `cars`, and added the `cars` directory to its public *include directories* with `target_include_directories()`. This allows `main.cpp` to include the `cars.h` file without providing a relative path:

```
#include "car.h"
```

We can see the `add_library()` command in the nested listfile, so did we start working with libraries in this example? Actually, no. Since we used the `OBJECT` keyword, we're indicating we're only interested in producing the *object files* (exactly as we did in the previous example). We just grouped them under a single logical target (`cars`). You may already have a sense of what a *target* is. Hold that thought – we'll get there in a second.

Nested projects

In the previous section, we briefly mentioned the `EXCLUDE_FROM_ALL` argument used in the `add_subdirectory()` command. The CMake documentation suggests that if we have such parts living inside the source tree, they should have their own `project()` commands in their `CMakeLists.txt` files so that they can generate their own buildsystems and can be built independently.

Are there any other scenarios where this would be useful? Sure. For example, one scenario would be when you're working with multiple C++ projects built in one **CI/CD** pipeline (perhaps when building a framework or a set of libraries). Alternatively, maybe you're porting the buildsystem from a legacy solution, such as GNU Make, which uses plain **makefiles**. In such a case, you might want an option to slowly break things down into more independent pieces – possibly to put them in a separate build pipeline, or just to work on a smaller scope, which could be loaded by an IDE such as **CLion**.

You can achieve that by adding the `project()` command to the listfile in the nested directory. Just don't forget to prepend it with `cmake_minimum_required()`.

Since project nesting is supported, could we somehow connect related projects that are built side by side?

External projects

It is technically possible to reach from one project to another, and CMake will support that to some extent. There's even a `load_cache()` command that allows you to load values from another project's cache. That said, this isn't a regular or a recommended use case, and it will lead to issues with cyclical dependencies and project coupling. It's best to avoid this command and make a decision: should our related projects be nested, connected through libraries, or merged into a single project?

These are the partitioning tools at our disposal: *including listfiles*, *adding subdirectories*, and *nesting projects*. But how should we use them so our projects stay maintainable and easy to navigate and extend? To do this, we need a well-defined project structure.

Thinking about the project structure

It's no secret that as a project grows, it becomes harder and harder to find things in it – both in listfiles and in the source code. Therefore, it is very important to maintain the project hygiene right from the get-go.

Imagine a scenario where you need to deliver some important, time-sensitive changes, and they don't fit well in either of the two directories in your project. Now, you need to quickly push a *cleanup commit* that introduces more directories and another level of hierarchy for your files so that your changes can have a nice place to fit. Or (what's worse), you decide to just shove them anywhere and create a ticket to deal with the issue later.

Over the course of the year, these tickets accumulate, the technical debt grows, and so does the cost of maintaining the code. This becomes extremely troublesome when there's a crippling bug in a live system that needs a quick fix and when people unfamiliar with the code base need to introduce their changes.

So, we need a good project structure. But what does this mean? There are a few rules that we can borrow from other areas of software development (for example, system design). The project should have the following characteristics:

- It should be easy to navigate and extend.
- It should be self-contained – for example, project-specific files should be in the project directory and nowhere else.
- The abstraction hierarchy should be expressed through executables and binaries.

There is no single agreed-upon solution, but among the many available project structure templates online, I recommend following this one, as it is simple and very extensible:

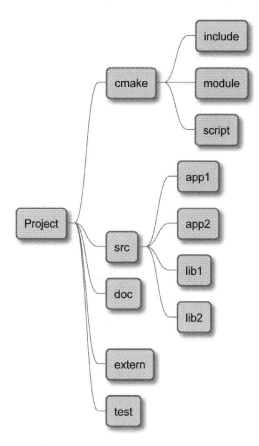

Figure 3.1 – An example of a project structure

This project outlines the directories for the following components:

- `cmake`: Includes macros and functions, find_modules, and one-off scripts
- `src`: Will store the source of our binaries and libraries
- `doc`: Used for building the documentation
- `extern`: Configuration for the external projects we are building from source
- `test`: Contains code for automated tests

In this structure, the `CMakeLists.txt` file should exist in the following directories: the top-level project directory, `src`, `doc`, `extern`, and `test`. The main listfile shouldn't declare any build steps on its own, but instead, it should use the `add_subdirectory()` command to execute all of the listfiles in the nested directories. In turn, these may delegate this work to even deeper layers if needed.

> **Note**
> Some developers suggest separating the executables from the libraries and creating two top-level directories instead of one: `src` and `lib`. CMake treats both artifacts the same, and separation at this level doesn't really matter.

Having multiple directories in the `src` directory comes in handy for bigger projects. But if you're building just a single executable or library, you may skip them and store your source files directly in `src`. In any case, remember to add a `CMakeLists.txt` file there and execute any nested listfiles as well.

This is how your file tree might look for a single target:

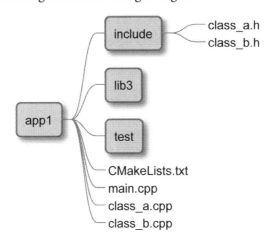

Figure 3.2 – The directory structure of an executable

We see a `CMakeLists.txt` file in the root of the `app1` directory – it will configure the key project settings and include all listfiles from nested directories. The `src` directory contains another `CMakeLists.txt` file along with the `.cpp` implementation files: two classes and the main file with the executable's entry point. The `CMakeLists.txt` file should define a target that uses these sources to build an executable – we'll learn how to do that in the next chapter.

Our header files go to the `include` directory – these are used by `.cpp` implementation files to declare symbols from other C++ translation units.

We have a `test` directory to store the source code for our automated tests, and we also have `lib3`, which contains a library specific to this executable only (libraries used elsewhere in the project or exported outside of it should live in the `src` directory).

This structure is pretty expressive and allows for many extensions of the project. As we keep adding more and more classes, we can easily group them in libraries to speed up the compilation process. Let's see what a library looks like:

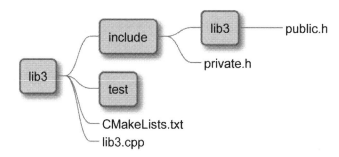

Figure 3.3 – The directory structure of a library

As it turns out, libraries follow the same structure as executables, with only a small difference: there is an optional `lib3` directory in the `include` directory. This should only be present if we use the library externally from the project. It provides the public header files that other projects will consume during compilation. We'll return to this subject when we start building our own libraries in *Chapter 5, Compiling C++ Sources with CMake*.

So, we have discussed how files are laid out in a directory structure. Now, it's time to take a look at how individual `CMakeFiles.txt` files come together to form a single project and what their role is in a bigger scenario.

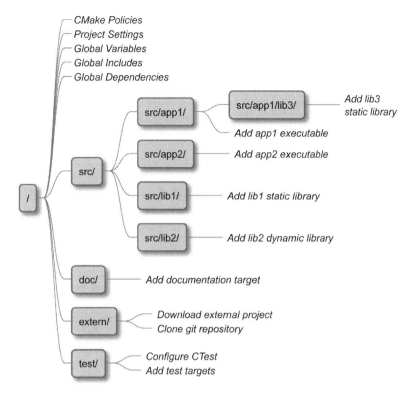

Figure 3.4 – How CMake merges listfiles together in a single project

In *Figure 3.4*, each box represents a `CMakeLists.txt` listfile residing in a given directory, while the labels in cursive text represent the actions executed by each file (from top to bottom). Let's analyze this project once more from CMake's perspective:

1. The execution starts from the root of the project – that is, from a listfile residing in the source tree. This file will set the minimum required CMake version with the appropriate policies, set the project name, supported languages, global variables, and include the files from the `cmake` directory so that their contents are available globally.

2. The next step is to enter the scope of the `src` directory by calling the `add_subdirectory(src bin)` command (we'd like to put compiled artifacts in `<binary_tree>/bin` rather than `<binary_tree>/src`).

3. CMake reads the `src/CMakeLists.txt` file and discovers that its only purpose is to add four nested subdirectories: `app1`, `app2`, `lib1`, and `lib2`.

4. CMake enters the variable scope of `app1` and learns about another nested library, `lib3`, which has its own `CMakeLists.txt` file; then the scope of `lib3` is entered.

5. The `lib3` library adds a static library target with the same name. CMake returns to the parent scope of `app1`.
6. The `app1` subdirectory adds an executable that depends on `lib3`. CMake returns to the parent scope of `src`.
7. CMake will continue entering the remaining nested scopes and executing their listfiles until all `add_subdirectory()` invocations have been completed.
8. CMake returns to the top-level scope and executes three remaining commands: `add_subdirectory(doc)`, `add_subdirectory(extern)`, and `add_subdirectory(test)`. Each time, CMake enters the new scope and executes commands from the appropriate listfile.
9. All of the targets are collected and checked for their correctness. CMake now has all of the necessary information to generate a buildsystem.

We need to remember that the preceding steps are happening in the exact order in which we wrote the commands in our listfiles. Sometimes this matters, while other times, not so much. We'll get to the bottom of that in the next chapter.

So, when is the right time to create the directories to contain all of the elements of the project? Should we do it right from the start – create everything needed for the future and keep the directories empty – or wait until we actually have the files that need to go in their own category? This is a choice – we could follow the extreme-programming rule **YAGNI** (**you aren't gonna need it**), or we could try to make our project future-proof and lay good foundations for new developers to come.

Try to aim for a good balance between these approaches – if you suspect that your project might one day need an `extern` directory, then add it (you may need to create an empty `.keep` file to check a directory into the repository). To help others know where to put their external dependencies, create a `readme` file, and lay the path for less experienced programmers who will travel this road in the future. You may have observed this yourself: developers are reluctant to create directories, especially in the root of the project. If we provide a good project structure, people will be inclined to follow it.

Some projects can be built in almost every environment, while others are quite particular about their specifics. The top-level listfile is the perfect place to assess how to proceed with the project, depending on what is available. Let's see how to do this.

Scoping the environment

CMake provides multiple ways of querying the environment with `CMAKE_` variables, `ENV` variables, and special commands. For example, collected information can be used to support cross-platform scripts. These mechanisms allow us to avoid using platform-specific shell commands that may not be easily portable or differ in naming across environments.

For performance-critical applications, it will be useful to know all the features of the destination platform (for example, instruction sets, CPU core count, and more). This information can then be passed to the compiled binaries so that they can be tuned to perfection (we'll learn how to do that in the next chapter). Let's see what information is available in CMake natively.

Discovering the operating system

There are many occasions when it is useful to know what the target operating system is. Even as mundane a thing as a filesystem differs greatly between Windows and Unix in things such as case sensitivity, file path structures, the presence of extensions, privileges, and so on. Most commands present on one system won't be available on another, or they could be named differently (even if it's by a single letter – for example, the `ifconfig` and `ipconfig` commands).

If you ever need to support multiple target operating systems with a single CMake script, just check the `CMAKE_SYSTEM_NAME` variable so that you can act accordingly. Here's a simple example:

```
if(CMAKE_SYSTEM_NAME STREQUAL "Linux")
   message(STATUS "Doing things the usual way")
elseif(CMAKE_SYSTEM_NAME STREQUAL "Darwin")
   message(STATUS "Thinking differently")
elseif(CMAKE_SYSTEM_NAME STREQUAL "Windows")
   message(STATUS "I'm supported here too.")
elseif(CMAKE_SYSTEM_NAME STREQUAL "AIX")
   message(STATUS "I buy mainframes.")
else()
   message(STATUS "This is ${CMAKE_SYSTEM_NAME} speaking.")
endif()
```

If needed, there's a variable containing the operating system version: `CMAKE_SYSTEM_VERSION`. However, my recommendation is to try and make your solutions as system-agnostic as possible and use the built-in CMake cross-platform functionality. Especially for operations on filesystems, you should use the `file()` command described in the *Appendix* section.

Cross-compilation – what are host and target systems?

Compiling code on one machine to be run on another is called *cross-compilation*. You can (with the right toolset) compile applications for Android by running CMake on a Windows machine. Cross-compilation isn't in the scope of this book, but it's important to understand how it impacts some parts of CMake.

One of the necessary steps to allow cross-compilation is setting the `CMAKE_SYSTEM_NAME` and `CMAKE_SYSTEM_VERSION` variables to the values appropriate for the operating system that you're compiling for targets (the CMake documentation refers to it as the **target system**). The operating system used to perform the build is called a **host system**.

Regardless of the configuration, the information on the host system is always accessible in variables with a `HOST` keyword in their name: `CMAKE_HOST_SYSTEM`, `CMAKE_HOST_SYSTEM_NAME`, `CMAKE_HOST_SYSTEM_PROCESSOR`, and `CMAKE_HOST_SYSTEM_VERSION`.

There are a few more variables with a `HOST` keyword in their name, so just keep in mind that they're explicitly referencing the host system. Otherwise, all variables reference the target system (which normally is the host system anyway, unless we're cross-compiling).

If you're interested in reading more about cross-compilation, I suggest referencing the CMake documentation at `https://cmake.org/cmake/help/latest/manual/cmake-toolchains.7.html`.

Abbreviated variables

CMake will predefine a few variables that will provide information about the host and target systems. If a specific system is used, an appropriate variable will be set to a non-false value (that is, `1` or `true`):

- `ANDROID`, `APPLE`, `CYGWIN`, `UNIX`, `IOS`, `WIN32`, `WINCE`, `WINDOWS_PHONE`
- `CMAKE_HOST_APPLE`, `CMAKE_HOST_SOLARIS`, `CMAKE_HOST_UNIX`, `CMAKE_HOST_WIN32`

The `WIN32` and `CMAKE_HOST_WIN32` variables will be `true` for 32- and 64-bit versions of Windows and MSYS (this value is kept for legacy reasons). Also, `UNIX` will be `true` for Linux, macOS, and Cygwin.

Host system information

CMake could provide more variables, but to save time, it doesn't query the environment for rarely needed information, such as *whether a processor supports MMX* or *what the total physical memory is*. That doesn't mean this information isn't available – you just need to ask for it explicitly with the following command:

`cmake_host_system_information(RESULT <VARIABLE> QUERY <KEY>...)`

We need to provide a target variable and a list of keys we're interested in. If we provide just one key, the variable will contain a single value; otherwise, it will be a list of values. We can ask for many details about the environment and the OS:

Key	Returned value
HOSTNAME	The hostname.
FQDN	The fully qualified domain name.
TOTAL_VIRTUAL_MEMORY	The total virtual memory in MiB.
AVAILABLE_VIRTUAL_MEMORY	The available virtual memory in MiB.
TOTAL_PHYSICAL_MEMORY	The total physical memory in MiB.
AVAILABLE_PHYSICAL_MEMORY	The available physical memory in MiB.
OS_NAME	The output of `uname -s` if this command is present, or one of `Windows`, `Linux`, or `Darwin` if it is not.
OS_RELEASE	The OS sub-type, for example, Windows Professional.
OS_VERSION	The OS build ID.
OS_PLATFORM	On Windows the `PROCESSOR_ARCHITECTURE` environment variable is returned. On Unix and macOS, the value contains the output of the `uname -m` command.

If needed, we can even query processor-specific information:

Key	Returned value
NUMBER_OF_LOGICAL_CORES	The number of logical cores
NUMBER_OF_PHYSICAL_CORES	The number of physical cores
HAS_SERIAL_NUMBER	1 if the processor has a serial number
PROCESSOR_SERIAL_NUMBER	The processor serial number
PROCESSOR_NAME	The human-readable processor name
PROCESSOR_DESCRIPTION	The human-readable full processor description
IS_64BIT	1 if the processor is 64 bit
HAS_FPU	1 if the processor has a floating-point unit
HAS_MMX	1 if the processor supports MMX instructions
HAS_MMX_PLUS	1 if the processor supports Ext. MMX instructions
HAS_SSE	1 if the processor supports SSE instructions
HAS_SSE2	1 if the processor supports SSE2 instructions
HAS_SSE_FP	1 if the processor supports SSE FP instructions
HAS_SSE_MMX	1 if the processor supports SSE MMX instructions
HAS_AMD_3DNOW	1 if the processor supports 3DNow instructions
HAS_AMD_3DNOW_PLUS	1 if the processor supports 3DNow+ instructions
HAS_IA64	1 if it is an IA-64 processor emulating x86

Does the platform have 32-bit or 64-bit architecture?

In 64-bit architecture, memory addresses, processor registers, processor instructions, address busses, and data buses are 64 bits wide. While this is a simplified definition, it gives a rough idea of how 64-bit platforms are different from 32-bit platforms.

In C++, different architectures mean different bit widths for some fundamental data types (`int` and `long`) and pointers. CMake utilizes the pointer size to gather information about the target machine. This information is available through the CMAKE_SIZEOF_VOID_P variable, and it will contain a value of 8 for 64 bits (because a pointer is 8 bytes wide) and 4 for 32 bits (4 bytes):

```
if(CMAKE_SIZEOF_VOID_P EQUAL 8)
  message(STATUS "Target is 64 bits")
endif()
```

What is the endianness of the system?

Architectures can be **big-endian** or **little-endian**. **Endianness** is the order of bytes in a **word** or the natural unit of data for a processor. A big-endian system stores the most significant byte at the lowest memory address and the least significant byte at the highest memory address. A little-endian system is the opposite of this.

In most cases, endianness doesn't matter, but when you're writing bit-wise code that needs to be portable, CMake will provide you with a `BIG_ENDIAN` or `LITTLE_ENDIAN` value stored in the `CMAKE_<LANG>_BYTE_ORDER` variable, where `<LANG>` is C, CXX, OBJC, or CUDA.

Now that we know how to query the environment, let's shift our focus to the key settings of the project.

Configuring the toolchain

For CMake projects, a toolchain consists of all of the tools used in building and running the application – for example, the working environment, the generator, the CMake executable itself, and the compilers.

Imagine what a less-experienced user feels when your build stops with some mysterious compilation and syntax errors. They have to dig into the source code and try to understand what happened. After an hour of debugging, they discover that the correct solution is to update their compiler. Could we provide a better experience for users and check if all of the required functions are present in the compiler before starting the build?

Sure! There are ways to specify these requirements. If the toolchain doesn't support all of the required features, CMake will stop early and show a clear message of what happened, asking the user to step in.

Setting the C++ standard

The first thing we might want to do is to set the C++ standard we require the compiler to support if the user wants to build our project. For new projects, this should be at least **C++14**, but preferably **C++17** or **C++20**. CMake also supports setting the standard to the experimental **C++23**, but that's just a draft version.

> **Note**
>
> It has been 10 years since the official release of **C++11**, and it is no longer considered to be *the modern C++ standard*. It's not recommended to start projects with this version unless your target environment is very old.
>
> Another reason to stick to old standards is if you are building legacy targets that are too hard to upgrade. However, the C++ committee works very hard to keep C++ backward compatible, and in most cases, you won't have any problems bumping the standard to a higher version.

CMake supports setting the standard on a target-per-target basis, which means that you can have any granularity you like. I believe it's better to converge to a single standard across the project. This can be done by setting the CMAKE_CXX_STANDARD variable to one of the following values: 98, 11, 14, 17, 20, or 23 (since CMake 3.20). This will be a default value for all subsequently defined targets (so it's best to set it close to the top of the root listfile). You can override it on a per-target basis if needed, like so:

```
set_property(TARGET <target> PROPERTY CXX_STANDARD <standard>)
```

Insisting on standard support

The CXX_STANDARD property mentioned in the previous section won't stop CMake from continuing with the build, even if the compiler isn't supporting the desired version – it's treated as a preference. CMake doesn't know if our code actually uses the brand-new features that aren't available in the previous compilers, and it will try to work with what it has available.

If we know for certain that this won't be successful, we can set another default flag (which is overridable in the same manner as the previous one) and explicitly require the standard we target:

```
set(CMAKE_CXX_STANDARD_REQUIRED ON)
```

In that case, if the latest compiler isn't present in the system (in this case, GNU GCC 11), the user will just see the following message and the build will stop:

```
Target "Standard" requires the language dialect "CXX23" (with
compiler extensions), but CMake does not know the compile flags
to use to enable it.
```

Asking for C++23 might be a bit excessive, even for a modern environment. But C++14 should be perfectly fine, as it has been fully supported in **GCC/Clang** since 2015.

Vendor-specific extensions

Depending on the policy you implement in your organization, you might be interested in allowing or disabling vendor-specific extensions. What are these? Well, let's just say that the C++ standard is moving a bit slow for the needs of some compiler producers, so they decided to add their own enhancements to the language – *plugins*, if you like. To achieve this, CMake will add `-std=gnu++14` instead of `-std=c++14` to the compile line.

On one hand, this may be desired, as it allows for some convenient functionality. But on the other, your code will fail to build if you switch to a different compiler (or if your users do!).

This is also a per-target property for which there is a default variable, `CMAKE_CXX_EXTENSIONS`. CMake is more liberal here, and allows the extensions unless we specifically tell it not to:

```
set(CMAKE_CXX_EXTENSIONS OFF)
```

I recommend doing so if possible, as this option will insist on having vendor-agnostic code. Such code won't impose any unnecessary requirements on the users. In a similar way, you can use `set_property()` to change this value on a per-target basis.

Interprocedural optimization

Usually, compilers optimize the code on the level of a single translation unit, which means that your `.cpp` file will be preprocessed, compiled, and then optimized. Later, these files will be passed to the linker to build a single binary. Modern compilers can perform optimization after linking (this is called *link time optimization*) so that all compilation units can be optimized as a single module.

If your compiler supports interprocedural optimization, it may be a good idea to use it. We'll follow the same method as previously. The default variable for this setting is called `CMAKE_INTERPROCEDURAL_OPTIMIZATION`. But before we set it, we need to make sure it is supported to avoid errors:

```
include(CheckIPOSupported)
check_ipo_supported(RESULT ipo_supported)
if(ipo_supported)
    set(CMAKE_INTERPROCEDURAL_OPTIMIZATION True)
endif()
```

As you can see, we had to include a built-in module to get access to the `check_ipo_supported()` command.

Checking for supported compiler features

As we discussed earlier, if our build is to fail, it's best if it fails early, so we can provide a clear feedback message to the user. What we're especially interested in is gauging which C++ features are supported (and which aren't). CMake will question the compiler during the configuration stage and store a list of the available features in the CMAKE_CXX_COMPILE_FEATURES variable. We may write a very specific check and ask if a certain feature is available:

chapter03/07-features/CMakeLists.txt

```
list(FIND CMAKE_CXX_COMPILE_FEATURES
    cxx_variable_templates result)
if(result EQUAL -1)
    message(FATAL_ERROR "I really need variable templates.")
endif()
```

As you may guess, writing one for every feature we use is a daunting task. Even the authors of CMake recommend to only check if certain high-level *meta-features* are present: cxx_std_98, cxx_std_11, cxx_std_14, cxx_std_17, cxx_std_20, and cxx_std_23. Each *meta-feature* indicates that the compiler supports a specific C++ standard. If you wish, you can use them exactly as we did in the previous example.

A full list of features known to CMake can be found in the documentation:

https://cmake.org/cmake/help/latest/prop_gbl/CMAKE_CXX_KNOWN_FEATURES.html

Compiling a test file

One particularly interesting scenario occurred to me when I was compiling an application with GCC 4.7.x. I had manually confirmed in the compiler's reference that all of the C++11 features we were using were supported. However, the solution still didn't work correctly. The code silently ignored the call to the standard <regex> header. As it turned out, GCC 4.7.x had a bug and the regex library wasn't implemented.

No single check can protect you from such bugs, but there's a chance to reduce such behavior by creating a test file that you can fill with all of the features that you'd like to check. CMake provides two configure-time commands, try_compile() and try_run(), to verify that everything you need is supported on the target platform.

The second command gives you more freedom, as you can ensure that the code is not only compiling but that it is also executing correctly (you could potentially test if `regex` is working). Of course, this won't work for cross-compilation scenarios (as the host won't be able to run an executable built for a different target). Just remember that the aim of this check is to provide a quick piece of feedback to the user if the compilation is working, so it's not meant to run any unit tests or anything complex – keep the file as basic as possible. For example, something like this:

chapter03/08-test_run/main.cpp

```cpp
#include <iostream>
int main()
{
    std::cout << "Quick check if things work." << std::endl;
}
```

Calling `test_run()` isn't very complicated at all. We start by setting the required standard, after which we call `test_run()` and print the collected information to the user:

chapter03/08-test_run/CMakeLists.txt

```cmake
set(CMAKE_CXX_STANDARD 20)
set(CMAKE_CXX_STANDARD_REQUIRED ON)
set(CMAKE_CXX_EXTENSIONS OFF)

try_run(run_result compile_result
        ${CMAKE_BINARY_DIR}/test_output
        ${CMAKE_SOURCE_DIR}/main.cpp
        RUN_OUTPUT_VARIABLE output)

message("run_result: ${run_result}")
message("compile_result: ${compile_result}")
message("output:\n" ${output})
```

This command has a lot of optional fields to set, which may seem overwhelming at first, but as we read and compare it with the call made in the example, everything comes together:

```
try_run(<runResultVar> <compileResultVar>
        <bindir> <srcfile> [CMAKE_FLAGS <flags>...]
        [COMPILE_DEFINITIONS <defs>...]
        [LINK_OPTIONS <options>...]
        [LINK_LIBRARIES <libs>...]
        [COMPILE_OUTPUT_VARIABLE <var>]
        [RUN_OUTPUT_VARIABLE <var>]
        [OUTPUT_VARIABLE <var>]
        [WORKING_DIRECTORY <var>]
        [ARGS <args>...])
```

Only a few fields are required to compile and run a very basic test file. I also used the optional `RUN_OUTPUT_VARIABLE` keyword to collect the output from `stdout`.

The next step is to extend this simple file by using some of the more modern C++ features that we're going to use throughout the actual project – perhaps by adding a variadic template to see if the compiler on the target machine can digest it. Each time we introduce a new feature to the actual project, we can put a tiny sample of the same feature into the test file. But remember – keep it lean. We want to check if the compilation works in the shortest time possible.

Finally, we can check in the conditional blocks if the collected output is meeting our expectations and `message(SEND_ERROR)` is printed when something isn't right. Remember that `SEND_ERROR` will continue through the configuration stage but won't start the generation. This is useful to show all of the encountered errors before aborting the build.

Disabling in-source builds

In *Chapter 1*, *First Steps with CMake*, we talked about in-source builds, and how it is recommended to always specify the build path to be out-of-source. This not only allows for a cleaner build tree and a simpler `.gitignore` file, but it also decreases the chances you'll accidentally overwrite or delete any source files.

Searching for the solution online, you may stumble on a StackOverflow thread that asks the same question: `https://stackoverflow.com/q/1208681/6659218`. Here, the author notices that no matter what you do, it seems like CMake will still create a `CMakeFiles/` directory and a `CMakeCache.txt` file. Some answers suggest using undocumented variables to make sure that the user can't write in the source directory under any circumstances:

```
# add this options before PROJECT keyword
set(CMAKE_DISABLE_SOURCE_CHANGES ON)
set(CMAKE_DISABLE_IN_SOURCE_BUILD ON)
```

I'd say to be cautious when using undocumented features of any software, as they may go away without warning. Setting the preceding variables in CMake 3.20 terminates the build with a rather ugly error:

```
CMake Error at /opt/cmake/share/cmake-3.20/Modules/
CMakeDetermineSystem.cmake:203 (file):
  file attempted to write a file:
  /root/examples/chapter03/09-in-source/CMakeFiles/CMakeOutput.
log into a source
  directory.
```

However, it still creates the mentioned files anyway! Therefore, my recommendation is to go with an older – but fully supported – mechanism:

chapter03/09-in-source/CMakeLists.txt

```
cmake_minimum_required(VERSION 3.20.0)
project(NoInSource CXX)
if(PROJECT_SOURCE_DIR STREQUAL PROJECT_BINARY_DIR)
    message(FATAL_ERROR "In-source builds are not allowed")
endif()
message("Build successful!")
```

If Kitware (company behind the CMake) ever decides to officially support CMAKE_DISABLE_SOURCE_CHANGES or CMAKE_DISABLE_IN_SOURCE_BUILD, then by all means, switch to that solution.

Summary

We introduced a lot of valuable concepts in this chapter that will give us a strong foundation to go forward and build hardened, future-proof projects. We discussed how to set the minimum CMake version and how to configure the key aspects of the project – that is, the name, languages, and metadata fields.

Laying good foundations will help ensure that our projects can grow quickly. This is why we discussed the partitioning of projects. We analyzed naïve code partitioning using `include()` and compared it with `add_subdirectory()`. At this point, we learned about the benefits of managing the directory scope of variables, and we explored the use of simpler paths and increased modularity. Having an option to create a nested project and build it separately is very useful when we need to slowly break code down into more independent units.

After an overview of the partitioning mechanisms we have at our disposal, we explored *how* we want to use them – for example, how to make transparent, resilient, and extensible project structures. Specifically, we analyzed how CMake will traverse the listfiles and the correct order of the different configuration steps.

Next, we studied how we can scope the environment of our target and host machines, what the differences are between them, and what kind of information about the platform and system is available through different queries.

Finally, we found out how to configure the toolchain – for example, how to specify the required C++ version, how to address the issue of vendor-specific compiler extensions, and how to enable important optimization. We wrapped up by discovering how to test our compiler for the required features and compile test files.

While this is all that a project technically requires, it's still not a very useful project. To change that, we need to introduce *targets*. So far, we've mentioned them here and there, but I tried to avoid the subject until we had learned more about some general concepts first. Now that's done, we'll look at them in detail.

Further reading

For more information on the topics covered in this chapter, you can refer to the following:

- *Separation of concerns*: `https://nalexn.github.io/separation-of-concerns/`
- *Complete CMake Variable reference*: `https://cmake.org/cmake/help/latest/manual/cmake-variables.7.html`
- *Try compile and try run references*:
  - `https://cmake.org/cmake/help/latest/command/try_compile.html`
  - `https://cmake.org/cmake/help/latest/command/try_run.html`

Section 2: Building With CMake

Now that we have the most essential skills, it's time to start diving a little deeper. The next part will allow you to solve most situations that come your way when building a project in CMake.

We purposely focus on modern, elegant practices and avoid bringing too much legacy into the picture. Specifically, we'll be dealing with logical build targets rather than manipulating individual files.

Next, we'll explain in detail all the steps that the toolchain takes to build a binary artifact from a target. That's the part many books about C++ are missing: how to configure and use preprocessors, compilers, and linkers properly, as well as how to optimize their behavior.

Lastly, this section will cover all the different ways in which CMake offers to manage dependencies, and will explain how to pick the best one for your specific use case.

This section comprises the following chapters:

- *Chapter 4, Working with Targets*
- *Chapter 5, Compiling C++ Sources with CMake*
- *Chapter 6, Linking with CMake*
- *Chapter 7, Managing Dependencies with CMake*

4
Working with Targets

The most basic target we can build in CMake is a single binary executable file that encompasses an entire application. It can be made out of a single piece of source code, such as the classic `helloworld.cpp`. Or it can be something complex – built with hundreds or even tens of thousands of files. This is what many beginner projects look like – create a binary with one source file, add another, and, before you know it, everything is linked to a single binary without any structure whatsoever.

As software developers, we deliberately draw boundaries and designate components to group one or more units of translation (`.cpp` files). We do it for multiple reasons: to increase code readability, manage coupling and connascence, speed up the build process, and finally, extract the reusable components.

Every project that is big enough will push you to introduce some form of partitioning. A target in CMake is an answer to exactly that problem – a high-level logical unit that forms a single objective for CMake. A target may depend on other targets, and they are produced in a declarative way. CMake will take care of determining in what order targets have to be built and then execute the necessary steps one by one. As a general rule, building a target will produce an artifact that will be fed into other targets or delivered as a final product of the build.

I deliberately use the inexact word *artifact* because CMake doesn't limit you to producing executables or libraries. In reality, we can use generated buildsystems to create many kinds of output: more source files, headers, *object files*, archives, and configuration files – anything really. All we need is a command-line tool (such as a compiler), optional input files, and an output path.

Targets are a very powerful concept and simplify building a project greatly. It is key to understand how they work and how to configure them in the most elegant and clean way.

In this chapter, we're going to cover the following main topics:

- The concept of a target
- Writing custom commands
- Understanding generator expressions

Technical requirements

You can find the code files that are present in this chapter on GitHub at https://github.com/PacktPublishing/Modern-CMake-for-Cpp/tree/main/examples/chapter04.

To build examples provided in this book always use recommended commands:

```
cmake -B <build tree> -S <source tree>
cmake --build <build tree>
```

Be sure to replace placeholders `<build tree>` and `<source tree>` with appropriate paths. As a reminder: **build tree** is the path to target/output directory, **source tree** is the path at which your source code is located.

The concept of a target

If you have ever used GNU Make, you will have already seen the concept of a target. Essentially, it's a recipe that a buildsystem uses to compile a list of files into another file. It can be a `.cpp` implementation file compiled into an `.o` *object file*, a group of `.o` files packaged into an `.a` static library, and many other combinations.

CMake, however, allows you to save time and skip the intermediate steps of those recipes; it works on a higher level of abstraction. It understands how to build an executable directly from source files. So, you don't need to write an explicit recipe to compile any *object files*. All that's required is an `add_executable()` command with the name of the executable target and a list of the files that are to be its elements:

```
add_executable(app1 a.cpp b.cpp c.cpp)
```

We already used this command in previous chapters and we already know how executable targets are used in practice – during the generation step, CMake will create a buildsystem and fill it with recipes to compile each of the source files and link them together into a single binary executable.

In CMake, we can create a target using one of three commands:

- `add_executable()`
- `add_library()`
- `add_custom_target()`

The first two are pretty self-explanatory; we briefly used them already in previous chapters to build executables and libraries (and we'll discuss them in depth in *Chapter 5, Compiling C++ Sources with CMake*). But what are those custom targets?

They allow you to specify your own command line that will be executed *without checking whether the produced output is up to date*, for example:

- Calculate the checksums of other binaries.
- Run the code-sanitizer and collect the results.
- Send a compilation report to the data processing pipeline.

Here's the full signature of the `add_custom_target()` command:

```
add_custom_target(Name [ALL] [command1 [args1...]]
                  [COMMAND command2 [args2...] ...]
                  [DEPENDS depend depend depend ... ]
                  [BYPRODUCTS [files...]]
                  [WORKING_DIRECTORY dir]
                  [COMMENT comment]
                  [JOB_POOL job_pool]
                  [VERBATIM] [USES_TERMINAL]
                  [COMMAND_EXPAND_LISTS]
                  [SOURCES src1 [src2...]])
```

We won't discuss every option here, as we want to quickly move on to other targets, but let's just say that custom targets don't necessarily have to produce tangible artifacts in the form of files.

One good use case for custom targets might be the need to remove specific files on every build – for example, to make sure that code-coverage reports don't contain stale data. All we need to do is define a custom target like so:

```
add_custom_target(clean_stale_coverage_files
        COMMAND find . -name "*.gcda" -type f -delete)
```

The preceding command will search for all files with a `.gcda` extension and remove them. There is one catch though; unlike executable and library targets, custom targets won't be built until they are added to a dependency graph. Let's find out what that is.

Dependency graph

Mature applications are often built from many components, and I don't mean external dependencies here. Specifically, I'm talking about internal libraries. Adding them to the project is useful from a structural perspective, as related things are packaged together in a single logical entity. And they can be linked with other targets – another library or an executable. This is especially convenient when multiple targets are using the same library. Take a look at *Figure 4.1*, which describes an exemplary dependency graph:

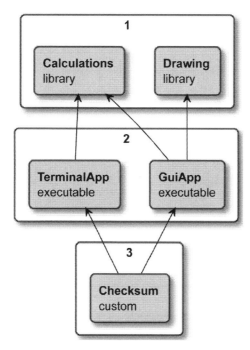

Figure 4.1 – Order of building dependencies in the BankApp project

In this project, we have two libraries, two executables, and a custom target. Our use case here is to provide a banking application with a nice GUI for users (**GuiApp**), and a command-line version to be used as part of an automated script (**TerminalApp**). Both executables are depending on the same **Calculations** library, but only one of them needs the **Drawing** library. To guarantee that our app wasn't modified when it was downloaded from the internet by an end user, we'll calculate a checksum, store it in a file, and distribute it through separate secure channels. CMake is pretty flexible when it comes to writing list files for such a solution:

chapter04/01-targets/CMakeLists.txt

```
cmake_minimum_required(VERSION 3.19.2)
project(BankApp CXX)

add_executable(terminal_app terminal_app.cpp)
add_executable(gui_app gui_app.cpp)

target_link_libraries(terminal_app calculations)
target_link_libraries(gui_app calculations drawing)
```

```
add_library(calculations calculations.cpp)
add_library(drawing drawing.cpp)

add_custom_target(checksum ALL
    COMMAND sh -c "cksum terminal_app>terminal.ck"
    COMMAND sh -c "cksum gui_app>gui.ck"
    BYPRODUCTS terminal.ck gui.ck
    COMMENT "Checking the sums..."
)
```

We connect our libraries with executables by using the `target_link_libraries()` command. Without it, the compilation for executables would fail because of undefined symbols. Have you noticed that we invoked this command before actually declaring any of the libraries? When CMake configures the project, it collects the information about targets and their properties – their names, dependencies, source files, and other details.

After parsing all the files, CMake will attempt to build a dependency graph. And like with all valid dependency graphs, they're directional acyclic graphs. This means that there is a clear direction of which target depends on which, and such dependencies cannot form cycles.

When we execute `cmake` in build mode, the generated buildsystem will check what top-level targets we have defined and recursively build their dependencies. Let's consider our example from *Figure 4.1*:

1. Start from the top, and build both libraries in group 1.
2. When the **Calculations** and **Drawing** libraries are complete, build group 2 – **GuiApp** and **TerminalApp**.
3. Build a checksum target; run specified command lines to generate checksums (`cksum` is a Unix checksum tool).

There's a slight issue though – the preceding solution doesn't guarantee that a checksum target will be built after executables. CMake doesn't know that a checksum depends on the executable binaries being present, so it's free to start building it first. To resolve this problem, we can put the `add_dependencies()` command at the end of the file:

```
add_dependencies(checksum terminal_app gui_app)
```

This will ensure that CMake understands the relation between the Checksum target and the executables.

That's great, but what's the difference between `target_link_libraries()` and `add_dependencies()`? The first is intended to be used with actual libraries and allows you to control property propagation. The second is meant to be used only with top-level targets to set their build order.

As projects grow in complexity, the dependency tree gets harder to understand. How can we simplify this process?

Visualizing dependencies

Even small projects can be difficult to reason about and share with other developers. The easiest way to do so is through a nice diagram. After all, a picture is worth a thousand words. We can do the work and draw a diagram ourselves, just like I did in *Figure 4.1*. But this is tedious and would require constant updates. Luckily, CMake has a great module to generate dependency graphs in the `dot`/`graphviz` format. And it supports both internal and external dependencies!

To use it, we can simply execute this command:

```
cmake --graphviz=test.dot .
```

The module will produce a text file that we can import to the Graphviz visualization software, which can render an image or produce a PDF or SVG file that can be stored as part of the software documentation. Everybody loves great documentation, but hardly anyone likes to create it – now, you don't need to!

If you're in a rush, you can even run Graphviz straight from your browser at this address:

`https://dreampuf.github.io/GraphvizOnline/`

> **Important Note**
> Custom targets are not visible by default and we need to create a special configuration file, `CMakeGraphVizOptions.cmake`, that will allow us to customize the graph. One handy customization command is `set(GRAPHVIZ_CUSTOM_TARGETS TRUE)`; add it to the special configuration file to enable reporting custom targets in your graph. You can find more options in the documentation for the module.

All you need to do is copy and paste the contents of the `test.dot` file into the window on the left and your project will be visualized. Quite convenient, isn't it?

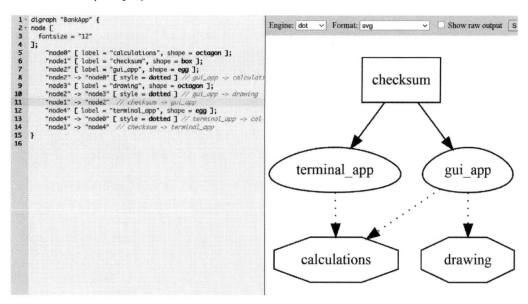

Figure 4.2 – A visualization of the BankApp example in Graphviz

I have removed the automatically generated legend section from the preceding figure for clarity.

Using this method, we can quickly see all the explicitly defined targets. Now that we have this global perspective, let's do a deep dive and see how to configure them.

Target properties

Targets have properties that work in a similar way to fields of C++ objects. We can modify some of these properties and others are read-only. CMake defines a large list of "known properties" (see the *Further reading* section) that are available depending on the type of the target (executable, library, or custom). You can also add your own properties if you like. Use the following commands to manipulate the properties of a target:

```
get_target_property(<var> <target> <property-name>)
set_target_properties(<target1> <target2> ...
                      PROPERTIES <prop1-name> <value1>
                      <prop2-name> <value2> ...)
```

To print a target property on screen, we first need to store it in the `<var>` variable and then `message()` it to the user; we have to read them one by one. On the other hand, setting properties on a target allows us to specify multiple properties at the same time, on multiple targets.

The concept of properties isn't unique to targets; CMake supports setting properties of other scopes as well: `GLOBAL`, `DIRECTORY`, `SOURCE`, `INSTALL`, `TEST`, and `CACHE`. To manipulate all kinds of properties, there are general `get_property()` and `set_property()` commands. You can use these low-level commands to do exactly what the `set_target_properties()` command does, just with a bit more work:

```
set_property(TARGET <target> PROPERTY <name> <value>)
```

Generally, it's better to use as many high-level commands as you can. CMake offers more of these, even narrower in their scope, such as setting specific properties on a target. For example, `add_dependencies(<target> <dep>)` is appending dependencies to the `MANUALLY_ADDED_DEPENDENCIES` target property. In this case, we can query it with `get_target_property()` exactly as with any other property. However, we can't use `set_target_property()` to change it (it's read-only), as CMake insists on using the `add_dependencies()` command to restrict operations to appending only.

We'll introduce more property setting commands when we discuss compiling and linking in upcoming chapters. Meanwhile, let's focus on how the properties of one target can transition to another.

What are transitive usage requirements?

Let's just agree that naming is hard, and sometimes one ends up with a result that's hard to understand. "Transitive usage requirements" is, unfortunately, one of those cryptic titles that you will encounter in the online CMake documents. Let's untangle this strange name and perhaps propose a term easier to understand.

I'll start by clarifying the middle bit of this puzzle. As we previously discussed, one target may depend on another. CMake documentation sometimes refers to such dependency as *usage*, as in one target *uses* another. This was straightforward, so on to the next one.

There will be cases when such a used target has specific *requirements* that a using target has to meet: link some libraries, include a directory, or require specific compile features. All of these are in fact requirements, so documentation is correct in a sense. The issue is that they aren't called requirements in any other context in the documentation. When you specify the same requirements for a single target, you set *properties* or *dependencies*. Therefore, the last part of the name should perhaps be simply "properties."

The last part is *–transitive*. This one I believe is correct (maybe a bit too smart). CMake appends some properties/requirements of used targets to properties of targets using them. You can say that some properties can transition (or simply propagate) across targets implicitly, so it's easier to express dependencies.

Simplifying this whole concept, I see it as *propagated properties* between *the source target* (targets that gets used) and *destination targets* (targets that use other targets).

Let's look at a concrete example to understand why it's there and how it works:

```
target_compile_definitions(<source> <INTERFACE|PUBLIC|PRIVATE>
[items1...])
```

This target command will populate the COMPILE_DEFINITIONS property of a <source> target. *Compile definitions* are simply -Dname=definition flags passed to the compiler that configure the C++ preprocessor definitions (we'll get to that in *Chapter 5, Compiling C++ Sources with CMake*). The interesting part here is the second argument. We need to specify one of three values, INTERFACE, PUBLIC, or PRIVATE, to control which targets the property should be passed to. Now, don't confuse these with C++ access specifiers – this is something else.

Propagation keywords work like this:

- PRIVATE sets the property of the source target.
- INTERFACE sets the property of the destination targets.
- PUBLIC sets the property of the source and destination targets.

When a property is not to be transitioned to any destination targets, set it to PRIVATE. When such a transition is needed, go with PUBLIC. If you're in a situation where the source target doesn't use the property in its implementation (.cpp files) and only in headers, and these are passed to the consumer targets, INTERFACE is the answer.

How does this work under the hood? To manage those properties, CMake provides a few commands such as the aforementioned target_compile_definitions(). When you specify a PRIVATE or PUBLIC keyword, CMake will store provided values in the property of the target matching the command – in this case, COMPILE_DEFINITIONS. Additionally, if a keyword was INTERFACE or PUBLIC, it will store the value in property with an INTERFACE_ prefix – INTERFACE_COMPILE_DEFINITIONS. During the configuration stage, CMake will read the interface properties of source targets and append their contents to destination targets. There you have it – propagated properties, or transitive usage requirements – as CMake calls them.

In CMake 3.20, there are 12 such properties managed with appropriate commands such as `target_link_options()` or directly with the `set_target_properties()` command:

- AUTOUIC_OPTIONS
- COMPILE_DEFINITIONS
- COMPILE_FEATURES
- COMPILE_OPTIONS
- INCLUDE_DIRECTORIES
- LINK_DEPENDS
- LINK_DIRECTORIES
- LINK_LIBRARIES
- LINK_OPTIONS
- POSITION_INDEPENDENT_CODE
- PRECOMPILE_HEADERS
- SOURCES

We'll discuss most of these options in the following pages, but remember that all of these options are, of course, described in the CMake manual. Find them on their own page under a URL in this format (replace <PROPERTY> with a property that interests you):

`https://cmake.org/cmake/help/latest/prop_tgt/<PROPERTY>.html`

The next question that comes to mind is how far this propagation goes. Are the properties set just on the first destination target, or are they sent to the very top of the dependency graph? Actually, you get to decide.

To create a dependency between targets, we use the `target_link_libraries()` command. The full signature of this command requires a propagation keyword:

```
target_link_libraries(<target>
                     <PRIVATE|PUBLIC|INTERFACE> <item>...
                     [<PRIVATE|PUBLIC|INTERFACE> <item>...]...)
```

As you can see, this signature also specifies a propagation keyword, but this one controls where properties from the source target get stored in the destination target. *Figure 4.3* shows what happens to a propagated property during the generation stage (after the configuration stage is completed):

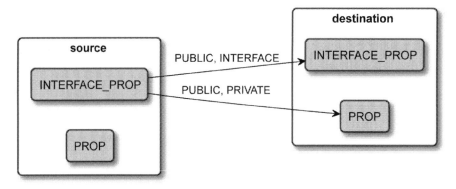

Figure 4.3 – How properties are propagated to destination targets

Propagation keywords work like this:

- `PRIVATE` appends the source value to the *private* property of the destination.
- `INTERFACE` appends the source value to the *interface* property of the destination.
- `PUBLIC` appends to both properties of the destination.

As we discussed before, interface properties are only used to propagate the properties further down the chain, and the destination target won't use them in its build process.

The basic `target_link_libraries(<target> <item>...)` command that we used before implicitly specifies the `PUBLIC` keyword.

If you correctly set propagation keywords for your source targets, properties will be automatically placed on destination targets for you – unless there's a conflict…

Dealing with conflicting propagated properties

When one target depends on multiple other targets, there may be a situation where propagated properties are in outright conflict with each other. Say that one used target specifies the `POSITION_INDEPENDENT_CODE` property as `true` and the other as `false`. CMake understands this as a conflict and will print an error similar to this:

```
CMake Error: The INTERFACE_POSITION_INDEPENDENT_CODE property
of "source_target2" does not agree with the value of POSITION_
INDEPENDENT_CODE already determined for "destination_target".
```

It is useful to receive such a message, as we explicitly know that we introduced this conflict and we need to resolve it. CMake has its own properties that have to "agree" between source and destination targets.

On rare occasions, this may become important – for example, if you're building software using the same library in multiple targets that are then linked to a single executable. If these source targets are using different versions of the same library, you may run into problems.

To make sure that we're only using the same specific version, we can create a custom interface property, `INTERFACE_LIB_VERSION`, and store the version there. This is not enough to solve the problem, as CMake won't propagate custom properties by default. We have to explicitly add a custom property to a list of "compatible" properties.

Each target has four such lists:

- `COMPATIBLE_INTERFACE_BOOL`
- `COMPATIBLE_INTERFACE_STRING`
- `COMPATIBLE_INTERFACE_NUMBER_MAX`
- `COMPATIBLE_INTERFACE_NUMBER_MIN`

Appending your property to one of them will trigger propagation and compatibility checks. The `BOOL` list will check whether all properties propagated to the destination target evaluate to the same Boolean value. Analogically, `STRING` will evaluate to a string. `NUMBER_MAX` and `NUMBER_MIN` are a bit different – propagated values don't have to match, but the destination target will just receive the highest or the lowest value instead.

This example will help us to understand how to apply this in practice:

chapter04/02-propagated/CMakeLists.txt

```
cmake_minimum_required(VERSION 3.20.0)
project(PropagatedProperties CXX)

add_library(source1 empty.cpp)
set_property(TARGET source1 PROPERTY INTERFACE_LIB_VERSION
    4)
set_property(TARGET source1 APPEND PROPERTY
  COMPATIBLE_INTERFACE_STRING LIB_VERSION
)
add_library(source2 empty.cpp)
```

```
set_property(TARGET source2 PROPERTY INTERFACE_LIB_VERSION
    4)
add_library(destination empty.cpp)
target_link_libraries(destination source1 source2)
```

We create three targets here; for simplicity, all are using the same empty source file. On both of the source targets, we specify our custom property with the INTERFACE_ prefix. And we set them to the same matching library version. Both of the source targets are linked to the destination target. Finally, we specify a STRING compatibility requirement as a property for source1 (we don't add the INTERFACE_ prefix here).

CMake will propagate this custom property to the destination target and check whether the version of all the source targets is an exact match (the compatibility property can be set on just one target).

Now that we understand what targets are, let's take a look at other things that look like targets, smell like targets, and sometimes act like targets but, as it turns out, aren't the real deal.

Meet the pseudo targets

The concept of a target is so useful that it would be great if some of its behaviors could be borrowed for other things too. This is, specifically, things that do not represent outputs of the buildsystem but rather inputs – external dependencies, aliases, and so on. These are the pseudo targets, or targets that don't make it to the generated buildsystem.

Imported targets

If you skimmed the table of contents, you know that we'll be talking about how CMake manages external dependencies – other projects, libraries, and so on. IMPORTED targets are essentially products of this process. CMake can define them as a result of the find_package() command.

You can adjust the target properties of such a target: *compile definitions*, *compile options*, *include directories*, and so on – and they will even support transitive usage requirements. However, you should treat them as immutable; don't change their sources or dependencies.

The scope of the definition of an IMPORTED target can be global or local to the directory where it was defined (visible in subdirectories but not in parent directories).

Alias targets

Alias targets do exactly what you expect – they create another reference to a target under a different name. You can create alias targets for executables and libraries with the following commands:

```
add_executable(<name> ALIAS <target>)
add_library(<name> ALIAS <target>)
```

Properties of alias targets are read-only, and you cannot install or export aliases (they aren't visible in the generated buildsystem).

So, what is the reason to have aliases at all? They come in handy in scenarios where some part of a project (such as a subdirectory) requires a target with a specific name, and the actual implementation may be available under different names depending on circumstances. For example, you may wish to build a library shipped with your solution or import it based on a user's choice.

Interface libraries

This is an interesting construct – a library that doesn't compile anything but instead serves as a utility target. Its whole concept is built around propagated properties (transitive usage requirements).

Interface libraries have two primary uses – to represent header-only libraries and to bundle a bunch of propagated properties into a single logical unit.

Header-only libraries are fairly easy to create with `add_library(INTERFACE)`:

```
add_library(Eigen INTERFACE
    src/eigen.h src/vector.h src/matrix.h
)
target_include_directories(Eigen INTERFACE
    $<BUILD_INTERFACE:${CMAKE_CURRENT_SOURCE_DIR}/src>
    $<INSTALL_INTERFACE:include/Eigen>
)
```

In the preceding snippet, we created an Eigen interface library with three headers. Next, with generator expressions (explained in the last section of this chapter), we set its *include directories* to be `${CMAKE_CURRENT_SOURCE_DIR}/src` when a target is exported and `include/Eigen` when it's installed (which will also be explained at the end of this chapter).

To use such a library, we just have to link it:

```
target_link_libraries(executable Eigen)
```

No actual linking occurs here, but CMake will understand this command as a request to propagate all the INTERFACE properties to the executable target.

The second use case leverages exactly the same mechanism but for a different purpose – it creates a logical target that can be a placeholder for propagated properties. We can then use this target as a dependency for other targets and set properties in a clean, convenient way. Here's an example:

```
add_library(warning_props INTERFACE)
target_compile_options(warning_props INTERFACE
    -Wall -Wextra -Wpedantic
)
target_link_libraries(executable warning_props)
```

The `add_library(INTERFACE)` command creates a logical `warning_props` target that is used to set *compile options* specified in the second command on the `executable` target. I recommend using these INTERFACE targets, as they improve the readability and reusability of your code. Think of it as refactoring a bunch of magic values to a well-named variable. I also suggest using the `_props` suffix to easily differentiate interface libraries from the regular ones.

Are pseudo targets exhausting the concept of the target? Of course not! That would simply be too easy. We still need to understand how these targets translate to produced buildsystems.

Build targets

Target is a bit of a loaded word. It means different things in the context of a project and the context of generated buildsystems. When CMake generates a buildsystem, it "compiles" list files from CMake language to the language of a chosen build tool; perhaps it creates a Makefile for GNU Make. Such Makefiles have their own targets – some of them are direct conversions of list file targets, and others are created implicitly.

One such buildsystem target is ALL, which CMake generates by default to contain all top-level list file targets, such as executables and libraries (not necessarily custom targets). ALL is built when we run `cmake --build <build tree>` without choosing a concrete target. As you might remember from the first chapter, you can choose one by adding the `--target <name>` parameter to the preceding command.

Some executables or libraries might not be needed in every build, but we'd like to keep them as part of the project for those rare occasions when they come in useful. To optimize our default build, we can exclude them from the ALL target like so:

```
add_executable(<name> EXCLUDE_FROM_ALL [<source>...])
add_library(<name> EXCLUDE_FROM_ALL [<source>...])
```

Custom targets work the other way around – by default, they're excluded from the ALL target unless you explicitly define them with an ALL keyword, as we did in the BankApp example.

Another implicitly defined build target is clean, which simply removes produced artifacts from the build tree. We use it to get rid of all old files and build everything from scratch. It's important though to understand that it don't just simply delete everything in the build directory. This means that for clean to work correctly, you need to manually specify any files that your custom targets might create as BYPRODUCTS (see the BankApp example).

There's also an interesting non-target mechanism to create custom artifacts that can be used in all *actual targets* – custom commands.

Writing custom commands

Using custom targets has one drawback – as soon as you add them to the ALL target or start depending on them for other targets, they will be built every single time (you may still enable them in an if block to limit that). Sometimes, this is what you want, but there are cases when custom behavior is necessary to produce files that shouldn't be recreated without reason:

- Generating a source code file that another target depends on
- Translating another language into C++
- Executing a custom action immediately before or after another target was built

There are two signatures for a custom command. The first one is an extended version of add_custom_target():

```
add_custom_command(OUTPUT output1 [output2 ...]
                   COMMAND command1 [ARGS] [args1...]
                   [COMMAND command2 [ARGS] [args2...] ...]
                   [MAIN_DEPENDENCY depend]
                   [DEPENDS [depends...]]
```

```
                    [BYPRODUCTS [files...]]
                    [IMPLICIT_DEPENDS <lang1> depend1
                                     [<lang2> depend2] ...]
                    [WORKING_DIRECTORY dir]
                    [COMMENT comment]
                    [DEPFILE depfile]
                    [JOB_POOL job_pool]
                    [VERBATIM] [APPEND] [USES_TERMINAL]
                    [COMMAND_EXPAND_LISTS])
```

As you might have guessed, a custom command doesn't create a logical target, but just like custom targets, it has to be added to a dependency graph. There are two ways of doing that – using its output artifact as a source for an executable (or library), or explicitly adding it to a DEPENDS list for a custom target.

Using a custom command as a generator

Admittedly, not every project needs to generate C++ code from other files. One such occasion might be a compilation of **Google's Protocol Buffer's** (**Protobuf**) .proto files. If you're not familiar with this library, protobuf is a platform-neutral binary serializer for structured data. To keep it cross-platform and fast at the same time, Google's engineers invented their own protobuf format that defines models in .proto files, such as this one:

```
message Person {
    required string name = 1;
    required int32 id = 2;
    optional string email = 3;
}
```

Such a file can be then shared across multiple languages – C++, Ruby, Go, Python, Java, and so on. Google provides compilers that read .proto files and output structure and serialization code valid for the chosen language. Smart engineers don't check those compiled files into a repository but will use the original protobuf format and add it to the build chain.

We don't know yet how to detect whether (and where) a protobuf compiler is available on the target host (we'll learn that in *Chapter 7, Managing Dependencies with CMake*). So, for now, let's just assume that the compiler's `protoc` command is residing in a location known to the system. We have prepared a `person.proto` file and we know that the protobuf compiler will output `person.pb.h` and `person.pb.cc` files. Here's how we would define a custom command to compile them:

```
add_custom_command(OUTPUT person.pb.h person.pb.cc
        COMMAND protoc ARGS person.proto
        DEPENDS person.proto
)
```

Then, to allow serialization in our executable, we can just add output files to the sources:

```
add_executable(serializer serializer.cpp person.pb.cc)
```

Assuming we dealt correctly with the inclusion of header files and linking the protobuf library, everything will compile and update automatically when we introduce changes to the `.proto` file.

A simplified (and much less practical) example would be to create the necessary header by copying it from another location:

chapter04/03-command/CMakeLists.txt

```
add_executable(main main.cpp constants.h)
target_include_directories(main PRIVATE
   ${CMAKE_BINARY_DIR})
add_custom_command(OUTPUT constants.h
COMMAND cp
ARGS "${CMAKE_SOURCE_DIR}/template.xyz" constants.h)
```

Our "compiler", in this case, is the `cp` command. It fulfills a dependency of the `main` target by creating a `constants.h` file in the build tree root, simply by copying it from the source tree.

Using a custom command as a target hook

The second version of the `add_custom_command()` command introduces a mechanism to execute commands before or after building a target:

```
add_custom_command(TARGET <target>
                   PRE_BUILD | PRE_LINK | POST_BUILD
                   COMMAND command1 [ARGS] [args1...]
                   [COMMAND command2 [ARGS] [args2...] ...]
                   [BYPRODUCTS [files...]]
                   [WORKING_DIRECTORY dir]
                   [COMMENT comment]
                   [VERBATIM] [USES_TERMINAL]
                   [COMMAND_EXPAND_LISTS])
```

We specify what target we'd like to "enhance" with new behavior in the first argument and under the following conditions:

- `PRE_BUILD` will run before any other rules for this target (Visual Studio generators only; for others, it behaves like `PRE_LINK`).
- `PRE_LINK` binds the command to be run just after all sources have been compiled but before the linking (or archiving) the target. It doesn't work for custom targets.
- `POST_BUILD` will run after all other rules have been executed for this target.

Using this version of `add_custom_command()`, we can replicate the generation of the checksum from the previous BankApp example:

chapter04/04-command/CMakeLists.txt

```
cmake_minimum_required(VERSION 3.20.0)
project(Command CXX)


add_executable(main main.cpp)
add_custom_command(TARGET main POST_BUILD
                   COMMAND cksum
                   ARGS "$<TARGET_FILE:main>" > "main.ck")
```

After the build of the main executable completes, CMake will execute cksum with provided arguments. But what is happening in the first argument? It's not a variable, as it would be wrapped in curly braces (${}), not in angle brackets ($<>). It's a generator expression evaluating a full path to the target's binary file. This mechanism is useful in the context of many target properties.

Understanding generator expressions

CMake builds the solution in three stages – configuration, generation, and running the build tool. Generally, we have all the required data during the configuration stage. But every once in a while, we encounter the chicken and the egg problem. Take an example from the previous section – a target needs to know the path of a binary artifact of another target. But that information is only available after all the list files are parsed and the configuration stage is complete.

How do we deal with that kind of problem? We could create a placeholder for that information and postpone its evaluation to the next stage – the generation stage.

This is what generator expressions (sometimes called genexes) do. They are built around target properties such as LINK_LIBRARIES, INCLUDE_DIRECTORIES, COMPILE_DEFINITIONS, propagated properties, and many others, but not all. They follow rules similar to conditional statements and variable evaluation.

It's worth noting that expressions are generally evaluated in the context of the target using the expression (unless explicitly stated otherwise).

> **Important Note**
>
> Generator expressions will be evaluated at the generation stage (when the configuration is complete and the buildsystem is created), which means that you can't capture their output into a variable and print it to the console very easily. To debug them, you can use either of these methods:
>
> • Write it to a file (this specific version of the file() command supports generator expressions): file(GENERATE OUTPUT filename CONTENT "$<...>")
>
> • Add a custom target and build it explicitly from the command line: add_custom_target(gendbg COMMAND ${CMAKE_COMMAND} -E echo "$<...>")

General syntax

Let's take the simplest possible example:

```
target_compile_definitions(foo PUBLIC
    BAR=$<TARGET_FILE:foo>)
```

The preceding command adds a -D definition flag to the compiler's arguments (ignore PUBLIC for now) that sets the BAR preprocessor definition to the **path of the binary artifact of the foo target**.

How is the generator expression formed?

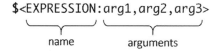

Figure 4.4 – The syntax of a generator expression

As you can see in *Figure 4.4*, the structure seems fairly simple and readable:

- Open with a dollar and a bracket ($<).
- Add the EXPRESSION name.
- If an expression requires arguments, add a colon (:) and provide the arg1, arg2, and arg3 values, separated with a comma (,).
- Close the expression with >.

There are even expressions that do not require any arguments, such as $<PLATFORM_ID>. However, generator expressions can quickly become very confusing and complicated when using their more advanced features.

Nesting

Let's start with the ability to pass a general expression as an argument to another expression or, in other words, general expression nesting:

```
$<UPPER_CASE:$<PLATFORM_ID>>
```

This isn't a very complex example, but it's easy to imagine what happens when we increase nesting levels and work with commands using multiple arguments.

As if that's not enough, you can technically add a variable expansion to this mix:

```
$<UPPER_CASE:${my_variable}>
```

A variable will be expanded at the configuration stage and a generation expression at the generation stage. There are some rare uses for this feature, but I strongly recommend avoiding it.

Conditional expressions

Boolean logic is supported in generator expressions. It's a great feature, but for legacy reasons, its syntax is inconsistent and can be hard to read. It's available in two forms. The first form supports both happy and sad paths:

```
$<IF:condition,true_string,false_string>
```

The syntax here is aligned with all other expressions and, like all expressions, nesting is allowed. So, you can replace any of the arguments with another expression and produce some very complex evaluations – you can even nest one condition in another. This form requires exactly three arguments, so we can't omit anything. Our best option to skip a value in case of an unmet condition is the following:

```
$<IF:condition,true_string,>
```

The second form is a shorthand for the preceding; it will only expand to a string if the condition is met:

```
$<condition:true_string >
```

As you can see, it breaks the convention of providing the EXPRESSION name as the first token. I assume that the intention here was to shorten the expression and skip those precious three characters, but the outcome can be really hard to rationalize. Here's one example from the CMake documentation:

```
$<$<AND:$<COMPILE_LANGUAGE:CXX>,$<CXX_COMPILER_ID:AppleClan
   g,Clang>>:COMPILING_CXX_WITH_CLANG>
```

I wish the syntax was aligned with conditions for the regular IF command, but sadly that's not the case.

Types of evaluation

Generator expressions are evaluated to one of two types – Boolean or string. Boolean is represented by 1 (true) and 0 (false). Everything else is just a string.

It's important to remember that nested expressions passed as conditions in conditional expressions are explicitly required to evaluate to Boolean.

There's an explicit logical operator to convert strings to Boolean, but Boolean types can be converted to strings implicitly.

Now that we know the basic syntax, let's take a look at what we can do with it.

Evaluation to Boolean

We started discussing conditional expressions in the previous section. I want to get the whole concept covered right off the bat so that there's no need to return to it later. There are three categories of expressions that get evaluated to Boolean.

Logical operators

There are four logical operators:

- `$<NOT:arg>` negates the Boolean argument.
- `$<AND:arg1,arg2,arg3...>` returns 1 if all the arguments are 1.
- `$<OR:arg1,arg2,arg3...>` returns 1 if any of the arguments is 1.
- `$<BOOL:string_arg>` converts arguments from a string to a Boolean type.

String conversion will evaluate to 1 if none of these conditions are met:

- The string is empty.
- The string is a case-insensitive equivalent of 0, FALSE, OFF, N, NO, IGNORE, or NOTFOUND.
- The string ends in the -NOTFOUND suffix (case-sensitive).

String comparison

Comparisons will evaluate to 1 if their condition is met and 0 otherwise:

- `$<STREQUAL:arg1,arg2>` is a case-sensitive string comparison.
- `$<EQUAL:arg1,arg2>` converts a string to a number and compares equality.
- `$<IN_LIST:arg,list>` checks whether the `arg` element is in the `list` list (case-sensitive).
- `$<VERSION_EQUAL:v1,v2>`, `$<VERSION_LESS:v1,v2>`, `$<VERSION_GREATER:v1,v2>`, `$<VERSION_LESS_EQUAL:v1,v2>`, and `$<VERSION_GREATER_EQUAL:v1,v2>` are component-wise version comparisons.

Variable queries

There are plenty of variables that contain Boolean-typed values. They also will evaluate to 1 if their condition is met and 0 otherwise.

There is one simple query:

- `$<TARGET_EXISTS:arg>` – does the `arg` target exist?

There are multiple queries scanning passed arguments for a specific value:

- `$<CONFIG:args>` is the current config (`Debug`, `Release`, and so on) in `args` (case-insensitive).
- `$<PLATFORM_ID:args>` is the current platform ID in `args`.
- `$<LANG_COMPILER_ID:args>` is CMake's LANG compiler ID in `args`, where LANG is one of C, CXX, CUDA, OBJC, OBJCXX, Fortran, or ISPC.
- `$<LANG_COMPILER_VERSION:args>` is the CMake's LANG compiler version in `args`, where LANG is one of C, CXX, CUDA, OBJC, OBJCXX, Fortran, or ISPC.
- `$<COMPILE_FEATURES:features>` will return `true` if `features` is supported by the compiler for this target.
- `$<COMPILE_LANG_AND_ID:lang,compiler_id1,compiler_id2...>` is the language of this `lang` target and is the compiler used for this target present in the `compiler_ids` list. This expression is useful to specify details of a configuration for specific compilers:

```
target_compile_definitions(myapp PRIVATE
  $<$<COMPILE_LANG_AND_ID:CXX,AppleClang,Clang>:CXX_CLAN
  G>
  $<$<COMPILE_LANG_AND_ID:CXX,Intel>:CXX_INTEL>
  $<$<COMPILE_LANG_AND_ID:C,Clang>:C_CLANG>
)
```

In the preceding example, if we compile the CXX compiler with `AppleClang` or `Clang`, the `-DCXX_CLANG` definition will be set. For the CXX compiler from Intel, the `-DCXX_INTEL` definition flag will be set. Lastly, for the C and Clang compiler, we'll get a `-DC_CLANG` definition.

- `$<COMPILE_LANGUAGE:args>` if a language is used for the compilation of this target in `args`. This can be used to provide language-specific flags to the compiler:

  ```
  target_compile_options(myapp
    PRIVATE $<$<COMPILE_LANGUAGE:CXX>:-fno-exceptions>
  )
  ```

  If we compile CXX, the compiler will use the `-fno-exceptions` flag.

- `$<LINK_LANG_AND_ID:lang,compiler_id1,compiler_id2...>` works similarly to `COMPILE_LANG_AND_ID` but checks the language used for the link step instead. Use this expression to specify link libraries, link options, link directories, and link dependencies of a particular language and a linker combination in a target.

- `$<LINK_LANGUAGE:args>` is the language used for the link step in `args`.

Evaluation to a string

There are plenty of expressions that get evaluated to a string. We can output them directly to the placeholder of the target or consume as an argument to another expression. We already learned about one – conditional expression evaluates to a string. What else is available?

Variable queries

These expressions will evaluate to a specific value at the generation stage:

- `$<CONFIG>` – the configuration (`Debug` and `Release`) name.
- `$<PLATFORM_ID>` – the current system's CMake platform ID (`Linux`, `Windows`, or `Darwin`). We discussed platform in the previous chapter, in the *Scoping the environment* section.
- `$<LANG_COMPILER_ID>` – CMake's compiler ID of the `LANG` compiler used, where `LANG` is one of C, CXX, CUDA, OBJC, OBJCXX, Fortran, or ISPC.
- `$<LANG_COMPILER_VERSION>` – CMake's compiler version of the `LANG` compiler used, where `LANG` is one of C, CXX, CUDA, OBJC, OBJCXX, Fortran, or ISPC.
- `$<COMPILE_LANGUAGE>` – the compiled language of source files when evaluating *compile options*.
- `$<LINK_LANGUAGE>` – the link language of a target when evaluating link options.

Target-dependent queries

With the following queries, you can evaluate properties of an executable or library target. Note that since CMake 3.19, for most expressions querying a target in the context of another target no longer creates an automated dependency between these targets (as was happening before 3.19):

- `$<TARGET_NAME_IF_EXISTS:target>` – the target name of `target` if it exists; it is an empty string otherwise.
- `$<TARGET_FILE:target>` – the full path to the `target` binary file.
- `$<TARGET_FILE_NAME:target>` – the `target` filename.
- `$<TARGET_FILE_BASE_NAME:target>` – the base name of `target`, or `$<TARGET_FILE_NAME:target>` without a prefix and suffix. For `libmylib.so`, the base name would be `mylib`.
- `$<TARGET_FILE_PREFIX:target>` – the prefix of the `target` filename (`lib`).
- `$<TARGET_FILE_SUFFIX:target>` – the suffix (or extension) of the `target` filename (`.so`, `.exe`).
- `$<TARGET_FILE_DIR:target>` – the directory of the `target` binary file.
- `$<TARGET_LINKER_FILE:target>` – the file used when linking to the `target` target. Usually, it is the library that `target` represents (`.a`, `.lib`, `.so`) on platforms with **Dynamically Linked Libraries** (**DLL**); for a shared library, it will be a `.lib` import library.

  `TARGET_LINKER_FILE` offers the same family of expressions as the regular `TARGET_FILE` expression:

  `$<TARGET_LINKER_FILE_NAME:target>`, `$<TARGET_LINKER_FILE_BASE_NAME:target>`, `$<TARGET_LINKER_FILE_PREFIX:target>`, `$<TARGET_LINKER_FILE_SUFFIX:target>`, `$<TARGET_LINKER_FILE_DIR:target>`

- `$<TARGET_SONAME_FILE:target>` – the full path to a file with a soname (`.so.3`).
- `$<TARGET_SONAME_FILE_NAME:target>` – the name of a file with a soname.
- `$<TARGET_SONAME_FILE_DIR:target>` – the directory of a file with a soname.
- `$<TARGET_PDB_FILE:target>` – the full path to the linker generated program database file (`.pdb`) for `target`.

PDB files offer the same expressions as a regular `TARGET_FILE`: `$<TARGET_PDB_FILE_BASE_NAME:target>`, `$<TARGET_PDB_FILE_NAME:target>`, `$<TARGET_PDB_FILE_DIR:target>`.

- `$<TARGET_BUNDLE_DIR:target>` – the full path to the bundle (Apple-specific package) directory (`my.app`, `my.framework`, or `my.bundle`) for `target`.
- `$<TARGET_BUNDLE_CONTENT_DIR:target>` – the full path to the bundle content directory for `target`. On macOS, it's `my.app/Contents`, `my.framework`, or `my.bundle/Contents`. Other **Software Developent Kits (SDKs)** (such as iOS) have a flat bundle structure – `my.app`, `my.framework`, or `my.bundle`.
- `$<TARGET_PROPERTY:target,prop>` – the `prop` value for `target`.
- `$<TARGET_PROPERTY:prop>` – the `prop` value for `target` for which the expression is being evaluated.
- `$<INSTALL_PREFIX>` – the install prefix when the target is exported with `install(EXPORT)` or when evaluated in `INSTALL_NAME_DIR`; otherwise, it is empty.

Escaping

On a rare occasion, you may need to pass a character to a generator expression that has a special meaning. To escape this behavior, use the following expressions:

- `$<ANGLE-R>` – a literal `>` symbol (which compares strings containing `>`)
- `$<COMMA>` – a literal `,` symbol (which compares strings containing `,`)
- `$<SEMICOLON>` – a literal `;` symbol (which prevents a list expansion on an argument with `;`)

String transformations

Working with strings in the generator stage is possible with the following expressions:

- `$<JOIN:list,d>` – join a semicolon-separated `list` using a `d` delimiter.
- `$<REMOVE_DUPLICATES:list>` – remove duplicates without sorting `list`.
- `$<FILTER:list,INCLUDE|EXCLUDE,regex>` – include/exclude items from a list using a `regex` regular expression.
- `$<LOWER_CASE:string>`, `$<UPPER_CASE:string>` – convert the string to another case.

- `$<GENEX_EVAL:expr>` – evaluate the `expr` string as a nested expression in the context of the current target. This is useful when an evaluation of a nested expression returns another expression (they aren't evaluated recursively).

- `$<TARGET_GENEX_EVAL:target,expr>` – evaluate `expr` similarly to the `GENEX_EVAL` transformation but in the context of `target`.

Output-related expressions

CMake documentation fails to provide a good explanation of what "output-related expressions" are. That leaves us a little lost; how are they related to output?

As per the v3.13 documentation (removed in newer revisions), *"These expressions generate output, in some cases depending on an input."*

It turns out that they are a little bit of everything really. Some are a legacy version of the shorthand conditional expression. Others are just a string transformation expression that hadn't yet made its way into the other section.

The following expressions will return their first arguments if a specific condition is met and an empty string otherwise:

- `$<LINK_ONLY:deps>` – sets implicitly with `target_link_libraries()` to store `PRIVATE` deps link dependencies, which won't be propagated as usage requirements
- `$<INSTALL_INTERFACE:content>` – returns `content` if used with `install(EXPORT)`
- `$<BUILD_INTERFACE:content>` – returns `content` if used with an `export()` command or by another target in the same buildsystem

The following output expressions will perform a string transformation on their arguments:

- `$<MAKE_C_IDENTIFIER:input>` – converts to a C identifier following the same behavior as `string(MAKE_C_IDENTIFIER)`.
- `$<SHELL_PATH:input>` – converts an absolute path (or list of paths) to a shell path style matching the target OS. Slashes are converted to backslashes in Windows shells and drive letters are converted to POSIX paths in MSYS shells.

Finally, we have a stray variable query expression:

- `$<TARGET_OBJECTS:target>` – returns a list of *object files* from a `target` object library

Examples to try out

Everything is easier to grasp when there's a good practical example to support the theory. Here are some of the uses for generator expressions:

Build configurations

In the first chapter, we discussed build type specifying which configuration we are building – `Debug`, `Release`, and so on. There may be cases where you'd like to act differently based on what kind of build you're making. A simple and easy way to do so is utilizing the `$<CONFIG>` generator expression:

```
target_compile_options(tgt $<$<CONFIG:DEBUG>:-ginline-
   points>)
```

The preceding example checks whether the config equals `DEBUG`; if that's the case, the nested expression is evaluated to `1`. The outer shorthand `if` expression then becomes `true`, and our `-ginline-points` debug flag gets added to the options.

System-specific one-liners

Generator expressions can also be used to compact verbose `if` commands into neat one-liners. Let's suppose we have the following code:

```
if (${CMAKE_SYSTEM_NAME} STREQUAL "Linux")
    target_compile_definitions(myProject PRIVATE LINUX=1)
endif()
```

It tells the compiler to add `-DLINUX=1` to the arguments if this is the target system. While this isn't terribly long, it could be easily replaced with an elegant expression:

```
target_compile_definitions(myProject PRIVATE
    $<$<CMAKE_SYSTEM_NAME:LINUX>:LINUX=1>)
```

Such code works well, but there's a limit to how much you can pack into a generator expression until it becomes too hard to read. In that case, it's better to stick to the long conditional blocks.

Interface libraries with compiler-specific flags

Interface libraries, as we discussed earlier in this chapter, can be used to provide flags to match the compiler:

```
add_library(enable_rtti INTERFACE)
target_compile_options(enable_rtti INTERFACE
    $<$<OR:$<COMPILER_ID:GNU>,$<COMPILER_ID:Clang>>:-rtti>
)
```

Even in such a simple example, we can already see what happens when we nest too many generator expressions. Unfortunately, sometimes this is the only way to achieve the desired effect. Here's what happens:

- We check whether `COMPILER_ID` is `GNU`; if that's the case, we evaluate `OR` to `1`.
- If it's not, we check whether `COMPILER_ID` is `Clang`, and evaluate `OR` to `1`. Otherwise, evaluate `OR` to `0`.
- If `OR` is evaluated to `1`, add `-rtti` to the `enable_rtti` *compile options*. Otherwise, do nothing.

Next, we can link our libraries and executables with the `enable_rtti` interface library. CMake will add the `-rtti` flag if a compiler supports it.

Nested generator expressions

Sometimes, it's not obvious what happens when we try to nest elements in a generator expression. We can debug the expressions by generating a test output to a debug file.

Let's try out a few things and see what happens:

chapter04/04-genex/CMakeLists.txt (fragment)

```
set(myvar "small text")
set(myvar2 "small > text")

file(GENERATE OUTPUT nesting CONTENT
    "1 $<PLATFORM_ID>
    2 $<UPPER_CASE:$<PLATFORM_ID>>
    3 $<UPPER_CASE:hello world>
    4 $<UPPER_CASE:${myvar}>
```

```
      5 $<UPPER_CASE:${myvar2}>
")
```

The output is as follows:

```
# cat nesting
1 Linux
  2 LINUX
  3 HELLO WORLD
  4 SMALL TEXT
  5 SMALL  text>
```

This is how each line works:

1. The `PLATFORM_ID` output value is regular case `Linux`.
2. The output from the nested value will get transformed correctly to uppercase `LINUX`.
3. We can transform plain strings.
4. We can transform the content of configuration-stage variables.
5. Variables will be interpolated first, and closing angle brackets (`>`) will be interpreted as part of the genex, in that only part of the string will get capitalized.

In other words, be aware that the content of variables may affect the behavior of your genex expansions. If you need an angle bracket in a variable, use `$<ANGLE-R>`.

The difference between a conditional expression and the evaluation of BOOL operator

Generator expressions can be a little confusing when it comes to evaluating Boolean types to strings. It is important to understand how they differ from regular conditional expressions, starting with an explicit `IF` keyword:

chapter04/04-genex/CMakeLists.txt (fragment)

```
file(GENERATE OUTPUT boolean CONTENT
    "1 $<0:TRUE>
     2 $<0:TRUE,FALSE> (won't work)
     3 $<1:TRUE,FALSE>
     4 $<IF:0,TRUE,FALSE>
```

```
    5 $<IF:0,TRUE,>
")
```

This produces a file like this:

```
# cat boolean
1
2   (won't work)
3 TRUE,FALSE
4 FALSE
5
```

Let's examine the output for each line:

1. This is a Boolean expansion, where BOOL is 0; therefore, the TRUE string isn't written.

2. This is a typical mistake – the author intended to print TRUE or FALSE depending on the BOOL value, but since it is a Boolean false expansion as well, two arguments are treated as one and not printed.

3. This is the same mistake for a reversed value – it is a Boolean true expansion that has both arguments written in a single line.

4. This is a proper conditional expression starting with IF – it prints FALSE because the first argument is 0.

5. This is the incorrect usage of a conditional expression – when we don't need to write values for Boolean false, we should use the first form.

Generator expressions are known for their convoluted syntax. The differences mentioned in this example can confuse even experienced builders. If in doubt, copy such an expression to another file and break it apart with added indentation and whitespace to understand it better.

Summary

Understanding targets is critical to writing clean, modern CMake projects. In this chapter, we not only discussed what constitutes a target and how targets depend on each other but also how to present that information in a diagram using the Graphviz module. With this general understanding, we were able to learn about the key feature of targets – properties (all kinds of properties). We not only went through a few commands to set regular properties on targets; we also solved the mystery of transitive usage requirements or propagated properties. This was a hard one to solve, as we not only needed to control which properties get propagated but also how to reliably propagate them to selected, further targets. Furthermore, we discovered how to guarantee that those propagated properties are compatible when they arrive from multiple sources.

We then briefly discussed pseudo targets – imported targets, alias targets, and interface libraries. All of them will come in handy in our projects, especially when we know how to connect them with propagated properties for our benefit. Then, we talked about generated build targets and how they are the immediate effect of our actions during the configuration stage. Afterward, we focused on custom commands (how they can generate files that can be consumed by other targets, compiled, translated, and so on) and their hook function – executing additional steps when a target is built.

The last part of the chapter was dedicated to the concept of a generator expression, or genex for short. We explained its syntax, nesting, and how its conditional expressions work. Then, we went through two types of evaluation – to Boolean and to string. Each had its own set of expressions, which we explored and commented on in detail. In addition, we have presented a few usage examples and clarified how they work in practice.

With such a solid foundation, we are ready for the next topic – compiling C++ sources to executables and libraries.

Further reading

For more information, use the following sites:

- *Graphviz module documentation:*

    `https://gitlab.kitware.com/cmake/community/-/wikis/doc/cmake/Graphviz`

    `https://cmake.org/cmake/help/latest/module/CMakeGraphVizOptions.html`

- *Graphviz software:*

  https://graphviz.org

- *CMake target properties:*

  https://cmake.org/cmake/help/latest/manual/cmake-properties.7.html#properties-on-targets

- *Transitive usage requirements:*

  https://cmake.org/cmake/help/latest/manual/cmake-buildsystem.7.html#transitive-usage-requirements

5
Compiling C++ Sources with CMake

Simple compilation scenarios are usually handled by a default configuration of a toolchain or just provided out of the box by an IDE. However, in a professional setting, business needs often call for something more advanced. It could be a requirement for higher performance, smaller binaries, more portability, testing support, or extensive debugging capabilities – you name it. Managing all of these in a coherent, future-proof way quickly becomes a complex, tangled mess (especially when there are multiple platforms to support).

The process of compilation is often not explained well enough in books on C++ (in-depth subjects such as virtual base classes seem to be more interesting). In this chapter, we'll go through the basics to ensure success when things don't go as planned. We'll discover how compilation works, what its internal stages are, and how they affect the binary output.

After that, we will focus on the prerequisites – we'll discuss what commands we can employ to tweak a compilation, how to require specific features from a compiler, and how to provide the compiler with the input files that it has to process.

Then, we'll focus on the first stage of compilation – the preprocessor. We'll be providing paths for included headers, and we'll study how to plug in variables from CMake and environments with preprocessor definitions. We'll cover some interesting use cases and learn how to expose CMake variables to C++ code in bulk.

Right after that, we'll talk about the optimizer and how different flags can affect performance. We'll also become painfully aware of the costs of optimization – how hard it is to debug mangled code.

Lastly, we'll explain how to manage the compilation process in terms of reducing the compilation time using precompiled headers and unity builds, preparing for the discovery of mistakes, debugging a build, and storing the debugging information in the final binary.

In this chapter, we're going to cover the following main topics:

- The basics of compilation
- Preprocessor configuration
- Configuring the optimizer
- Managing the process of compilation

Technical requirements

You can find the code files present in this chapter on GitHub at https://github.com/PacktPublishing/Modern-CMake-for-Cpp/tree/main/examples/chapter05.

To build examples provided in this book always use recommended commands:

```
cmake -B <build tree> -S <source tree>
cmake --build <build tree>
```

Be sure to replace placeholders `<build tree>` and `<source tree>` with appropriate paths. As a reminder: **build tree** is the path to target/output directory, **source tree** is the path at which your source code is located.

The basics of compilation

Compilation can be roughly described as a process of translating instructions written in a higher-level programming language to a low-level machine code. This allows us to create our applications using abstract concepts such as classes and objects and not bother with the tedious details of processor-specific assembly languages. We don't need to work directly with CPU registers, think about short or long jumps, and manage stack frames. Compiled languages are more expressive, readable, secure, and foster more maintainable code (but are still as performant as possible).

In C++, we rely on static compilation – an entire program has to be translated into native code before it is executed. This is an alternative approach to languages such as Java or Python, which compile a program on the fly with a special, separate interpreter every time a user runs it. There are certain advantages to each method. The policy of C++ is to provide as many high-level tools as possible while still being able to deliver native performance in a complete, self-contained application for almost every architecture out there.

It takes a few steps to create and run a C++ program:

1. Design your application and carefully write the source code.
2. Compile individual .cpp implementation files (called translation units) to *object files*.
3. Link *object files* together in a single executable and add all other dependencies – dynamic and static libraries.
4. To run the program, the OS will use a tool called *loader* to map its machine code and all required dynamic libraries to the virtual memory. The loader then reads the headers to check where the program starts and hands over control to the code.
5. C++ runtime kicks in; a special _start function is executed to collect the command-line arguments and environment variables. It starts threading, initializes static symbols, and registers cleanup callbacks. Only then will it call main(), which is filled with code by the programmer.

As you can see, quite a lot of work happens behind the scenes. This chapter is about the second step in the preceding list. By taking the whole picture into consideration, we can understand better where some of the possible issues come from. After all, there's no black magic in software (even if the impenetrable complexity makes it seem that way). Everything has an explanation and a reason. Things may fail during the runtime of a program because of how we compiled it (even if the compilation step itself has passed successfully). It's just not possible for a compiler to check all the edge cases during its work.

How compilation works

As mentioned before, compilation is the process of translating a higher-level language into a lower-level language – specifically, by producing machine code (instructions that a specific processor can directly execute) in a binary *object file* format specific for a given platform. On Linux, the most popular format is the **Executable and Linkable Format (ELF)**. Windows uses a PE/COFF format specification. On macOS, we'll find Mach objects (the Mach-O format).

Object files are the direct translation of a single source file. Each one of them has to be compiled separately and later joined by a linker into one executable or library. Thanks to this, when you change your code, you can save time by recompiling only the affected files.

The compiler has to execute the following stages to create an *object file*:

- Preprocessing
- Linguistic analysis
- Assembly
- Optimization
- Code emission

Preprocessing (despite being automatically invoked by most compilers) is thought of as a preliminary step to actual compilation. Its role is to manipulate source code in a very rudimentary way; it executes `#include` directives, replaces identifiers with defined values (`#define` directives and `-D` flags), invokes simple macros, and conditionally includes or excludes parts of code based on the `#if`, `#elif`, and `#endif` directives. The preprocessor is blissfully unaware of the actual C++ code and, in general, is just a slightly more advanced find-and-replace tool. Nevertheless, its job is critical in building advanced programs; the ability to break code up into parts and share declarations across multiple translation units is the foundation of code reusability.

Next up is **linguistic analysis**. This is where more interesting things happen. The compiler will scan the file (containing all the headers included by the preprocessor) character by character and perform lexical analysis, grouping them into meaningful tokens – keywords, operators, variable names, and so on. Then, tokens are grouped into token chains and verified if their order and presence follow the rules of C++ – this process is called syntax analysis or parsing (usually, it's the most vocal part in terms of printed errors). Finally, semantic analysis is performed – the compiler tries to detect whether statements in a file actually make sense. For example, they have to meet type correctness checks (you can't assign an integer to a string variable).

Assembly is nothing more than a translation of these tokens to CPU-specific instructions based on an instruction set available for the platform. Some compilers actually create an assembler output file, which is later passed to a dedicated assembler program to produce machine code that the CPU can execute. Others produce the same machine code directly from memory. Usually, such compilers include an option to produce a textual output of human-readable assembly code (although, just because you can read it, it doesn't mean that it's worth it).

Optimization happens throughout the whole compilation, little by little, at every stage. There's an explicit stage after producing the first assembly version, which is responsible for minimizing the usage of registers and removing unused code. One interesting and important optimization is in-line expansion or *inlining*. The compiler will "cut" the body of a function and "paste" it instead of its call (standard doesn't define in which cases this happens – it depends on the implementation of the compiler). This process speeds up execution and reduces memory usage but has significant disadvantages for debugging (the executed code is no longer at the original line).

Code emission consists of writing the optimized machine code into an *object file* according to the format specified by the target platform. This *object file* is not ready to be executed – it has to be passed to the next tool, the linker, which will appropriately relocate the sections of our *object file* and resolve references to external symbols. This is the transformation from the ASCII source code into binary *object files* that are digestible by processors.

Each of these stages is significant and can be configured to meet our specific needs. Let's look at how we can manage this process with CMake.

Initial configuration

CMake offers multiple commands to affect each stage:

- `target_compile_features()`: Require a compiler with specific features to compile this target.
- `target_sources()`: Add sources to an already defined target.
- `target_include_directories()`: Set up the preprocessor *include paths*.
- `target_compile_definitions()`: Set up preprocessor definitions.
- `target_compile_options()`: Compiler-specific options for the command line.
- `target_precompile_headers()`: Optimize the compilation of external headers.

All of the preceding commands accept similar arguments:

```
target_...(<target name> <INTERFACE|PUBLIC|PRIVATE>
    <value>)
```

This means that they support property propagation, as discussed in the previous chapter, and can be used both for executables and libraries. Also, a reminder here – all of these commands support generator expressions.

Requiring specific features from the compiler

As discussed in the *Checking for supported compiler features* section in *Chapter 3, Setting Up Your First CMake Project*, prepare for things going wrong and aim to provide the user of your software with a clear message – **available compiler X isn't providing required feature Y**. This is a much better experience than the user deciphering whatever error is produced by the incompatible toolchain they might have. We don't want users to assume that your code is at fault instead of their outdated environment.

The following command allows you to specify all the features that your target needs to build:

```
target_compile_features(<target> <PRIVATE|PUBLIC|INTERFACE>
                        <feature> [...])
```

CMake understands C++ standards and supported compiler features for these `compiler_ids`:

- `AppleClang`: Apple Clang for Xcode versions 4.4+
- `Clang`: Clang Compiler versions 2.9+
- `GNU`: GNU Compiler versions 4.4+
- `MSVC`: Microsoft Visual Studio versions 2010+
- `SunPro`: Oracle Solaris Studio versions 12.4+
- `Intel`: Intel Compiler versions 12.1+

> **Important Note**
> You can, of course, use any of the `CMAKE_CXX_KNOWN_FEATURES` variable, but I recommend sticking to a general C++ standard – `cxx_std_98`, `cxx_std_11`, `cxx_std_14`, `cxx_std_17`, `cxx_std_20`, or `cxx_std_23`. Check out the *Further reading* section for more details.

Managing sources for targets

We already know how to tell CMake which source files make up a single target – an executable or a library. We provide the list of files whenever we use `add_executable()` or `add_library()`.

As you grow your solution, the list of files for each target grows too. We can end up with some really lengthy `add_...()` commands. How do we deal with that? One temptation might be to utilize the `file()` command in `GLOB` mode – it can collect all the files from subdirectories and store them in a variable. We could pass it as an argument to the target declaration and not bother with list files again:

```
file(GLOB helloworld_SRC "*.h" "*.cpp")
add_executable(helloworld ${helloworld_SRC})
```

However, the previously mentioned approach is not recommended. Let's figure out why. CMake generates buildsystems based on changes in the list files, so if no changes are made, your builds might break without any warning (which, as we know from long hours spent debugging, is the worst kind of breakage). Other than that, not having all sources listed in the target declaration will break code inspection in IDEs such as CLion (CLion only parses some of the commands to understand your project).

If it's not recommended to use variables in target declarations, how can we add source files conditionally, for example, when dealing with platform-specific implementation files such as `gui_linux.cpp` and `gui_windows.cpp`?

We can use the `target_sources()` command to append files to a previously created target:

chapter05/01-sources/CMakeLists.txt

```
add_executable(main main.cpp)
if(CMAKE_SYSTEM_NAME STREQUAL "Linux")
    target_sources(main PRIVATE gui_linux.cpp)
elseif(CMAKE_SYSTEM_NAME STREQUAL "Windows")
    target_sources(main PRIVATE gui_windows.cpp)
endif()
```

This way, each platform gets its own set of compatible files. That's great, but what about long lists of sources? Well, we'll just have to accept that some things aren't perfect just yet and keep adding them manually.

Now that we have established the key facts about compilation, let's take a closer look at the first step – preprocessing. As with all things in computer science, the devil is in the details.

Preprocessor configuration

The preprocessor plays a huge role in the process of building. Maybe this is a little surprising, given how simple and limited its functionality is. In following sections, we'll cover providing paths to included files and using the preprocessor definitions. We'll also explain how we can use CMake to configure included headers.

Providing paths to included files

The most basic feature of the preprocessor is the ability to include .h/.hpp header files with the #include directive. It comes in two forms:

- #include <path-spec>: Angle-bracket form
- #include "path-spec": Quoted form

As we know, the preprocessor will replace these directives with the contents of the file specified in path-spec. Finding these files may be an issue. Which directories do we search and in what order? Unfortunately, the C++ standard doesn't exactly specify that; we need to check the manual for the compiler we use.

Typically, the angle-bracket form will check standard *include directories*, including the directories where standard C++ library and standard C library headers are stored in the system.

The quoted form will start searching for the included file in the directory of the current file and then check directories for the angle-bracket form.

CMake provides a command to manipulate paths being searched for the included files:

```
target_include_directories(<target> [SYSTEM] [AFTER|BEFORE]
    <INTERFACE|PUBLIC|PRIVATE> [item1...]
    [<INTERFACE|PUBLIC|PRIVATE> [item2...] ...])
```

We can add custom paths that we'd like the compiler to check. CMake will add them to compiler invocations in the generated buildsystem. They will be provided with a flag appropriate for the specific compiler (usually, it's -I).

Using BEFORE or AFTER determines whether the path should be prepended or appended to the target INCLUDE_DIRECTORIES property. It's still up to the compiler to decide whether directories provided here will be checked before or after the default ones (usually, it's before).

The SYSTEM keyword informs the compiler that the provided directories are meant as standard system directories (to be used with the angle-bracket form). For many compilers, this value will be provided as a `-isystem` flag.

Preprocessor definitions

Remember how I mentioned the preprocessor's `#define` and `#if`, `#elif`, and `#endif` directives when describing the stages of compilation? Let's consider the following example:

chapter05/02-definitions/definitions.cpp

```cpp
#include <iostream>
int main() {
#if defined(ABC)
    std::cout << "ABC is defined!" << std::endl;
#endif

#if (DEF < 2*4-3)
    std::cout << "DEF is greater than 5!" << std::endl;
#endif
}
```

As it is, this example does nothing; neither ABC nor DEF is defined (DEF would default to 0 in this example). We can easily change that by adding two lines at the top of this code:

```cpp
#define ABC
#define DEF 8
```

After compiling and executing this code, we can see both messages in the console:

```
ABC is defined!
DEF is greater than 5!
```

This seems easy enough, but what happens if we want to condition these sections based on external factors, such as an operating system, architecture, or something else? Good news! You can pass values from CMake to a C++ compiler, and it's not complicated at all.

The `target_compile_definitions()` command will do the trick:

chapter05/02-definitions/CMakeLists.txt

```
set(VAR 8)
add_executable(defined definitions.cpp)
target_compile_definitions(defined PRIVATE ABC
  "DEF=${VAR}")
```

The preceding code will behave exactly like the two `#define` statements, but we have the freedom to use CMake's variables and generator expressions, and we can put the command in a conditional block.

> **Important Note**
>
> These definitions are traditionally passed to the compiler with the `-D` flag – `-DFOO=1` – and some programmers still use that flag in this command:
>
> `target_compile_definitions(hello PRIVATE -DFOO)`
>
> CMake recognizes this and will remove any leading `-D` flags. It will also ignore empty strings, so it's even okay to write the following:
>
> `target_compile_definitions(hello PRIVATE -D FOO)`
>
> `-D` is a separate argument; it will become an empty string after removal, and then get ignored, correctly behaving as a result.

Common gotchas in unit-testing private class fields

Some online resources recommend using a combination of specific `-D` definitions with `#ifdef/ifndef` directives for the purposes of unit testing. The simplest possible approach is to wrap access specifiers in conditional inclusion and ignore them when `UNIT_TEST` is defined:

```
class X {
#ifndef UNIT_TEST
  private:
#endif
    int x_;
}
```

While this use case is very convenient (it allows tests to directly access private members), it's not very clean code. Unit tests should only test whether methods in the public interface work as expected and treat underlying implementation as a black-box mechanism. I recommend that you only use this as a last resort.

Using git commit to track a compiled version

Let's think about use cases that benefit from knowing details about the environment or filesystem. One great example for professional settings might be passing the revision or commit SHA that was used to build the binary:

chapter05/03-git/CMakeLists.txt

```cmake
add_executable(print_commit print_commit.cpp)
execute_process(COMMAND git log -1 --pretty=format:%h
                OUTPUT_VARIABLE SHA)
target_compile_definitions(print_commit PRIVATE
  "SHA=${SHA}")
```

We can then use it in our application, like so:

chapter05/03-git/print_commit.cpp

```cpp
#include <iostream>
// special macros to convert definitions into c-strings:
#define str(s) #s
#define xstr(s) str(s)
int main()
{
#if defined(SHA)
    std::cout << "GIT commit: " << xstr(SHA) << std::endl;
#endif
}
```

Of course, the preceding code requires a user to have `git` installed and available in their PATH. This is useful when programs running on our production hosts come from a continuous integration/deployment pipeline. If there's an issue with our software, we can quickly check which exact Git commit was used to build the faulty product.

Keeping track of an exact commit is really useful for debugging purposes. For a single variable, it's not a lot of work, but what happens when we have dozens of variables we'd like to pass to our headers?

Configuring the headers

Passing definitions through `target_compile_definitions()` can be a bit of overhead if we have multiple variables. Can't we just provide a header file with placeholders referencing various variables and get CMake to fill them in?

Sure we can! With the `configure_file(<input> <output>)` command, we can generate new files from templates like this one:

chapter05/04-configure/configure.h.in

```
#cmakedefine FOO_ENABLE
#cmakedefine FOO_STRING1 "@FOO_STRING1@"
#cmakedefine FOO_STRING2 "${FOO_STRING2}"
#cmakedefine FOO_UNDEFINED "@FOO_UNDEFINED@"
```

We can then use the command, like so:

chapter05/04-configure/CMakeLists.txt

```
add_executable(configure configure.cpp)
set(FOO_ENABLE ON)
set(FOO_STRING1 "abc")
set(FOO_STRING2 "def")
configure_file(configure.h.in configured/configure.h)
target_include_directories(configure PRIVATE
                           ${CMAKE_CURRENT_BINARY_DIR})
```

We can have CMake build an output file, like this:

chapter05/04-configure/<build_tree>/configure.h

```
#define FOO_ENABLE
#define FOO_STRING1 "abc"
#define FOO_STRING2 "def"
/* #undef FOO_UNDEFINED "@FOO_UNDEFINED@" */
```

As you can see, the @VAR@ and ${VAR} variable placeholders were replaced with the values from the CMake list file. Additionally, #cmakedefine was replaced with #define for defined variables and /* #undef VAR */ for undefined.

If you need an explicit #define 1 or #define 0 for #if blocks, use #cmakedefine01 instead.

How do we use such a configured header in the application? We can simply include it in our implementation file:

chapter05/04-configure/configure.cpp

```cpp
#include <iostream>
#include "configured/configure.h"

// special macros to convert definitions into c-strings:
#define str(s) #s
#define xstr(s) str(s)

using namespace std;
int main()
{
#ifdef FOO_ENABLE
  cout << "FOO_ENABLE: ON" << endl;
#endif
  cout << "FOO_STRING1: " << xstr(FOO_STRING1) << endl;
  cout << "FOO_STRING2: " << xstr(FOO_STRING2) << endl;
  cout << "FOO_UNDEFINED: " << xstr(FOO_UNDEFINED) << endl;
}
```

And because we have added the binary tree to our *include paths* with the target_include_directories() command, we can compile the example and receive output populated from CMake:

```
FOO_ENABLE: ON
FOO_STRING1: "abc"
FOO_STRING2: "def"
FOO_UNDEFINED: FOO_UNDEFINED
```

The `configure_file()` command also has a number of formatting and file-permission options. Describing them here would be a bit too lengthy. If you're interested, check out the online documentation for details (the link is in the *Further reading* section).

After preparing a complete composite of our headers and source file, we can talk about how the output code is shaped during the next steps. As we can't influence the linguistic analysis or assembling directly (these steps follow strict standards), we definitely have access to the configuration of the optimizer. Let's learn how it can affect the end result.

Configuring the optimizer

The optimizer will analyze the output of previous stages and use a multitude of tricks, which programmers would consider dirty, as they don't adhere to clean-code principles. That's okay – the critical role of the optimizer is to make code performant (that is, use few CPU cycles, few registers, and less memory). As the optimizer goes through the source code, it will transform it heavily so that it almost becomes unrecognizable. It turns into a specially prepared version for the target CPU.

The optimizer will not only decide which functions could be removed or compacted; it will also move code around or even significantly duplicate it! If it can determine with full certainty that some lines of code are meaningless, it will wipe them out from the middle of an important function (you won't even notice). It will reuse memory, so numerous variables can occupy the same slot in different periods of time. And it will transform your control structures into totally different ones if that means it can shave off a few cycles here and there.

The techniques described here, if applied manually to source code by a programmer, would turn it into a horrible, unreadable mess. It would be hard to write and reason about. On the other hand, they are great if applied by compilers, which will follow the orders exactly as written. The optimizer is a ruthless beast that serves only one purpose: make the execution fast, no matter how mangled the output will be. Such output may contain some debugging information if we are running it in our test environment, or it may not, in order to make it difficult for unauthorized people to tamper with it.

Each compiler has its own tricks up its sleeve, aligned with the platform and philosophy it follows. We'll take a look at the most common ones, available in GNU GCC and LLVM Clang, so that we can understand what is useful and possible.

Here's the thing – many compilers won't enable any optimization by default (GCC included). This is okay in some cases but not so much in others. Why go slow when you can go fast? To change things, we can use the `target_compile_options()` command and specify exactly what we want from the compiler.

The syntax of this command is similar to others in this chapter:

```
target_compile_options(<target> [BEFORE]
    <INTERFACE|PUBLIC|PRIVATE> [items1...]
    [<INTERFACE|PUBLIC|PRIVATE> [items2...] ...])
```

We provide the `target` command-line options to add and we specify the propagation keyword. When this command is executed, CMake will append the given options to the appropriate `COMPILE_OPTIONS` variable of the target. The optional `BEFORE` keyword may be used to specify that we'd like to prepend them instead. Order matters in some cases, so it's good that we can choose.

> **Important Note**
>
> `target_compile_options()` is a general command. It can also be used to provide other arguments to compiler-like `-D` definitions, for which CMake offers the `target_compile_definition()` command as well. It is always recommended to use the CMake commands wherever possible, as they work the same way across all supported compilers.

Time to discuss the details. The subsequent sections will introduce various kinds of optimizations you can enable in most compilers.

General level

All the different behaviors of the optimizer can be configured in depth by specific flags that we can pass as *compile options*. Getting to know all of them is time-consuming and requires a lot of knowledge about the internal workings of compilers, processors, and memory. What can we do if we just want the best possible scenario that works well in most cases? We can reach for a general solution – an optimization-level specifier.

Most compilers offer four basic levels of optimization, from 0 to 3. We specify them with the `-O<level>` option. `-O0` means *no optimization* and, usually, it's the default level for compilers. On the other hand, `-O2` is considered a *full optimization*, one that generates highly optimized code but at the cost of the slowest compilation time.

There's an in-between `-O1` level, which (depending on your needs) can be a good compromise – it enables a reasonable amount of optimization mechanisms without slowing the compilation too much.

Finally, we can reach for `-O3`, which is *full optimization*, like `-O2`, but with a more aggressive approach to subprogram inlining and loop vectorization.

There are also some variants of the optimization that will optimize for the size (not necessarily the speed) of the produced file – `-Os`. There is a super-aggressive optimization, `-Ofast`, which is an `-O3` optimization that doesn't comply strictly with C++ standards. The most obvious difference is the usage of `-ffast-math` and `-ffinite-math` flags, meaning that if your program is about precise calculations (as most are), you might want to avoid it.

CMake knows that not all compilers are made equal, and for that reason, it standardizes the experience for developers by providing some default flags for compilers. They are stored in system-wide (not target-specific) variables for used language (`CXX` for C++) and build configuration (`DEBUG` or `RELEASE`):

- `CMAKE_CXX_FLAGS_DEBUG` equals `-g`.
- `CMAKE_CXX_FLAGS_RELEASE` equals `-O3 -DNDEBUG`.

As you can see, the debug configuration doesn't enable any optimizations and the release configuration goes straight for O3. If you like, you can change them directly with the `set()` command or just add a target compilation option, which will override this default behavior. The other two flags (`-g, -DNDEBUG`) are related to debugging – we'll discuss them in the *Providing information for the debugger* section.

Variables such as `CMAKE_<LANG>_FLAGS_<CONFIG>` are global – they apply to all targets. It is recommended to configure your targets through properties and commands such as `target_compile_options()` rather than relying on global variables. This way, you can control your targets at higher granularity.

By choosing an optimization level with `-O<level>`, we indirectly set a long list of flags, each controlling a specific optimization behavior. We can then fine-tune the optimization by appending more flags, like so:

- Enable them with an `-f` option: `-finline-functions`.
- Disable them with an `-fno` option: `-fno-inline-functions`.

Some of these flags are worth understanding better as they will often impact how your program works and how you can debug it. Let's take a look.

Function inlining

As you will recall, compilers can be encouraged to inline some functions, either by *defining* a function inside a class *declaration* block or by explicitly using the `inline` keyword:

```
struct X {
   void im_inlined(){ cout << "hi\n"; };
   void me_too();
};
inline void X::me_too() { cout << "bye\n"; };
```

It's up to the compiler to decide whether a function will be inlined. If inlining is enabled and the function is used in a single place (or is a relatively small function used in a few places), then inlining will most likely happen.

It's a really curious optimization technique. It works by extracting the code from the function in question and putting it in all the places the function was called, replacing the original call and saving precious CPU cycles.

Let's consider the following example using the class we just defined:

```
int main() {
   X x;
   x.im_inlined();
   x.me_too();
   return 0;
}
```

Without inlining, the code would execute in the `main()` frame until a method call. Then, it would create a new frame for `im_inlined()`, execute in a separate scope, and go back to the `main()` frame. The same would happen for the `me_too()` method.

However, when inlining takes place, the compiler will replace the calls, like so:

```
int main() {
   X x;
   cout << "hi\n";
   cout << "bye\n";
   return 0;
}
```

This isn't an exact representation because inlining happens at the level of assembly or machine code (and not the source code), but it conveys a general picture.

The compiler does it to save time; it won't have to go through the creation and teardown of a new call frame, it doesn't have to look up the address of the next instruction to execute (and return to), and it can cache the instructions better as they are nearby.

Of course, inlining has some important side effects; if the function is used more than once, it has to be copied to all places (meaning a bigger file size and more memory being used). Nowadays, this may not be so critical as it was in the past, but it's still relevant, as we constantly develop software that has to run on low-end devices without much RAM to spare.

Other than that, it affects us critically when we're debugging the code we wrote. Inlined code is no longer at the line number it was originally written, so it's not as easy (or sometimes even possible) to track. This is the exact reason why a debugger breakpoint placed in a function that was inlined never gets hit (although the code is still somehow executed). To avoid this issue, we simply have to disable inlining for debug builds (at the cost of not testing the exact same version as the release build).

We can do that by specifying the `-O0` level for the target or going straight after the flags responsible:

- `-finline-functions-called-once`: GCC only
- `-finline-functions`: Clang and GCC
- `-finline-hint-functions`: Clang only

You can explicitly disable inlining with `-fno-inline-...`. In any case, for details, refer to the documentation of the specific version of your compiler.

Loop unrolling

Loop unrolling is an optimization technique that is also known as loop unwinding. The general approach is to transform loops into a set of statements that achieve the same effect. By doing so, we'll trade the size of the program for execution speed, as we'll reduce or eliminate the instruction that controls the loop – pointer arithmetic or end-of-loop tests.

Consider the following example:

```
void func() {
    for(int i = 0; i < 3; i++)
        cout << "hello\n";
}
```

The previous code will be transformed into something like this:

```
void func() {
    cout << "hello\n";
    cout << "hello\n";
    cout << "hello\n";
}
```

The outcome will be the same, but we no longer have to allocate the i variable, increment it, or compare it three times with a value of 3. If we call func() enough times in the lifetime of the program, unrolling even such a short and small function will make a significant difference.

However, it is important to understand two limiting factors. Loop unrolling will only work if the compiler knows or can effectively estimate the amount of iterations. Secondly, loop unrolling can produce undesirable effects on modern CPUs, as increased code size might prevent effective caching.

Each compiler offers a slightly different version of this flag:

- -floop-unroll: GCC
- -funroll-loops: Clang

If you're in doubt, test extensively whether this flag is affecting your particular program and explicitly enable or disable it. Do note that on GCC, it is implicitly enabled with -O3 as part of the implicitly enabled -floop-unroll-and-jam flag.

Loop vectorization

Single Instruction Multiple Data (**SIMD**) is one of the mechanisms developed in the early 1960s to achieve parallelism. It works exactly as the name suggests; it can perform the same operation on multiple pieces of information at the same time. What does it mean in practice? Let's consider the following example:

```
int a[128];
int b[128];
// initialize b
for (i = 0; i<128; i++)
    a[i] = b[i] + 5;
```

Normally, the preceding code would loop 128 times, but with a capable CPU, we can execute the code much faster by calculating two or more elements of the array at the same time. This works because there's no dependency between consecutive elements and no overlap of data between arrays. Smart compilers can transform the preceding loop into something similar to this (which happens on the assembly level):

```
for (i = 0; i<32; i+=4) {
    a[ i ] = b[ i ] + 5;
    a[i+1] = b[i+1] + 5;
    a[i+2] = b[i+2] + 5;
    a[i+3] = b[i+3] + 5;
}
```

GCC will enable such automatic vectorization of loops at -O3. Clang enables it by default. Both compilers offer different flags to enable/disable vectorization in particular:

- `-ftree-vectorize -ftree-slp-vectorize` to enable in GCC
- `-fno-vectorize -fno-slp-vectorize` to disable in Clang (if things break)

The performance of vectorization comes from utilizing special instructions that CPU manufacturers provide, rather than just simply replacing the original form of the loop with the unrolled version. Therefore, it's not possible to achieve the same level of performance by doing it manually (also, it's not very clean code).

The role of the optimizer is important in enhancing the performance of the program during runtime. By employing its strategies effectively, we'll get more bang for our buck. Efficiency is important not only after the coding is completed but also as we work on the software. If the compilation times are lengthy, we can improve them by managing the process better.

Managing the process of compilation

As programmers and build engineers, we need to consider the other aspects of compilation as well – the time it takes to complete, and how easy it is to spot and fix mistakes made during the process of building a solution.

Reducing compilation time

In busy projects that require many dozens of recompilations per day (or per hour), it's paramount that compilation is as quick as possible. This not only affects how tight your code-compile-test loop is but also affects your concentration and flow of work. Luckily, C++ is already pretty good at managing compilation time, thanks to separate translation units. CMake will take care of recompiling only sources that were impacted by recent changes. However, if we need to improve things even more, there are a couple of techniques we can use – header precompilation and unity builds.

Precompilation of headers

Header files (.h) are included in the translation unit by the preprocessor before the actual compilation begins. It means that they have to be recompiled every time the .cpp implementation files change. On top of that, if multiple translation files are using the same shared header, it has to be compiled every time it's included. This is wasteful, but that's how things were for a long time.

Luckily, since version 3.16, CMake offers a command to enable header precompilation. This allows a compiler to process headers separately from the implementation file and speed up the compilation. This is the syntax for the provided command:

```
target_precompile_headers(<target>
    <INTERFACE|PUBLIC|PRIVATE> [header1...]
    [<INTERFACE|PUBLIC|PRIVATE> [header2...] ...])
```

The list of added headers is stored in the `PRECOMPILE_HEADERS` target property. As you'll know from *Chapter 4, Working with Targets*, we can use the propagated properties to share the headers with any depending targets by using the `PUBLIC` or `INTERFACE` keyword; however, this shouldn't be done for targets exported with the `install()` command. Other projects shouldn't be forced to consume our precompiled headers (as it's unconventional).

> **Important Note**
> If you need precompiled headers internally and still want to install-export the target, the `$<BUILD_INTERFACE:...>` generator expression described in *Chapter 4, Working with Targets*, will prevent headers from appearing in usage requirements. However, they will still be added to targets exported from the build tree with the `export()` command.

CMake will put all headers' names in a `cmake_pch.h|xx` file, which will then be precompiled to a compiler-specific binary file with a `.pch`, `.gch`, or `.pchi` extension.

We can use it like so:

chapter05/06-precompile/CMakeLists.txt

```
add_executable(precompiled hello.cpp)
target_precompile_headers(precompiled PRIVATE <iostream>)
```

chapter05/06-precompile/hello.cpp

```
int main() {
    std::cout << "hello world" << std::endl;
}
```

Note that in our `main.cpp` file, we don't need to include `cmake_pch.h` or any other header – it will be force-included by CMake with compiler-specific command-line options.

In the previous example, I have used a built-in header; however, you can easily add your own headers with class or function definitions:

- `header.h` is interpreted as relative to the current source directory and will be included with an absolute path.
- `[["header.h"]]` is interpreted according to the compiler's implementation and is usually found in the `INCLUDE_DIRECTORIES` variable. Use `target_include_directories()` to configure it.

Some online references will discourage precompiling headers that aren't part of a standard library, such as `<iostream>`, or using precompiled headers altogether. This is because changing the list or editing a custom header will cause recompilation of all translation units in the target. With CMake, you don't need to worry as much, especially if you structure your project right (with relatively small targets, focused on a narrow domain). Every target has a separate precompiled header file that limits the fallout of header changes.

On the other hand, if your headers are considered fairly stable, you might decide that it's a good idea to reuse precompiled headers from one target in another. CMake provides a handy command for this purpose:

```
target_precompile_headers(<target> REUSE_FROM
    <other_target>)
```

This sets the `PRECOMPILE_HEADERS_REUSE_FROM` property of the target reusing the headers and creates a dependency between these targets. By using this method, the consuming target can no longer specify its own precompiled headers. Additionally, all *compile options*, *compile flags*, and *compile definitions* must match between targets. Pay attention to requirements, especially if you have any headers that use the double bracket format (`[["header.h"]]`). Both targets need to set their *include paths* appropriately to make sure those headers are found by the compiler.

Unity builds

CMake 3.16 also introduced another compilation time optimization feature – unity builds, also known as *unified build* or *jumbo build*. Unity builds combine multiple implementation source files with the `#include` directive (after all, a compiler doesn't know whether it's including headers or implementation). This has a few interesting implications – some are really useful and others are potentially harmful.

Let's start with the most obvious one – avoiding recompilation of headers in different translation units when CMake creates a unified build file:

```
#include "source_a.cpp"
#include "source_b.cpp"
```

When both of these sources contain a `#include "header.h"` line, it will only be parsed once thanks to *include guards* (assuming we didn't forget to add those). This isn't as elegant as precompiled headers, but it's an option.

The second benefit from this type of build is the fact that the optimizer may now act on a greater scale and optimize interprocedural calls across all bundled sources. This is similar to link-time optimization, as we discussed in *Chapter 2, The CMake Language*.

However, these benefits come at a price. As we reduced the number of *object files* and processing steps, we also increased the amount of necessary memory to process much larger files. Additionally, we reduced the amount of parallelizable work. Compilers aren't really that great at multithreaded compiling because they don't need to be – the buildsystem will usually kick-start many compilation tasks to execute all the files simultaneously on different threads. When we clump all files together, we make it much harder, as CMake will now schedule parallel builds across however many jumbo builds we create.

With unity builds, you also need to consider some C++ semantic implications that might not be so obvious to catch – anonymous namespaces hiding symbols across files are now scoped to the group. The same thing happens with static global variables, functions, and macro definitions. It may cause name collisions, or incorrect function overloads to be executed.

Jumbo builds are not desirable when recompiling, as they will compile many more files than needed. They work best when the code is meant to compile all files as fast as possible as a whole. Tests done on Qt Creator show that you can expect an improvement anywhere between 20% to 50% (depending on the compiler used).

To enable unity builds, we have two options:

- Set the `CMAKE_UNITY_BUILD` variable to `true` – it will initialize the `UNITY_BUILD` property on every target defined thereafter.
- Manually define `UNITY_BUILD` as `true` on every target that should use unity builds.

The second option is achieved by calling the following:

```
set_target_properties(<target1> <target2> ...
                PROPERTIES UNITY_BUILD true)
```

By default, CMake will create builds containing eight source files, as specified by the `UNITY_BUILD_BATCH_SIZE` property of a target (copied at the creation of a target from the `CMAKE_UNITY_BUILD_BATCH_SIZE` variable). You can change the target property or default variable.

Since version 3.18, you may decide that you'd like to explicitly define how files should be bundled with named groups. To do so, change the target's `UNITY_BUILD_MODE` property to `GROUP` (the default is always `BATCH`). Then, you'll need to assign your source files to groups by setting their `UNITY_GROUP` property to the name of your choosing:

```
set_property(SOURCE <src1> <src2>...
            PROPERTY UNITY_GROUP "GroupA")
```

CMake will then disregard `UNITY_BUILD_BATCH_SIZE` and add all files from the group to a single jumbo build.

CMake's documentation advises against enabling unity builds for public projects by default. It is recommended that the end user of your application should be able to decide whether they want jumbo builds or not by providing the `DCMAKE_UNITY_BUILD` command-line argument. What's more, if they cause issues because of how your code is written, you should explicitly set the target's property to `false`. However, nothing is stopping you from enabling this feature for code that will be used internally, such as inside a company or for your private project.

Unsupported C++20 modules

If you follow the C++ standard releases closely, you will be aware of the new feature introduced in C++20 – modules. This is a significant game changer. It allows you to avoid many nuisances when using headers, reduces build time, and allows for cleaner, more compact code that is easier to navigate and reason about.

Essentially, instead of creating a separate header and implementation file, we can create a single file with module declaration:

```
export module hello_world;
import <iostream>;
export void hello() {
```

```
    std::cout << "Hello world!\n";
}
```

Then, you can use it in your code by simply importing it:

```
import hello_world;
int main() {
    hello();
}
```

Note how we aren't relying on a preprocessor anymore; modules have their own keywords – `import`, `export`, and `module`. The latest versions of the most popular compilers can already perform all the necessary tasks to support modules as the new method of writing and building C++ solutions. It was my hope that by the time this chapter was started, some early support for modules would already have been provided in CMake. Unfortunately, this hasn't happened just yet.

However, it might be available by the time you have bought this book (or soon after). There are some really good indicators; Kitware developers have created (and released in 3.20) a new, experimental feature to support C++20 module dependency scanning for the Ninja generator. For now, it's only intended for compiler writers so that they can test their dependency scanning tools as they are being developed.

When this much-anticipated feature is finished and available in a stable release, I suggest researching it thoroughly. I expect it will simplify and speed up the compilation way beyond anything available today.

Finding mistakes

As programmers, we spend a lot of time bug hunting. It's a sad fact. Finding errors and solving them can often get under our skin, especially if it takes long hours. It's even more difficult when we are flying blind, without instruments to help us navigate through the storm. This is why we should apply great care to set our environment in a way that makes this process as easy and as bearable as possible. We do this by configuring the compiler with `target_compile_options()`. Which *compile options* could help us then?

Configuring errors and warnings

There are many great stressful things about software development – fixing critical bugs in the middle of the night, working on high-visibility, costly failures in large systems, and dealing with annoying compilation errors, especially with those that are hard to understand or impossibly tedious to fix. When researching a subject in order to simplify your work and reduce the chance of failure, you'll find a lot of recommendations on how to configure the compiler's warnings.

One such fine piece of advice is to enable the `-Werror` flag as default for all builds. What this flag does is innocently simple – all warnings are treated as errors, and the code won't compile unless you resolve all of them. While it may seem like a good idea, it hardly ever is.

You see, warnings aren't errors for a reason. They're meant to warn you about things. It's up to you to decide what to do about that. Having the freedom to ignore a warning, especially when you experiment with and prototype your solution, is often a blessing.

On the other hand, if you have a perfect, no-warnings, all-shiny piece of code, it's a shame to allow future changes to ruin this state of things. What harm could come from enabling it and just keeping it there? Seemingly none. At least until your compiler gets upgraded, that is. New versions of compilers tend to be stricter about deprecated features or just get better about suggesting things to improve. This is great when you don't treat all warnings as errors, but when you do, you'll discover one day that your build starts breaking without changes in the code or, even more frustrating, when you need to quickly fix a problem totally unrelated to a new warning.

What is this "hardly ever" case, when you actually should enable all the warnings possible? The quick answer is when you're writing a public library. Then, you really want to avoid issue tickets complaining about your code being naughty just because it is compiled in a stricter environment than yours. If you decide to enable it, make sure that you're up to speed with new versions of the compiler and the warnings it introduces.

Otherwise, let warnings be warnings, and focus on errors. If you feel an internal need to be pedantic, use the `-Wpedantic` flag. This is an interesting one – it enables all the warnings demanded by strict ISO C and ISO C++. Do note that you can't check whether the code is conforming to the standard with this flag – it will only find non-ISO practices that require a diagnostic message.

More lenient and down-to-earth coders will be satisfied with `-Wall` and optionally with `-Wextra` for that extra-fancy feel. These are considered to be actually useful and meaningful warnings that you should fix in your code when you have a spare moment.

There are plenty of other warning flags, which might be useful depending on the kind of project. I recommend that you read the manual for your chosen compiler and see what's available.

Debugging the build

Occasionally, compilation will break. This usually happens when we try to refactor a bunch of code or clean up our buildsystem. Sometimes, things get resolved easily, but then there are much more complex problems that require a deep dive into the steps of the configuration. We already know how to print more verbose CMake outputs (as discussed in *Chapter 1, First Steps with CMake*), but how do we analyze what actually happens under the hood at each stage?

Debugging individual stages

There is a `-save-temps` flag we can pass to the compilers (both GCC and Clang have it) that will force the output of each stage to be stored in a file instead of memory:

chapter05/07-debug/CMakeLists.txt

```
add_executable(debug hello.cpp)
target_compile_options(debug PRIVATE -save-temps=obj)
```

The preceding snippet will usually produce two extra files:

- `<build-tree>/CMakeFiles/<target>.dir/<source>.ii`: Stores the output of the preprocessing stage, with comments explaining where each part of the source code comes from:

```
# 1 "/root/examples/chapter05/06-debug/hello.cpp"
# 1 "<built-in>"
# 1 "<command-line>"
# 1 "/usr/include/stdc-predef.h" 1 3 4
# / / / ... removed for brevity ... / / /
# 252 "/usr/include/x86_64-linux-
    gnu/c++/9/bits/c++config.h" 3
namespace std
{
    typedef long unsigned int size_t;
    typedef long int ptrdiff_t;
```

```
        typedef decltype(nullptr) nullptr_t;
}
...
```

- `<build-tree>/CMakeFiles/<target>.dir/<source>.s`: The output of the linguistic analysis stage, ready for the assembler stage:

```
        .file   "hello.cpp"
        .text
        .section        .rodata
        .type   _ZStL19piecewise_construct, @object
        .size   _ZStL19piecewise_construct, 1
_ZStL19piecewise_construct:
        .zero   1
        .local  _ZStL8__ioinit
        .comm   _ZStL8__ioinit,1,1
.LC0:
        .string "hello world"
        .text
        .globl  main
        .type   main, @function
main:
( ... )
```

Depending on the kind of problem, we can usually discover what the actual issue is. The output of the preprocessor can be useful to discover bugs such as incorrect *include paths* (providing the wrong version of libraries) and mistakes with definitions causing incorrect `#ifdef` evaluations.

The output of the linguistic analysis is useful for targeting specific processors and solving critical optimization problems.

Debugging issues with header file inclusion

Incorrectly included files can be a really hard problem to debug. I should know – it was my first corporate job to port an entire code base from one buildsystem to another. If you ever find yourself in a position that requires an exact understanding of which paths are being used to include a requested header, use -H:

chapter05/07-debug/CMakeLists.txt

```
add_executable(debug hello.cpp)
target_compile_options(debug PRIVATE -H)
```

The printed output will look similar to this:

```
[ 25%] Building CXX object
    CMakeFiles/inclusion.dir/hello.cpp.o
. /usr/include/c++/9/iostream
.. /usr/include/x86_64-linux-gnu/c++/9/bits/c++config.h
... /usr/include/x86_64-linux-gnu/c++/9/bits/os_defines.h
.... /usr/include/features.h
-- removed for brevity --
.. /usr/include/c++/9/ostream
```

After the name of *object file*, each row in the output contains a path to a header. A single dot at beginning of the line means top-level inclusion (the `#include` directive is in `hello.cpp`). Two dots mean that this file is included by `<iostream>`. Every further dot indicates yet another level of nesting.

At the end of this output, you may also find suggestions of possible improvements to your code:

```
Multiple include guards may be useful for:
/usr/include/c++/9/clocale
/usr/include/c++/9/cstdio
/usr/include/c++/9/cstdlib
```

You're not required to fix the standard library, but you might see some of your own headers. You may want to correct them.

Providing information for the debugger

Machine code is a cryptic list of instructions and data encoded in binary format. It doesn't convey any meaning or objective. This is because the CPU doesn't care what the goal of the program is or what the sense of all of the instructions is. The only requirement is the correctness of the code. The compiler will translate all of the preceding into numeric identifiers of CPU instructions, some data to initialize the memory, and thousands of memory addresses. In other words, the final binary doesn't need to contain the actual source code, variable names, signatures of functions, or any other details that programmers care about. And that's the default output of the compiler – raw and dry.

This is done primarily to save space and execute without too much overhead. By coincidence, we are also (somewhat) protecting our application from reverse engineering. Yes, you can understand what each CPU instruction does without the source code (for example, copy this integer to that register). But in the end, even basic programs contain too many of them to easily think about the big picture.

If you're a particularly driven individual, you can use a tool called a **disassembler**, and with a lot of knowledge (and a little luck), you'll be able to understand what might be going on. This approach isn't very practical, as disassembled code doesn't have original symbols, so it's extremely hard and slow to untangle what goes where.

Instead, we can ask the compiler to store the source code in the produced binary along with the map containing references between compiled and original code. Then, we can hook a debugger to a running program and see which source line is being executed at any given moment. This is indispensable when we're working on code, such as writing new functionality or correcting mistakes.

These two use cases are the reason for two configs: Debug and Release. As we saw earlier, CMake will provide some flags to the compiler by default to manage this process, storing them first in global variables:

- CMAKE_CXX_FLAGS_DEBUG contains -g.
- CMAKE_CXX_FLAGS_RELEASE contains -DNDEBUG.

The -g flag simply means *add debugging information*. It's provided in the operating system's native format – stabs, COFF, XCOFF, or DWARF. These formats can be then accessed by debuggers such as gdb (the GNU debugger). Usually, this is good enough for IDEs such as CLion (as they use gdb under the hood). In other cases, refer to the manual of the provided debugger and check what the appropriate flag is for the compiler of your choice.

For the `RELEASE` config, CMake will add the `-DNDEBUG` flag. It's a preprocessor definition, which simply means *not a debug build*. Some debug-oriented macros may not work when this option is enabled. One of them is `assert`, available in the `<assert.h>` header file. If you decide to use assertions in your production code, they simply won't work:

```
int main(void)
{
    bool my_boolean = false;
    assert(my_boolean);
    std::cout << "This shouldn't run. \n";
    return 0;
}
```

The `assert(my_boolean)` call won't have any effect in the `Release` config, but it will work just fine in `Debug`. What do you do if you're practicing assertive programming and still need to use `assert()` for release builds? Either change the defaults that are provided by CMake (remove `NDEBUG` from `CMAKE_CXX_FLAGS_RELEASE`) or implement a hardcoded override by undefining the macro before the header inclusion:

```
#undef NDEBUG
#include <assert.h>
```

Refer to the assert reference for more information: https://en.cppreference.com/w/c/error/assert.

Summary

We have completed yet another chapter! There is no doubt that compilation is a complex process. With all its edge cases and specific requirements, it can be difficult to manage without a good tool. Thankfully, CMake is doing a great job in supporting us here.

What have we learned so far? We started by discussing what compilation is and where it fits in the larger story of building and running applications in the operating system. We then examined what the stages of compilation are and the internal tools that manage them. This is very useful in resolving all the issues in more advanced cases that we might encounter down the line.

Then, we looked at how to ask CMake to verify whether the compiler available on the host is meeting all the necessary requirements for our code to build. As we have already established, it's a much better experience for users of our solution to see a friendly message asking them to upgrade, rather than some arcane error printed by an old compiler that is confused by the new features of the language.

We shortly discussed how to add sources to already defined targets, and moved on to the configuration of the preprocessor. This was quite a big subject, as this stage brings all bits of the code together and decides which of them will be ignored. We talked about providing paths to files and adding custom definitions as single arguments and in bulk (along with some use cases).

Then, we discussed the optimizer; we explored all the general levels of optimization and what kind of flags they imply, but we also went into details about a few of them – `finline`, `floop-unroll`, and `ftree-vectorize`.

Finally, it was time to research the bigger picture again and study how to manage the viability of compilation. We tackled two main aspects here – reducing the time of compilation (and, by extension, strengthening the focus of the programmer) and finding mistakes. The latter is extremely important for discovering what is broken and how. Setting the tools correctly and understanding why things happen goes a long way in ensuring the quality of the code (and our mental health).

In the next chapter, we'll learn about linking, and all the things we need to consider to build libraries and use them in our projects.

Further reading

- For more information on the topics covered in this chapter, you can refer to the following: *CMake-supported compile features and compilers:* `https://cmake.org/cmake/help/latest/manual/cmake-compile-features.7.html#supported-compilers`

- *Managing sources for targets:*

    - `https://stackoverflow.com/questions/32411963/why-is-cmake-file-glob-evil`

    - `https://cmake.org/cmake/help/latest/command/target_sources.html`

- *Providing paths to included files:*
  - `https://en.cppreference.com/w/cpp/preprocessor/include`
  - `https://cmake.org/cmake/help/latest/command/target_include_directories.html`
- *Configuring headers:* `https://cmake.org/cmake/help/latest/command/configure_file.html`
- *Pre-compilation of headers:* `https://cmake.org/cmake/help/latest/command/target_precompile_headers.html`
- *Unity builds:*
  - `https://cmake.org/cmake/help/latest/prop_tgt/UNITY_BUILD.html`
  - `https://www.qt.io/blog/2019/08/01/precompiled-headers-and-unity-jumbo-builds-in-upcoming-cmake`
- *Finding mistakes – compiler flags:* `https://interrupt.memfault.com/blog/best-and-worst-gcc-clang-compiler-flags`
- *Why use libraries and not object files:* `https://stackoverflow.com/questions/23615282/object-files-vs-library-files-and-why`
- *Separation of concerns:* `https://nalexn.github.io/separation-of-concerns/`

6
Linking with CMake

You might think that after we have successfully compiled the source code into a binary file, our job as build engineers is done. That's almost the case – binary files contain all the code for a CPU to execute, but the code is scattered across multiple files in a very complex way. Linking is a process that simplifies things and makes machine code neat and quick to consume.

A quick glance at the list of commands will tell you that CMake doesn't provide that many related to linking. Admittedly, `target_link_libraries()` is the only one that actually configures this step. Why dedicate a whole chapter to a single command then? Unfortunately, almost nothing is ever easy in computer science, and linking is no exception.

To achieve the correct results, we need to follow the whole story – understand how exactly a linker works and get the basics right. We'll talk about the internal structure of *object files*, how the relocation and reference resolution works, and what it is for. We'll discuss how the final executable differs from its components and how the process image is built by the system.

Then, we'll introduce you to all kinds of libraries – static, shared, and shared modules. They all are called libraries, but in reality, they are almost nothing alike. Building a correctly linked executable heavily depends on a valid configuration (and taking care of such minute details as **position-independent code** (**PIC**).

We'll learn about another nuisance of linking – the **One Definition Rule** (**ODR**). We need to get the amount of definitions exactly right. Dealing with duplicated symbols can sometimes be very tricky, especially when shared libraries come into play. Then, we'll learn why linkers sometimes can't find external symbols, even when the executable is linked with the appropriate library.

Finally, we'll discover how we can save time and use a linker to prepare our solution for testing with dedicated frameworks.

In this chapter, we're going to cover the following main topics:

- Getting the basics of linking right
- Building different library types
- Solving problems with the One Definition Rule
- The order of linking and unresolved symbols
- Separating `main()` for testing

Technical requirements

You can find the code files that are present in this chapter on GitHub at https://github.com/PacktPublishing/Modern-CMake-for-Cpp/tree/main/examples/chapter06.

To build examples provided in this book always use recommended commands:

```
cmake -B <build tree> -S <source tree>
cmake --build <build tree>
```

Be sure to replace placeholders `<build tree>` and `<source tree>` with appropriate paths. As a reminder: **build tree** is the path to target/output directory, **source tree** is the path at which your source code is located.

Getting the basics of linking right

We discussed the life cycle of a C++ program in *Chapter 5, Compiling C++ Sources with CMake*. It consists of five main stages – writing, compiling, linking, loading, and execution. After correctly compiling all the sources, we need to put them together into an executable. *Object files* produced in a compilation can't be executed by a processor directly. But why?

To answer this, let's take a look at how a compiler structures an *object file* in the popular ELF format (used by Unix-like systems and many others):

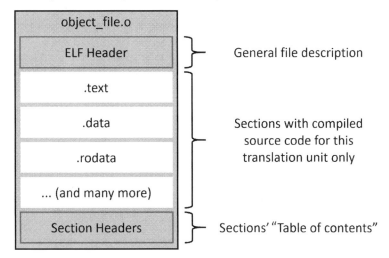

Figure 6.1 – The structure of an object file

The compiler will prepare an *object file* for every unit of translation (for every .cpp file). These files will be used to build an in-memory image of our program. *Object files* contain the following elements:

- An ELF header identifying the target operating system, ELF file type, target instruction set architecture, and information on the position and size of two header tables found in ELF files – the program headers table (not present in *object files*) and the section headers table.
- Sections containing information grouped by type (described next).
- A section headers table, containing information about the name, the type, flags, the destination address in memory, the offset in the file, and other miscellaneous information. It is used to understand what sections are in this file and where they are, just like a table of contents.

As the compiler processes your source code, it groups the collected information into a few separate bins, which will be put in their own separate section. Some of them are as follows:

- .text section: Machine code, with all the instructions to be executed by the processor
- .data section: All values of the initialized global and static objects (variables)

- `.bss` section: All values of the uninitialized global and static objects (variables), which will be initialized to zero on program start
- `.rodata` section: All values of the constants (read-only data)
- `.strtab` section: A string table containing all constant strings such as *Hello World* that we put in our basic `hello.cpp` example
- `.shstrtab` section: A string table containing the names of all the sections

These groups very closely resemble the final version of the executable, which will be put in the RAM to run our application. However, we can't just load this file to memory as it is. This is because every *object file* has its own set of sections. If we were to just concatenate them together, we'd run into all sorts of issues. We'd be wasting a lot of space and time, as we'd need many more pages of RAM. Instructions and data would be much harder to copy to a CPU cache. An entire system would have to be much more complex and would waste precious cycles jumping around many (possibly tens of thousands) of `.text`, `.data`, and other sections during runtime.

So, what we'll do instead is take each section of the *object file* and put it together with the same type of section from all other *object files*. This process is called **relocation** (that's why the ELF file type is `Relocatable` for *object files*). Apart from just bringing appropriate sections together, it has to update internal associations in the file – that is, addresses of variables, functions, symbol table indexes, or string table indexes. All of these values are local to the *object file*, and their numbering starts from zero. When we bundle files together, we need to offset these values so that they are pointing at the correct addresses in the combined file.

Figure 6.2 shows relocation in action – the `.text` section is relocated, `.data` is being built from all linked files, and `.rodata` and `.strtab` will follow (for simplicity, the figure doesn't contain headers):

Getting the basics of linking right 189

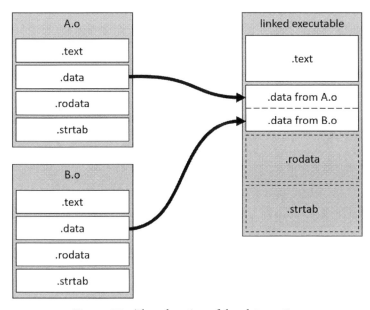

Figure 6.2 – The relocation of the .data section

Secondly, a linker needs to **resolve references**. Whenever a piece of code from one translation unit references a symbol defined in another (such as through including its header or by using the `extern` keyword), the compiler reads the declaration and *trusts* that the definition is somewhere out there and will be provided at a later time. A linker is responsible for collecting such *unresolved references* to external symbols, finding and filling the addresses at which they reside after merging into the executable. *Figure 6.3* shows a simple example of reference resolution:

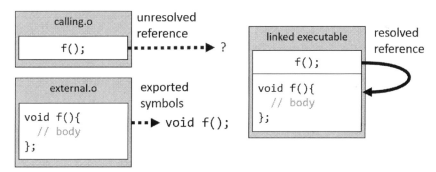

Figure 6.3 – A reference resolution

This part of the linking can be a source of problems if a programmer is unaware of how it works. We may end up with unresolved references that won't find their external symbols, or the opposite – we provided too many definitions and the linker doesn't know which one to pick.

The final *executable file* looks very similar to the *object file*; it contains relocated sections with resolved references, a section headers table, and of course, the ELF Header describing the whole file. The main difference is the presence of the Program Header (as pictured in *Figure 6.4*).

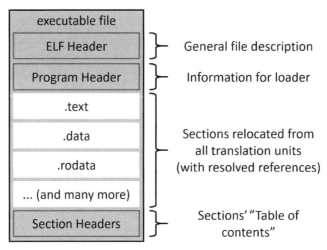

Figure 6.4 – The structure of the executable file in ELF

The Program Header is placed right after the ELF Header. A system loader will read this header to create a process image. The header contains some general information and a description of the memory layout. Each entry in the layout represents one fragment of memory called a **segment**. Entries specify which sections will be read, in what order, to which addresses in the virtual memory, what their flags are (read, write, or execute), and a few other useful details.

Object files may also be bundled in a library, which is an intermediate product that can be used in a final executable or another library. In the next section, we'll discuss three types of libraries.

Building different library types

After source code is compiled, we might want to avoid compiling it again for the same platform or even share it with external projects wherever possible. Of course, you could just simply provide all of your *object files* as they were originally created, but that has a few downsides. It is harder to distribute multiple files and add them individually to a buildsystem. It can be a hassle, especially if they are numerous. Instead, we could simply bring all *object files* into a single object and share that. CMake helps greatly with this process. We can create these libraries with a simple `add_library()` command (which is consumed with the `target_link_libraries()` command). By convention, all libraries have a common prefix, `lib`, and use system-specific extensions that denote what kind of library they are:

- A static library has a `.a` extension on Unix-like systems and `.lib` on Windows.
- Shared libraries have a `.so` extension on Unix-like systems and `.dll` on Windows.

When building libraries (static, shared, or shared modules), you'll often encounter the name *linking* for this process. Even CMake calls it that in the build output of the `chapter06/01-libraries` project:

```
[ 33%] Linking CXX static library libmy_static.a
[ 66%] Linking CXX shared library libmy_shared.so
[100%] Linking CXX shared module libmy_module.so
[100%] Built target module_gui
```

Contrary to how it may seem, a linker isn't used to create all of the preceding libraries. There are exceptions to performing relocation and reference resolution. Let's take a look at each library type to understand how each works.

Static libraries

To build a static library, we can simply use the command we already saw in previous chapters:

```
add_library(<name> [<source>...])
```

The preceding code will produce a static library if the `BUILD_SHARED_LIBS` variable isn't set to `ON`. If we want to build a static library regardless, we can provide an explicit keyword:

```
add_library(<name> STATIC [<source>...])
```

What are static libraries? They are essentially a collection of raw *object files* stored in an archive. On Unix-like systems, such archives can be created by the `ar` tool. Static libraries are the oldest and most basic mechanism to provide a compiled version of code. Use them if you want to avoid separating your dependencies from the executable, at the price of the executable increasing in size and used memory.

The archive may contain some additional indexes to speed up the final linking process. Each platform uses its own methods to generate those. Unix-like systems use a tool called `ranlib` for this purpose.

Shared libraries

It's not surprising to learn that we can build shared libraries with the `SHARED` keyword:

```
add_library(<name> SHARED [<source>...])
```

We can also do it by setting the `BUILD_SHARED_LIBS` variable to `ON` and using the short version:

```
add_library(<name> SHARED [<source>...])
```

The difference from static libraries is significant. Shared libraries are built using a linker, and they will perform both stages of linking. This means that we'll receive a file with proper section headers, sections, and a section header table (*Figure 6.1*).

Shared libraries (also known as shared objects) can be shared between multiple different applications. An operating system will load a single instance of such a library into memory with the first program that uses it, and all subsequently started programs will be provided with the same address (thanks to the complex mechanisms of virtual memory). Only the `.data` and `.bss` segments will be created separately for every process consuming the library (so that each process can modify its own variables without affecting other consumers).

Thanks to this approach, the overall memory usage in the system is better. And if we're using a very popular library, we might not need to ship it with our program. Chances are that it's already available on the target machine. However, if that's not the case, a user is expected to explicitly install it before running the application. This opens up the possibility of some issues when an installed version of a library is different from expected (this type of problem is called *dependency hell*; more information can be found in the *Further reading* section).

Shared modules

To build shared modules, we need to use the MODULE keyword:

```
add_library(<name> MODULE [<source>...])
```

This is a version of a shared library that is intended to be used as a plugin loaded during runtime, rather than something that is linked with an executable during compilation. A shared module isn't loaded automatically with the start of the program (like regular shared libraries). This only happens when a program explicitly requests it by making a system call such as LoadLibrary (Windows) or dlopen()/dlsym() (Linux/macOS).

You shouldn't try to link your executable with a module, as this isn't guaranteed to work on all platforms. If you need to do that, use regular shared libraries.

Position-independent code

All sources for shared libraries and modules should be compiled with a *position-independent code* flag enabled. CMake checks the POSITION_INDEPENDENT_CODE property of targets and appropriately adds compiler-specific compilation flags such as -fPIC for gcc or clang.

PIC is a bit of a confusing term. Nowadays, programs are already *position-independent* in a sense, in that they use virtual memory to abstract away actual physical addresses. When calling a function, a CPU uses a **memory management unit** (**MMU**) to translate a virtual address (starting from 0 for every process) to a physical address that was available at the time of allocation. These mappings don't have to point to consecutive physical addresses or follow any other specific order.

PIC is about mapping symbols (references to functions and global variables) to their runtime addresses. During compilation of a library, it is not known which processes might use it. It's not possible to predetermine where in the virtual memory the library will be loaded or in what order. This, in turn, means that the addresses of the symbols are unknown, as is their relative position to the library's machine code.

To deal with that, we need another level of indirection. PIC will add a new section to our output – the **Global Offset Table** (**GOT**). Eventually, this section will become a segment containing runtime addresses for all the symbols needed by shared libraries. The position of the GOT relative to the `.text` section is known during linking; therefore, all symbol references can be pointed (through an offset) to a placeholder GOT at that time. The actual values pointing to symbols in memory will only be filled when an instruction accessing a referenced symbol is first executed. At that time, a loader will set up that particular entry in the GOT (this is where the term *lazy loading* comes from).

Shared libraries and modules will have the `POSITION_INDEPENDENT_CODE` property automatically set to `ON` by CMake. However, it is important to remember that if your shared library is linked against another target, such as a static or object library, you need to set this property on that target too. Here's how:

```
set_target_properties(dependency_target
                      PROPERTIES POSITION_INDEPENDENT_CODE
                      ON)
```

Failing to do so will get you into trouble with CMake, as this property is by default checked for conflicts in a manner described in the *Dealing with conflicting propagated properties* section of *Chapter 4, Working With Targets*.

Speaking of symbols, there's another problem to discuss. The next section is about name collisions leading to ambiguity and inconsistency in definitions.

Solving problems with the One Definition Rule

Phil Karlton was right on point when he said the following:

> *"There are two hard things in computer science: cache invalidation and naming things."*

Names are difficult for a few reasons – they have to be precise, simple, short, and expressive at the same time. That makes them meaningful and allows programmers to understand the concepts behind the raw implementation. C++ and many other languages impose one more requirement – many names have to be unique.

This is manifested in a few different ways. A programmer is required to follow the ODR. This says that in the scope of a single translation unit (a single `.cpp` file), you are required to *define* it exactly once, even if you *declare* the same name (of a variable, function, class type, enumeration, concept, or template) multiple times.

This rule is extended to the scope of an entire program for all variables you effectively use in your code and non-inlined functions. Consider the following example:

chapter06/02-odr-fail/shared.h

```
int i;
```

chapter06/02-odr-fail/one.cpp

```
#include <iostream>
#include "shared.h"

int main() {
    std::cout << i << std::endl;
}
```

chapter06/02-odr-fail/two.cpp

```
#include "shared.h"
```

chapter06/02-odr-fail/two.cpp

```
cmake_minimum_required(VERSION 3.20.0)
project(ODR CXX)
set(CMAKE_CXX_STANDARD 20)
add_executable(odr one.cpp two.cpp)
```

As you can see, it's very straightforward – we created a shared.h header file used in two separate translation units:

- one.cpp, which simply prints i to the screen
- two.cpp, which does nothing except include the header

We then link the two into a single executable and receive the following error:

```
[100%] Linking CXX executable odr
/usr/bin/ld: CMakeFiles/odr.dir/two.cpp.o:(.bss+0x0): multiple definition of 'i'
; CMakeFiles/odr.dir/one.cpp.o:(.bss+0x0): first defined here
collect2: error: ld returned 1 exit status
```

You can't define these things twice. However, there's a notable exception – types, templates, and extern inline functions can repeat their definitions in multiple translation units if they are exactly the same (that is, they have the same sequence of tokens). We can prove that by replacing a simple definition, `int i;`, with a definition of a class:

chapter06/03-odr-success/shared.h

```
struct shared {
   static inline int i = 1;
};
```

Then, we use it like so:

chapter06/03-odr-success/one.cpp

```
#include <iostream>
#include "shared.h"

int main() {
    std::cout << shared::i << std::endl;
}
```

The other two files, `two.cpp` and `CMakeLists.txt`, remain the same, as in the `02odrfail` example. Such a change will allow the linking to succeed:

```
-- Build files have been written to: /root/examples/
chapter06/03-odr-success/b
[ 33%] Building CXX object CMakeFiles/odr.dir/one.cpp.o
[ 66%] Building CXX object CMakeFiles/odr.dir/two.cpp.o
[100%] Linking CXX executable odr
[100%] Built target odr
```

Alternatively, we can mark the variable as local to a translation unit (it won't be exported outside of the *object file*). To do so, we'll use the `static` keyword, like so:

chapter06/04-odr-success/shared.h

```
static int i;
```

All other files will remain the same, as in the original example, and linking will still succeed. This, of course, means that the variable in the preceding code is stored in separate memory for each translation unit, and changes to one won't affect the other.

Dynamically linked duplicated symbols

The ODR rule works exactly the same for static libraries as it does for *object files*, but things aren't so clear when we build our code with SHARED libraries. A linker will allow duplicated symbols here. In the following example, we'll create two shared libraries, A and B, with one `duplicated()` function and two unique `a()` and `b()` functions:

chapter06/05-dynamic/a.cpp

```cpp
#include <iostream>
void a() {
   std::cout << "A" << std::endl;
}
void duplicated() {
   std::cout << "duplicated A" << std::endl;
}
```

The second implementation file is almost an exact copy of the first:

chapter06/05-dynamic/b.cpp

```cpp
#include <iostream>
void b() {
   std::cout << "B" << std::endl;
}
void duplicated() {
   std::cout << "duplicated B" << std::endl;
}
```

Now, let's use each function to see what happens (we'll declare them locally with `extern` for simplicity):

chapter06/05-dynamic/main.cpp

```cpp
extern void a();
extern void b();
```

```
extern void duplicated();

int main() {
  a();
  b();
  duplicated();
}
```

The preceding code will run unique functions from each library and then call a function defined with the same signature in both dynamic libraries. What do you think will happen? Would the linking order matter in this case? Let's test it for two cases:

- `main_1` linked with the `a` library first
- `main_2` linked with the `b` library first

Here's the code for such a project:

chapter06/05-dynamic/CMakeLists.txt

```
cmake_minimum_required(VERSION 3.20.0)
project(Dynamic CXX)

add_library(a SHARED a.cpp)
add_library(b SHARED b.cpp)

add_executable(main_1 main.cpp)
target_link_libraries(main_1 a b)

add_executable(main_2 main.cpp)
target_link_libraries(main_2 b a)
```

After building and running both executables, we'll see the following output:

```
root@ce492a7cd64b:/root/examples/chapter06/05-dynamic# b/main_1
A
B
duplicated A
root@ce492a7cd64b:/root/examples/chapter06/05-dynamic# b/main_2
A
```

```
B
duplicated B
```

Aha! So, a linker does care about the order of the linked libraries. This may create some confusion if we aren't careful. In practice, naming collisions aren't as rare as they seem.

There are some exceptions to this behavior; if we define locally visible symbols, they will take precedence over those available from dynamically linked libraries. Adding the following function to `main.cpp` will change the last line of output of both binaries to **duplicated MAIN**, as shown here:

```
#include <iostream>
void duplicated() {
    std::cout << "duplicated MAIN" << std::endl;
}
```

Always take great care when exporting names from libraries, as you're bound to encounter name collisions sooner or later.

Use namespaces – don't count on a linker

The concept of namespaces was invented to avoid such weird problems and deal with the ODR in a manageable way. It comes as no surprise that it is recommended to wrap your library code in a namespace named after the library. This way, we can escape all the problems of duplicated symbols.

In our projects, we might experience situations where one shared library is linking another and then another in a lengthy chain. These aren't that rare, especially in more complex setups. It is important to remember that simply linking one library to another doesn't imply any kind of namespace inheritance. Symbols in each link of this chain remain unprotected, kept in the namespaces in which they were originally compiled.

The quirks of a linker are interesting and useful to know on a couple of occasions, but let's talk about a not-so-uncommon problem – what to do when correctly defined symbols go missing without an explanation.

The order of linking and unresolved symbols

A linker can often seem whimsical and start complaining about things for no apparent reason. This is an especially difficult ordeal for programmers starting out who don't know their way around this tool. It's no wonder, since they usually try to avoid touching build configuration for as long as they possibly can. Eventually, they're forced to change something (perhaps add a library they worked on) in the executable, and all hell breaks loose.

Let's consider a fairly simple dependency chain – the `main` executable depends on the `outer` library, which depends on the `nested` library (containing the necessary `int b` variable). Suddenly, an inconspicuous message appears on the programmer's screen:

```
outer.cpp:(.text+0x1f): undefined reference to 'b'
```

This isn't such a rare diagnostic – usually, it means that we forgot to add a necessary library to the linker. But in this case, the library is actually added correctly to the `target_link_libraries()` command:

chapter06/06-order/CMakeLists.txt

```
cmake_minimum_required(VERSION 3.20.0)
project(Order CXX)

add_library(outer outer.cpp)
add_library(nested nested.cpp)

add_executable(main main.cpp)
target_link_libraries(main nested outer)
```

What then!? Very few errors can be as infuriating to debug and understand. What we're seeing here is an incorrect order of linking. Let's dive into the source code to figure out the reason:

chapter06/06-order/main.cpp

```
#include <iostream>
extern int a;
int main() {
    std::cout << a << std::endl;
}
```

The preceding code seems easy enough – we'll print an a external variable, which can be found in the outer library. We're declaring it ahead of time with the extern keyword. Here is the source for that library:

chapter06/06-order/outer.cpp

```
extern int b;
int a = b;
```

This is quite simple too – outer is depending on the nested library to provide the b external variable, which gets assigned to the a exported variable. Let's see the source of nested to confirm that we're not missing the definition:

chapter06/06-order/nested.cpp

```
int b = 123;
```

So indeed, we have provided the definition for b, and since it's not marked as local with the static keyword, it's correctly exported from the nested target. As we saw previously, this target is linked with the main executable in CMakeLists.txt:

```
target_link_libraries(main nested outer)
```

So where does the undefined reference to 'b' error come from?

Resolving undefined symbols works like this – a linker processes the binaries from left to right. As the linker iterates through the binaries, it will do the following:

1. Collect all undefined symbols exported from this binary and store them for later
2. Try to resolve undefined symbols (collected from all binaries processed so far) with symbols defined in this binary
3. Repeat this process for the next binary

If any symbols remain undefined after the whole operation is completed, the linking fails.

This is the case in our example (CMake puts the *object files* of the executable target before the libraries):

1. We processed `main.o`, got an undefined reference to a, and collected it for future resolution.
2. We processed `libnested.a`, no undefined references were found, so there was nothing to resolve.
3. We processed `libouter.a`, got an undefined reference to b, and resolved a reference to a.

We did correctly resolve the reference to the a variable, but not for b. All we need to do is reverse the order of linking so that nested comes after outer:

```
target_link_libraries(main outer nested)
```

Another less elegant option is to repeat the library (which is useful for cyclic references):

```
target_link_libraries(main nested outer nested)
```

Finally, we can try using linker-specific flags such as `--start-group` or `--end-group`. Go to the documentation of your linker for details, as these specifics are outside of the scope of this book.

Now that we know how to solve common problems, let's talk about how we could use the linker to our advantage.

Separating main() for testing

As we established so far, a linker enforces the ODR and makes sure that all external symbols provide their definitions in the process of linking. One interesting problem that we might encounter is the correct testing of the build.

Ideally, we should test exactly the same source code that is being run in production. An exhaustive testing pipeline should build the source code, run its tests on produced binary, and only then package and distribute the executable (without the tests themselves).

But how do we actually make this happen? Executables have a very specific flow of execution, which often requires reading command-line arguments. C++'s compiled nature doesn't really support pluggable units that can be temporarily injected into the binary for test purposes only. It seems like we'll need a very complex approach to solve this.

Luckily, we can use a linker to help us deal with this in an elegant manner. Consider extracting all logic from your program's `main()` to an external function, `start_program()`, like so:

chapter06/07-testing/main.cpp

```
extern int start_program(int, const char**);
int main(int argc, const char** argv) {
  return start_program(argc, argv);
}
```

It's reasonable to skip testing this new `main()` function now; it is only forwarding arguments to a function defined elsewhere (in another file). We can then create a library containing the original source from `main()` wrapped in a new function – `start_program()`. In this example, I'm going to use a simple program to check whether the command-line argument count is higher than 1:

chapter06/07-testing/program.cpp

```
#include <iostream>
int start_program(int argc, const char** argv) {
  if (argc <= 1) {
    std::cout << "Not enough arguments" << std::endl;
    return 1;
  }
  return 0;
}
```

We can now prepare a project that builds this application and links together those two translation units:

chapter06/07-testing/CMakeLists.cpp

```
cmake_minimum_required(VERSION 3.20.0)
project(Testing CXX)

add_library(program program.cpp)
```

```
add_executable(main main.cpp)
```
`target_link_libraries(main program)`

The `main` target is just providing the required `main()` function. It's the `program` target that contains all the logic. We can now test it by creating another executable with its own `main()` containing the test logic.

In a real-world scenario, frameworks such as **GoogleTest** or **Catch2** will provide their own `main()` method that can be used to replace your program's entry point and run all the defined tests. We'll dive deep into the subject of actual testing in *Chapter 8, Testing Frameworks*. For now, let's focus on the general principle and write our own tests in another `main()` function:

chapter06/07-testing/test.cpp

```cpp
#include <iostream>
extern int start_program(int, const char**);
using namespace std;
int main() {
    auto exit_code = start_program(0, nullptr);
    if (exit_code == 0)
        cout << "Non-zero exit code expected" << endl;

    const char* arguments[2] = {"hello", "world"};
    exit_code = start_program(2, arguments);
    if (exit_code != 0)
        cout << "Zero exit code expected" << endl;
}
```

The preceding code will call `start_program` twice, with and without arguments, and check whether the returned exit codes are correct. This unit test leaves much to be desired in terms of clean code and elegant testing practices, but at least it's a start. The important thing is that we have now defined `main()` twice:

- In `main.cpp` for production use
- In `test.cpp` for test purposes

We'll add the second executable to the bottom of our `CMakeLists.txt` now:

```
add_executable(test test.cpp)
target_link_libraries(test program)
```

This creates another target, which is linked against the exact same binary code as the production, but it grants us the freedom to call all exported functions however we like. Thanks to this, we can run all code paths automatically and check whether they work as expected. Great!

Summary

Linking in CMake does seem simple and insignificant, but in reality, there's much more to it than meets the eye. After all, linking executables isn't as simple as putting puzzle pieces together. As we learned about the structure of *object files* and libraries, we discovered that things need to move around a bit before a program is runnable. These things are called sections and they have distinct roles in the life cycle of the program – store different kinds of data, instructions, symbol names, and so on. A linker needs to combine them together in the final binary accordingly. This process is called relocation.

We also need to take care of symbols – resolve references across all the translation units and make sure that nothing's missing. Then, a linker can create the program header and add it to the final executable. It will contain instructions for the system loader, describing how to turn consolidated sections into segments that make up the runtime memory image of the process.

We also discussed three different kinds of libraries (static, shared, and shared modules), and we explained how they differ and which scenarios fit some better than others. We also touched on the subject of PIC – a powerful concept that allows for the lazy binding of symbols.

The ODR is a C++ concept, but as we already know, it's heavily enforced by linkers. After introducing this subject, we briefly explored how to deal with the most basic symbol duplication, in both static and dynamic libraries. This was followed by some short advice to use namespaces wherever possible and not to rely on a linker too much when it comes to preventing symbol collisions.

For such a seemingly straightforward step (CMake offers only a few commands dedicated to a linker), it sure has a lot of quirks! One tricky thing to get right is the order of linking, especially when libraries have nested dependencies. We now know how to handle some basic situations and what other methods we could research to deal with more complex ones.

Lastly, we investigated how to take advantage of a linker to prepare our program for testing – by separating the `main()` function into another translation unit. This enabled us to introduce another executable, which ran tests against the exact same machine code that will be run in production.

Now that we know how to link, we can retrieve external libraries and use them in our CMake projects. In the next chapter, we'll study how to manage dependencies in CMake.

Further reading

For more information on the topics covered in this chapter, you can refer to the following:

- *The structure of ELF files:*

    `https://en.wikipedia.org/wiki/Executable_and_Linkable_Format`

- *The CMake manual for* `add_library()`:

    `https://cmake.org/cmake/help/latest/command/add_library.html`

- *Dependency hell:*

    `https://en.wikipedia.org/wiki/Dependency_hell`

- *The differences between modules and shared libraries:*

    `https://stackoverflow.com/questions/4845984/difference-between-modules-and-shared-libraries`

7
Managing Dependencies with CMake

It doesn't really matter whether your solution is big or small; as it matures, you'll eventually decide to bring in external dependencies. It's important to avoid the costs of creating and maintaining code using prevailing business logic. This way, you can devote your time to things that matter to you and your customers.

External dependencies are used not only to provide frameworks and features and solve quirky problems. They can also play an important part in the process of building and controlling the quality of your code – whether it is in the form of special compilers such as **Protobuf** or testing frameworks such as **GTest**.

Whether you're working with open source projects or using projects written by other developers in your company, you still need a good, clean process to manage external dependencies. Solving this on your own would take countless hours of setup and a lot of additional support work later. Fortunately, CMake does an excellent job in accommodating different styles and historical approaches to dependency management while keeping up with the constant evolution of industry-approved standards.

To supply an external dependency, we should first check whether the host system already has the dependency available, since it's best to avoid unnecessary downloads and lengthy compilations. We'll explore how to find and turn such dependencies into CMake targets to use in our project. This can be done in many ways, specifically when packages support CMake out of the box or at least provide files for a slightly older PkgConfig tool. If that's not the case, we can still write our own file to detect and include such a dependency.

We'll discuss what to do when a dependency isn't present on a system. As you can imagine, we can take alternative steps to automatically provide the necessary files. We'll consider tackling this problem using different Git methods and bringing in entire CMake projects as part of our build.

In this chapter, we're going to cover the following main topics:

- How to find installed packages
- Discovering legacy packages with `FindPkgConfig`
- Writing your own find-modules
- Working with Git repositories
- Using `ExternalProject` and `FetchContent` modules

Technical requirements

You can find the code files that are present in this chapter on GitHub at https://github.com/PacktPublishing/Modern-CMake-for-Cpp/tree/main/examples/chapter07.

To build examples provided in this book always use recommended commands:

```
cmake -B <build tree> -S <source tree>
cmake --build <build tree>
```

Be sure to replace placeholders `<build tree>` and `<source tree>` with appropriate paths. As a reminder: **build tree** is the path to target/output directory, **source tree** is the path at which your source code is located.

How to find installed packages

Alright, let's say that you have decided to up your game with network communication or storing data at rest. Plaintext files, JSON, or even good old XML won't do. You want to serialize your data straight to binary format, preferably with a library known very well in the industry – say, protocol buffers (Protobuf) from Google. You find the documentation, install the dependencies in the system, and now what? How do we actually tell CMake to find and use this external dependency you're introducing? Luckily, there's a `find_package()` command. It works like a charm in most cases.

Let's rewind and start by setting the scene – we have to install the dependencies we want to use because `find_package()`, as the name suggests, is only about discovering packages in a system. We're assuming that dependencies are already installed or that users of our solution know how to install specific, necessary dependencies when prompted. To cover other scenarios, you'll need to provide a backup plan (more on which can be found in the *Working with Git repositories* section).

In the case of Protobuf, the situation is fairly straightforward: you can either download, compile, and install the library yourself from the official repository (https://github.com/protocolbuffers/protobuf) or use the package manager in your operating system. If you're following these examples using the Docker image mentioned in *Chapter 1, First Steps with CMake*, you'll be using Debian Linux. The commands to install the Protobuf library and compiler are as follows:

```
$ apt update
$ apt install protobuf-compiler libprotobuf-dev
```

Every system has its own way of installing packages and managing them. Finding the path where a package is residing can be tricky and time-consuming, especially when you want to support most of the operating systems used today. Fortunately, `find_package()` can often do it for you if the package in question provides an appropriate **config-file** that allows CMake to determine variables necessary to support the package.

Today, many projects are compatible with this requirement and provide this file for CMake during installation. If you plan to use some popular library that doesn't provide it, don't worry just yet. Chances are that CMake authors have bundled the file with CMake itself (these are called **find-modules**, to differentiate from config-files). If that's not the case, we still have some options:

- Provide our own find-modules for a specific package and bundle it with our project.
- Write a config-file and ask package maintainers to ship the package with it.

You might say that you're not quite ready to create such merge requests yourself, and that's fine because it's most likely you won't have to. CMake ships with over 150 find-modules that can find libraries such as Boost, bzip2, curl, curses, GIF, GTK, iconv, ImageMagick, JPEG, Lua, OpenGL, OpenSSL, PNG, PostgreSQL, Qt, SDL, Threads, XML-RPC, X11, and zlib, and luckily, also the Protobuf file that we're going to use in this example. A full list is available in the CMake documentation: `https://cmake.org/cmake/help/latest/manual/cmake-modules.7.html#find modules`.

Both find-modules and config-files can be used in CMake projects with a single `find_package()` command. CMake looks for matching find-modules, and if it can't find any, it will turn to config-files. The search will start from the path stored in the `CMAKE_MODULE_PATH` variable (which is empty by default). This variable can be configured by a project when it wants to add and use external find-modules. Next, CMake will scan the list of built-in find-modules available in the installed version of CMake.

If no applicable module is found, it's time to search for corresponding package config-files. CMake has a long list of paths appropriate for a host operating system, which can be scanned for filenames matching the following pattern:

- `<CamelCasePackageName>Config.cmake`
- `<kebab-case-package-name>-config.cmake`

Let's talk a little about the project files; in this example, I don't really intend to design a full network-based solution with remote procedure calls and all the bells and whistles. Instead, I just want to prove that I can build and run a project that depends on Protobuf. To accomplish this, I'm going to create a `.proto` file with as small a contract as possible. If you're not that familiar with Protobuf, just know that this library provides a mechanism to serialize structured data in a binary form. To do so, we need to provide a schema of such a structure, which will be used to write and read from binary form into C++ objects.

This is what I came up with:

chapter07/01-find-package-variables/message.proto

```
syntax = "proto3";
message Message {
    int32 id = 1;
}
```

Don't worry if you're not familiar with Protobuf syntax (this isn't really what this example is about). This is just a simple `message` that contains just one 32-bit integer. Protobuf has a special compiler that will read these files and generate C++ sources and headers that can be then used by our application. This means we'll need to somehow add this compilation step to our process. We'll return to that. For now, let's see what our `main.cpp` file looks like:

chapter07/01-find-package-variables/main.cpp

```cpp
#include "message.pb.h"
#include <fstream>
using namespace std;
int main()
{
  Message m;
  m.set_id(123);
  m.PrintDebugString();
  fstream fo("./hello.data", ios::binary | ios::out);
  m.SerializeToOstream(&fo);
  fo.close();
  return 0;
}
```

As I've mentioned, `Message` contains a single `id` field. In the `main.cpp` file, I'm creating an object representing this message, setting the field to `123`, and printing its debug information to the standard output. Next, I'm creating a file stream, writing a binary version of this object to it, and closing the stream – the simplest possible use for a serialization library.

Note that I've included a `message.pb.h` header. This file doesn't yet exist; it needs to be created by `protoc`, the Protobuf compiler, during compilation of `message.proto`. This scenario sounds pretty complex, implying that the list file of such a project must be incredibly long. Not at all! This is where the CMake magic happens:

chapter07/01-find-package-variables/CMakeLists.txt

```cmake
cmake_minimum_required(VERSION 3.20.0)
project(FindPackageProtobufVariables CXX)

find_package(Protobuf REQUIRED)
```

```
protobuf_generate_cpp(GENERATED_SRC GENERATED_HEADER
  message.proto)

add_executable(main main.cpp
  ${GENERATED_SRC} ${GENERATED_HEADER})
target_link_libraries(main PRIVATE ${Protobuf_LIBRARIES})
target_include_directories(main PRIVATE
  ${Protobuf_INCLUDE_DIRS}
  ${CMAKE_CURRENT_BINARY_DIR})
```

Let's break this down:

- The first two lines we know already; they create the project and declare its language.
- `find_package(Protobuf REQUIRED)` asks CMake to run the bundled `FindProtobuf.cmake` find-module and set up the Protobuf library for us. That find-module will scan commonly used paths and (because we provided the `REQUIRED` keyword) terminate if a library is not found. It will also specify useful variables and functions (such as the one on the next line).
- `protobuf_generate_cpp` is a custom function defined in the Protobuf find-module. Under the hood, it calls `add_custom_command()`, which invokes the `protoc` compiler with appropriate arguments. We use this function by providing two variables that will be filled with paths to the generated source (`GENERATED_SRC`) and header (`GENERATED_HEADER`) files, and a list of files to compile (`message.proto`).
- `add_executable`, as we already know, will create our executable using `main.cpp` and Protobuf files configured in the previous command.
- `target_link_libraries` adds libraries (static or shared) found by `find_package()` to the linking command of our `main` target.
- `target_include_directories()` adds to *include paths* the necessary `INCLUDE_DIRS` provided by the package and `CMAKE_CURRENT_BINARY_DIR`. The latter is needed so that the compiler can find the generated `message.pb.h` header.

In other words, it achieves the following:

- Finds the location of the library and the compiler
- Provides helper functions to teach CMake how to call a custom compiler for `.proto` files
- Adds variables containing the necessary paths for inclusion and linking

In most cases, you can expect some variables to be set when you call `find_package()`, whether you're using a built-in find-module or a config-file bundled with a package (assuming that the package was found):

- `<PKG_NAME>_FOUND`
- `<PKG_NAME>_INCLUDE_DIRS` or `<PKG_NAME>_INCLUDES`
- `<PKG_NAME>_LIBRARIES` or `<PKG_NAME>_LIBS`
- `<PKG_NAME>_DEFINITIONS`
- `IMPORTED` targets specified by the find-module or config-file

The last point is really interesting – if a package supports so-called "modern CMake" (built around targets), it will provide those `IMPORTED` targets instead (or alongside) of these variables, which allows for cleaner, simpler code. It is recommended to prioritize targets over variables.

Protobuf is a great example, as it offers both variables and `IMPORTED` targets (since CMake 3.10): `protobuf::libprotobuf`, `protobuf::libprotobuf-lite`, `protobuf::libprotoc`, and `protobuf::protoc`. This allows us to write even more concise code:

chapter07/02-find-package-targets/CMakeLists.txt

```
cmake_minimum_required(VERSION 3.20.0)
project(FindPackageProtobufTargets CXX)

find_package(Protobuf REQUIRED)
protobuf_generate_cpp(GENERATED_SRC GENERATED_HEADER
   message.proto)

add_executable(main main.cpp
   ${GENERATED_SRC} ${GENERATED_HEADER})
```

```
target_link_libraries(main PRIVATE protobuf::libprotobuf)
target_include_directories(main PRIVATE
                           ${CMAKE_CURRENT_BINARY_DIR})
```

The `protobuf::libprotobuf` imported target implicitly specifies *include directories* and, thanks to transitive dependencies (or propagated properties as I call them), they are shared with our `main` target. The same process happens with the linker and compiler flags.

If you need to know what exactly is provided from a specific find-module, it's best to visit its online documentation. One for Protobuf can be found here: `https://cmake.org/cmake/help/latest/module/FindProtobuf.html`.

> **Important Note**
> To keep things simple, examples in this section will simply fail if the protobuf library (or its compiler) was not found in the user's system. But a really robust solution should verify that by checking the `Protobuf_FOUND` variable and acting accordingly, either by printing a clear diagnostic message for the user (so they can install it) or performing the installation automatically.

The last thing to mention about the `find_package()` command is its options. A full list is a bit extensive, so we'll just focus on the basic signature. It looks like this:

```
find_package(<Name> [version] [EXACT] [QUIET] [REQUIRED])
```

The most important options are as follows:

- `[version]`, which allows us to optionally request a specific version. Use the `major.minor.patch.tweak` format (such as `1.22`) or provide a range – `1.22...1.40.1` (use three dots as a separator).
- The `EXACT` keyword means that we want an exact version (a range is not supported here).
- The `QUIET` keyword silences all messages about a found/not found package.
- The `REQUIRED` keyword will stop execution if a package is not found and print a diagnostic message (even if `QUIET` is enabled).

More information on the command can be found on the documentation page here: `https://cmake.org/cmake/help/latest/command/find_package.html`.

The concept of providing config-files for a package that could be automatically consumed by buildsystems isn't that new. And it certainly wasn't invented by CMake. There are other tools and formats for this very purpose. PkgConfig is one of them. CMake provides a useful wrapper module to support it as well.

Discovering legacy packages with FindPkgConfig

The problem of managing dependencies and discovering all the compile flags that they require is as old as C++ libraries themselves. There are many tools to deal with it, ranging from very small and minimal mechanisms to very versatile solutions offered as parts of buildsystems and IDEs. One of the (once very popular) tools is called PkgConfig (`freedesktop.org/wiki/Software/pkg-config/`). It is often available on Unix-like systems (although it works on macOS and Windows too).

`pkg-config` is slowly being phased out by other more modern solutions. A question arises here – should you invest your time in supporting it? The answer is as usual – it depends:

- If a library is really popular, it might already have its find-module in CMake; in that case, you probably won't need it.
- If there's no find-module (or it doesn't work for your library) and a PkgConfig `.pc` file is all that library provides, just use what's readily available.

Many (if not most) libraries have embraced CMake and provide a package config-file in current versions. If you're not publishing your solution and you control the environment, use `find_package()` and don't worry about legacy versions.

Sadly, not all environments can be quickly updated to the latest versions of a library. A lot of companies are still using legacy systems in production, which are no longer getting the latest packages. In that case, users might be stuck with an older (but hopefully compatible) version. And very often, it will provide a `.pc` file.

Additionally, efforts to support the older PkgConfig format might be worthwhile if it means that your project will work out of the box for most users.

In any case, start by using `find_package()`, as described in the previous section, and if `<PKG_NAME>_FOUND` is false, fall back on PkgConfig. This way, we cover a scenario where an environment gets upgraded and we can just use the main method without changing the code.

The concept of this *helper tool* is quite simple – the author of the library provides a small `.pc` file containing details necessary for compilation and linking, such as this one:

```
prefix=/usr/local
exec_prefix=${prefix}
includedir=${prefix}/include
libdir=${exec_prefix}/lib

Name: foobar
Description: A foobar library
Version: 1.0.0
Cflags: -I${includedir}/foobar
Libs: -L${libdir} -lfoobar
```

The format is pretty straightforward, lightweight, and it even supports a basic variable expansion. This is why many developers prefer it over complex, robust solutions such as CMake. While PkgConfig is extremely easy to use, its features are quite limited:

- Checks to see whether a library exists in the system and if a `.pc` file is provided with it
- Checks whether a sufficient version of a library is available
- Gets linker flags for a library by running `pkg-config --libs libfoo`
- Gets the *include directories* for a library (this field can technically contain other compiler flags) – `pkg-config --cflags libfoo`

To properly use PkgConfig in a build scenario, your buildsystem has to find the `pkg-config` executable in the OS, run it a few times and provide appropriate arguments, and store the responses in variables so they can be passed later to the compiler. We already know how to do that in CMake – scan paths known for storing helper tools to check whether PkgConfig is installed and then use a few `exec_program()` commands to discover how to link dependencies. Even though the steps are limited, it seems excessive to do it every time when we'd like to use PkgConfig.

Fortunately, CMake provides a handy built-in find-module just for that purpose – `FindPkgConfig`. It follows most of the rules for regular find modules, but instead of providing `PKG_CONFIG_INCLUDE_DIRS` or `PKG_CONFIG_LIBS` variables, it sets a variable with a direct path to the binary – `PKG_CONFIG_EXECUTABLE`. Unsurprisingly, the `PKG_CONFIG_FOUND` variable is set too – we'll use it to confirm that the tool is available in the system and then scan for a package with a `pkg_check_modules()` helper command defined in the module.

Let's see that in practice. One example of a somewhat popular library that offers a `.pc` file is a client for the PostgreSQL database – `libpqxx`.

To install it on Debian, you can use the `libpqxx-dev` package (your OS might need a different package):

```
apt-get install libpqxx-dev
```

We'll create the shortest possible `main.cpp` file, which utilizes a dummy connection class:

chapter07/02-find-pkg-config/main.cpp

```cpp
#include <pqxx/pqxx>
int main()
{
    // We're not actually connecting, but
    // just proving that pqxx is available.
    pqxx::nullconnection connection;
}
```

And we can now provide the necessary dependencies for the previous code by using the PkgConfig find-module:

chapter07/03-find-pkg-config/CMakeLists.txt

```cmake
cmake_minimum_required(VERSION 3.20.0)
project(FindPkgConfig CXX)

find_package(PkgConfig REQUIRED)
pkg_check_modules(PQXX REQUIRED IMPORTED_TARGET libpqxx)
message("PQXX_FOUND: ${PQXX_FOUND}")
```

```
add_executable(main main.cpp)
target_link_libraries(main PRIVATE PkgConfig::PQXX)
```

Let's break down what happens:

- We ask CMake to find the PkgConfig executable with the `find_package()` command. It will fail if `pkg-config` is not present because of the `REQUIRED` keyword.

- A `pkg_check_modules()` custom macro defined in the `FindPkgConfig` find-module is called to create a new `IMPORTED` target with PQXX as the chosen name. The find-module will search for a dependency called `libpxx`, and again, it will fail if the library isn't available because of the `REQUIRED` keyword. Note the `IMPORTED_TARGET` keyword – without it, no target would be automatically created, and we would have to define it manually with variables created by the macro.

- We confirm that everything is correct with a diagnostic message by printing `PQXX_FOUND`. If we didn't specify `REQUIRED` in the previous command, we can check here whether this variable was set (perhaps to allow other fallback mechanisms to kick in).

- We create the `main` executable.

- We link the `PkgConfig::PQXX IMPORTED` target created by `pkg_check_modules()`. Note that `PkgConfig::` is a constant prefix, and `PQXX` comes from the first argument passed to that command.

This was a fairly convenient method to bring in dependencies that don't support CMake yet. This find-module has a few other methods and options; if you're interested in learning more, I recommend referring to the official documentation: https://cmake.org/cmake/help/latest/module/FindPkgConfig.html.

Find-modules are meant as a very convenient way of providing CMake with information on installed dependencies. Most popular libraries are widely supported by CMake on all major platforms. What can we do though when we want to use a third-party library that doesn't have a dedicated find-module yet?

Writing your own find-modules

On a rare occasion, the library that you really want to use in your project doesn't provide a config-file or a PkgConfig file, and there's no find-module readily available in CMake already. You can then write a custom find-module for that library and ship it with your project. This situation is not ideal, but in the interest of taking care of the users of your project, it has to be done.

Since we have already become familiar with `libpqxx` in the previous section, let's write a nice find-module for it. We start by writing in a new `FindPQXX.cmake` file, which we'll store in the `cmake/module` directory of our project source tree. We need to make sure that the find-module gets discovered by the CMake when `find_package()` is called, so we'll add this path to the `CMAKE_MODULE_PATH` variable in our `CMakeLists.txt` with `list(APPEND)`. The whole list file should look like this:

chapter07/04-find-package-custom/CMakeLists.txt

```
cmake_minimum_required(VERSION 3.20.0)
project(FindPackageCustom CXX)

list(APPEND CMAKE_MODULE_PATH
  "${CMAKE_SOURCE_DIR}/cmake/module/")
find_package(PQXX REQUIRED)
add_executable(main main.cpp)
target_link_libraries(main PRIVATE PQXX::PQXX)
```

Now that's done, we need to write the actual find-module. Technically speaking, nothing will happen if the `FindPQXX.cmake` file is empty: CMake won't complain if some specific variables aren't set (including `PQXX_FOUND`), even if a user calls `find_package()` with `REQUIRED`. It's up to the author of the find-module to respect conventions outlined in CMake's documentation:

- CMake will provide a `<PKG_NAME>_FIND_REQUIRED` variable set to `1` when `find_package(<PKG_NAME> REQUIRED)` is called. A find-module should call `message(FATAL_ERROR)` when a library is not found.

- CMake will provide a `<PKG_NAME>_FIND_QUIETLY` variable set to `1` when `find_package(<PKG_NAME> QUIET)` is called. A find-module should avoid printing diagnostic messages (other than the one mentioned previously).

- CMake will provide a `<PKG_NAME>_FIND_VERSION` variable set to the version required by calling the list file. A find-module should find the appropriate version or issue `FATAL_ERROR`.

Of course, it's best to follow the preceding rules for consistency with other find-modules. Let's discuss the steps needed to create an elegant find-module for PQXX:

1. If paths to library and headers are known (either provided by a user or coming from the cache of a previous run), use these paths and create an `IMPORTED` target. End here.
2. Otherwise, find the library and headers of the nested dependency – PostgreSQL.
3. Search the known paths for the binary version of the PostgreSQL client library.
4. Search the known paths for the PostgreSQL client *include headers*.
5. Check whether the library and *include headers* were found; if so, create an `IMPORTED` target.

The creation of an `IMPORTED` target happens twice – if the user provides the library's paths from the command line or if they're found automatically. We'll start by writing a function to handle the result of our search process and keep our code DRY.

To create an `IMPORTED` target, we'll simply need a library with an `IMPORTED` keyword (to use it in the `target_link_libraries()` command in `CMakeLists.txt`). The library has to provide a type – we mark it as `UNKNOWN` to say that we don't want to detect whether a found library was static or dynamic; we just want to provide an argument to a linker.

Next, we set the required properties of the `IMPORTED_LOCATION` and `INTERFACE_INCLUDE_DIRECTORIES IMPORTED` targets to arguments the function was called with. We can specify other properties too (such as `COMPILE_DEFINITIONS`); they just aren't necessary for PQXX.

After that, we'll store the paths in cache variables so that we don't need to perform the search again. It's worth mentioning that `PQXX_FOUND` is set explicitly in the cache, and therefore it's visible in the global variable scope (so it can be accessed by the user's `CMakeLists.txt`).

Finally, we mark cache variables as advanced, which means they won't be visible in the CMake GUI unless the "advanced" option is enabled. This is a common practice for these variables and we should follow the convention too:

chapter07/04-find-package-custom/cmake/module/FindPQXX.cmake

```
function(add_imported_library library headers)
   add_library(PQXX::PQXX UNKNOWN IMPORTED)
   set_target_properties(PQXX::PQXX PROPERTIES
     IMPORTED_LOCATION ${library}
     INTERFACE_INCLUDE_DIRECTORIES ${headers}
   )
   set(PQXX_FOUND 1 CACHE INTERNAL "PQXX found" FORCE)
   set(PQXX_LIBRARIES ${library}
       CACHE STRING "Path to pqxx library" FORCE)
   set(PQXX_INCLUDES ${headers}
       CACHE STRING "Path to pqxx headers" FORCE)
   mark_as_advanced(FORCE PQXX_LIBRARIES)
   mark_as_advanced(FORCE PQXX_INCLUDES)
endfunction()
```

Next, we cover the first case – a user who has their PQXX installed in a non-standard location can provide necessary paths through the command line, with -D arguments. If that's the case, we just call the function we just defined and abandon the search by escaping with return(). We trust that the user knows best and provides us with correct paths to the library and its dependencies (PostgreSQL).

This condition will also be true if the configuration stage was performed in the past, as the PQXX_LIBRARIES and PQXX_INCLUDES variables are cached.

```
if (PQXX_LIBRARIES AND PQXX_INCLUDES)
  add_imported_library(${PQXX_LIBRARIES} ${PQXX_INCLUDES})
  return()
endif()
```

It's time to find some nested dependencies. To use PQXX, the host machine also needs PostgreSQL. It's completely legal to use another find-module in our find-module, but we should forward the REQUIRED and QUIET flags to it (so that the nested search behaves consistently with the outer one). It's not complex logic, but we should try to avoid unnecessary code.

CMake has a built-in helper macro that does just that – `find_dependency()`. Interestingly, the documentation states that it's not a right fit for find-modules, as it calls the `return()` command if the dependency is not found. Because this is a macro (and not a function), `return()` will exit the scope of the caller, the `FindPQXX.cmake` file, stopping the execution of the outer find-module. There may be cases when that's undesirable, but in this one, this is exactly what we want to do – prevent CMake from going down the rabbit hole and looking for the components of PQXX when we already know that PostgreSQL isn't available:

```
# deliberately used in mind-module against the
  documentation
include(CMakeFindDependencyMacro)
find_dependency(PostgreSQL)
```

To find the `PQXX` library, we'll set up a `_PQXX_DIR` helper variable (transformed to a CMake-style path) and use the `find_library()` command to scan a list of paths we'll provide after the `PATHS` keyword. The command will check for the presence of library binaries that match names provided after another keyword, `NAMES`. If a matching file is found, its path will be stored in the `PQXX_LIBRARY_PATH` variable. Otherwise, the variable will be set to `<VAR>-NOTFOUND`, or `PQXX_HEADER_PATH-NOTFOUND` in this case.

The `NO_DEFAULT_PATH` keyword disables the default behavior, which will scan a long list of default paths provided by CMake for this host environment. It's not recommended to skip those default paths (they'll work in most cases), but if you're sure that dependency you're after resides elsewhere, `NO_DEFAULT_PATH` will allow you to list the search paths explicitly:

```
file(TO_CMAKE_PATH "$ENV{PQXX_DIR}" _PQXX_DIR)
find_library(PQXX_LIBRARY_PATH NAMES libpqxx pqxx
  PATHS
    ${_PQXX_DIR}/lib/${CMAKE_LIBRARY_ARCHITECTURE}
    # (...) many other paths - removed for brevity
    /usr/lib
  NO_DEFAULT_PATH
)
```

Next, we'll search for all known header files with the `find_path()` command, which works very similarly to `find_library()`. The main difference is that `find_library()` knows the system-specific extensions for the libraries and will implicitly append those as needed, and for `find_path()`, we'll need to provide exact names.

Also, don't get confused here with pqxx/pqxx. It's an actual header file, but the extension was deliberately omitted by library authors to comply with #include directives in C++ style (rather than following the C-style .h extension):#include <pqxx/pqxx>:

```
find_path(PQXX_HEADER_PATH NAMES pqxx/pqxx
  PATHS
    ${_PQXX_DIR}/include
    # (...) many other paths - removed for brevity
    /usr/include
  NO_DEFAULT_PATH
)
```

Now it's time to check whether the PQXX_LIBRARY_PATH and PQXX_HEADER_PATH variables contain any -NOTFOUND value. Again, we can do this manually and then print diagnostic messages or terminate the build execution, according to the convention, or we could use the find_package_handle_standard_args() helper function available in the FindPackageHandleStandardArgs list file provided by CMake. It's a helper command that sets the <PKG_NAME>_FOUND variable to 1 if path variables are filled and provides the correct diagnostic message about success and failure (it will respect the QUIET keyword). It will also terminate execution with FATAL_ERROR if one of the provided path variables is empty when the REQUIRED keyword was passed to the find-module.

If a library was found, we'll call the function to define the IMPORTED targets and store the paths in the cache:

```
include(FindPackageHandleStandardArgs)
find_package_handle_standard_args(
  PQXX DEFAULT_MSG PQXX_LIBRARY_PATH PQXX_HEADER_PATH
)
if (PQXX_FOUND)
  add_imported_library(
    "${PQXX_LIBRARY_PATH};${POSTGRES_LIBRARIES}"
    "${PQXX_HEADER_PATH};${POSTGRES_INCLUDE_DIRECTORIES}"
  )
endif()
```

That's it. This find-module will find PQXX and create the appropriate PQXX::PQXX targets. You can find the whole file in the book examples repository: `chapter07/04-find-package-custom/cmake/module/FindPQXX.cmake`.

This method works great if a library is popular and most likely already installed in the system. However, not all libraries will be available all the time. Can we make this easy for our users and fetch and build these dependencies with CMake?

Working with Git repositories

Many projects rely on Git as a version control system. Assuming that our project and external library are both using it, is there some kind of Git magic that would allow us to link these repositories together? Can we build a specific (or latest) version of the library as a step toward building our project? If so, how?

Providing external libraries through Git submodules

One possible solution is to use a mechanism built into Git called **Git submodules**. Submodules allow a project repository to use other Git repositories without actually adding the referenced files to the project repository. They work similarly to soft links – they point to a specific branch or commit in an external repository (but you need to update them explicitly). To add a submodule to your repository (and clone its repository), execute the following command:

```
git submodule add <repository-url>
```

If you pulled a repository that already has submodules, you'll need to initialize them:

```
git submodule update --init -- <local-path-to-submodule>
```

As you can tell, this is a versatile mechanism to leverage third-party code in our solution. The small drawback is that submodules don't get automatically pulled when a user clones the repository with the root project. An explicit `init/pull` command is required. Hold that thought – we'll solve it with CMake too. First, let's see how we can use a freshly created submodule in our code.

For this example, I've decided to write a tiny program that reads a name from a YAML file and prints it out in a welcome message. YAML is a great, simple format to store human-readable configuration, but it's quite complex to parse by machines. I've found a neat, small project that solves this problem by Jesse Beder (and 92 other contributors at the time) called yaml-cpp (https://github.com/jbeder/yaml-cpp).

The example is fairly straightforward. It's a greeting program that prints a `Welcome <name>` message. The default value of `name` will be `Guest`, but we can specify a different name in a YAML configuration file. Here's the code:

chapter07/05-git-submodule-manual/main.cpp

```cpp
#include <string>
#include <iostream>
#include "yaml-cpp/yaml.h"

using namespace std;
int main() {
  string name = "Guest";
  YAML::Node config = YAML::LoadFile("config.yaml");
  if (config["name"])
    name = config["name"].as<string>();

  cout << "Welcome " << name << endl;
  return 0;
}
```

The configuration file for this example is just a single line:

chapter07/05-git-submodule-manual/config.yaml

```
name: Rafal
```

Let's get back to `main.cpp` for a second – it includes the `"yaml-cpp/yaml.h"` header. To make it available, we need to clone the `yaml-cpp` project and build it. Let's make an `extern` directory to store all third-party dependencies (as suggested in the *Thinking about the project structure* section in *Chapter 3, Setting Up Your First CMake Project*) and add a Git submodule, referencing the library's repository:

```
$ mkdir extern
$ cd extern
$ git submodule add https://github.com/jbeder/yaml-cpp.git
Cloning into 'chapter07/01-git-submodule-manual/extern/yaml-cpp'...
remote: Enumerating objects: 8134, done.
```

```
remote: Total 8134 (delta 0), reused 0 (delta 0), pack-reused
8134
Receiving objects: 100% (8134/8134), 3.86 MiB | 3.24 MiB/s,
done.
Resolving deltas: 100% (5307/5307), done.
```

Git has cloned the repository; we can now add it as a dependency to our project and have CMake take care of building:

chapter07/05-git-submodule-manual/CMakeLists.txt

```
cmake_minimum_required(VERSION 3.20.0)
project(GitSubmoduleManual CXX)

add_executable(welcome main.cpp)
configure_file(config.yaml config.yaml COPYONLY)

add_subdirectory(extern/yaml-cpp)
target_link_libraries(welcome PRIVATE yaml-cpp)
```

Let's break down what instructions we are giving to CMake here:

1. Set up the project and add our `welcome` executable.

2. Next, call `configure_file` but don't actually configure anything. By providing the `COPYONLY` keyword, we just copy our `config.yaml` to the build tree so that the executable can find it in runtime.

3. Add the subdirectory of the yaml-cpp repository. CMake will treat it as part of the project and recursively execute any nested `CMakeLists.txt` files.

4. Link the `yaml-cpp` target provided by the library with the `welcome` target.

Authors of yaml-cpp follow the practices outlined in *Chapter 3, Setting Up Your First CMake Project* and store public headers in a separate directory – `<project-name>/include/<project-name>`. This allows clients of the library (such as `main.cpp`) to address the files with paths containing the `"yaml-cpp/yaml.h"` library name. Such naming practices are great for discovery – we know immediately which library is providing this header.

As you can see, this isn't a very complex process, but it isn't ideal – the user has to manually initialize the submodule we have added after cloning the repository. What's worse is that it doesn't take into account the fact that the user might already have this library installed in their system. That means a wasteful download and build of this dependency. There has to be a better way.

Automatic Git submodule initialization

Providing a neat experience to the users doesn't always have to be painful for developers. If a library provides a package config-file, we can just ask `find_package()` to search for it in the installed libraries. As promised, CMake will start by checking whether there's an appropriate find-module, and if there's not, it will look for config-files.

We already know that if the `<LIB_NAME>_FOUND` variable is set to 1, the library was found and we can just use it. We can also act when library wasn't found and provide convenient workaround to silently improve the user's experience: fall back to fetching submodules and building the library from source. Suddenly, the fact that a freshly cloned repository doesn't automatically download and initialize nested submodules doesn't look so bad, does it?

Let's take the code from the previous example and extend it:

chapter07/06-git-submodule-auto/CMakeLists.txt

```cmake
cmake_minimum_required(VERSION 3.20.0)
project(GitSubmoduleAuto CXX)

add_executable(welcome main.cpp)
configure_file(config.yaml config.yaml COPYONLY)

find_package(yaml-cpp QUIET)
if (NOT yaml-cpp_FOUND)
  message("yaml-cpp not found, initializing git submodule")
  execute_process(
    COMMAND git submodule update --init -- extern/yaml-cpp
    WORKING_DIRECTORY ${CMAKE_CURRENT_SOURCE_DIR}
  )
  add_subdirectory(extern/yaml-cpp)
endif()
target_link_libraries(welcome PRIVATE yaml-cpp)
```

We added the highlighted lines:

- We'll try to quietly find yaml-cpp and use it.
- If it's not present, we'll print a short diagnostic message and use the `execute_process()` command to initialize the submodule. This effectively clones the files from the referenced repository.
- Finally, we'll `add_subdirectory()` to build the dependency from the source.

This is short and sweet. This also works for libraries that aren't built with CMake – we can follow the example of `git submodule` and call `execute_process()` again to kick off any external build tools in the same fashion.

Sadly, this method falls apart if your company works with **Concurrent Versions System (CVS)**, **Subversion (SVN)**, Mercurial, or anything else to ship code to your users. If you cannot rely on Git submodules, what's the alternative?

Git-cloning dependencies for projects that don't use Git

If you're using another VCS or offer your source in an archive, you might have a hard time relying on Git submodules bringing in external dependencies to your repository. Chances are that the environment that will build your code has Git installed and could execute the `git clone` command.

Let's see how we can go about this:

chapter07/07-git-clone/CMakeLists.txt

```
cmake_minimum_required(VERSION 3.20.0)
project(GitClone CXX)

add_executable(welcome main.cpp)
configure_file(config.yaml config.yaml COPYONLY)

find_package(yaml-cpp QUIET)
if (NOT yaml-cpp_FOUND)
  message("yaml-cpp not found, cloning git repository")
  find_package(Git)
  if (NOT Git_FOUND)
    message(FATAL_ERROR "Git not found, can't initialize!")
```

```
    endif ()
   execute_process(
     COMMAND ${GIT_EXECUTABLE} clone
     https://github.com/jbeder/yaml-cpp.git
     WORKING_DIRECTORY ${CMAKE_CURRENT_SOURCE_DIR}/extern
   )
   add_subdirectory(extern/yaml-cpp)
endif()
target_link_libraries(welcome PRIVATE yaml-cpp)
```

Again, the highlighted lines are new parts in our YAML project. Here's what happens:

1. We start by checking if Git is available through the `FindGit` find-module.
2. If it's not, we're stuck. We'll issue `FATAL_ERROR` and hope that the user knows what to do next.
3. Otherwise, we'll call `execute_process()` with the `GIT_EXECUTABLE` variable that was set by `find_package()` and clone the repository we're interested in.

Git is especially attractive for developers who have some experience with it. It can be a good fit for a smaller project that doesn't contain nested references to the same repositories. However, if it does, you'll find that you might need to clone and build the same project multiple times. If the dependency project doesn't use Git at all, you'll need another solution.

Using ExternalProject and FetchContent modules

Online reference books on CMake will suggest `ExternalProject` and `FetchContent` modules to deal with the management of dependencies in more complex projects. That's actually good advice, but it's often given without appropriate context. Suddenly, we're facing a lot of questions. What are these modules for? When to choose one over the other? How exactly do they work, and how do they interact with each other? Some answers are harder to find than others, and surprisingly, CMake's documentation doesn't provide a smooth introduction to the subject. Not to worry – we'll take care of it here.

ExternalProject

CMake 3.0.0 introduced a module called `ExternalProject`. As you can guess, its purpose was to add support for external projects available in online repositories. Over the years, the module was gradually extended for different needs, resulting in quite a complicated command – `ExternalProject_Add()`. And I mean complicated – it accepts over 85 different options. No wonder, as it provides an impressive set of features:

- Management of directory structure for an external project
- Downloading of sources from a URL (and extracting from archives if needed)
- Support for Git, Subversion, Mercurial, and CVS repositories
- Fetching updates if needed
- Configuring and building the project with CMake, Make, or with a user-specified tool
- Performing installations and running tests
- Logging to files
- Asking for user input from terminals
- Depending on other targets
- Adding custom commands/steps to the build

The `ExternalProject` module populates the dependencies during the build stage. For every external project added with `ExternalProject_Add()`, CMake will execute the following steps:

1. `mkdir` – create a subdirectory for the external project
2. `download` – get the project files from a repository or URL
3. `update` – refresh the files on rerun for download methods that support delta updates
4. `patch` – optionally execute a *patch command* that alters downloaded files for the needs of the project
5. `configure` – execute the configure stage for CMake projects or manually specified command for non-CMake dependencies
6. `build` – perform the build stage for CMake projects, and for other dependencies, execute the `make` command

7. `install` – install CMake projects, and for other dependencies, execute the `make install` command
8. `test` – execute the dependency's tests if any of the `TEST_...` options are defined

The steps follow the preceding exact order, with the exception of the `test` step, which can be optionally enabled before or after the `install` step with the `TEST_BEFORE_INSTALL <bool>` or `TEST_AFTER_INSTALL <bool>` option.

Downloading the step options

We're mostly interested in options controlling the `download` step or how the dependency will get fetched by CMake. Firstly, we may choose to not use the CMake built-in method for that but rather provide a custom command (generator expressions are supported here):

```
DOWNLOAD_COMMAND <cmd>...
```

By doing so, we tell CMake to ignore all other options for this step and just execute a system-specific command. An empty string is accepted too, and it is used to disable this step.

Downloading dependencies from a URL

We can provide a list of URLs to be scanned in sequence until a download succeeds. CMake will recognize whether the downloaded file is an archive and will unpack it by default:

```
URL <url1> [<url2>...]
```

Additional options allow us to customize the behavior of this method further:

- `URL_HASH <algo>=<hashValue>` – checks whether a downloaded file's checksum generated by `<algo>` matches the provided `<hashValue>`. It is recommended to guarantee the integrity of downloads. The `MD5`, `SHA1`, `SHA224`, `SHA256`, `SHA384`, `SHA512`, `SHA3_224`, `SHA3_256`, `SHA3_384`, and `SHA3_512` supported algorithms are defined by the `string(<HASH>)` command. For MD5, we can use a shorthand option, `URL_MD5 <md5>`.
- `DOWNLOAD_NO_EXTRACT <bool>` – explicitly disables extraction after downloading. We may consume the filename of downloaded files in the follow-up steps by accessing the `<DOWNLOADED_FILE>` variable.
- `DOWNLOAD_NO_PROGRESS <bool>` – don't log download progress.
- `TIMEOUT <seconds>` and `INACTIVITY_TIMEOUT <seconds>` – timeouts to terminate the download after a fixed total time or period of inactivity.

- `HTTP_USERNAME <username>` and `HTTP_PASSWORD <password>` – options to provide values for HTTP authentication. Always be sure to avoid hardcoding any credentials in your projects.
- `HTTP_HEADER <header1> [<header2>...]` – sends additional headers with your HTTP request. Use this to access content in AWS or pass some custom tokens.
- `TLS_VERIFY <bool>` – verifies the SSL certificate. If this is not set, CMake will read this setting from the `CMAKE_TLS_VERIFY` variable, which is set to `false` by default. Skipping TLS verification is an unsafe, bad practice and should be avoided, especially in production environments.
- `TLS_CAINFO <file>` – this is useful if your company is issuing self-signed SSL certificates. This option provides a path to the authority file; if it isn't specified, CMake will read this setting from the `CMAKE_TLS_CAINFO` variable.

Downloading dependencies from Git

To download dependencies from Git, you'll need to make sure that the host has Git 1.6.5 or later installed. The following options are required to clone from Git:

```
GIT_REPOSITORY <url>
```
```
GIT_TAG <tag>
```

Both `<url>` and `<tag>` should be in formats understood by the `git` command. Additionally, it is recommended to use a specific git hash to make sure that produced binaries can be traced to a specific commit and no unnecessary `git fetch` executions are made. If you insist on using a branch, use remote names such as `origin/main`. This guarantees the correct synchronization of the local clone.

Additional options are as follows:

- `GIT_REMOTE_NAME <name>` – the remote name, which defaults to `origin`.
- `GIT_SUBMODULES <module>...` – specifies which submodules should be updated. Since 3.16, this value defaults to none (previously, all submodules were updated).
- `GIT_SUBMODULES_RECURSE 1` – enables the recursive update of submodules.
- `GIT_SHALLOW 1` – performs a shallow clone (don't download historical commits). This option is recommended for performance.
- `TLS_VERIFY <bool>` – this option was explained in the *Downloading dependencies from a URL* section. It is also available for Git, and should be enabled for security.

Downloading dependencies from Subversion

To download from Subversion, we should specify the following options:

```
SVN_REPOSITORY <url>
```
```
SVN_REVISION -r<rev>
```

Additionally, we may provide the following:

- `SVN_USERNAME <user>` and `SVN_PASSWORD <password>` – credentials for checkout and update. As always, avoid hardcoding them in your projects.
- `SVN_TRUST_CERT <bool>` – skips the verification of the Subversion server site certificate. Only use this option if the network path to the server and its integrity are trustworthy. It is disabled by default.

Downloading dependencies from Mercurial

This mode is very straightforward. We need to provide two options and we're done:

```
HG_REPOSITORY <url>
```
```
HG_TAG <tag>
```

Downloading dependencies from CVS

To check out modules from CVS, we need to provide these three options:

```
CVS_REPOSITORY <cvsroot>
```
```
CVS_MODULE <module>
```
```
CVS_TAG <tag>
```

Update step options

By default, the `update` step will re-download the external project's files if the download method supports updates. We can override this behavior in two ways:

- Provide a custom command to be executed during the update with `UPDATE_COMMAND <cmd>`.
- Completely disable the `update` step (to allow building with a disconnected network) – `UPDATE_DISCONNECTED <bool>`. Do note that the `download` step (during the first build) will still happen.

Patch step options

`Patch` is an optional step that will execute after the source is fetched. To enable it, we need to specify the exact command we want to execute with:

```
PATCH_COMMAND <cmd>...
```

CMake documentation warns that some patches may be more "sticky" than others. For example, in Git, changed files don't get restored to the original state during the update, and we need to be careful to avoid incorrectly patching the file twice. Ideally, the `patch` command should be really robust and idempotent.

> **Important Note**
> The previously mentioned lists of options contain only the most useful entries. Be sure to reference the official documentation for more details and a description of options for other steps: https://cmake.org/cmake/help/latest/module/ExternalProject.html.

Using ExternalProject in practice

The fact that dependency is populated at the build stage is very important, and it has two effects – the namespaces of projects are completely separate, and targets defined by any external project are not visible in the main project. The latter is especially painful, as we can't use `target_link_libraries()` in the same fashion as we would after using the `find_package()` command. This is because of a disjoint of two configuration stages. The main project has to finish the configuration stage and start the build stage before the dependency is downloaded and configured. This is an issue, but we'll learn how to deal with that in a second. For now, let's see how `ExternalProject_Add()` would work with the yaml-cpp library that we used in the previous examples:

chapter07/08-external-project-git/CMakeLists.txt

```
cmake_minimum_required(VERSION 3.20.0)
project(ExternalProjectGit CXX)

add_executable(welcome main.cpp)
configure_file(config.yaml config.yaml COPYONLY)

include(ExternalProject)
```

```
ExternalProject_Add(external-yaml-cpp
    GIT_REPOSITORY      https://github.com/jbeder/yaml-cpp.git
    GIT_TAG             yaml-cpp-0.6.3
)
target_link_libraries(welcome PRIVATE yaml-cpp)
```

These are the steps taken to build this project:

- We included the `ExternalProject` module to access its functions.
- We called the `FindExternalProject_Add()` command, which tasks the build stage with downloading the necessary files, and configuring, building, and installing the dependency in our system.

We need to be cautious here and understand that this example only works because the yaml-cpp library has an installation stage defined in its `CMakeLists.txt`. This stage copies the library files to the standard locations in the system. The `yaml-cpp` argument to the `target_link_libraries()` command is interpreted by CMake as a direct argument to the linker – `-lyaml-cpp`. This behavior differs from the previous examples, where we explicitly defined the `yaml-cpp` target. If the library wouldn't provide an installation stage (or the name of the binary version wouldn't match), the linker would throw an error.

At this point, we should dive deeper into the configuration of each stage and explain how to use different download methods. We'll get to that in the *FetchContent* section, but first, let's get back to the problem of late dependency fetching by `ExternalProject`. We cannot use targets of external projects in the compilation stage because that stage has already finished by the time these projects are being fetched. CMake will explicitly protect the target created with `FindExternalProject_Add()` by marking it with a special `UTILITY` type. When you mistakenly try to use such a target in the main project (perhaps to link it), CMake will throw an error:

```
Target "external-yaml-cpp-build" of type UTILITY may not be
linked into another target.
```

To get around this limitation, we can technically create another target, an IMPORTED library, and use that instead (just as we did earlier in this chapter with `FindPQXX.cmake`). But this is an awful lot of work. What's worse is that CMake actually understands the targets created by the external CMake projects (since it builds them). Repeating those declarations in the main project wouldn't be a very DRY practice.

Another possible solution is to extract whole dependency fetching and building to a separate sub-project and build that during the configuration stage. To make it happen, we'd need to start another instance of CMake with `execute_process()`. With some trickery and the `add_subdirectory()` command, we can then consume this sub-project's list files and binaries into the main project. This approach (sometimes called *the super-build*) is outdated and unnecessarily complex. I won't go into the details here, as it wouldn't be very useful for beginners. If you're curious, read this great article by Craig Scott: https://crascit.com/2015/07/25/cmake-gtest/.

To sum it up, `ExternalProject` can get us out of a bind when there are namespacing collisions across projects, but in all other cases, `FetchContent` is far superior. Let's figure out why.

FetchContent

Nowadays, it is recommended to go with the `FetchContent` module to import external projects. This module has been available in CMake since version 3.11, but we recommend using at least 3.14 to work with it effectively.

Essentially, it's a high-level wrapper around `ExternalProject`, offering similar functionality and more. The key difference is in the stage of execution – unlike `ExternalProject`, `FetchContent` populates dependencies during the configuration stage, bringing all the targets declared by an external project to the scope of the main project. This way, we can use them exactly like the ones we defined ourselves.

The usage of `FetchContent` module requires three steps:

1. Include the module in your project with `include(FetchModule)`.
2. Configure dependencies with the `FetchContent_Declare()` command.
3. Populate dependencies with the `FetchContent_MakeAvailable()` command – download, build, install, and add its list files to the main project and parse.

You may ask yourself why the `Declare` and `MakeAvailable` commands were separated. This was done to enable configuration overrides in hierarchical projects. Here's a scenario – a parent project depends on the **A** and **B** external libraries. The **A** library also depends on **B**, but authors of the **A** library are still using an old version, different from the parent project (*Figure 7.1*):

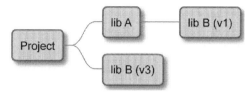

Figure 7.1 – The hierarchical project

What's more, the dependency on the **B** library is optional, depending on the configuration (let's say it's OS-specific). `MakeAvailable` can't both configure and populate the dependency because to override the version in the **A** library, the parent project would be forced to populate the dependency regardless of its final necessity in the **A** library.

By virtue of having a separate configuration step, we're able to specify a single version in the parent project and have it used in all sub-projects and dependencies:

```
FetchContent_Declare(
  googletest
  GIT_REPOSITORY https://github.com/google/googletest.git
  # release-1.11.0
  GIT_TAG        e2239ee6043f73722e7aa812a459f54a28552929
)
```

Any subsequent calls to `FetchContent_Declare()` with `googletest` as the first argument will be ignored to allow the project highest in the hierarchy to decide how to handle this dependency.

The signature of the `FetchContent_Declare()` command is exactly the same as `ExternalProject_Add()`:

```
FetchContent_Declare(<depName> <contentOptions>...)
```

This is no coincidence – these arguments will be stored by CMake until the `FetchContent_MakeAvailable()` is called and population is necessary. Then, they will be forwarded internally to the `ExternalProject_Add()` command. However, not all of the options are allowed. We can specify any options of the `download`, `update`, or `patch` steps but not the `configure`, `build`, `install`, or `test` steps.

When the configuration is ready, we'll populate the dependencies like so:

```
FetchContent_MakeAvailable(<depName>)
```

This will download the files and read the targets into the project, but what actually happens during this call? `FetchContent_MakeAvailable()` was added to CMake 3.14 to wrap the most commonly used scenario in a single command. In *Figure 7.2*, you can see the details of this process:

1. Call `FetchContent_GetProperties()` to read the configuration set by `FetchContent_Declare()` from the global variables to local variables.
2. Check (case-insensitively) whether the dependency with this name was already populated to avoid downloading it twice. If so, stop here.
3. Call `FetchContent_Populate()`. It will configure the wrapped `ExternalProject` module by forwarding options we have set (but skipping the disabled ones) and downloading the dependency. It will also set some variables to prevent re-downloading on subsequent calls and forward the necessary paths to the next command.
4. Finally, `add_subdirectory()` is called with source and build trees as arguments to tell the parent project where the list files are and where to put the build artifacts.

By calling `add_subdirectory()`, CMake effectively performs the configuration stage of the fetched project and retrieves any targets defined there in the current scope. How convenient!

Using ExternalProject and FetchContent modules

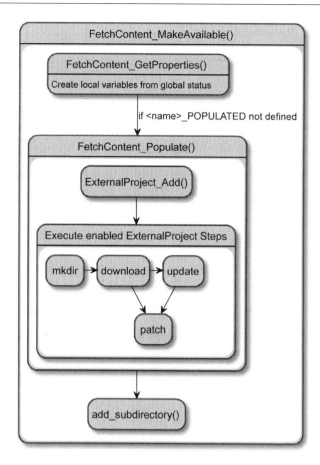

Figure 7.2 – How FetchContent_MakeAvailable() wraps calls to ExternalProject

Obviously, we may have a situation where two unrelated projects declare a target with the same name. This is a problem that can only be solved by falling back to `ExternalProject` or other methods. Luckily, it doesn't happen too often.

For this explanation to be complete, it has to be complemented with a practical example. Let's see how the list file from the previous section changes when we switch to `FetchContent`:

chapter07/09-fetch-content/CMakeLists.txt

```
cmake_minimum_required(VERSION 3.20.0)
project(ExternalProjectGit CXX)


add_executable(welcome main.cpp)
```

```
configure_file(config.yaml config.yaml COPYONLY)

include(FetchContent)
FetchContent_Declare(external-yaml-cpp
    GIT_REPOSITORY    https://github.com/jbeder/yaml-cpp.git
    GIT_TAG           yaml-cpp-0.6.3
)
FetchContent_MakeAvailable(external-yaml-cpp)
target_link_libraries(welcome PRIVATE yaml-cpp)
```

`ExternalProject_Add` was directly replaced with `FetchContent_Declare`, and we added another command – `FetchContent_MakeAvailable`. The changes in code are minuscule, but the practical differences are huge! We can explicitly access the targets created by the yaml-cpp library. To prove it, we'll use a `CMakePrintHelpers` helper module and add these lines to the previous file:

```
include(CMakePrintHelpers)
cmake_print_properties(TARGETS yaml-cpp
    PROPERTIES TYPE SOURCE_DIR)
```

Now, the configuration stage will print the following output:

```
Properties for TARGET yaml-cpp:
    yaml-cpp.TYPE = "STATIC_LIBRARY"
    yaml-cpp.SOURCE_DIR = "/tmp/b/_deps/external-yaml-cpp-src"
```

The target exists; it's a static library, and its source directory resides inside the build tree. Using the same helper to debug the target in the `ExternalProject` example simply returns:

```
No such TARGET "yaml-cpp" !
```

The target isn't recognized during the configuration stage. This is why `FetchContent` is much better and should be used wherever possible.

Summary

Managing dependencies isn't complicated when we use modern, well-supported projects. In most cases, we'd simply rely on the library being available in the system and fall back to `FetchContent` if it's not. This would be appropriate if dependencies are relatively small and quick to build.

For some really big libraries out there (such as Qt), it would take a significant amount of time to build from the source. To provide automatic dependency resolution in these cases, we'd have to resort to package managers offering compiled versions of libraries matching the user's environment. External tools such as Apt or Conan aren't within the scope of this book, as they are either too system-dependent or too complex.

The good news is that most users know how to install dependencies that your project might require, as long as you provide them with clear instructions to do so. From this chapter, you already know how to detect packages installed in the system with CMake's find-modules and config files bundled with the library.

We also learned what to do if a library is a bit older and doesn't support CMake but is distributed with the `.pc` files instead – we'll rely on the PkgConfig tool and the `FindPkgConfig` find-module bundled with CMake. We can expect that CMake will automatically create build targets when a library is found with one of the aforementioned methods, which is convenient and elegant. We also discussed relying on Git, and its submodules and cloning entire repositories. This method comes in useful when others won't do or are impractical to implement.

Finally, we explored the `ExternalProject` module and its functionalities and limitations. We studied how `FetchContent` extends the `ExternalProject` module, which things it has in common with the module, where it differs from the module, and why `FetchContent` is preferable.

You're now ready to use regular libraries in your projects; however, there's another kind of dependency that we should cover – testing frameworks. Every serious project needs to be tested for correctness, and CMake is a great tool to automate this process. We'll learn how to do it in the next chapter.

Further reading

For more information on the topics covered in this chapter, you can refer to the following:

- *CMake documentation – Using Dependencies Guide:* https://cmake.org/cmake/help/latest/guide/using-dependencies/index.html

- *Tutorial: Easy dependency management for C++ with CMake and Git:* https://www.foonathan.net/2016/07/cmake-dependency-handling/

- *CMake and using git-submodule for dependence projects:* https://stackoverflow.com/questions/43761594/

- *Piggybacking on PkgConfig:* https://gitlab.kitware.com/cmake/community/-/wikis/doc/tutorials/How-To-Find-Libraries#piggybacking-on-pkg-config
- *Discussion on the UNKNOWN type of imported libraries in findmodules:* https://gitlab.kitware.com/cmake/cmake/-/issues/19564
- *What Git submodules are:* https://git-scm.com/book/en/v2/Git-Tools-Submodules
- *How to use ExternalProject:* https://www.jwlawson.co.uk/interest/2020/02/23/cmake-external-project.html
- *CMake FetchContent vs. ExternalProject:* https://www.scivision.dev/cmake-fetchcontent-vs-external-project/
- *Using CMake with External Projects:* http://www.saoe.net/blog/using-cmake-with-external-projects/

Section 3: Automating With CMake

Completing the previous sections has turned you into a self-sufficient build engineer capable of building all kinds of projects with CMake. The final step in becoming a CMake professional is learning how to introduce and automate various quality checks and prepare your projects for collaborative work and publication. High-quality projects developed within large companies often share the same philosophy: automate repetitive tasks that drain mental energy from important decisions.

To achieve that, we're leveraging the power of the CMake ecosystem to add all kinds of tests done during the build: code-style checks, unit tests, and static and dynamic analyses of our solutions. We'll also simplify the documentation process by using tooling to generate pretty web pages, and we'll package and install our project to make its consumption a breeze, both for other developers and end users.

As a summary, we will put together everything we have learned into one coherent unit: a professional project that will stand the test of time.

This section comprises the following chapters:

- Chapter 8, *Testing Frameworks*
- Chapter 9, *Program Analysis Tools*
- Chapter 10, *Generating Documentation*
- Chapter 11, *Installing and Packaging*
- Chapter 12, *Creating Your Professional Project*

8
Testing Frameworks

Tenured professionals know that testing has to be automated. Someone explained that to them years ago or they learned the hard way. This practice isn't as obvious to inexperienced programmers: it seems unnecessary, additional work that doesn't bring much value. No wonder: when someone is just starting writing code, they'll avoid writing complex solutions and contributing to vast code bases. Most likely, they're the sole developer on their pet project. These early projects hardly ever need more than a few months to complete, so there's hardly any opportunity to see how code rots over a longer period.

All these factors contribute toward the notion that writing tests is a waste of time and effort. The programming apprentice may say to themselves that they actually do test their code each time they execute the "build-and-run" routine. After all, they have manually confirmed that their code works and does what's expected. It's finally time to move on to the next task, right?

Automated testing guarantees that new changes don't accidentally break our program. In this chapter, we'll learn why tests are important and how to use CTest (a tool bundled with CMake) to coordinate test execution. CTest is capable of querying available tests, filtering execution, shuffling, repeating, and time-limiting. We'll explore how to use those features, control the output of CTest, and handle test failures.

Next, we'll adapt our project's structure to support testing and create our own test runner. After discussing the basic principles, we'll move on to adding popular testing frameworks: Catch2 and GoogleTest with its mocking library. Lastly, we'll introduce detailed test coverage reporting with LCOV.

In this chapter, we're going to cover the following main topics:

- Why are automated tests worth the trouble?
- Using CTest to standardize testing in CMake
- Creating the most basic unit test for CTest
- Unit-testing frameworks
- Generating test coverage reports

Technical requirements

You can find the code files present in this chapter on GitHub at the following link:

https://github.com/PacktPublishing/Modern-CMake-for-Cpp/tree/main/examples/chapter08

To build examples provided in this book always use recommended commands:

```
cmake -B <build tree> -S <source tree>
cmake --build <build tree>
```

Be sure to replace placeholders `<build tree>` and `<source tree>` with appropriate paths. As a reminder: **build tree** is the path to target/output directory, **source tree** is the path at which your source code is located.

Why are automated tests worth the trouble?

Imagine a factory line that has a machine putting holes in sheets of steel. These holes have to be of specific size and shape so that they can house bolts that will hold the finished product together. The designer of such a factory line will set up the machine, test if the holes are correct, and move on. Sooner or later, something will change: the factory will use different, thicker steel; a worker will accidentally change the hole size; or, simply, more holes need to be punched and the machine has to be upgraded. A smart designer will put quality-control checks at certain points on the line to make sure that the product follows the specification and retains its key qualities. Holes have to conform to particular requirements but it doesn't really matter how they are created: drilled, punched, or laser-cut.

The same approach finds application in software development: it's very hard to predict which pieces of code will remain unchanged for years and which will see multiple revisions. As the functionality of the software expands, we need to make sure that we don't accidentally break things. But we will. Even the best programmers will make mistakes because they can't foresee all the implications of every change they make. As if that weren't enough, developers often work on code written by someone else and they don't know any of the intricate assumptions made earlier. They will read the code, build a rough mental model, add necessary changes, and hope they got it right. Most times, that's true—until it isn't. In such cases, an introduced bug can consume hours if not days to fix, not to mention the damage it can do to the product and the customers.

On occasion, you will stumble upon some code that is really hard to understand and follow. You will not only question how the code came to be and what it does, but you will also start a witch-hunt to figure out who's to blame for creating such a mess. Don't be too surprised if it turns out that you're the author. It has happened to me, and it will happen to you. Sometimes, code is created in a hurry, without a full understanding of the problem. As developers, we're not only under pressure from deadlines or budgets. Woken up in the middle of the night to fix a critical failure, you'll be appalled at how certain errors can slip past code review.

Most of this can be avoided with automated tests. These are pieces of code that check if another piece of code (used in production) is behaving correctly. As the name suggests, automated tests should be executed without prompts every time someone makes a change. It usually happens as part of the build process and is often added as a step to control the code quality before merging it into the repository.

You may be tempted to avoid automated tests to save time. That would be a very costly lesson. Steven Wright rightfully said: *"Experience is something you don't get until just after you need it."* Trust me: unless you're writing a one-off script for personal purposes or prototyping a non-production experiment, don't skip writing tests. Initially, you might get annoyed by the fact that the code you meticulously crafted is constantly failing tests. But if you really think about it, that failed test just stopped you from adding a breaking change to production. The effort invested now will pay off as time is saved on bug-fixing (and full nights of sleep). Tests are not as hard to add and maintain as they may seem.

Using CTest to standardize testing in CMake

Ultimately, automated testing involves nothing other than running an executable that sets your **system under test** (or **SUT**) in a given state, performs tested operations, and checks if the results match expectations. You can think of them as a codified way of filling the blanks in the sentence "*GIVEN _ WHEN _ THEN _*" and checking if it's true for SUT. As you can imagine, there's more than one way of doing this—actually, there are lots. Everything depends on the kind of framework you're going to use, how you are hooking it up to your SUT, and what is the exact configuration. Even things as minuscule as the filename of your testing binary will impact the experience of the person using your software. As there are no agreed-upon standards to these things, one developer will use the name `test_my_app`, another will go with `unit_tests`, and a third will use something obscure or not provide tests at all. Discovering which file needs to be run, which framework is used, which arguments should be passed to the runner, and how to collect results are problems that users would like to avoid.

CMake solves this by introducing a separate `ctest` command-line tool. It's configured by the project's author through listfiles and provides a unified way of executing tests: the same, standardized interface for every project built with CMake. If you follow this convention, you will enjoy other benefits down the line: adding the project to a (CI/CD) pipeline will be easier, surfacing them in (IDEs) such as Visual Studio or CLion—all of these things will be streamlined and more convenient. More importantly, you'll get a more powerful test-running utility with very little investment.

How to execute tests with CTest on an already configured project? We'll need to pick one of the following three modes of operation:

- Test
- Build-and-test
- Dashboard client

The last mode allows you to send the results of the test to a separate tool called CDash (also from Kitware). CDash collects and aggregates software-quality test results in an easy-to-navigate dashboard, as illustrated in the following screenshot:

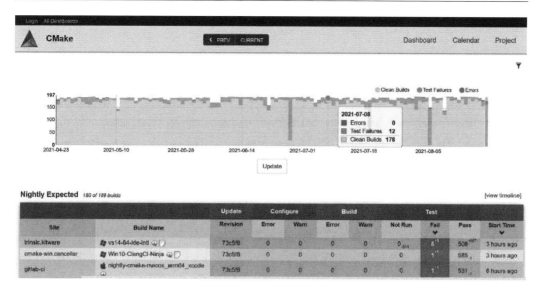

Figure 8.1 – Screenshot of the CDash dashboard timeline view

CDash isn't in the scope of this book since it's an advanced solution used as a shared server, accessible for all developers in a company.

> **Note**
>
> If you're interested in learning more online, reference the official documentation of CMake and visit the CDash website:
>
> https://cmake.org/cmake/help/latest/manual/ctest.1.html#dashboard-client
>
> https://www.cdash.org/

Let's get back to the first two modes. The command line for test mode looks like this:

```
ctest [<options>]
```

In this mode, CTest should be executed in the build tree, after building the project with cmake. This is slightly cumbersome during the development cycle, as you'd need to execute multiple commands and change the working directory back and forth. To simplify the process, CTest added a second mode: build-and-test mode.

Build-and-test mode

To use this mode, we need to execute `ctest` starting with `--build-and-test`, as follows:

```
ctest --build-and-test <path-to-source> <path-to-build>
      --build-generator <generator> [<options>...]
      [--build-options <opts>...]
      [--test-command <command> [<args>...]]
```

Essentially, this is a simple wrapper around the regular test mode that accepts a few build configuration options and allows us to append the command for the first mode— in other words, all options that can be passed to `ctest <options>` will work when passed to `ctest --build-and-test`. The only requirement here is to pass the full command after the `--test-command` argument. Contrary to what you might think, build-and-test mode won't actually run any tests unless provided with `ctest` keyword after `--test-command`, like so:

```
ctest --build-and-test project/source-tree /tmp/build-tree
     --build-generator "Unix Makefiles" --test-command ctest
```

In this command, we specify source and build paths, and select a build generator. All three are required and follow the rules for the `cmake` command, described in detail in *Chapter 1, First Steps with CMake*.

You may pass additional arguments to this mode. They come in three groups, controlling the configuration, the build process, or the tests.

Here are the arguments for controlling the configuration stage:

- `--build-options`—Any extra options for the `cmake` configuration (not the build tool) should be provided just before `--test-command`, which comes last.
- `--build-two-config`—Run the configuration stage for CMake twice.
- `--build-nocmake`—Skip the configuration stage.
- `--build-generator-platform`, `--build-generator-toolset`— Provide a generator-specific platform and toolset.
- `--build-makeprogram`—Specify a `make` executable when using Make- or Ninja-based generators.

Here are the arguments for controlling the build stage:

- `--build-target`—Build the specified target (instead of the `all` target).
- `--build-noclean`—Build without building the `clean` target first.
- `--build-project`—Provide the name of the built project.

This is the argument used to control the test stage:

- `--test-timeout`—Limit the execution of tests (provided in seconds).

All that's left is to configure the regular testing mode after the `--test-command` cmake argument.

Test mode

Assuming that we have built our project and we're executing `ctest` in the build tree (or we're using the `build-and-test` wrapper), we can finally execute our tests.

A simple `ctest` command without any arguments is usually enough to get satisfactory results in most scenarios. If all tests pass, `ctest` will return a 0 exit code. Use this in your CI/CD pipeline to prevent faulty commits from merging to your repository's production branch.

Writing good tests can be as challenging as writing the production code itself. We set up our SUT to be in a specific state, run a single test, and then tear down the SUT instance. This process is rather complex and can generate all sorts of issues: cross-test pollution, temporal and concurrency disruptions, resource contention, frozen execution due to deadlocks, and many others.

We can employ strategies that help detect and solve some of these problems. CTest allows you to affect test selection, their order, produced output, time limits, repetition, and so on. The following sections will provide the necessary context and a brief overview of the most useful options. As always, refer to the CMake documentation for an exhaustive list.

Querying tests

The first thing we might need to do is to understand which tests are actually written for the project. CTest offers an `-N` option, which disables execution and only prints a list, as follows:

```
# ctest -N
Test project /tmp/b
    Test #1: SumAddsTwoInts
    Test #2: MultiplyMultipliesTwoInts
Total Tests: 2
```

You might want to use `-N` with the filters described in the next section to check which tests would be executed when a filter is applied.

If you need a JSON format that can be consumed by automated tooling, execute `ctest` with `--show-only=json-v1`.

CTest also offers a mechanism to group tests with `LABELS` keyword. To list all available labels (without actually executing any tests), use `--print-labels`. This option is helpful when tests are defined manually with the `add_test(<name> <test-command>)` command in your listfile, as you are then able to specify individual labels through test properties, like this:

```
set_tests_properties(<name> PROPERTIES LABELS "<label>")
```

On the other hand, the frameworks we'll discuss later provide automatic test discovery, which unfortunately doesn't support such a granular level of labeling yet.

Filtering tests

There are plenty of reasons to run only a subset of all tests—the most common one might be the need to debug a single failing test or a module you're working on. There's no point in waiting for all other tests in that case. Other advanced testing scenarios will even go as far as partitioning test cases and distributing the load across a fleet of test runners.

These flags will filter tests according to the provided `<r>` **regular expression** (**regex**), as follows:

- `-R <r>, --tests-regex <r>`—Only run tests with names matching `<r>`
- `-E <r>, --exclude-regex <r>`—Skip tests with names matching `<r>`
- `-L <r>, --label-regex <r>`—Only run tests with labels matching `<r>`
- `-LE <r>, --label-exclude <regex>`—Skip tests with labels matching `<r>`

Advanced scenarios can be achieved with the `--tests-information` option (or the shorter form, `-I`). Use this filter to provide a range in a comma-separated format: `<start>`, `<end>`, `<step>`. Any of the fields can be empty, and after one more comma, you can append individual `<test-id>` values to run them additionally. Here are some examples:

- `-I 3,,` will skip tests 1 and 2 (execution starts from the third test)
- `-I ,2,` will only run the first and second test
- `-I 2,,3` will run every third test, starting from the second test in the row
- `-I ,0,,3,9,7` will only run the third, ninth, and seventh test

Optionally, CTest will accept the filename containing the specification in the same format. As you might imagine, users prefer filtering tests by name. This option can be used to distribute tests across multiple machines for really large suites.

By default, the `-I` option used with `-R` will narrow the execution (only tests matching both requirements will run). Add the `-U` option if you need the union of the two to execute instead (any of the requirements will suffice).

As mentioned before, you can use the `-N` option to check the outcome of filtering.

Shuffling tests

Writing unit tests can be tricky. One of the more surprising problems to encounter is test coupling, which is a situation where one test affects another by incompletely setting or clearing the state of SUT. In other words, the first test to execute can "leak" its state and pollute the second test. Such coupling is bad news because it introduces unknown, implicit relations between tests.

What's worse, this kind of error is known to hide really well in the complexities of testing scenarios. We might detect it when it causes one of the tests to fail when it shouldn't, but the opposite is equally possible: an incorrect state causes the test to pass when it shouldn't. Such falsely passing tests give developers an illusion of security, which is even worse than not having tests at all. The assumption that the code is correctly tested may encourage bolder actions, leading to unexpected outcomes.

One way of discovering such problems is by running each test in isolation. Usually, this is not the case when executing test runners straight from the testing framework without CTest. To run a single test, you'll need to pass a framework-specific argument to the test executable. This allows you to detect tests that are passing in the suite but are failing when executed on their own.

CTest, on the other hand, effectively removes all memory-based cross-contamination of tests by implicitly executing every test case in a child CTest instance. You may even go further and add the `--force-new-ctest-process` option to enforce separate processes.

Unfortunately, this alone won't work if your tests are using external, contested resources such as GPUs, databases, or files. An additional precaution we can take is to simply randomize the order of test execution. Such disturbance is often enough to eventually detect such spuriously passing tests. CTest supports this strategy with the `--schedule-random` option.

Handling failures

Here's a famous quote from John C. Maxwell: "*Fail early, fail often, but always fail forward.*" This is exactly what we want to do when running unit tests (and perhaps in other areas of life). Unless you're running your tests with a debugger attached, it's not easy to learn where you made a mistake as CTest will keep things brief and only list tests that failed, without actually printing any of their output.

Messages printed to `stdout` by the test case or the SUT might be invaluable to determine what was wrong exactly. To see them, we can run `ctest` with `--output-on-failure`. Alternatively, setting the `CTEST_OUTPUT_ON_FAILURE` environment variable will have the same effect.

Depending on the size of the solution, it might make sense to stop execution after any of the tests fail. This can be done by providing the `--stop-on-failure` argument to `ctest`.

CTest stores the names of failed tests. In order to save time in lengthy test suites, we can focus on these failed tests and skip running the passing tests until the problem is solved. This feature is enabled with the `--rerun-failed` option (any other filters will be ignored). Remember to run all tests after solving all issues to make sure that no regression has been introduced in the meantime.

When CTest doesn't detect any tests, it may mean two things: either tests aren't there or there's an issue with the project. By default, `ctest` will print a warning message and return a 0 exit code, to avoid muddying the waters. Most users will have enough context to understand which case they encountered and what to do next. However, in some environments, `ctest` will be executed always, as part of an automated pipeline. Then, we might need to explicitly say that a lack of tests should be interpreted as an error (and return a nonzero exit code). We can configure this behavior by providing the `--no-tests=error` argument. For the opposite behavior (no warning), use the `--no-tests=ignore` option.

Repeating tests

Sooner or later in your career, you'll encounter tests that work correctly most of the time. I want to emphasize the word *most*. Once in a blue moon, these tests will fail for environmental reasons: because of incorrectly mocked time, issues with event loops, poor handling of asynchronous execution, parallelism, hash collisions, and other really complicated scenarios that don't occur on every run. These unreliable tests are called "flaky tests".

Such inconsistency seems a not-so-important problem. We might say that tests aren't a real production environment and this is the ultimate reason why they sometimes fail. There is a grain of truth in this: tests aren't meant to replicate every little detail, because it's not viable. Tests are a simulation, an approximation of what might happen, and that's usually good enough. Does it hurt to rerun tests if they'll pass on the next execution?

Actually, it does. There are three main concerns, as outlined here:

- If you have gathered enough flaky tests in your code base, they will become a serious obstacle to the smooth delivery of code changes. It's especially frustrating when you're in a hurry: either getting ready to go home on a Friday afternoon or delivering a critical fix to a severe issue impacting your customers.

- You can't be truly sure that your flaky tests are failing because of the inadequacy of the testing environment. It may be the opposite: they fail because they replicated a rare scenario that already occurs in production. It's just not obvious enough to raise an alert... yet.

- It's not the test that's flaky—it's your code! The environment is wonky from time to time—as programmers, we deal with that in a deterministic manner. If SUT behaves this way, it's a sign of a serious error—for example, the code might be reading from uninitialized memory.

There isn't a perfect way to address all of the preceding cases—the multitude of possible reasons is simply too great. However, we might increase our chance of identifying flaky tests by running them repeatedly with the `-repeat <mode>:<#>` option. Three modes are available, as outlined here:

- `until-fail`—Run test `<#>` times; all runs have to pass.
- `until-pass`—Run test up to `<#>` times; it has to pass at least once. This is useful when dealing with tests that are known to be flaky, but too difficult and important to debug or disable.
- `after-timeout`—Run test up to `<#>` times but retry only if the test is timing out. Use it in busy test environments.

A general recommendation is to debug flaky tests as quickly as possible or get rid of them if they can't be trusted to produce consistent results.

Controlling output

Printing every piece of information to the screen every time would instantly get incredibly busy. CTest reduces the noise and collects the outputs of tests it executes to the log files, providing only the most useful information on regular runs. When things go bad and tests fail, you can expect a summary and possibly some logs if you enabled `--output-on-failure`, as mentioned earlier.

I know from experience that "enough information" is enough until it isn't. Sometimes, we may want to see the output of passed tests too, perhaps to check if they're truly working (and not just silently stopping without an error). To get access to more verbose output, add the `-V` option (or `--verbose` if you want to be explicit in your automated pipelines). If that's not enough, you might want `-VV` or `--extra-verbose`. For extremely in-depth debugging, use `--debug` (but be prepared for walls of text with all the details).

If you're looking for the opposite, CTest also offers "Zen mode" enabled with `-Q`, or `--quiet`. No output will be printed then (you can stop worrying and learn to love the calm). It seems that this option has no other use than to confuse people, but be aware that the output will still be stored in test files (in `./Testing/Temporary` by default). Automated pipelines can check if the exit code is a nonzero value and collect the log files for further processing without littering the main output with details that may confuse developers not familiar with the product.

To store the logs in a specific path, use the `-O <file>`, `--output-log <file>` option. If you're suffering from lengthy outputs, there are two limit options to cap them to the given number of bytes per test: `--test-output-size-passed <size>` and `--test-output-size-failed <size>`.

Miscellaneous

There are a few other useful options that can be useful for your everyday testing needs, as outlined here:

- `-C <cfg>`, `--build-config <cfg>` (multi-configuration generators only)—Use this to specify which configuration to test. The `Debug` configuration usually has debugging symbols, making things easier to understand, but `Release` should be tested too, as heavy optimization options could potentially affect the behavior of SUT.

- `-j <jobs>`, `--parallel <jobs>`—This sets the number of tests executed in parallel. It's very useful to speed up the execution of long tests during development. Be mindful that in a busy environment (on a shared test runner), it might have an adverse effect due to scheduling. This can be slightly mitigated with the next option.

- `--test-load <level>`—Use this to schedule parallel tests in a fashion that CPU load doesn't exceed the `<level>` value (on a best-effort basis).

- `--timeout <seconds>`—Use this to specify the default limit of time for a single test.

Now that we understand how to execute `ctest` in many different scenarios, let's learn how to add a simple test.

Creating the most basic unit test for CTest

Writing unit tests is technically possible without any kind of framework. All we have to do is create an instance of the class we want to test, execute one of its methods, and check if the new state or value returned meets our expectations. Then, we report the result and delete the object under test. Let's try it out.

We'll use the following structure:

```
- CMakeLists.txt
- src
    |- CMakeLists.txt
    |- calc.cpp
    |- calc.h
    |- main.cpp
- test
    |- CMakeLists.txt
    |- calc_test.cpp
```

Starting from main.cpp, we can see it will use a Calc class, as illustrated in the following code snippet:

chapter08/01-no-framework/src/main.cpp

```cpp
#include <iostream>
#include "calc.h"
using namespace std;

int main() {
  Calc c;
  cout << "2 + 2 = " << c.Sum(2, 2) << endl;
  cout << "3 * 3 = " << c.Multiply(3, 3) << endl;
}
```

Nothing too fancy—main.cpp simply includes the calc.h header and calls two methods of the Calc object. Let's quickly glance at the interface of Calc, our SUT, as follows:

chapter08/01-no-framework/src/calc.h

```cpp
#pragma once
class Calc {
 public:
    int Sum(int a, int b);
    int Multiply(int a, int b);
};
```

The interface is as simple as possible. We're using #pragma once here—it works exactly like commonly seen preprocessor include guards and is understood by almost all modern compilers, despite not being part of the official standard. Let's see the class implementation, as follows:

chapter08/01-no-framework/src/calc.cpp

```cpp
#include "calc.h"
int Calc::Sum(int a, int b) {
  return a + b;
}
```

```cpp
int Calc::Multiply(int a, int b) {
  return a * a; // a mistake!
}
```

Uh-oh! We introduced a mistake! `Multiply` is ignoring the b argument and returns a squared instead. That should be detected by correctly written unit tests. So, let's write some! Here we go:

chapter08/01-no-framework/test/calc_test.cpp

```cpp
#include "calc.h"
#include <cstdlib>

void SumAddsTwoIntegers() {
  Calc sut;
  if (4 != sut.Sum(2, 2))
    std::exit(1);
}

void MultiplyMultipliesTwoIntegers() {
  Calc sut;
  if(3 != sut.Multiply(1, 3))
    std::exit(1);
}
```

We start our `calc_test.cpp` file by writing two test methods, one for each tested method of SUT. If the value returned from the called method doesn't match expectations, each function will call `std::exit(1)`. We could use `assert()`, `abort()`, or `terminate()` here, but that would result in a less explicit `Subprocess aborted` message in the output of `ctest`, instead of the more readable `Failed` message.

Time to create a test runner. Ours will be simple as possible because doing it correctly would require a ridiculous amount of work. Just look at the `main()` function we had to write in order to run just two tests:

chapter08/01-no-framework/test/unit_tests.cpp

```cpp
#include <string>
void SumAddsTwoIntegers();
```

```cpp
void MultiplyMultipliesTwoIntegers();

int main(int argc, char *argv[]) {
  if (argc < 2 || argv[1] == std::string("1"))
    SumAddsTwoIntegers();

  if (argc < 2 || argv[1] == std::string("2"))
    MultiplyMultipliesTwoIntegers();
}
```

Here's a breakdown of what happens here:

- We declare two external functions that will be linked from another translation unit.
- If no arguments were provided, execute both tests (the zeroth element in `argv[]` is always the program name).
- If the first argument is an identifier of the test, execute it.
- If any of the tests fail, it internally calls `exit()` and returns with a `1` exit code.
- If no tests were executed or all passed, it implicitly returns with a `0` exit code.

To run the first test, we'll execute `./unit_tests 1`; to run the second, we'll execute `./unit_tests 2`. We simplified the code as much as we could, and it still turned out to be pretty hard to read. Anyone who might need to maintain this section isn't going to have a great time after adding a few more tests, not to mention that this functionality is pretty raw—debugging such a test suite will be a lot of work. Nevertheless, let's see how we can use it with CTest, as follows:

chapter08/01-no-framework/CMakeLists.txt

```cmake
cmake_minimum_required(VERSION 3.20.0)
project(NoFrameworkTests CXX)
enable_testing()
add_subdirectory(src bin)
add_subdirectory(test)
```

We start with the usual heading and `enable_testing()`. This is to tell CTest that we'd like to enable tests in this directory and its subdirectories. Next, we'll include two nested listfiles in each of the subdirectories: `src` and `test`. The highlighted `bin` value states that we'd like the binary output of `src` subdirectories to be placed in `<build_tree>/bin`. Otherwise, binary files would end up in `<build_tree>/src`, which could be confusing. After all, build artifacts are no longer source files.

The listfile for the `src` directory is very straightforward and contains a simple `main` target definition, as illustrated here:

chapter08/01-no-framework/src/CMakeLists.txt

```
add_executable(main main.cpp calc.cpp)
```

We also need a listfile for the `test` directory, as follows:

chapter08/01-no-framework/test/CMakeLists.txt

```
add_executable(unit_tests
               unit_tests.cpp
               calc_test.cpp
               ../src/calc.cpp)
target_include_directories(unit_tests PRIVATE ../src)

add_test(NAME SumAddsTwoInts COMMAND unit_tests 1)
add_test(NAME MultiplyMultipliesTwoInts COMMAND unit_tests 2)
```

We have now defined a second `unit_tests` target that also uses the `src/calc.cpp` implementation file and respective header. Finally, we explicitly add two tests: `SumAddsTwoInts` and `MultiplyMultipliesTwoInts`. Each provides its ID as an argument to the `add_test()` command. CTest will simply take anything provided after the `COMMAND` keyword and execute it in a subshell, collecting the output and exit code. Don't get too attached to `add_test()` — in the *Unit-testing frameworks* section, we'll discover a much better way of dealing with test cases, so we'll skip describing it in detail here.

This is how `ctest` works in practice when executed in the build tree:

```
# ctest
Test project /tmp/b
    Start 1: SumAddsTwoInts
1/2 Test #1: SumAddsTwoInts ..................   Passed    0.00 sec
    Start 2: MultiplyMultipliesTwoInts
2/2 Test #2: MultiplyMultipliesTwoInts ........***Failed  0.00 sec

50% tests passed, 1 tests failed out of 2
Total Test time (real) =   0.00 sec
The following tests FAILED:
          2 - MultiplyMultipliesTwoInts (Failed)
Errors while running CTest
Output from these tests are in: /tmp/b/Testing/Temporary/LastTest.log
Use "--rerun-failed --output-on-failure" to re-run the failed cases verbosely.
```

CTest executed both tests and reported that one of them is failing—the returned value from `Calc::Multiply` didn't meet expectations. Very good. We now know that our code has a bug, and someone should fix it.

> **Note**
>
> You may have noticed that in most examples so far, we didn't necessarily employ the project structure described in *Chapter 3*, *Setting Up Your First CMake Project*. This was done to keep things brief. This chapter discusses more advanced concepts, and therefore using a full structure is warranted. In your projects (no matter how small), it's best to follow this structure from the start. As a wise man once said: "*You step onto the road, and if you don't keep your feet, there's no knowing where you might be swept off to.*"

It's no secret that you should avoid building a testing framework as part of your own project. Even the most basic example is hard on the eyes, has a lot of overhead, and doesn't add any value. However, before we can adopt a unit-testing framework, we'll need to rethink the structure of the project.

Structuring our projects for testing

C++ has some limited introspection capabilities, but cannot offer such powerful retrospection features as Java can. This might be the very reason why writing tests and unit-testing frameworks for C++ code is much harder than in other, richer environments. One implication of such an economic approach is the fact that the programmer has to be more involved in crafting testable code. We'll not only have to design our interfaces more carefully, but also answer questions about the practicalities, such as this: *How do we avoid doubling the compilation, and reuse artifacts between tests and production?*

Compilation time might not be a significant problem for smaller projects, but as time flies, the projects grow. The need for short compilation loops does not go away. In the previous example, we appended all the sut sources to the unit-test executable apart from the main.cpp file. If you were reading closely, you will have noticed that we had some code in that file that didn't get tested (the contents of main() itself). By compiling the code twice, there's a slight chance that the produced artifacts won't be *exactly the same*. These things can potentially diverge over time (due to the addition of compilation flags and preprocessor directives). This may be especially dangerous when engineers contributing to the code base are in a rush, inexperienced, or simply unfamiliar with the project.

There are multiple ways of dealing with the problem, but the most elegant is to build your entire solution as a library and link it with unit tests. You might ask: "*How are we going to run it then?*" We'll need a bootstrap executable that will link with the library and run its code.

Begin by renaming your current main() function to run(), start_program(), or something similar. Then, create another implementation file (bootstrap.cpp) with a new main() function, and this function only. This will be our adapter (or wrapper, if you will): its sole role is to provide an entry point and call the run() forwarding command-line arguments (if any). All that's left is to link everything together, and we've got ourselves a testable project.

By renaming main(), we can now link SUT with tests and test its primary function too. Otherwise, we'd be in violation of the **One Definition Rule (ODR)** discussed in *Chapter 6, Linking with CMake*, as the test runner needs its own entry point, a separate main() function. As promised in the *Separating main() for testing* section of *Chapter 6*, we'll explain this subject in detail.

The testing framework may provide its own implementation of the main() function out of the box, so we don't need to write it. Usually, it will detect all tests that we've linked and execute them according to the desired configuration.

Artifacts produced by this approach can be grouped into the following targets:

- A sut library with production code
- bootstrap with a main() wrapper calling run() from sut
- unit tests with a main() wrapper that runs all the tests on sut

The following diagram shows the symbol relations between targets:

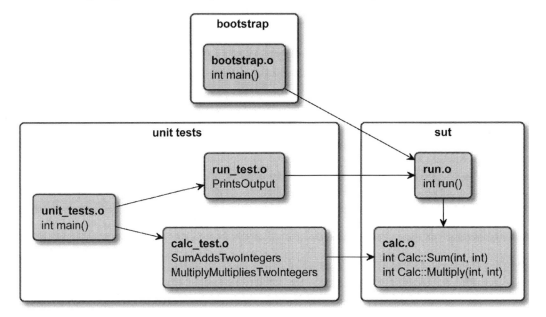

Figure 8.2 – Sharing artifacts between test and production executables

We end up with six implementation files that will produce their respective (.o) *object files*, as follows:

- calc.cpp—The Calc class to be unit-tested. This is called a **unit under test (UUT)** because UUT is a specialization of SUT.
- run.cpp—Original entry point renamed run(), which can be now tested.
- bootstrap.cpp—New main() entry point calling run().
- calc_test.cpp—Tests the Calc class.
- run_test.cpp—New tests for run() can go here.
- unit_tests.o—Entry point for unit tests, extended to call tests for run().

The library that we're about to build doesn't actually need to be a factual library: static or shared. By creating an object library, we can avoid unnecessary archiving or linking. Technically speaking, it's possible to shave a few moments by relying on dynamic linking for SUT, but more often than not, we're making changes in both targets: `tests` and `sut`, canceling out any potential gains.

Let's see how our files have changed, starting with the file previously named `main.cpp`, as follows:

chapter08/02-structured/src/run.cpp

```cpp
#include <iostream>
#include "calc.h"
using namespace std;

int run() {
  Calc c;
  cout << "2 + 2 = " << c.Sum(2, 2) << endl;
  cout << "3 * 3 = " << c.Multiply(3, 3) << endl;
  return 0;
}
```

Not too many differences: renamed file and function. We also added a `return` statement as the compiler won't do this implicitly for functions that are not `main()`.

The new `main()` function looks like this:

chapter08/02-structured/src/bootstrap.cpp

```cpp
int run(); // declaration
int main() {
  run();
}
```

As simple as possible—we're declaring that the linker will provide the `run()` function from another translation unit, and we're calling it. Next to change is the `src` listfile, which you can see here:

chapter08/02-structured/src/CMakeLists.txt

```
add_library(sut STATIC calc.cpp run.cpp)
target_include_directories(sut PUBLIC .)

add_executable(bootstrap bootstrap.cpp)
target_link_libraries(bootstrap PRIVATE sut)
```

First, we created a `sut` library and marked `.` as a `PUBLIC` *include directory* so that it will be propagated to all targets that will link `sut` (that is, `bootstrap` and `unit_tests`). Note that *include directories* are relative to the listfile, therefore we can use a dot (`.`) to refer to the current `<source_tree>/src` directory.

Time to update our `unit_tests` target. Here, we'll remove the direct reference to the `../src/calc.cpp` file with a linking reference to `sut` for the `unit_tests` target. We'll also add a new test for the primary function in the `run_test.cpp` file. We'll skip discussing that for brevity, but if you're interested, check out the online examples. Meanwhile, here's the whole `test` listfile:

chapter08/02-structured/test/CMakeLists.txt

```
add_executable(unit_tests
               unit_tests.cpp
               calc_test.cpp
               run_test.cpp)
target_link_libraries(unit_tests PRIVATE sut)
```

We should also register the new test, as follows:

```
add_test(NAME SumAddsTwoInts COMMAND unit_tests 1)
add_test(NAME MultiplyMultipliesTwoInts COMMAND unit_tests 2)
add_test(NAME RunOutputsCorrectEquations COMMAND unit_tests 3)
```

Done! By following this practice, you can be sure that your tests are executed on the very machine code that will be used in production.

> **Note**
> The target names we're using here, `sut` and `bootstrap`, are chosen to make it very clear what they're about from the perspective of testing. In real-life projects, you should pick names that match the context of the production code (rather than tests). For example, for a FooApp, name your target `foo` instead of `bootstrap`, and `lib_foo` instead of `sut`.

Now that we know how to structure a testable project in appropriate targets, let's shift our focus to the testing frameworks themselves. We don't want to add every test case to our listfiles manually, do we?

Unit-testing frameworks

The previous section proves that it isn't extremely complicated to write a tiny unit-testing driver. It wasn't pretty, but believe it or not, professional developers actually *do like* to reinvent the wheel (theirs will be fancier, rounder, and faster than the legacy one). Don't fall into this trap: you'll create so much boilerplate that it could become a separate project. Introducing a popular unit-test framework to your solution aligns it to a standard that transcends projects and companies and will get you free updates and extensions for cheap. You can't lose.

How do we add a unit-testing framework to our project? Well, write tests in implementation files according to the chosen framework's rules and link these tests with a test runner provided by the framework. Test runners are your entry points that will start the execution of selected tests. Unlike the basic `unit_tests.cpp` file we saw earlier in the chapter, many of them will detect all the tests automatically. Beautiful.

There are two unit-testing frameworks I decided to introduce in this chapter. I picked them for the following reasons:

- **Catch2** is a relatively easy-to-learn and well-supported and -documented project. It offers simple test cases, but also provides elegant macros for **behavior-driven development** (**BDD**). It lacks some features but can be coupled with external tools when needed. You can visit its home page here: https://github.com/catchorg/Catch2.

- **GTest** is also very convenient, but much more advanced. Its key features are a rich set of assertions, user-defined assertions, death tests, fatal and non-fatal failures, value- and type-parametrized tests, XML test report generation, and mocking. The last one is delivered in the GMock module available from the same repository: https://github.com/google/googletest.

Which framework you should choose depends on your learning approach and the size of the project. If you prefer a slow, gradual process and don't need all the bells and whistles, go with Catch2. Developers who prefer starting from the deep end and need a lot of firepower will benefit from choosing GTest.

Catch2

This framework, maintained by Martin Hořeňovský, is great for beginners and smaller projects. This is not to say that it can't handle the bigger applications, as long as you keep in mind that there will be areas where additional tooling may be necessary. I would deviate too much from the topic of this book if I went into it in detail, but I still want to give you an overview. To start, let's take a brief look at the implementation of a unit test we can write for our `Calc` class, as follows:

chapter08/03-catch2/test/calc_test.cpp

```
#include <catch2/catch_test_macros.hpp>
#include "calc.h"

TEST_CASE("SumAddsTwoInts", "[calc]") {
  Calc sut;
  CHECK(4 == sut.Sum(2, 2));
}

TEST_CASE("MultiplyMultipliesTwoInts", "[calc]") {
  Calc sut;
  CHECK(12 == sut.Multiply(3, 4));
}
```

That's it. These few lines are much more powerful than what we wrote in the previous examples. `CHECK()` macros will not only verify if the expectation is met—they will actually collect all failed assertions and present them in a single output so that you can do a single fix and avoid constant recompilation.

Now, to the best part: we don't need to add these tests anywhere or even inform CMake they exist; you can forget about `add_test()` because you won't need it again. Catch2 will automatically register your tests with CTest if you let it. Adding the framework is very easy after configuring the project as described in the previous section. We need to bring it into the project with `FetchContent()`.

There are two major versions to choose from: v2 and v3. Version 2 is offered as a single-header library (just #include <catch2/catch.hpp>) for C++11, and will be eventually deprecated by Version 3. This one has multiple headers, is compiled as a static library, and requires C++14. Of course, it's recommended to go with the newer release if you can use modern C++ (yes—C++11 is no longer considered "modern"). When working with Catch2, you should pick a Git tag and pin it in your listfile. In other words, it is not guaranteed that an upgrade won't break your code (it likely won't, but don't risk going with the devel branch if you don't need to). To fetch Catch2, we need to provide a URL to the repository, as follows:

chapter08/03-catch2/test/CMakeLists.txt

```
include(FetchContent)
FetchContent_Declare(
  Catch2
  GIT_REPOSITORY https://github.com/catchorg/Catch2.git
  GIT_TAG        v3.0.0
)
FetchContent_MakeAvailable(Catch2)
```

Then, we need to define our unit_tests target and link it with sut and with a framework-provided entry point and Catch2::Catch2WithMain library. Since Catch2 provides its own main() function, we no longer use the unit_tests.cpp file (this file can be removed). The code is illustrated in the following snippet:

chapter08/03-catch2/test/CMakeLists.txt (continued)

```
add_executable(unit_tests
               calc_test.cpp
               run_test.cpp)
target_link_libraries(unit_tests PRIVATE
                      sut Catch2::Catch2WithMain)
```

Lastly, we use a `catch_discover_tests()` command defined in the module provided by Catch2 that will detect all test cases from `unit_tests` and register them with CTest, as follows:

chapter08/03-catch2/test/CMakeLists.txt (continued)

```
list(APPEND CMAKE_MODULE_PATH ${catch2_SOURCE_DIR}/extras)
include(Catch)
catch_discover_tests(unit_tests)
```

Done. We just added a unit-testing framework to our solution. Let's now see it in practice. The output from the test runner looks like this:

```
# ./test/unit_tests
unit_tests is a Catch v3.0.0 host application.
Run with -? for options
-------------------------------------------------------------------
MultiplyMultipliesTwoInts
-------------------------------------------------------------------
examples/chapter08/03-catch2/test/calc_test.cpp:9
...................................................................
examples/chapter08/03-catch2/test/calc_test.cpp:11: FAILED:
  CHECK( 12 == sut.Multiply(3, 4) )
with expansion:
  12 == 9
===================================================================
test cases: 3 | 2 passed | 1 failed
assertions: 3 | 2 passed | 1 failed
```

The direct execution of the runner (compiled `unit_test` executable) is slightly faster, but normally, you'd like to use the `ctest --output-on-failure` command instead of executing the test runner directly to get all the CTest benefits mentioned earlier. Note also that Catch2 was able to conveniently expand the `sut.Multiply(3, 4)` expression to 9, providing us with more context.

This concludes the setup of Catch2. If you ever need to add more tests, just create implementation files and insert their paths to the list of sources for the `unit_tests` target.

This framework has quite a few interesting tricks up its sleeve: event listeners, data generators, and micro benchmarking, but it doesn't provide a mocking functionality. If you don't know what mocks are, read on—we'll cover that in a moment. Nevertheless, if you find yourself in need of mocks, you can always add one of the mocking frameworks next to Catch2, as listed here:

- FakeIt (`https://github.com/eranpeer/FakeIt`)
- Hippomocks (`https://github.com/dascandy/hippomocks`)
- Trompeloeil (`https://github.com/rollbear/trompeloeil`)

That said, for a more streamlined, advanced experience, there is another framework worth looking at.

GTest

There are a few important advantages when it comes to using GTest: it's been around quite a long time and is highly recognized in the C++ community (thus, multiple IDEs support it natively). The company behind the biggest search engine on the planet is maintaining and using it extensively, so it's quite unlikely it will become stale or abandoned any time soon. It can test C++11 and up, so if you're stuck in a bit older environment, you're in luck.

The GTest repository comprises two projects: GTest (the main testing framework) and GMock (a library adding the mocking functionality). That means you can download both with a single `FetchContent()` call.

Using GTest

To use GTest, our project needs to follow the directions from the *Structuring our projects for testing* section. This is how we'd write a unit test in this framework:

chapter08/04-gtest/test/calc_test.cpp

```cpp
#include <gtest/gtest.h>
#include "calc.h"

class CalcTestSuite : public ::testing::Test {
 protected:
  Calc sut_;
};
```

```cpp
TEST_F(CalcTestSuite, SumAddsTwoInts) {
    EXPECT_EQ(4, sut_.Sum(2, 2));
}

TEST_F(CalcTestSuite, MultiplyMultipliesTwoInts) {
    EXPECT_EQ(12, sut_.Multiply(3, 4));
}
```

Since this example will be used also in GMock, I decided to put tests in a single `CalcTestSuite` class. Test suites are group related tests, so they can reuse the same fields, methods, setup (initialization), and teardown (cleanup) steps. To create a test suite, we need to declare a new class inheriting from `::testing::Test` and put reused elements (fields, methods) in its `protected` section.

Each test case in a test suite is declared with a `TEST_F()` preprocessor macro that stringifies provided names for the test suite and test case (there's also a simple `TEST()` macro that defines unaffiliated tests). Because we defined `Calc sut_` in the class, each test case can access it as if the test were a method of `CalcTestSuite`. In reality, each test case is run in its own class implicitly inheriting from `CalcTestSuite` (that's why we need the `protected` keyword). Note that reused fields are not meant to share any data between consecutive tests—their function is to keep the code *DRY*.

GTest doesn't offer natural syntax for assertions like Catch2 does. Instead, we need to use an explicit comparison, such as `EXPECT_EQ()`. By convention, we put the expected value as the first argument and the actual value as the second argument. There are many other assertions, helpers, and macros worth learning about.

> **Note**
> For detailed information on GTest, see the official reference material (https://google.github.io/googletest/).

To add this dependency to our project, we need to decide which version to use. Unlike Catch2, GTest is leaning toward a "live at head" philosophy (originating from the Abseil project that GTest depends on). It states: "*If you build our dependency from source and follow our API, you shouldn't have any issues.*" (Refer to the *Further reading* section for more details.)

If you're comfortable following this rule (and building from source isn't an issue), set your Git tag to the `master` branch. Otherwise, pick a release from the GTest repository. We can also choose to search the host machine for the installed copy first, as CMake offers a bundled `FindGTest` module to find the local installation. Since v3.20, CMake will use the upstream `GTestConfig.cmake` config-file, if it exists, instead of relying on the find-module, which might become outdated.

In any case, adding a dependency on GTest looks like this:

chapter08/04-gtest/test/CMakeLists.txt

```cmake
include(FetchContent)
FetchContent_Declare(
  googletest
  GIT_REPOSITORY https://github.com/google/googletest.git
  GIT_TAG master
)
set(gtest_force_shared_crt ON CACHE BOOL "" FORCE)
FetchContent_MakeAvailable(googletest)
```

We're following the same method as with Catch2—execute `FetchContent()` and build the framework from source. The only difference is the addition of the `set(gtest...)` command, as recommended by GTest authors to prevent overriding the parent project's compiler and linker settings on Windows.

Finally, we can declare our test runner executable, link it with `gtest_main`, and have our test cases automatically discovered thanks to the built-in CMake `GoogleTest` module, as illustrated here:

chapter08/04-gtest/test/CMakeLists.txt (continued)

```cmake
add_executable(unit_tests
               calc_test.cpp
               run_test.cpp)
target_link_libraries(unit_tests PRIVATE sut gtest_main)
include(GoogleTest)
gtest_discover_tests(unit_tests)
```

This completes the setup of GTest. The output of the test runner is much more verbose than from Catch2, but we can pass `--gtest_brief=1` to limit it to failures only, as follows:

```
# ./test/unit_tests --gtest_brief=1
~/examples/chapter08/04-gtest/test/calc_test.cpp:15: Failure
Expected equality of these values:
  12
  sut_.Multiply(3, 4)
    Which is: 9
[  FAILED  ] CalcTestSuite.MultiplyMultipliesTwoInts (0 ms)
[==========] 3 tests from 2 test suites ran. (0 ms total)
[  PASSED  ] 2 tests.
```

Luckily, even the noisy output will be suppressed when running from CTest (unless we explicitly enable it on the `ctest --output-on-failure` command line).

Now that we have the framework in place, let's discuss mocking. After all, no test can be truly "unit" when it's coupled with other elements.

GMock

Writing true unit tests is about executing a piece of code in isolation from other pieces of code. Such a unit is understood as a self-contained element, either a class or a component. Of course, hardly any programs written in C++ have all of their units in clear isolation from others. Most likely, your code will rely heavily on some form of association relationship between classes. There's only one problem with that: objects of such a class will require objects of another class, and those will require yet another. Before you know it, your entire solution is participating in a "unit test". Even worse, your code might be coupled to an external system and be dependent on its state—for example, specific records in a database, network packets coming in, or specific files stored on the disk.

To decouple units for the purpose of testing, developers use **test doubles** or a special version of classes that are used by a class under test. Some examples include fakes, stubs, and mocks. Here are some rough definitions of these:

- A **fake** is a limited implementation of some more complex class. An example could be an in-memory map instead of an actual database client.
- A **stub** provides specific, canned answers to method calls, limited to responses used by tests. It can also record which methods were called and how many times this occurred.

- A **mock** is a bit more extended version of a stub. It will additionally verify if methods were called during the test as expected.

Such a test double is created at the beginning of a test and provided as an argument to the constructor of a tested class to be used instead of a real object. This mechanism is called **dependency injection**.

The problem with simple test doubles is the fact that they are *too simple*. To simulate behaviors for different test scenarios, we would have to provide many different doubles, one for every state in which the coupled object can be. This isn't very practical and would scatter testing code across too many files. This is where GMock comes in: it allows developers to create a generic test double for a specific class and define its behavior for every test in line. GMock calls these doubles "mocks", but in reality, they're a mixture of all the aforementioned types, depending on the occasion.

Consider the following example: let's add a functionality to our `Calc` class that would add a random number to the provided argument. It will be represented by an `AddRandomNumber()` method that returns this sum as an `int`. How would we confirm the fact that the returned value is really an exact sum of something random and the value provided to the class? As we know, relying on randomness is key to many important processes, and if we're using it incorrectly, we might suffer all kinds of consequences. Checking all random numbers until we exhaust all possibilities isn't very practical.

To test it, we need to wrap a random number generator in a class that could be mocked (or, in other words, replaced with a mock). Mocks will allow us to force a specific response, which is to "fake" generation of a random number. `Calc` will use that value in `AddRandomNumber()` and allow us to check if the returned value from that method meets expectations. The clean separation of random number generation to another unit is an added value (as we'll be able to exchange one type of generator for another).

Let's start with the public interface for the abstract generator. This will allow us to implement it in the actual generator and a mock, enabling us to use them interchangeably. We'll execute the following code:

chapter08/05-gmock/src/rng.h

```
#pragma once
class RandomNumberGenerator {
 public:
  virtual int Get() = 0;
  virtual ~RandomNumberGenerator() = default;
};
```

Classes implementing this interface will provide us with a random number from the `Get()` method. Note the `virtual` keyword—it has to be on all methods to be mocked unless we'd like to get involved with more complex template-based mocking. We also need to remember to add a virtual destructor. Next, we have to extend our `Calc` class to accept and store the generator, as follows:

chapter08/05-gmock/src/calc.h

```cpp
#pragma once
#include "rng.h"

class Calc {
  RandomNumberGenerator* rng_;
 public:
    Calc(RandomNumberGenerator* rng);
    int Sum(int a, int b);
    int Multiply(int a, int b);
    int AddRandomNumber(int a);
};
```

We included the header and added a method to provide random additions. Additionally, a field to store the pointer to the generator was created, along with a parameterized constructor. This is how dependency injection works in practice. Now, we implement these methods, as follows:

chapter08/05-gmock/src/calc.cpp

```cpp
#include "calc.h"

Calc::Calc(RandomNumberGenerator* rng) {
  rng_ = rng;
}

int Calc::Sum(int a, int b) {
  return a + b;
}

int Calc::Multiply(int a, int b) {
```

```
    return a * b; // now corrected
}
```

```
int Calc::AddRandomNumber(int a) {
    return a + rng_->Get();
}
```

In the constructor, we're assigning the provided pointer to a class field. We're then using this field in AddRandomNumber() to fetch the generated value. The production code will use a real number generator; the tests will use mocks. Remember that we need to dereference pointers to enable polymorphism. As a bonus, we could possibly create different generator classes for different implementations. I just need one: a Mersenne Twister pseudo-random generator with uniform distribution, as illustrated in the following code snippet:

chapter08/05-gmock/src/rng_mt19937.cpp

```
#include <random>
#include "rng_mt19937.h"

int RandomNumberGeneratorMt19937::Get() {
    std::random_device rd;
    std::mt19937 gen(rd());
    std::uniform_int_distribution<> distrib(1, 6);
    return distrib(gen);
}
```

This code isn't very efficient, but it will suffice for this simple example. The purpose is to generate numbers from 1 to 6 and return them to the caller. The header for this class is as simple as possible, as we can see here:

chapter08/05-gmock/src/rng_mt19937.h

```
#include "rng.h"
class RandomNumberGeneratorMt19937
        : public RandomNumberGenerator {
 public:
    int Get() override;
};
```

And this is how we're using it in the production code:

chapter08/05-gmock/src/run.cpp

```cpp
#include <iostream>
#include "calc.h"
#include "rng_mt19937.h"
using namespace std;

int run() {
  auto rng = new RandomNumberGeneratorMt19937();
  Calc c(rng);
  cout << "Random dice throw + 1 = "
       << c.AddRandomNumber(1) << endl;
  delete rng;
  return 0;
}
```

We have created a generator and passed a pointer to it to the constructor of `Calc`. Everything is ready, and we can start writing our mock. To keep things organized, developers usually put mocks in a separate `test/mocks` directory. To prevent ambiguity, the header name has a `_mock` suffix. Here is the code we will execute:

chapter08/05-gmock/test/mocks/rng_mock.h

```cpp
#pragma once
#include "gmock/gmock.h"

class RandomNumberGeneratorMock : public
  RandomNumberGenerator {
 public:
  MOCK_METHOD(int, Get, (), (override));
};
```

After adding the gmock.h header, we can declare our mock. As planned, it's a class implementing the RandomNumberGenerator interface. Instead of writing methods ourselves, we need to use MOCK_METHOD macros provided by GMock. These are informing the framework as to which methods from the interface should be mocked. Use the following format (note the parentheses):

```
MOCK_METHOD(<return type>, <method name>,
            (<argument list>), (<keywords>))
```

We're ready to use the mock in our test suite (previous test cases are omited for brevity), as follows:

chapter08/05-gmock/test/calc_test.cpp

```cpp
#include <gtest/gtest.h>
#include "calc.h"
#include "mocks/rng_mock.h"

using namespace ::testing;
class CalcTestSuite : public Test {
 protected:
   RandomNumberGeneratorMock rng_mock_;
   Calc sut_{&rng_mock_};
};

TEST_F(CalcTestSuite, AddRandomNumberAddsThree) {
   EXPECT_CALL(rng_mock_,
Get()).Times(1).WillOnce(Return(3));
   EXPECT_EQ(4, sut_.AddRandomNumber(1));
}
```

Let's break down the changes: we added the new header and created a new field for rng_mock_ in the test suite. Next, the mock's address is passed to the constructor of sut_. We can do that because fields are initialized in order of declaration (rng_mock_ precedes sut_).

In our test case, we call GMock's `EXPECT_CALL` macro on the `Get()` method of `rng_mock_`. This tells the framework to fail the test if the `Get()` method isn't called during execution. The `Times` chained call explicitly states how many calls must happen for the test to pass. `WillOnce` determines what the mocking framework does after the method is called (it returns 3).

By virtue of using GMock, we're able to express mocked behavior alongside the expected outcome. This greatly improves readability and eases the maintenance of tests. Most importantly, though, it provides elasticity in each test case, as we get to differentiate what happens with a single, expressive statement.

Finally, we need to make sure that the `gmock` library is linked with a test runner. To achieve that, we add it to the `target_link_libraries()` list, as follows:

chapter08/05-gmock/test/CMakeLists.txt

```cmake
include(FetchContent)
FetchContent_Declare(
  googletest
  GIT_REPOSITORY https://github.com/google/googletest.git
  GIT_TAG release-1.11.0
)
# For Windows: Prevent overriding the parent project's
  compiler/linker settings
set(gtest_force_shared_crt ON CACHE BOOL "" FORCE)
FetchContent_MakeAvailable(googletest)

add_executable(unit_tests
               calc_test.cpp
               run_test.cpp)
target_link_libraries(unit_tests PRIVATE sut gtest_main
gmock)
include(GoogleTest)
gtest_discover_tests(unit_tests)
```

Now, we can enjoy all the benefits of GTest frameworks. Both GTest and GMock are very advanced tools with a vast multitude of concepts, utilities, and helpers for different occasions. This example (despite being a bit lengthy) only touches the surface of what's possible. I encourage you to incorporate them in your projects as they will greatly increase the quality of your code. A good place to start with GMock is the *Mocking for Dummies* page in the official documentation (you can find a link to this in the *Further reading* section).

Having tests in place, we should somehow measure what's tested and what isn't and strive to improve the situation. It's best to use automated tools that will collect and report this information.

Generating test coverage reports

Adding tests to such a small solution isn't incredibly challenging. The real difficulty comes with slightly more advanced and longer programs. Over the years, I have found that as I approach over 1,000 lines of code, it slowly becomes hard to track which lines and branches are executed during tests and which aren't. After crossing 3,000 lines, it is nearly impossible. Most professional applications will have much more code than that. To deal with this problem, we can use a utility to understand which code lines are "covered" by test cases. Such code coverage tools hook up to the SUT and gather the information on the execution of each line during tests to present it in a convenient report like the one shown here:

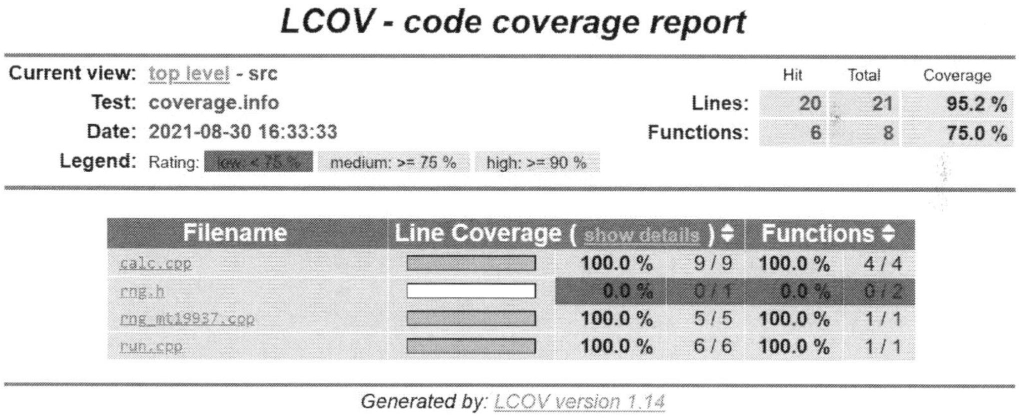

Figure 8.3 – Code coverage report generated by LCOV

These reports will show you which files are covered by tests and which aren't. More than that, you can also take a peek inside the details of each file and see exactly which lines of code are executed and how many times this occurs. In the following screenshot, the **Line data** column says that the `Calc` constructor was run 4 times, one time for each of the tests:

LCOV - code coverage report

Current view:	top level - src - calc.cpp (source / functions)		Hit	Total	Coverage
Test:	coverage.info	Lines:	9	9	100.0 %
Date:	2021-08-30 16:33:33	Functions:	4	4	100.0 %
Legend:	Lines: hit not hit				

Line	Line data	Source code
1	:	#include "calc.h"
2	:	
3	4 :	Calc::Calc(RandomNumberGenerator* rng) {
4	4 :	rng_ = rng;
5	4 :	}
6	:	
7	1 :	int Calc::Sum(int a, int b) {
8	1 :	return a + b;
9	:	}
10	:	
11	1 :	int Calc::Multiply(int a, int b) {
12	1 :	return a * b;
13	:	}
14	:	
15	2 :	int Calc::AddRandomNumber(int a) {
16	2 :	return a + rng_->Get();
17	:	}

Generated by: LCOV version 1.14

Figure 8.4 – Detailed view of a code coverage report

There are multiple ways of generating similar reports and they differ across platforms and compilers, but they generally follow the same procedure: prepare the SUT to be measured, and get the baseline, measure, and report.

The simplest tool for the job is called **LCOV**, and it's a graphical frontend for `gcov`, a coverage utility from the **GNU Compiler Collection (GCC)**. LCOV will generate HTML coverage reports and internally use `gcov` to measure coverage. If you're using Clang, don't worry—Clang supports producing metrics in this format. You can get LCOV from the official repository maintained by the *Linux Test Project* (`https://github.com/linux-test-project/lcov`) or simply use a package manager. As the name suggests, it is a Linux-targeted utility. It's possible to run it on macOS, but the Windows platform is not supported. End users often don't care about test coverage, so it's usually fine to install LCOV manually in your own build environment instead of bolting it to the project.

To measure coverage, we'll need to do the following:

1. Compile in the Debug configuration with compiler flags enabling code coverage. This will generate coverage note (.gcno) files.
2. Link the test executable with the gcov library.
3. Gather coverage metrics for the baseline, without any tests being run.
4. Run the tests. This will create coverage data (.gcda) files.
5. Collect the metrics to an aggregated information file.
6. Generate a (.html) report.

We should start by explaining why the code has to be compiled in the Debug configuration. The most important reason is the fact that usually, Debug configurations have disabled any optimization with a -O0 flag. CMake does this by default in the CMAKE_CXX_FLAGS_DEBUG variable (despite not stating this anywhere in the documentation). Unless you decided to override this variable, your debug build should be unoptimized. This is desired to prevent any inlining and other kinds of implicit code simplification. Otherwise, it would be really hard to trace which machine instruction came from which line of source code.

In the first step, we need to instruct the compiler to add the necessary instrumentation to our SUT. The exact flag to add is compiler-specific; however, two major compilers—GCC and Clang—offer the same --coverage flag that enables coverage, producing data in a GCC-compatible gcov format.

This is how we can add the coverage instrumentation to our exemplary SUT from the previous section:

chapter08/06-coverage/src/CMakeLists.txt

```
add_library(sut STATIC calc.cpp run.cpp rng_mt19937.cpp)
target_include_directories(sut PUBLIC .)

if (CMAKE_BUILD_TYPE STREQUAL Debug)
   target_compile_options(sut PRIVATE --coverage)
   target_link_options(sut PUBLIC --coverage)
   add_custom_command(TARGET sut PRE_BUILD COMMAND
                      find ${CMAKE_BINARY_DIR} -type f
                      -name '*.gcda' -exec rm {} +)
```

```
endif()

add_executable(bootstrap bootstrap.cpp)
target_link_libraries(bootstrap PRIVATE sut)
```

Let's break this down step by step, as follows:

1. Ensure that we're running in the Debug configuration with the `if(STREQUAL)` command. Remember that you won't be able to get any coverage unless you run cmake with the `-DCMAKE_BUILD_TYPE=Debug` option.
2. Add `--coverage` to the `PRIVATE` *compile options* for all *object files* that are part of the sut library.
3. Add `--coverage` to the `PUBLIC` linker options: both GCC and Clang interpret this as a request to link the gcov (or compatible) library with all targets that depend on sut (due to propagated properties).
4. The `add_custom_command()` command is introduced to clean any stale .gcda files. Reasons to add this command are discussed in detail in the *Avoiding the SEGFAULT gotcha* section.

This is enough to produce code coverage. If you're using an IDE such as Clion, you'll be able to run your unit tests with coverage and get the results in a built-in report view. However, this won't work in any automated pipeline that might be run in your CI/CD. To get reports, we'll need to generate them ourselves with LCOV.

For this purpose, it's best to define a new target called coverage. To keep things clean, we'll define a separate function, AddCoverage, in another file to be used in the test listfile, as follows:

chapter08/06-coverage/cmake/Coverage.cmake

```
function(AddCoverage target)
  find_program(LCOV_PATH lcov REQUIRED)
  find_program(GENHTML_PATH genhtml REQUIRED)

  add_custom_target(coverage
    COMMENT "Running coverage for ${target}..."
    COMMAND ${LCOV_PATH} -d . --zerocounters
    COMMAND $<TARGET_FILE:${target}>
    COMMAND ${LCOV_PATH} -d . --capture -o coverage.info
    COMMAND ${LCOV_PATH} -r coverage.info '/usr/include/*'
```

```
                    -o filtered.info
    COMMAND ${GENHTML_PATH} -o coverage filtered.info
        --legend
    COMMAND rm -rf coverage.info filtered.info
    WORKING_DIRECTORY ${CMAKE_BINARY_DIR}
  )
endfunction()
```

In the preceding snippet, we first detect the paths for `lcov` and `genhtml` (two command-line tools from the LCOV package). The `REQUIRED` keyword instructs CMake to throw an error when they're not found. Next, we add a custom `coverage` target with the following steps:

1. Clear the counters from any previous runs.
2. Run the `target` executable (using generator expressions to get its path). `$<TARGET_FILE:target>` is an exceptional generator expression, and it will implicitly add a dependency on `target` in this case, causing it to be built before executing all commands. We'll provide `target` as an argument to this function.
3. Collect metrics for the solution from the current directory (`-d .`) and output to a file (`-o coverage.info`).
4. Remove (`-r`) unwanted coverage data on system headers (`'/usr/include/*'`) and output to another file (`-o filtered.info`).
5. Generate an HTML report in the `coverage` directory, and add a `--legend` color.
6. Remove temporary `.info` files.
7. Specifying the `WORKING_DIRECTORY` keyword sets binary tree as working directory for all commands.

These are the general steps for both GCC and Clang, but it's important to know that the `gcov` tool's version has to match the version of the compiler. In other words, you can't use GCC's `gcov` tool for Clang-compiled code. To point `lcov` to Clang's `gcov` tool, we can use the `--gcov-tool` argument. The only problem here is that it has to be a single executable. To deal with that, we can provide a simple wrapper script (remember to mark it as an executable with `chmod +x`), as follows:

cmake/gcov-llvm-wrapper.sh

```
#!/bin/bash
exec llvm-cov gcov "$@"
```

All of our calls to `${LCOV_PATH}` in the previous function should receive the following additional flag:

```
--gcov-tool ${CMAKE_SOURCE_DIR}/cmake/gcov-llvm-wrapper.sh
```

Make sure that this function is available for inclusion in the `test` listfile. We can do this by extending the *include search path* in the main listfile, as follows:

chapter08/06-coverage/CMakeLists.txt

```
cmake_minimum_required(VERSION 3.20.0)
project(Coverage CXX)
enable_testing()
list(APPEND CMAKE_MODULE_PATH "${CMAKE_SOURCE_DIR}/cmake")
add_subdirectory(src bin)
add_subdirectory(test)
```

This small line allows us to include all `.cmake` files from the `cmake` directory in our project. We can now use `Coverage.cmake` in the `test` listfile, like so:

chapter08/06-coverage/test/CMakeLists.txt (fragment)

```
# ... skipped unit_tests target declaration for brevity

include(Coverage)
AddCoverage(unit_tests)

include(GoogleTest)
gtest_discover_tests(unit_tests)
```

To build this target, use the following commands (notice that first command ends with a `DCMAKE_BUILD_TYPE=Debug` build type selection):

```
# cmake -B <binary_tree> -S <source_tree>
   -DCMAKE_BUILD_TYPE=Debug
# cmake --build <binary_tree> -t coverage
```

After executing all of the mentioned steps, you will see a short summary like this:

```
Writing directory view page.
Overall coverage rate:
```

```
   lines......: 95.2% (20 of 21 lines)
   functions..: 75.0% (6 of 8 functions)
[100%] Built target coverage
```

Next, open the `coverage/index.html` file in your browser and enjoy the reports! There's only one small issue though…

Avoiding the SEGFAULT gotcha

We may get ourselves into trouble when we start editing sources in such a solution. This is because the coverage information is split into two parts, as follows:

- gcno files, or **GNU Coverage Notes**, generated during the compilation of the SUT
- gcda files, or **GNU Coverage Data**, generated **and updated** during test runs

The "update" functionality is a potential source of segmentation faults. After we run our tests initially, we're left with a bunch of gcda files that don't get removed at any point. If we make some changes to the source code and recompile the *object files*, new gcno files will be created. However, there's no wipe step—the old gcda files still follow the stale source. When we execute the `unit_tests` binary (it happens in the `gtest_discover_tests` macro), the coverage information files won't match, and we'll receive a SEGFAULT (segmentation fault) error.

To avoid this problem, we should erase any stale gcda files. Since our sut instance is a STATIC library, we can hook the `add_custom_command(TARGET)` command to building events. The clean will be executed before the rebuild starts.

Find links to more information in the *Further reading* section.

Summary

On the surface, it may seem that complexities associated with proper testing are so great, they aren't worth the effort. It's striking how much code out there is running without any tests at all, the primary argument being that testing your software is a daunting endeavor. I'll add: even more so if done manually. Unfortunately, without rigorous automated testing, visibility of any issues in the code is incomplete or non-existent. Untested code is often quicker to write (not always), but it's definitely much slower to read, refactor, and fix.

In this chapter, we outlined some key reasons for going forward with tests from the get-go. One of the most compelling is mental health and a good night's sleep. Not one developer lies in their bed thinking: *I can't wait to be woken up in a few hours to put out some fires and fix bugs*. But seriously: catching errors before deploying them to production can be a life-saver for you (and the company).

When it comes to testing utilities, CMake really shows its true strength. CTest can do wonders in detecting faulty tests: isolation, shuffling, repetition, timeouts. All these techniques are extremely handy and available through a simple flag straight from the command line. We also learned how we can use CTest to list tests, filter them, and control the output of test cases, but most importantly, we now know the true power of adopting a standard solution across the board. Any project built with CMake can be tested exactly the same, without investigating any details about its internals.

Next, we structured our project to simplify the process of testing and reuse the same *object files* between production code and test runners. It was interesting to write our own test runner, but maybe let's focus on the actual problem our program should solve and invest time in embracing a popular third-party testing framework.

Speaking of which, we learned the very basics of Catch2 and GTest. We further dove into details of the GMock library and understood how test doubles work to make true unit tests possible. Lastly, we set up some reporting with LCOV. After all, there's nothing better than hard data to prove that our solution is, in fact, fully tested.

In the next chapter, we'll discuss more useful tooling to improve the quality of our source code and find issues we didn't even know existed.

Further reading

For more information you can refer to the following links:

- *CMake documentation on CTest*: `https://cmake.org/cmake/help/latest/manual/ctest.1.html`

- *Catch2 documentation*:

  `https://github.com/catchorg/Catch2/blob/devel/docs/cmake-integration.md`

  `https://github.com/catchorg/Catch2/blob/devel/docs/tutorial.md`

- *GMock tutorial*: `https://google.github.io/googletest/gmock_for_dummies.html`

- *Abseil:* https://abseil.io/
- *Live at head with Abseil:* https://abseil.io/about/philosophy#we-recommend-that-you-choose-to-live-at-head
- *Why Abseil is becoming a dependency of GTest:* https://github.com/google/googletest/issues/2883
- *Coverage in GCC:*

  https://gcc.gnu.org/onlinedocs/gcc/Instrumentation-Options.html

  https://gcc.gnu.org/onlinedocs/gcc/Invoking-Gcov.html

  https://gcc.gnu.org/onlinedocs/gcc/Gcov-Data-Files.html
- *Coverage in Clang:* https://clang.llvm.org/docs/SourceBasedCodeCoverage.html
- *LCOV documentation for command-line tools:*

  http://ltp.sourceforge.net/coverage/lcov/lcov.1.php

  http://ltp.sourceforge.net/coverage/lcov/genhtml.1.php
- *GCOV update functionality:* https://gcc.gnu.org/onlinedocs/gcc/Invoking-Gcov.html#Invoking-Gcov

9
Program Analysis Tools

Producing high-quality code is not an easy task, even for very experienced developers. By adding tests to our solution, we reduce the risk of making obvious mistakes in the business code. But that won't be enough to avoid more intricate problems. Every piece of software consists of so many details that keeping track of them all becomes a full-time job. There are dozens of conventions and multiple special design practices agreed upon by teams maintaining the product.

Some questions relate to consistent coding style: should we use 80 or 120 columns in our code? Should we allow `std::bind` or commit to Lambda functions? Is it okay to use C-style arrays? Should small functions be defined in a single line? Should we insist on using `auto` always, or only when it increases readability?

Ideally, we also avoid any statements that are known to be incorrect in general: infinite loops, usage of identifiers reserved by a standard library, unintended loss of precision, redundant `if` statements, and anything else that isn't considered a "best practice" (see the *Further reading* section for references).

Another thing to look at is the modernization of code: as C++ evolves, it offers new features. It can be difficult to track all the places we can refactor to the latest standard. Additionally, manual effort costs time and introduces the risk of bugs, which can be considerable for a large code base.

Finally, we should inspect how things work when they're put into motion: executing the program and examining its memory. Is the memory freed properly after use? Do we access data that was initialized correctly? Or maybe the code tries to dereference some dangling pointers?

Managing all these issues and questions by hand is inefficient and error-prone. Thankfully, we can employ automatic utilities to check and enforce rules, fix mistakes, and modernize code for us. It's time to discover tools for program analysis. Our code will be inspected on every build to ensure that it adheres to industry standards.

In this chapter, we're going to cover the following main topics:

- Enforcing the formatting
- Using static checkers
- Dynamic analysis with Valgrind

Technical requirements

You can find the code files present in this chapter on GitHub at https://github.com/PacktPublishing/Modern-CMake-for-Cpp/tree/main/examples/chapter09.

To build examples provided in this book always use recommended commands:

```
cmake -B <build tree> -S <source tree>
cmake --build <build tree>
```

Be sure to replace placeholders `<build tree>` and `<source tree>` with appropriate paths. As a reminder: **build tree** is the path to target/output directory, **source tree** is the path at which your source code is located.

Enforcing the formatting

Professional developers generally follow rules. They say that senior developers know when to break one (as they can justify the need to). On the other hand, it is said that very senior developers don't break rules because it's a waste of time having to keep explaining their reasons to others. I say, pick your battles and focus on things that actually matter and have a tangible impact on the product.

When it comes to coding style and formatting, programmers are presented with a myriad of choices: should we use tabs or spaces for indentation? If spaces, how many? What is the limit of characters in a column? How about in a file? Such choices don't impact the behavior of the program in most cases, but they do generate a lot of noise and start lengthy discussions that don't bring much value to a product.

Some practices are commonly agreed upon, but most of the time, we're debating personal preference and anecdotal evidence. After all, enforcing 80 characters in a column over 120 is an arbitrary choice. It doesn't really matter what we're going to choose as long as we're consistent. Inconsistency in style is bad, as it affects an important aspect of the software – the readability of the code.

The best way to avoid it is to use a formatting tool such as `clang-format`. This can alert us that the code isn't formatted properly and even fix things that stand out if we let it. Here's an example of a command that formats code:

```
clang-format -i --style=LLVM filename1.cpp filename2.cpp
```

The `-i` option tells ClangFormat to edit files in place. `--style` selects which supported formatting style should be used: `LLVM`, `Google`, `Chromium`, `Mozilla`, `WebKit`, or custom, provided from `file` (there are links to details in the *Further reading* section).

Of course, we don't want to execute this command manually every time we make a change; CMake should take care of this as part of the building process. We already know how to find `clang-format` in the system (we'll need to install it manually beforehand). What we haven't discussed yet is the process of applying an external tool to all of our source files. To do it, we'll create a convenient function that can be included from the `cmake` directory:

chapter09/01-formatting/cmake/Format.cmake

```cmake
function(Format target directory)
   find_program(CLANG-FORMAT_PATH clang-format REQUIRED)
   set(EXPRESSION h hpp hh c cc cxx cpp)
   list(TRANSFORM EXPRESSION PREPEND "${directory}/*.")
   file(GLOB_RECURSE SOURCE_FILES FOLLOW_SYMLINKS
        LIST_DIRECTORIES false ${EXPRESSION}
   )
   add_custom_command(TARGET ${target} PRE_BUILD COMMAND
        ${CLANG-FORMAT_PATH} -i --style=file ${SOURCE_FILES}
```

```
    )
endfunction()
```

The `Format` function takes two arguments: `target` and `directory`. It will format all source files from `directory`, right before `target` is built.

Technically, not all files in `directory` must necessarily belong to `target` (and target sources can potentially be in multiple directories). However, finding all the source files and headers that belong to the target (and possible dependent targets) is a very complex process, especially when we need to filter out headers that belong to external libraries and shouldn't be formatted. It's just more manageable to work on directories in this scenario. We can just call the function for each directory of the formatted target.

This function has the following steps:

1. Find the `clang-format` binary installed in the system. The `REQUIRED` keyword will stop the configuration with an error if the binary wasn't found.
2. Create a list of file extensions to format (to be used as a *globbing expression*).
3. Prepend each expression with a path to `directory`.
4. Recursively search for sources and headers (using the previously created list), skip directories, and put their paths into the `SOURCE_FILES` variable.
5. Hook the formatting command as the `PRE_BUILD` step of `target`.

This command will work well for small-to-medium code bases. For high amounts of files, we'd need to transform absolute file paths to relative paths and execute formatting using `directory` as a working directory (the `list(TRANSFORM)` command is useful here). This might be necessary because commands passed to the shell have a limit on their length (usually about 13,000 characters) and too many long paths simply won't fit.

Let's see how we can use this function in practice. We'll use the following project structure:

```
- CMakeLists.txt
- .clang-format
- cmake
  |- Format.cmake
- src
  |- CMakeLists.txt
  |- header.h
  |- main.cpp
```

First, we'll need to set up the project and add the cmake directory to the module path so that we can include it later:

chapter09/01-formatting/CMakeLists.txt

```cmake
cmake_minimum_required(VERSION 3.20.0)
project(Formatting CXX)
enable_testing()
list(APPEND CMAKE_MODULE_PATH "${CMAKE_SOURCE_DIR}/cmake")
add_subdirectory(src bin)
```

Having that set, let's fill in the list file for the `src` directory:

chapter09/01-formatting/src/CMakeLists.txt

```cmake
add_executable(main main.cpp)
include(Format)
Format(main .)
```

This is simple and to the point. We have created an executable target `main`, included the `Format.cmake` module, and called the `Format()` function for the `main` target in the current directory (`src`).

Now, we need some unformatted source files. The header is just a simple `unused` function:

chapter09/01-formatting/src/header.h

```cpp
int unused() { return 2 + 2; }
```

We'll also add a source file with way too much whitespace:

chapter09/01-formatting/src/main.cpp

```cpp
#include <iostream>
  using namespace std;
    int main() {

        cout << "Hello, world!" << endl;
    }
```

We're almost set. All that's left is the configuration file of the formatter (which is enabled with the `--style=file` argument in the command line):

chapter09/01-formatting/.clang-format

```
BasedOnStyle: Google
ColumnLimit: 140
UseTab: Never
AllowShortLoopsOnASingleLine: false
AllowShortFunctionsOnASingleLine: false
AllowShortIfStatementsOnASingleLine: false
```

Clang Format will scan the parent directories for the `.clang-format` file, which specifies the exact formatting rules. This allows us to specify every little detail, or to customize one of the standards mentioned earlier. In my case, I've chosen to start with Google's coding style and throw in a few tweaks: limit columns to 140 characters, remove tabs, and allow short loops, functions, and `if` statements.

Let's see how files have changed after building this project (formatting happens automatically before compilation):

chapter09/01-formatting/src/header.h (formatted)

```
int unused() {
  return 2 + 2;
}
```

The header file was formatted, even though it isn't used by the target; short functions aren't allowed on a single line. The formatter added new lines, just as expected. The `main.cpp` file also looks pretty slick now:

chapter09/01-formatting/src/main.cpp (formatted)

```
#include <iostream>
using namespace std;
int main() {
  cout << "Hello, world!" << endl;
}
```

Unnecessary whitespace was removed and indentations were standardized.

Adding the automated formatter isn't too big of an effort and will save you a bunch of time in code reviews. If you've ever had to amend a commit to correct some whitespace, you know the feeling. Consistent formatting keeps your code neat without any effort.

> **Note**
> Applying formatting to an existing code base will most likely introduce a big one-off change to the majority of the files in the repository. This may cause *a lot* of merge conflicts if you (or your teammates) have some ongoing work. It's best to coordinate such efforts to happen after all pending changes are done. If this isn't possible, consider gradual adoption, perhaps on a per-directory basis. Your fellow developers will thank you.

The formatter is a great and simple tool to bring the visual aspect of the code together, but it isn't a fully fledged program analysis tool (it focuses mostly on whitespace). To deal with more advanced scenarios, we need to reach for utilities capable of understanding the program's source to perform a static analysis.

Using static checkers

Static program analysis is the process of checking the source code without actually running the compiled version. The rigorous application of static checkers dramatically improves the quality of the code: it becomes more consistent and less bug-prone. The chance of introducing known security vulnerabilities is reduced too. The C++ community has created dozens of static checkers: Astrée, Clang-Tidy, CLazy, CMetrics, Cppcheck, Cpplint, CQMetrics, ESBMC, FlawFinder, Flint, IKOS, Joern, PC-Lint, Scan-Build, Vera++, and so on.

Many of them recognize CMake as the industry standard and will provide out-of-the-box support (or an integration tutorial). Some build engineers don't want to go to the trouble of writing CMake code, and they add static checkers by including external modules available online, such as those collected by Lars Bilke in his GitHub repository: `https://github.com/bilke/cmake-modules`.

It's no wonder, as the general misconception is that you'd need to jump through many hoops to get your code checked. The reason for this complexity is in the nature of static checkers: they often mimic the behavior of a real compiler to understand what happens in the code.

Cppcheck recommends the following steps in its manual:

1. Find the static checker's executable.
2. Generate a *compile database* with the following:

   ```
   cmake -DCMAKE_EXPORT_COMPILE_COMMANDS=ON .
   ```

3. Run the checker on the produced JSON file:

   ```
   <path-to-cppcheck> --project=compile_commands.json
   ```

All that should happen as part of the build so that it doesn't get forgotten.

Since CMake understands exactly how we want our targets built, can't it support some of these utilities? At least the most popular? Sure, it can! This gem of a feature is hard to find among the online noise, despite being so simple to use. CMake supports enabling checkers on a per-target basis for the following tools:

- include-what-you-use (`https://include-what-you-use.org`)
- Clang-Tidy (`https://clang.llvm.org/extra/clang-tidy`)
- link what you use (a built-in CMake checker)
- cpplint (`https://github.com/cpplint/cpplint`)
- Cppchecker (`https://cppcheck.sourceforge.io`)

All we need to do is set an appropriate target property to a semicolon-separated list containing the path to the checker's executable, followed by any command-line options that should be forwarded to the checker:

- `<LANG>_CLANG_TIDY`
- `<LANG>_CPPCHECK`
- `<LANG>_CPPLINT`
- `<LANG>_INCLUDE_WHAT_YOU_USE`
- `LINK_WHAT_YOU_USE`

As usual, `<LANG>` should be replaced with the language used, so use C for C sources and CXX for C++. If you don't need to control the checker on a per-target basis, you can specify a default value for all targets in the project by setting an appropriate global variable prefixed with `CMAKE_`, such as the following:

```
set(CMAKE_CXX_CLANG_TIDY /usr/bin/clang-tidy-3.9;-checks=*)
```

Any target defined after this statement will have its CXX_CLANG_TIDY property set the same way. Just keep in mind that this adds the analysis to regular builds, which will make them slightly longer.

On the other hand, there's some value in more granular control of how targets should be tested by the checker. We can write a simple function to solve this for us:

chapter09/02-clang-tidy/cmake/ClangTidy.cmake

```
function(AddClangTidy target)
  find_program(CLANG-TIDY_PATH clang-tidy REQUIRED)
  set_target_properties(${target}
    PROPERTIES CXX_CLANG_TIDY
    "${CLANG-TIDY_PATH};-checks=*;--warnings-as-errors=*"
  )
endfunction()
```

The AddClangTidy function has two simple steps:

1. Find the Clang-Tidy binary and store its path in CLANG-TIDY_PATH. The REQUIRED keyword will stop the configuration with an error if the binary wasn't found.
2. Enable Clang-Tidy on target, provide the path to the binary and custom options to enable all checks, and treat warnings as errors.

To use this function, we just need to include the module and call it for the chosen target:

chapter09/02-clang-tidy/src/CMakeLists.txt

```
add_library(sut STATIC calc.cpp run.cpp)
target_include_directories(sut PUBLIC .)

add_executable(bootstrap bootstrap.cpp)
target_link_libraries(bootstrap PRIVATE sut)

include(ClangTidy)
AddClangTidy(sut)
```

This is short and extremely powerful. As we build the solution, we can see the output from Clang-Tidy:

```
[  6%] Building CXX object bin/CMakeFiles/sut.dir/calc.cpp.o
/root/examples/chapter09/04-clang-tidy/src/calc.cpp:3:11:
warning: method 'Sum' can be made static [readability-convert-
member-functions-to-static]
int Calc::Sum(int a, int b) {
          ^
[ 12%] Building CXX object bin/CMakeFiles/sut.dir/run.cpp.o
/root/examples/chapter09/04-clang-tidy/src/run.cpp:1:1:
warning: #includes are not sorted properly [llvm-include-order]
#include <iostream>
^      ~~~~~~~~~~~
/root/examples/chapter09/04-clang-tidy/src/run.cpp:3:1:
warning: do not use namespace using-directives; use using-
declarations instead [google-build-using-namespace]
using namespace std;
^
/root/examples/chapter09/04-clang-tidy/src/run.cpp:6:3:
warning: initializing non-owner 'Calc *' with a newly created
'gsl::owner<>' [cppcoreguidelines-owning-memory]
    auto c = new Calc();
    ^
```

Note that unless you add the `--warnings-as-errors=*` option to the command-line arguments, the build will succeed. It is recommended to agree on a list of rules that will be enforced and fail builds that break them; this way, we'll prevent non-compliant code from tainting the repository.

`clang-tidy` also offers an interesting `--fix` option, which will automatically correct your code where possible. This is definitely a great timesaver and can be used whenever you're increasing the number of checks. As with formatting, be sure to avoid merge conflicts when introducing any changes generated by static analysis tools to legacy code bases.

Depending on your use case, the size of the repository, and team preferences, you should probably choose a few checkers that are a good match. Adding too many will become a nuisance. Here's a short introduction to checkers supported by CMake out-of-the-box.

Clang-Tidy

Here is a description of Clang-Tidy from the official website:

> *clang-tidy is a clang-based C++ "linter" tool. Its purpose is to provide an extensible framework for diagnosing and fixing typical programming errors, like style violations, interface misuse, or bugs that can be deduced via static analysis. clang-tidy is modular and provides a convenient interface for writing new checks.*

The versatility of this tool is really impressive, as it offers over 400 checks. It works well paired with ClangFormat, as the fixes applied automatically (over 150 available) can follow the same format file. Offered checks include improvements in performance, readability, modernization, cpp-core-guidelines, and bug-prone namespaces.

Cpplint

Here is a description of Cpplint from the official website:

> *Cpplint is a command-line tool to check C/C++ files for style issues following Google's C++ style guide. Cpplint is developed and maintained by Google Inc. at google/styleguide.*

This linter is meant to get your code in line with the aforementioned Google style. It is written in Python, which might be an unwanted dependency for some projects. The fixes are offered in formats consumable by Emacs, Eclipse, VS7, Junit, and as `sed` commands.

Cppcheck

Here is a description of Cppcheck from the official website:

> *Cppcheck is a static analysis tool for C/C++ code. It provides unique code analysis to detect bugs and focuses on detecting undefined behaviour and dangerous coding constructs. The goal is to have very few false positives. Cppcheck is designed to be able to analyze your C/C++ code even if it has non-standard syntax (common in embedded projects).*

This tool is worth recommending for peace of mind when it comes to avoiding unnecessary noise generated by false positives. It is quite well established (over 14 years in the making) and still very actively maintained. Also, you might find it useful if your code doesn't compile with Clang.

include-what-you-use

Here is a description of include-what-you-use from the official website:

> *The main goal of include-what-you-use is to remove superfluous #includes. It does this both by figuring out what #includes are not actually needed for this file (for both .cc and .h files), and replacing #includes with forward-declares when possible.*

Too many included headers might not seem like a really big problem if your code base is slim. In larger projects, time saved by avoiding unnecessary compilation of header files quickly adds up.

Link what you use

Here is a description of link-what-you-use on CMake's blog:

> *This is a built in CMake feature that uses options of ld and ldd to print out if executables link more libraries than they actually require.*

This also speeds up the build time; only in this case we're focusing on the unneeded binary artifacts.

Static analysis is critical where software errors can affect people's safety, especially in medical, nuclear, aviation, automotive, and machine industries. Smart developers know that it doesn't hurt to follow similar practices in less demanding environments, most of all when the costs of adoption are so low. Using static analyzers during the build is not only much cheaper than finding and fixing bugs manually; it's also easy to enable with CMake. I'd even go as far to say that there's almost no excuse to skip these checks in quality-sensitive software (that is, all software involving someone else other than the programmer).

Unfortunately, not all bugs can be caught before a program is executed. What can we do to get an even better insight into our projects?

Dynamic analysis with Valgrind

Valgrind (https://www.valgrind.org) is an instrumentation framework that allows building dynamic analysis utilities – that is, analysis performed during a program's runtime. It offers an extensive tool suite that allows all kinds of investigations and checks. Some of the tools are as follows:

- Memcheck – detects memory-management problems
- Cachegrind – profiles CPU caches, and pinpoints cache misses and other cache issues
- Callgrind – an extension of Cachegrind with extra information on call graphs
- Massif – a heap profiler that shows which parts of the program use heap over time
- Helgrind – a thread debugger, which helps with data race issues
- DRD – a lighter, limited version of Helgrind

Every single tool from this list is extremely handy when the occasion is right. Most package managers know Valgrind and can install it on your OS with ease (it's possible that it's already installed if you're using Linux). In any case, the official website offers the source code, so you can build it yourself.

We'll limit our focus to the most useful application from the suite. When people refer to Valgrind, they very often mean Valgrind's Memcheck. Let's figure out how to use it with CMake – it will pave the way for the adoption of other tools, should you need them.

Memcheck

Memcheck can be indispensable when debugging memory issues. This subject is particularly tricky in C++, as programmers have tremendous control over how they manage memory. All kinds of mistakes are possible: reading unallocated memory, reading memory that was already freed, attempting to free memory more than once, and writing to incorrect addresses. Developers obviously try to avoid these, but since these bugs are so inconspicuous, they can sneak into even the simplest programs. Sometimes, all it takes is a forgotten variable initialization and we're in a pinch.

Invoking Memcheck looks like this:

```
valgrind [valgrind-options] tested-binary [binary-options]
```

Memcheck is the default tool of Valgrind, but you can also select it explicitly:

```
valgrind --tool=memcheck tested-binary
```

Running Memcheck is expensive; the manual (see the link in *Further reading*) says that programs instrumented with it can be 10–15 times slower. To avoid waiting for Valgrind every time we run tests, we'll create a separate target that will be called from the command line whenever we need to test our code. Ideally, the developer will run it before merging their change to the default branch of the repository. This can be done with an early Git hook or added as a step in the CI pipeline. To build a custom target, we'll use the following command after the generation stage has been completed:

```
cmake --build <build-tree> -t valgrind
```

Adding such a target isn't very difficult:

chapter09/03-valgrind/cmake/Valgrind.cmake

```
function(AddValgrind target)
    find_program(VALGRIND_PATH valgrind REQUIRED)
    add_custom_target(valgrind
        COMMAND ${VALGRIND_PATH} --leak-check=yes
            $<TARGET_FILE:${target}>
        WORKING_DIRECTORY ${CMAKE_BINARY_DIR}
    )
endfunction()
```

In this example, we created a CMake module (so we can reuse the same file across projects) wrapping function that will accept the target to be tested. Two things happen here:

- CMake searches default system paths for the `valgrind` executable and stores it in the `VALGRIND_PATH` variable. The `REQUIRED` keyword will stop the configuration with an error if the binary wasn't found.

- A custom target, `valgrind`, is created; it will execute the Memcheck tool on the `target` binary. We also added an option to always check for memory leaks.

When it comes to Valgrind options, we can provide them as command-line arguments and also in the following:

1. The `~/.valgrindrc` file (in your home directory)
2. The `$VALGRIND_OPTS` environment variable
3. The `./.valgrindrc` file (in the working directory)

These are checked in that order. Also, note that the last file will only be considered if it belongs to the current user, is a regular file, and isn't marked as world-writable. This is a safety mechanism, as options given to Valgrind can be potentially harmful.

To use the `AddValgrind` function, we should provide it with a unit_tests target:

chapter09/03-valgrind/test/CMakeLists.txt (fragment)

```
# ...
add_executable(unit_tests calc_test.cpp run_test.cpp)
# ...
include(Valgrind)
AddValgrind(unit_tests)
```

Remember that generating build trees with the `Debug` config allows Valgrind to tap into the debug information, which makes its output much clearer. Let's see how this works in practice:

```
# cmake --build <build-tree> -t valgrind
```

This will build the `sut` and `unit_tests` targets:

```
[100%] Built target unit_tests
```

Start the execution of Memcheck, which will provide us with general information:

```
==954== Memcheck, a memory error detector
==954== Copyright (C) 2002-2017, and GNU GPL'd, by Julian Seward et al.
==954== Using Valgrind-3.15.0 and LibVEX; rerun with -h for copyright info
==954== Command: ./unit_tests
```

The `==954==` prefix contains the process ID. This is added to distinguish Valgrind commentary from the output of the tested process.

Next, tests are run as usual with `gtest`:

```
[==========] Running 3 tests from 2 test suites.
[----------] Global test environment set-up.
...
[==========] 3 tests from 2 test suites ran. (42 ms total)
[  PASSED  ] 3 tests.
```

At the end, a summary is presented:

```
==954==
==954== HEAP SUMMARY:
==954==     in use at exit: 1 bytes in 1 blocks
==954==   total heap usage: 209 allocs, 208 frees, 115,555 bytes allocated
```

Uh-oh! We are still using at least 1 byte. Allocations made with `malloc()` and `new` aren't matched with appropriate `free()` and `delete` operations. It seems we have a memory leak in our program. Valgrind provides more details to find it:

```
==954== 1 bytes in 1 blocks are definitely lost in loss record 1 of 1
==954==    at 0x483BE63: operator new(unsigned long) (in /usr/lib/x86_64-linux-gnu/valgrind/vgpreload_memcheck-amd64-linux.so)
==954==    by 0x114FC5: run() (run.cpp:6)
==954==    by 0x1142B9: RunTest_RunOutputsCorrectEquations_Test::TestBody() (run_test.cpp:14)
```

Lines starting with `by 0x<address>` indicate individual functions in a call stack. I've truncated the output (it had some noise from GTest) to focus on the interesting bit – the topmost function and source reference, `run() (run.cpp:6)`:

Finally, the summary is found at the bottom:

```
==954== LEAK SUMMARY:
==954==    definitely lost: 1 bytes in 1 blocks
==954==    indirectly lost: 0 bytes in 0 blocks
==954==      possibly lost: 0 bytes in 0 blocks
==954==    still reachable: 0 bytes in 0 blocks
==954==         suppressed: 0 bytes in 0 blocks
```

```
==954==
==954== ERROR SUMMARY: 1 errors from 1 contexts (suppressed: 0
from 0)
```

Valgrind does a very good job of finding very intricate issues. On occasion, it's capable of digging even deeper to find questionable situations that can't be categorized automatically. Such discoveries will be accounted for in the `possibly lost` row.

Let's see what the issue found by Memcheck was in this case:

chapter09/03-valgrind/src/run.cpp

```cpp
#include <iostream>
#include "calc.h"
using namespace std;

int run() {
    auto c = new Calc();
    cout << "2 + 2 = " << c->Sum(2, 2) << endl;
    cout << "3 * 3 = " << c->Multiply(3, 3) << endl;
    return 0;
}
```

That's right: the highlighted code is faulty. We do, in fact, create an object that isn't deleted before the test ends. This is the exact reason why having extensive test coverage is so important.

Valgrind is an extremely useful tool, but it can get a bit verbose when dealing with more complex programs. There must be a way to collect that information in a more manageable form.

Memcheck-Cover

Commercial IDEs such as CLion natively support parsing Valgrind's output to something that can be easily navigated through GUI without scrolling through the console window to find the right message. If your editor doesn't have this option, you still can get a much clearer view of the errors by using a third-party report generator. Memcheck-cover, written by David Garcin, offers a nicer experience in the form of a generated HTML file, as shown in *Figure 9.1*:

Figure 9.1 – A report generated by memcheck-cover

This neat little project is available on GitHub (`https://github.com/Farigh/memcheck-cover`); it requires Valgrind and `gawk` (GNU AWK tool). To use it, we'll prepare a setup function in a separate CMake module. It will consist of two parts:

- Fetching and configuring the tool
- Adding a custom target that executes Valgrind and generates a report

The configuration looks as follows:

chapter09/04-memcheck/cmake/Memcheck.cmake

```
function(AddMemcheck target)
  include(FetchContent)
  FetchContent_Declare(
    memcheck-cover
    GIT_REPOSITORY https://github.com/Farigh/memcheck-cover.git
    GIT_TAG        release-1.2
  )
  FetchContent_MakeAvailable(memcheck-cover)
  set(MEMCHECK_PATH ${memcheck-cover_SOURCE_DIR}/bin)
```

In the first part, we follow the same practices as with a regular dependency: include the `FetchContent` module, and specify the project's repository and desired Git tag with `FetchContent_Declare`. Next, we initiate the fetch process and configure the path to the binary using the `memcheck-cover_SOURCE_DIR` variable set by `FetchContent_Populate` (called implicitly by `FetchContent_MakeAvailable`).

The second part of the function is creating the target to generate reports. We'll call it `memcheck` (so that it doesn't overlap with the previous `valgrind` target if we want to keep both options for some reason):

chapter09/04-memcheck/cmake/Memcheck.cmake (continued)

```
  add_custom_target(memcheck
    COMMAND ${MEMCHECK_PATH}/memcheck_runner.sh -o
      "${CMAKE_BINARY_DIR}/valgrind/report"
      -- $<TARGET_FILE:${target}>
    COMMAND ${MEMCHECK_PATH}/generate_html_report.sh
      -i "${CMAKE_BINARY_DIR}/valgrind"
      -o "${CMAKE_BINARY_DIR}/valgrind"
    WORKING_DIRECTORY ${CMAKE_BINARY_DIR}
  )
endfunction()
```

This happens in two commands:

1. First, we'll run the `memcheck_runner.sh` wrapper script, which will execute Valgrind's Memcheck and collect the output to the file provided with the `-o` argument.
2. Then, we'll parse the output and create the report with `generate_html_report.sh`. This script requires input and output directories provided with the `-i` and `-o` arguments.

Both steps should be executed in the `CMAKE_BINARY_DIR` working directory so that the unit test binary can access files through relative paths if needed.

The last thing we need to add to our list files is, of course, a call to this function. It has the same pattern as `AddValgrind`:

chapter09/04-memcheck/test/CMakeLists.txt (fragment)

```
include(Memcheck)
AddMemcheck(unit_tests)
```

After generating a buildsystem with the `Debug` config, we can build the target with the following:

```
cmake --build <build-tree> -t memcheck
```

And then we can enjoy our formatted report. Well, to truly enjoy it we'll need to add that missing `delete c;` in `run.cpp` so that it stops complaining (or, better yet, use a smart pointer instead).

Summary

> *"You'll spend more time studying the code than creating it – therefore, you should optimize for reading rather than writing."*

This sentence is repeated like a mantra in more than one book discussing clean code practices. No wonder, as this is very true, as tested in practice by many software developers – so much so that rules for even minuscule things such as the numbers of spaces, newlines, and the ordering of `#import` statements have been codified. This isn't done out of pettiness, but to save time. By following the practices outlined in this chapter, we don't need to worry about formatting code correctly by hand. It will automatically get formatted as a side effect of building – a step that we have to do anyway to check whether the code is working correctly. By introducing ClangFormat, we can also ensure that it looks proper.

Of course, we want more than a simple whitespace correction; code has to conform to dozens of other small regulations. This is done by the addition of Clang-Tidy and configuring it to enforce the coding style of our choosing. We discussed this static checker in detail, but we also mentioned other options: Cpplint, Cppcheck, Include-what-you-use, and Link-what-you-use. Since static linkers are relatively fast, we can add them to builds with little investment, and it will usually be well worth the price.

Lastly, we looked at the Valgrind utilities, specifically Memcheck, which allows debugging problems related to memory management: incorrect reads, writes, deallocations, and so on. This is a very handy tool that can save hours of manual investigation and prevent bugs from sneaking into production. As mentioned, it can be a bit slow to execute, which is why we created a separate target to run it explicitly before submitting the code. We also learned how to present the output of Valgrind in a more approachable form with Memcheck-Cover, an HTML report generator. This can be really useful in environments that don't support running an IDE (such as CI pipelines).

Of course, we aren't limited to these tools; there's plenty more: both free and open source projects, as well as commercial products coming with extensive support. This is merely an introduction to the subject. Be sure to explore what's right for you. In the next chapter, we'll take a closer look at documentation generation.

Further reading

For more information, you can refer to the following links:

- *C++ Core guidelines curated by Bjarne Stroustrup, author of C++:* https://github.com/isocpp/CppCoreGuidelines
- *The ClangFormat reference:* https://clang.llvm.org/docs/ClangFormat.html
- *Static analyzers for C++ – a curated list:* https://github.com/analysis-tools-dev/static-analysis#cpp
- *Built-in static checker support in CMake:* https://blog.kitware.com/static-checks-with-cmake-cdash-iwyu-clang-tidy-lwyu-cpplint-and-cppcheck/
- *A target property enabling ClangTidy:* https://cmake.org/cmake/help/latest/prop_tgt/LANG_CLANG_TIDY.html
- *The Valgrind manual:* https://www.valgrind.org/docs/manual/manual-core.html

10
Generating Documentation

High-quality code is not only well written, working, and tested—it is also thoroughly documented. Documentation allows us to share information that could otherwise get lost, draw a bigger picture, give context, reveal intent, and—finally—educate both external users and maintainers.

Do you remember the last time you joined a new project and got lost for hours in a maze of directories and files? This can be avoided. Truly excellent documentation will lead a complete newcomer to the exact line of code they're looking for in seconds. Sadly, the subject of missing documentation is often swept under the rug. No wonder—it takes a lot of skill and many of us aren't very good at it. On top of that, documentation and code can really part ways very quickly. Unless a strict update and review process is put in place, it's easy to forget that documentation needs work too.

Some teams (in the interest of time or encouraged by managers) follow a practice of writing "self-documenting code". By picking meaningful, readable identifiers for filenames, functions, variables, and whatnot, they hope to avoid the chore of documenting. While the habit of good naming is absolutely correct, it won't replace documentation. Even the best function signatures don't guarantee that all necessary information is conveyed—for example, `int removeDuplicates();` is quite descriptive, but it doesn't reveal what is returned! It may be the number of duplicates found, the number of items left, or something else—it's not certain. Remember: there's no such thing as a free lunch.

To make things easier, professionals use automatic documentation generators that can analyze the code and comments in source files to produce comprehensive documentation in multiple different formats. Adding such generators to a CMake project is very simple—let's see how!

In this chapter, we're going to cover the following main topics:

- Adding Doxygen to your project
- Generating documentation with a modern look

Technical requirements

You can find the code files present in this chapter on GitHub at the following link: https://github.com/PacktPublishing/Modern-CMake-for-Cpp/tree/main/examples/chapter10

To build examples provided in this book always use recommended commands:

```
cmake -B <build tree> -S <source tree>
cmake --build <build tree>
```

Be sure to replace placeholders <build tree> and <source tree> with appropriate paths. As a reminder: **build tree** is the path to target/output directory, **source tree** is the path at which your source code is located.

Adding Doxygen to your project

One of the most established and popular tools that can generate documentation from C++ sources is Doxygen. And when I say "established", I mean it: the first version was released by Dimitri van Heesch in October 1997. Since then, it has grown immensely, and it is actively supported by over 180 contributors to its repository (https://github.com/doxygen/doxygen).

Doxygen can produce documentation in the following formats:

- **HyperText Markup Language (HTML)**
- **Rich Text Format (RTF)**
- **Portable Document Format (PDF)**
- **Lamport's TeX (LaTeX)**

- **PostScript (PS)**
- **Unix manual (man pages)**
- **Microsoft Compiled HTML Help (CHM)**

If you decorate your code with comments providing additional information in the format specified by Doxygen, it will be parsed to enrich the output file. What's more, the code structure will be analyzed to produce helpful charts and diagrams. The latter is optional, as it requires an external Graphviz tool (https://graphviz.org/).

The developer should first answer the following question: *Do users of the project just get the documentation or will they generate it themselves (perhaps when they build from source)?* The first option implies that documentation is shipped with the binaries, available online, or (less elegantly) checked in with the source code into the repository.

The answer matters, because if we want users to generate documentation during the build, they will need the dependencies present in their system. This isn't too large a problem since Doxygen is available through most package managers (as well as Graphviz), and all that's needed is a simple command, such as this one for Debian:

```
apt-get install doxygen graphviz
```

There are also binaries available for Windows (check the project's website).

To summarize: generate documentation for users or handle adding the dependencies if needed. This is covered in *Chapter 7, Managing Dependencies with CMake*, so we won't repeat the steps here. Note that Doxygen is built with CMake, so you can easily compile it from source as well.

When Doxygen and Graphviz are installed in the system, we can add the generation to our project. Unlike as suggested by online sources, this isn't as hard or involved as we might think. We don't need to create external configuration files, provide paths to the doxygen executable, or add custom targets. Since CMake 3.9, we can use the doxygen_add_docs() function from FindDoxygen find-module, which sets the documentation target up.

The signature looks like this:

```
doxygen_add_docs(targetName [sourceFilesOrDirs...]
    [ALL] [USE_STAMP_FILE] [WORKING_DIRECTORY dir]
    [COMMENT comment])
```

The first argument specifies the target name, which we'll need to build explicitly with the `-t` argument to `cmake` (after generating a build tree), as follows:

```
cmake --build <build-tree> -t targetName
```

Or, we can always have it be built by adding the `ALL` argument (usually not necessary). Other options are pretty self-explanatory, except maybe `USE_STAMP_FILE`. This allows CMake to skip regeneration of documentation if none of the source files have changed (but requires `sourceFilesOrDirs` to only contain files).

We'll follow the practice from previous chapters and create a utility module with a helper function (so that it can be reused in other projects), as follows:

chapter-10/01-doxygen/cmake/Doxygen.cmake

```cmake
function(Doxygen input output)
    find_package(Doxygen)
    if (NOT DOXYGEN_FOUND)
        add_custom_target(doxygen COMMAND false
            COMMENT "Doxygen not found")
        return()
    endif()
    set(DOXYGEN_GENERATE_HTML YES)
    set(DOXYGEN_HTML_OUTPUT
        ${PROJECT_BINARY_DIR}/${output})

    doxygen_add_docs(doxygen
        ${PROJECT_SOURCE_DIR}/${input}
        COMMENT "Generate HTML documentation"
    )
endfunction()
```

The function accepts two arguments—`input` and `output` directories—and will create a custom `doxygen` target. Here's what happens:

1. First, we'll use CMake's built-in Doxygen find-module to figure out if Doxygen is available in the system.
2. If it isn't available, we'll create a dummy `doxygen` target that will inform the user and run a `false` command, which (on Unix-like systems) returns 1, causing the build to fail. We terminate the function at that time with `return()`.
3. If Doxygen is available, we'll configure it to generate HTML output in the provided `output` directory. Doxygen is extremely configurable (find out more in the official documentation). To set any option, just follow the example by calling `set()` and prepend its name with `DOXYGEN_`.
4. Set up the actual `doxygen` target: all the `DOXYGEN_` variables will be forwarded to Doxygen's configuration file, and documentation will be generated from the provided `input` directory in the source tree.

If your documentation is to be generated by users, *Step 2* should probably involve installing the necessary dependencies instead.

To use this function, we can add it to the main listfile of our project, as follows:

chapter-10/01-doxygen/CMakeLists.txt

```
cmake_minimum_required(VERSION 3.20.0)
project(Doxygen CXX)
enable_testing()
list(APPEND CMAKE_MODULE_PATH "${CMAKE_SOURCE_DIR}/cmake")
add_subdirectory(src bin)

include(Doxygen)
Doxygen(src docs)
```

Not difficult at all. Building the doxygen target generates HTML documentation that looks like this:

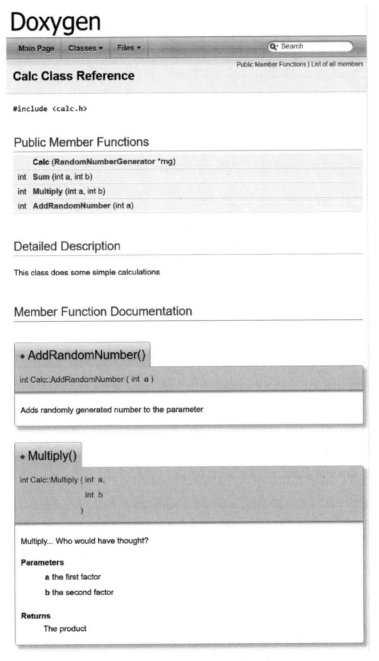

Figure 10.1 – Class reference generated with Doxygen

The additional description you can see in **Member Function Documentation** is added by prepending the method with an appropriate comment in the header file, as follows:

chapter-10/01-doxygen/src/calc.h (fragment)

```
/**
    Multiply... Who would have thought?
    @param a the first factor
    @param b the second factor
    @result The product
*/
int Multiply(int a, int b);
```

This format is known as Javadoc. It is important to open the comment block with double asterisks: /**. More information can be found in the description of Doxygen's docblocks (see the link in the *Further reading* section).

As mentioned earlier, if Graphviz is installed, Doxygen will detect it and generate dependency diagrams, as illustrated here:

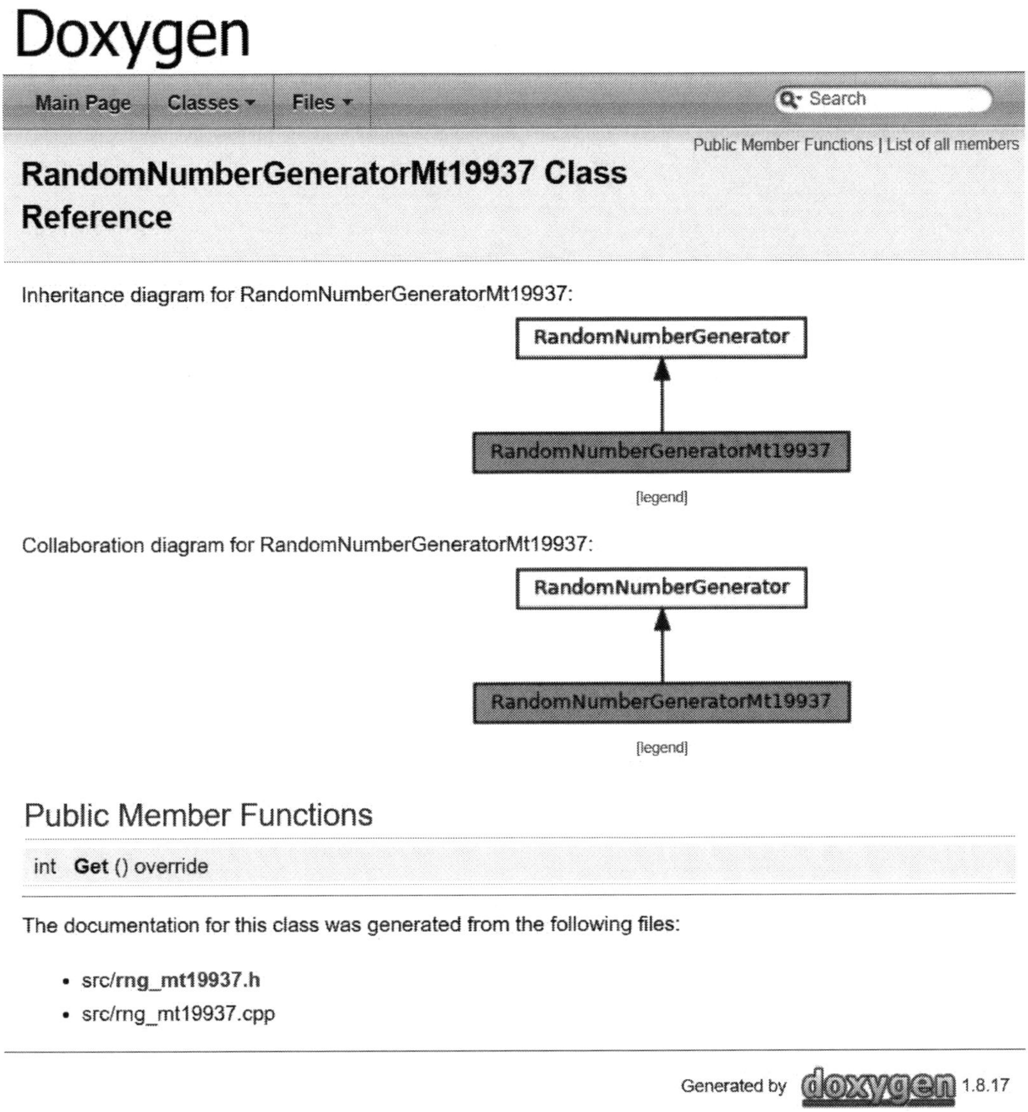

Doxygen

Main Page | **Classes ▼** | **Files ▼** | Search

Public Member Functions | List of all members

RandomNumberGeneratorMt19937 Class Reference

Inheritance diagram for RandomNumberGeneratorMt19937:

```
      RandomNumberGenerator
                ▲
                │
   RandomNumberGeneratorMt19937
```
[legend]

Collaboration diagram for RandomNumberGeneratorMt19937:

```
      RandomNumberGenerator
                ▲
                │
   RandomNumberGeneratorMt19937
```
[legend]

Public Member Functions

int **Get** () override

The documentation for this class was generated from the following files:

- src/rng_mt19937.h
- src/rng_mt19937.cpp

Generated by **doxygen** 1.8.17

Figure 10.2 – Inheritance and collaboration diagrams generated by Doxygen

By generating documentation straight from the source, we create a mechanism to quickly update it with any code changes happening throughout the development cycle. Also, any missed updates in the comments have a chance of being spotted during the code review.

Many developers will complain that the design offered by Doxygen is dated, which makes them hesitant to present generated documentation to their customers. Don't worry—there's an easy solution to this problem.

Generating documentation with a modern look

Having your project documented with a clean, fresh design is also important. After all, if we put all this work into writing high-quality documentation for our cutting-edge project, it is imperative that the user perceives it as such. Doxygen has all the bells and whistles, but it isn't known for following the latest visual trends. That doesn't mean we'll need a lot of effort to change this, however.

Luckily, a developer known as *jothepro* created a theme called doxygen-awesome-css that offers a modern, customizable design. It even comes with a dark mode! You can see this in the following screenshot:

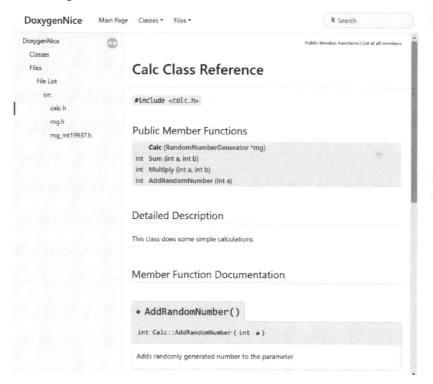

Figure 10.3 – HTML documentation in doxygen-awesome-css theme

The theme doesn't require any additional dependencies and can be easily fetched from its GitHub page at `https://github.com/jothepro/doxygen-awesome-css`.

> **Note**
>
> Online sources suggest using multiple applications executed in series to upgrade the experience. One popular approach proposes transforming Doxygen's output with Sphinx using Breathe and Exhale extensions. This process seems a little busy and will pull in a lot of other dependencies (such as Python). I recommend keeping tooling simple where possible. Chances are that not every developer on your project will understand CMake very well, and such a complex process will give them a hard time.

We'll go straight to the automated adoption of this theme. Let's see how we can extend our `Doxygen.cmake` file to use it by adding a new macro, as follows:

chapter-10/02-doxygen-nice/cmake/Doxygen.cmake (fragment)

```cmake
macro(UseDoxygenAwesomeCss)
    include(FetchContent)
    FetchContent_Declare(doxygen-awesome-css
        GIT_REPOSITORY
            https://github.com/jothepro/doxygen-awesome-css.git
        GIT_TAG
            v1.6.0
    )
    FetchContent_MakeAvailable(doxygen-awesome-css)
    set(DOXYGEN_GENERATE_TREEVIEW     YES)
    set(DOXYGEN_HAVE_DOT              YES)
    set(DOXYGEN_DOT_IMAGE_FORMAT      svg)
    set(DOXYGEN_DOT_TRANSPARENT       YES)
    set(DOXYGEN_HTML_EXTRA_STYLESHEET
        ${doxygen-awesome-css_SOURCE_DIR}/doxygen-awesome.css)
endmacro()
```

We already know all of these commands from previous chapters of the book, but let's reiterate what happens for perfect clarity, as follows:

1. `doxygen-awesome-css` is pulled from Git and made available to the project with the `FetchContent` module.

2. Extra options for Doxygen are configured, as recommended in the theme's `README` file.
3. `DOXYGEN_HTML_EXTRA_STYLESHEET` configures the path to the theme's `.css` file. It will be copied to the output directory.

As you can imagine, it's best to call this macro in the `Doxygen` function right before `doxygen_add_docs()`, like this:

chapter-10/02-doxygen-nice/cmake/Doxygen.cmake

```
function(Doxygen input output)
    ...
    UseDoxygenAwesomeCss()
    doxygen_add_docs (...)
endfunction()

macro(UseDoxygenAwesomeCss)
    ...
endmacro()
```

As a reminder, all variables in macros are set in the scope of the calling function.

We can now enjoy modern style in our generated HTML documentation and share it proudly with the world.

Summary

In this short chapter, we covered adding Doxygen, the documentation generation tool, to a CMake project, and making it elegant. This process isn't too involved and will greatly improve the flow of information in your solution. Time spent on adding documentation will be a worthwhile investment, especially if you find that you or your teammates have trouble in understanding complex relations in the application.

You may worry that it will be hard to add Doxygen to a bigger project that didn't use documentation generation from the start. The sheer amount of work required to add comments to every function can be overwhelming for developers. Don't strive for immediate completeness: start small, by only filling in a description of elements you touched in your latest commit. Even largely incomplete documentation is better than no documentation at all.

Keep in mind that by generating documentation, you'll enforce its proximity to the actual code: it's way easier to maintain written explanations in sync with the logic if they're both in the same file. Also, realize that as with most programmers, you're probably a very busy person and you will eventually forget some of the small details of your project. Remember: the shortest pencil is longer than the longest memory. Do yourself a favor—write things down and prosper.

In the next chapter, we'll learn how to automate the packaging and installation of our projects with CMake.

Further reading

- Official website of Doxygen: `https://www.doxygen.nl/`
- FindDoxygen find-module documentation: `https://cmake.org/cmake/help/latest/module/FindDoxygen.html`
- Doxygen's docblocks: `https://www.doxygen.nl/manual/docblocks.html#specialblock`

Other documentation generation utilities

There are dozens of other tools that are not covered in this book, as we're focusing on projects supported by CMake. Nevertheless, some of them may be more appropriate for your use case. If you're feeling adventurous, visit the websites of two projects I found interesting that are listed here:

- Adobe's Hyde (`https://github.com/adobe/hyde`)

  Aimed at the Clang compiler, Hyde produces Markdown files that can be consumed by tools such as Jekyll (`https://jekyllrb.com/`), a static page generator supported by GitHub.

- Standardese (`https://github.com/standardese/standardese`)

  This uses `libclang` to compile your code and provides output in HTML, Markdown, LaTex, and man pages. It aims (quite boldly) to be the next Doxygen.

11
Installing and Packaging

Our project has been built, tested, and documented. Now, it's finally time to release it to our users. This chapter is mainly about the two last steps we'll need to take to do that: installation and packaging. These are advanced techniques that build on top of everything we've learned so far: managing targets and their dependencies, transient usage requirements, generator expressions, and much more.

Installation allows our project to be discoverable and accessible system-wide. In this chapter, we will cover how to export targets so that another project can use them without installation, as well as how to install our projects so that they can easily be used by any program on the system. In particular, we'll learn how to configure our project so that it can automatically put different artifact types in the correct directory. To handle more advanced scenarios, we'll introduce low-level commands for installing files and directories, as well as for executing custom scripts and CMake commands.

Next, we'll learn how to set up reusable CMake packages so that they can be discovered by calling `find_package()` from other projects. Specifically, we'll explain how to make sure that targets and their definitions are not fixed to a specific location on the filesystem. We'll also discuss how to write basic and advanced config files, along with the *version files* associated with packages.

Then, to make things modular, we'll briefly introduce the concept of components, both in terms of CMake packages and the `install()` command. All this preparation will pave the way for the final aspect we'll be covering in this chapter: using CPack to generate archives, installers, bundles, and packages that are recognized by all kinds of package managers in different operating systems. These can be used to carry pre-built artifacts, executables, and libraries. It's the easiest way for end users to start using our software.

In this chapter, we're going to cover the following main topics:

- Exporting without installation
- Installing projects on the system
- Creating reusable packages
- Defining components
- Packaging with CPack

Technical requirements

You can find the code files for this chapter on GitHub at https://github.com/PacktPublishing/Modern-CMake-for-Cpp/tree/main/examples/chapter11.

To build examples provided in this book always use recommended commands:

```
cmake -B <build tree> -S <source tree>
cmake --build <build tree>
```

Be sure to replace placeholders `<build tree>` and `<source tree>` with appropriate paths. As a reminder: **build tree** is the path to target/output directory, **source tree** is the path at which your source code is located.

Exporting without installation

How can we make the targets of project A available to the consuming project B? Usually, we'd reach for the `find_package()` command, but that would mean that we'd need to create a package and install it on the system. That approach is useful, but it takes some work. Sometimes, we just need a really quick way to build a project and make its targets available for other projects.

We could save some time by including the main listfile of A: it contains all the target definitions already. Unfortunately, it also potentially contains a lot of other things: global configuration, requirements, CMake commands with side effects, additional dependencies, and perhaps targets that we don't want in B (such as unit tests). So, let's not do that. It's better to achieve this by providing **a target export file** that the consuming project, B, can include with the `include()` command:

```cmake
cmake_minimum_required(VERSION 3.20.0)
project(B)
include(/path/to/project-A/ProjectATargets.cmake)
```

Doing this will provide definitions (commands such as `add_library()` and `add_executable()`) for all the targets of A with the correct properties set.

Of course, we're not going to write such a file manually – that wouldn't be a very DRY approach. CMake can generate these files for us with the `export()` command, which has the following signature:

```cmake
export(TARGETS [target1 [target2 [...]]]
   [NAMESPACE <namespace>] [APPEND] FILE <path>
   [EXPORT_LINK_INTERFACE_LIBRARIES])
```

We must supply all the targets that we'd like to export after the TARGET keyword and provide the destination filename after FILE. The other arguments are optional:

- NAMESPACE is recommended as a hint, stating that the target has been imported from other projects.
- APPEND tells CMake that it shouldn't erase the contents of the file before writing.
- EXPORT_LINK_INTERFACE_LIBRARIES will export target link dependencies (including imported and config-specific variants).

Let's see this in action with our example Calc library, which provides two simple methods:

chapter-11/01-export/src/include/calc/calc.h

```cpp
#pragma once
int Sum(int a, int b);
int Multiply(int a, int b);
```

We declare its target like so:

chapter-11/01-export/src/CMakeLists.txt

```
add_library(calc STATIC calc.cpp)
target_include_directories(calc INTERFACE include)
```

Then, we ask CMake to generate the export file with the `export(TARGETS)` command:

chapter-11/01-export/CMakeLists.txt (fragment)

```
cmake_minimum_required(VERSION 3.20.0)
project(ExportCalcCXX)
add_subdirectory(src bin)
set(EXPORT_DIR "${CMAKE_CURRENT_BINARY_DIR}/cmake")
export(TARGETS calc
  FILE "${EXPORT_DIR}/CalcTargets.cmake"
  NAMESPACE Calc::
)
...
```

In the preceding code, we can see that the `EXPORT_DIR` variable has been set to the `cmake` subdirectory of the build tree (as per the convention for `.cmake` files). Then, we export the target declaration file, `CalcTargets.cmake`, with a single target `calc` that's visible as `Calc::calc` for projects that will include this file.

Note that this export file is not a package yet. And, more importantly, all the paths in this file are absolute and hardcoded to the build tree. In other words, they're non-relocatable (we'll discuss this in the *Understanding the issues with relocatable targets* section).

The `export()` command also has a shorter version:

```
export(EXPORT <export> [NAMESPACE <namespace>] [FILE
  <path>])
```

However, it requires a `<export>` name rather than a list of exported targets. Such `<export>` instances are named lists of targets that are defined by `install(TARGETS)` (we'll cover this command in the *Installing logical targets* section). Here's a tiny example demonstrating how this shorthand is used in practice:

chapter-11/01-export/CMakeLists.txt (continued)

```
...
install(TARGETS calc EXPORT CalcTargets)
export(EXPORT CalcTargets
  FILE "${EXPORT_DIR}/CalcTargets2.cmake"
  NAMESPACE Calc::
)
```

The preceding code works exactly like the previous one, but now, a single target list between the `export()` and `install()` commands is being shared.

Both ways of generating export files will produce the same results. They will contain some boilerplate code and a few lines defining the target. With `/tmp/b` set to the build tree path, they'll look like this:

/tmp/b/cmake/CalcTargets.cmake (fragment)

```
# Create imported target Calc::calc
add_library(Calc::calc STATIC IMPORTED)
set_target_properties(Calc::calc PROPERTIES
  INTERFACE_INCLUDE_DIRECTORIES
    "/root/examples/chapter11/01-export/src/include"
)
# Import target "Calc::calc" for configuration ""
set_property(TARGET Calc::calc APPEND PROPERTY
  IMPORTED_CONFIGURATIONS NOCONFIG
)
set_target_properties(Calc::calc PROPERTIES
  IMPORTED_LINK_INTERFACE_LANGUAGES_NOCONFIG "CXX"
  IMPORTED_LOCATION_NOCONFIG "/tmp/b/libcalc.a"
)
```

Normally, we wouldn't edit this file or even open it, but I wanted to highlight the hardcoded paths in this generated file. In its current form, the package is not relocatable. If we want to change that, we'll need to jump through some hoops first. We'll explore why that's important in the next section.

Installing projects on the system

In *Chapter 1*, *First Steps with CMake*, we indicated that CMake offers a command-line mode that installs built projects on the system:

```
cmake --install <dir> [<options>]
```

`<dir>` is the path to the generated build tree (required). Our `<options>` are as follows:

- `--config <cfg>`: This picks the build configuration for a multi-configuration generator.
- `--component <comp>`: This limits the installation to the given component.
- `--default-directory-permissions <permissions>`: This sets the default permissions for the installed directories (in `<u=rwx,g=rx,o=rx>` format).
- `--prefix <prefix>`: This specifies the non-default installation path (stored in the `CMAKE_INSTALL_PREFIX` variable). It defaults to `/usr/local` for Unix-like systems and `c:/Program Files/${PROJECT_NAME}` for Windows.
- `-v, --verbose`: This makes the output verbose (this can also be achieved by setting the `VERBOSE` environment variable).

Installations can consist of many steps, but at their core, they copy the generated artifacts and the necessary dependencies to a directory somewhere on the system. Using CMake for installation not only introduces a convenient standard to all CMake projects but also does the following:

- Provides a platform-specific installation path for artifacts, depending on their types (by following *GNU Coding Standards*)
- Enhances the installation process by generating target export files, which allow project targets to be directly reused by other projects
- Creates discoverable packages through config files, which wrap the target export files and package-specific CMake macros and functions defined by the author

These features are quite powerful as they save a lot of time and simplify the usage of projects that are prepared this way. The first step in performing a basic installation is copying the built artifacts to their destination directory.

This brings us to the `install()` command and its various modes:

- `install(TARGETS)`: This installs output artifacts such as libraries and executables.
- `install(FILES|PROGRAMS)`: This installs individual files and sets their permissions.
- `install(DIRECTORY)`: This installs whole directories.
- `install(SCRIPT|CODE)`: This runs a CMake script or a snippet during installation.
- `install(EXPORT)`: This generates and installs a target export file.

Adding these commands to your listfile will generate a `cmake_install.cmake` file in your build tree. While it's possible to invoke this script manually with `cmake -P`, it isn't recommended. This file is meant to be used by CMake internally when `cmake --install` is executed.

> **Note**
> Upcoming CMake versions will also support installing runtime artifacts and dependency sets, so be sure to check the latest documentation to learn more.

Every `install()` mode has an extensive set of options. A few of them are shared and work the same way:

- DESTINATION: This specifies the installation path. Relative paths will be prepended with `CMAKE_INSTALL_PREFIX`, while absolute paths are used verbatim (and not supported by `cpack`).
- PERMISSIONS: This sets file permissions on platforms that support them. The available values are `OWNER_READ`, `OWNER_WRITE`, `OWNER_EXECUTE`, `GROUP_READ`, `GROUP_WRITE`, `GROUP_EXECUTE`, `WORLD_READ`, `WORLD_WRITE`, `WORLD_EXECUTE`, `SETUID`, and `SETGID`. The default permissions for directories that are created during installation time can be set by specifying the `CMAKE_INSTALL_DEFAULT_DIRECTORY_PERMISSIONS` variable.

- `CONFIGURATIONS`: This specifies a list of configurations (`Debug`, `Release`). Any of the options in this command that follow this keyword will only be applied if the current build config is in this list.
- `OPTIONAL`: This disables raising errors when the installed files don't exist.

Two shared options are also used in component-specific installations: `COMPONENT` and `EXCLUDE_FROM_ALL`. We'll discuss these in detail in the *Defining components* section.

Let's take a look at the first installation mode: `install(TARGETS)`.

Installing logical targets

Targets defined by `add_library()` and `add_executable()` can easily be installed with the `install(TARGETS)` command. This means copying the artifacts that have been produced by the buildsystem to the appropriate destination directories and setting suitable file permissions for them. The general signature for this mode is as follows:

```
install(TARGETS <target>... [EXPORT <export-name>]
        [<output-artifact-configuration> ...]
        [INCLUDES DESTINATION [<dir> ...]]
        )
```

After the initial mode specifier – that is, `TARGETS` – we must provide a list of targets we'd like to install. Here, we may optionally assign them to a **named export** with the `EXPORT` option, which can be used in `export(EXPORT)` and `install(EXPORT)` to produce a target export file. Then, we must configure the installation of output artifacts (grouped by type). Optionally, we can provide a list of directories that will be added to the target export file for each target in its `INTERFACE_INCLUDE_DIRECTORIES` property.

`[<output-artifact-configuration>...]` provides a list of configuration blocks. The full syntax of a single block is as follows:

```
<TYPE> [DESTINATION <dir>] [PERMISSIONS permissions...]
       [CONFIGURATIONS [Debug|Release|...]]
       [COMPONENT <component>]
       [NAMELINK_COMPONENT <component>]
       [OPTIONAL] [EXCLUDE_FROM_ALL]
       [NAMELINK_ONLY|NAMELINK_SKIP]
```

Every output artifact block has to start with `<TYPE>` (this is the only required element). CMake recognizes several of them:

- `ARCHIVE`: Static libraries (`.a`) and DLL import libraries for Windows-based systems (`.lib`).
- `LIBRARY`: Shared libraries (`.so`), but not DLLs.
- `RUNTIME`: Executables and DLLs.
- `OBJECTS`: *Object files* from `OBJECT` libraries.
- `FRAMEWORK`: Static and shared libraries that have the `FRAMEWORK` property set (this excludes them from `ARCHIVE` and `LIBRARY`). This is macOS-specific.
- `BUNDLE`: Executables marked with `MACOSX_BUNDLE` (also not part of `RUNTIME`).
- `PUBLIC_HEADER`, `PRIVATE_HEADER`, `RESOURCE`: Files specified in the target properties with the same name (on Apple platforms, they should be set on the `FRAMEWORK` or `BUNDLE` targets).

The CMake documentation claims that if you only configure one artifact type (for example, `LIBRARY`), only this type will be installed. For CMake version 3.20.0, this is not true: all the artifacts will be installed as if they were configured with the default options. This can be solved by specifying `<TYPE> EXCLUDE_FROM_ALL` for all unwanted artifact types.

> **Note**
>
> A single `install(TARGETS)` command can have multiple artifact configuration blocks. However, be aware that you may only specify one of each type per call. That is, if you'd like to configure different destinations of `ARCHIVE` artifacts for the `Debug` and `Release` configurations, then you must make two separate `install(TARGETS ... ARCHIVE)` calls.

You may also omit the type name and specify options for all the artifacts:

```
install(TARGETS executable, static_lib1
    DESTINATION /tmp
)
```

Installation would be then performed for every file that's produced by these targets, regardless of their type.

Also, you don't always need to provide an installation directory with `DESTINATION`. Let's see why.

Working out the correct destination for different platforms

The formula for a destination path is as follows:

```
${CMAKE_INSTALL_PREFIX} + ${DESTINATION}
```

If `DESTINATION` isn't provided, CMake will use a built-in default for every type:

Artifact Type	Built-In Guess	Install Directory Variable
`RUNTIME`	`bin`	`CMAKE_INSTALL_BINDIR`
`LIBRARY`, `ARCHIVE`	`lib`	`CMAKE_INSTALL_LIBDIR`
`PRIVATE_HEADER`, `PUBLIC_HEADER`	`include`	`CMAKE_INSTALL_INCLUDEDIR`

While default paths are sometimes useful, they aren't correct for every situation. For example, by default, CMake will "guess" that `DESTINATION` for libraries should be `lib`. The full path for libraries will be computed to `/usr/local/lib` for all Unix-like systems, and something like `C:\Program Files (x86)\<project-name>\lib` on Windows. This won't be a very good choice for Debian with multi-arch support, which requires a path to a specific architecture (for example, `i386-linux-gnu`) when `INSTALL_PREFIX` is `/usr`. Figuring out the correct path for every platform is a common problem for Unix-like systems. To get it right, we need to follow *GNU Coding Standards* (a link to this can be found in the *Further reading* section).

Before going with a "guess," CMake will check if a `CMAKE_INSTALL_<DIR>DIR` variable for this artifact type was set and use the path from there. What we need is an algorithm that will detect the platform and fill the install directory variables with the appropriate paths. CMake simplifies this by providing the `GNUInstallDirs` utility module, which handles most platforms by setting the install directory variables accordingly. Just `include()` it before calling any `install()` commands and you'll be set.

Users that need custom configuration can provide install directory variables through the command line with `-DCMAKE_INSTALL_BINDIR=/path/in/the/system`.

However, installing the public headers of libraries can be a little tricky. Let's see why.

Dealing with public headers

The `install(TARGETS)` documentation recommends that we specify public headers (as a semicolon-separated list) in the `PUBLIC_HEADER` property of the library target:

chapter-11/02-install- targets/src/CMakeLists.txt

```
add_library(calc STATIC calc.cpp)
target_include_directories(calc INTERFACE include)
set_target_properties(calc PROPERTIES
   PUBLIC_HEADER src/include/calc/calc.h
)
```

If we're using the default "guess" for Unix, files will end up in `/usr/local/include`. This isn't necessarily the best practice. Ideally, we'd like to put these public headers in a directory that would indicate their origin and introduce namespacing; for example, `/usr/local/include/calc`. This will allow us to use them in all the projects on this system, like so:

```
#include <calc/calc.h>
```

Most preprocessors recognize directives with angle brackets as a request to scan standard system directories. This is where the `GNUInstallDirs` module, which we mentioned earlier, comes in. It defines the installation variables for the `install()` command, though we can also use them explicitly. In this case, we want to prepend the public header's destination, `calc`, with `CMAKE_INSTALL_INCLUDEDIR`:

chapter-11/02-install-targets/CMakeLists.txt

```
cmake_minimum_required(VERSION 3.20.0)
project(InstallTargets CXX)
add_subdirectory(src bin)

include(GNUInstallDirs)
install(TARGETS calc
   ARCHIVE
   PUBLIC_HEADER
   DESTINATION ${CMAKE_INSTALL_INCLUDEDIR}/calc
)
```

After including the listfile from `src`, which defined our `calc` target, we must configure the installation of the static library and its public headers. We have included the `GNUInstallDirs` module and explicitly specified `DESTINATION` for `PUBLIC_HEADERS`. Running `cmake` in install mode will work exactly as expected:

```
# cmake -S <source-tree> -B <build-tree>
# cmake --build <build-tree>
# cmake --install <build-tree>
-- Install configuration: ""
-- Installing: /usr/local/lib/libcalc.a
-- Installing: /usr/local/include/calc/calc.h
```

This works well for this basic case, but there's a slight drawback: files specified in this way don't retain their directory structure. They will all be installed in the same destination, even if they're nested in different base directories.

There are plans for newer versions (CMake 3.23.0) to manage headers better with the `FILE_SET` keyword:

```
target_sources(<target>
  [<PUBLIC|PRIVATE|INTERFACE>
    [FILE_SET <name> TYPE <type> [BASE_DIR <dir>] FILES]
    <files>...
  ]...
)
```

See the *Further reading* section for a link to the discussion on official forums. Until that option is released, we can use this mechanism with the `PRIVATE_HEADER` and `RESOURCE` artifact types. But how can we specify a more complex installation directory structure?

Low-level installation

Modern CMake is moving away from the concept of manipulating files directly. Ideally, we'd always add them to a logical target and use that as a higher level of abstraction to represent all the underlying assets: source files, headers, resources, configuration, and so on. The main advantage is the dryness of the code: usually, we won't need to change more than one line to add a file to the target.

Unfortunately, adding every installed file to a target isn't always possible or convenient. For such cases, three choices are available: `install(FILES)`, `install(PROGRAMS)`, and `install(DIRECTORY)`.

Installing file sets with install(FILES|PROGRAMS)

The `FILES` and `PROGRAMS` modes are very similar. They can be used to install public header files, documentation, shell scripts, configuration, and all kinds of assets, including images, audio files, and datasets to be used at runtime.

Here's the command signature:

```
install(<FILES|PROGRAMS> files...
        TYPE <type> | DESTINATION <dir>
        [PERMISSIONS permissions...]
        [CONFIGURATIONS [Debug|Release|...]]
        [COMPONENT <component>]
        [RENAME <name>] [OPTIONAL] [EXCLUDE_FROM_ALL])
```

The main difference between `FILES` and `PROGRAMS` is the default file permission set on newly copied files. `install(PROGRAMS)` will also set `EXECUTE` for all users, while `install(FILES)` will not (both will set `OWNER_WRITE`, `OWNER_READ`, `GROUP_READ`, and `WORLD_READ`). You can change this behavior by providing the optional `PERMISSIONS` keyword, then picking the leading keyword as an indicator of what's installed: `FILES` or `PROGRAMS`. We've already discussed how `PERMISSIONS`, `CONFIGURATIONS`, and `OPTIONAL` work. `COMPONENT` and `EXCLUDE_FROM_ALL` will be discussed later in the *Defining components* section.

Right after the initial keyword, we need to list all the files we want to install. CMake supports relative and absolute paths, as well as generator expressions. Just keep in mind that if your file path starts with a generator expression, it must be absolute.

The next required keyword is `TYPE` or `DESTINATION`. We can explicitly provide the `DESTINATION` path or ask CMake to look it up for a specific `TYPE` file. Unlike in `install(TARGETS)`, `TYPE` doesn't claim to selectively install any subset of the provided files to be installed. Nevertheless, computing the installation path follows the same pattern (the + symbol denotes a platform-specific path separator):

```
${CMAKE_INSTALL_PREFIX} + ${DESTINATION}
```

And similarly, every `TYPE` will have built-in guesses:

File Type	Built-In Guess	Installation Directory Variable
BIN	bin	CMAKE_INSTALL_BINDIR
SBIN	sbin	CMAKE_INSTALL_SBINDIR
LIB	lib	CMAKE_INSTALL_LIBDIR
INCLUDE	include	CMAKE_INSTALL_INCLUDEDIR
SYSCONF	etc	CMAKE_INSTALL_SYSCONFDIR
SHAREDSTATE	com	CMAKE_INSTALL_SHARESTATEDIR
LOCALSTATE	var	CMAKE_INSTALL_LOCALSTATEDIR
RUNSTATE	$LOCALSTATE/run	CMAKE_INSTALL_RUNSTATEDIR
DATA	$DATAROOT	CMAKE_INSTALL_DATADIR
INFO	$DATAROOT/info	CMAKE_INSTALL_INFODIR
LOCALE	$DATAROOT/locale	CMAKE_INSTALL_LOCALEDIR
MAN	$DATAROOT/man	CMAKE_INSTALL_MANDIR
DOC	$DATAROOT/doc	CMAKE_INSTALL_DOCDIR

The behavior here follows the same principle that was described in the *Working out the correct destination for different platforms* section: if no installation directory variable for this `TYPE` file is set, CMake will fall back to the default "guess" path. Again, we can use the `GNUInstallDirs` module for portability.

Some of the built-in guesses in the table are prefixed with installation directory variables:

- $LOCALSTATE is CMAKE_INSTALL_LOCALSTATEDIR or defaults to `var`
- $DATAROOT is CMAKE_INSTALL_DATAROOTDIR or defaults to `share`

As with `install(TARGETS)`, if the `GNUInstallDirs` module is included, it will provide platform-specific installation directory variables. Let's look at an example:

chapter-11/03-install-files/CMakeLists.txt

```
cmake_minimum_required(VERSION 3.20.0)
project(InstallFiles CXX)

include(GNUInstallDirs)
install(FILES
    src/include/calc/calc.h
    src/include/calc/nested/calc_extended.h
```

```
      DESTINATION ${CMAKE_INSTALL_INCLUDEDIR}/calc
)
```

In this case, CMake will install the two header-only libraries – that is, `calc.h` and `nested/calc_extended.h` – in the project-specific subdirectory in the system-wide *include directory*.

> **Note**
>
> We know from the `GNUInstallDirs` source that `CMAKE_INSTALL_INCLUDEDIR` contains the same path for all supported platforms. However, it's still recommended to use it for readability and consistency with more dynamic variables. For example, `CMAKE_INSTALL_LIBDIR` will vary by architecture and distribution – `lib`, `lib64`, or `lib/<multiarch-tuple>`.

CMake 3.20 also adds a somewhat useful `RENAME` keyword to the `install(FILES|PROGRAMS)` command, which has to be followed by a new filename (this only works if the `files...` list contains a single file).

The example in this section shows how easy it can be to install files in the appropriate directory. There's one problem, though – take a look at the installation output:

```
# cmake -S <source-tree> -B <build-tree>
# cmake --build <build-tree>
# cmake --install <build-tree>
-- Install configuration: ""
-- Installing: /usr/local/include/calc/calc.h
-- Installing: /usr/local/include/calc/calc_extended.h
```

Both files were installed in the same directory, regardless of nesting. Sometimes, that's not what we want. In the next section, we'll learn how to deal with this.

Working with whole directories

If you don't want to add individual files to your installation command, you can choose the broader approach and work with entire directories instead. The `install(DIRECTORY)` mode was created for this purpose. It will copy the listed directories verbatim to the chosen destination. Let's see what it looks like:

```
install(DIRECTORY dirs...
        TYPE <type> | DESTINATION <dir>
```

```
            [FILE_PERMISSIONS permissions...]
            [DIRECTORY_PERMISSIONS permissions...]
            [USE_SOURCE_PERMISSIONS] [OPTIONAL] [MESSAGE_NEVER]
            [CONFIGURATIONS [Debug|Release|...]]
            [COMPONENT <component>] [EXCLUDE_FROM_ALL]
            [FILES_MATCHING]
            [[PATTERN <pattern> | REGEX <regex>] [EXCLUDE]
            [PERMISSIONS permissions...]] [...])
```

As you can see, many options are repeated from `install(FILES|PROGRAMS)`. They work the same way. There's one detail worth noting: if the paths that are provided after the `DIRECTORY` keyword do not end with `/`, the last directory of the path will be appended to the destination, like so:

```
install(DIRECTORY a DESTINATION /x)
```

This will create a directory called `/x/a` and copy the contents of a to it. Now, look at the following code:

```
install(DIRECTORY a/ DESTINATION /x)
```

This will copy the contents of a directly to `/x`.

`install(DIRECTORY)` also introduces other mechanisms that are not available for files:

- Output silencing
- Extended permission control
- File/directories filtering

Let's start with the output silencing option, `MESSAGE_NEVER`. It disables output diagnostics during installation. It is very useful when we have many files in the directories we're installing and it would be too noisy to print them all.

Next up are permissions. This `install()` mode supports three options for setting permissions:

- `USE_SOURCE_PERMISSIONS` works exactly as expected – it sets the permissions on installed files that follow the original files. This only works when `FILE_PERMISSIONS` is not set.

- `FILE_PERMISSIONS` is pretty self-explanatory as well. It allows us to specify the permissions we want to set on installed files and directories. The default permissions are `OWNER_WRITE`, `OWNER_READ`, `GROUP_READ`, and `WORLD_READ`.
- `DIRECTORY_PERMISSIONS` works similarly to the previous option, but it will set additional `EXECUTE` permissions for all users (this is because `EXECUTE` on directories is understood by Unix-like systems as permission to list their contents).

Note that CMake will ignore permissions options on platforms that don't support them. More permission control can be achieved by adding the `PERMISSIONS` keyword after every filtering expression: any files or directories that are matched by it will receive permissions that are specified after this keyword instead.

Let's talk about filters or "globbing" expressions. You can set multiple filters that control which files/directories get installed from source directories. They have the following syntax:

```
PATTERN <p> | REGEX <r> [EXCLUDE] [PERMISSIONS
  <permissions>]
```

There are two matching methods to pick from:

- With `PATTERN`, which is the simpler option, we're allowed to provide a pattern with `?` placeholders (matches any character) and wildcards, `*` (matches any string). Only paths that end with `<pattern>` will be matched.
- On the other hand, the `REGEX` option is more advanced – it supports regular expressions. It also allows us to match any part of the path (we can still use the `^` and `$` anchors to denote the beginning and end of the path).

Optionally, we can set the `FILES_MATCHING` keyword before the first filter, which will specify that any filters will be applied to files and not directories.

Remember two caveats:

- `FILES_MATCHING` requires an inclusive filter in that you may exclude some files, but unless you also add an expression to include some of them, no files will be copied. However, all directories will be created, regardless of filtering.
- All subdirectories are filtered in by default; you may only filter out.

For each filtering method, we may choose to `EXCLUDE` matched paths (this only works when `FILES_MATCHING` isn't used).

We can set specific permissions for all matched paths by adding the `PERMISSIONS` keyword and a list of desired permissions after any filter. Let's try this out. In this example, we'll install three directories in three different ways. We'll have some static data files that will be used at runtime:

```
data
- data.csv
```

We also need some public headers that live in the `src` directory among other, unrelated files:

```
src
- include
  - calc
    - calc.h
    - ignored
      - empty.file
    - nested
      - calc_extended.h
```

Finally, we will need two configuration files at two levels of nesting. To make things more interesting, we are going to make the contents of `/etc/calc/` accessible only to the file owner:

```
etc
- calc
  - nested.conf
- sample.conf
```

To install the directory with static data files, we'll start our project with the most basic form of the `install(DIRECTORY)` command:

chapter-11/04-install-directories/CMakeLists.txt (fragment)

```
cmake_minimum_required(VERSION 3.20.0)
project(InstallDirectories CXX)
install(DIRECTORY data/ DESTINATION share/calc)
...
```

This command will simply take all the contents of our `data` directory and put it in `${CMAKE_INSTALL_PREFIX}` and `share/calc`. Note that our source path ends with a `/` symbol to indicate we don't want to copy the `data` directory itself, only its contents.

The second case is the opposite: we don't add the trailing `/` because the directory should be included. This is because we're relying on a system-specific path for the `INCLUDE` file type, which is provided by `GNUInstallDirs` (note how the `INCLUDE` and `EXCLUDE` keywords represent unrelated concepts):

chapter-11/04-install-directories/CMakeLists.txt (fragment)

```
...
include(GNUInstallDirs)
install(DIRECTORY src/include/calc TYPE INCLUDE
  PATTERN "ignored" EXCLUDE
  PATTERN "calc_extended.h" EXCLUDE
)
...
```

Additionally, we have excluded two paths from this operation: the entire `ignored` directory and all files ending with `calc_extended.h` (remember how `PATTERN` works).

The third case installs some default configuration files and sets their permissions:

chapter-11/04-install-directories/CMakeLists.txt (fragment)

```
...
install(DIRECTORY etc/ TYPE SYSCONF
  DIRECTORY_PERMISSIONS
    OWNER_READ OWNER_WRITE OWNER_EXECUTE
  PATTERN "nested.conf"
    PERMISSIONS OWNER_READ OWNER_WRITE
)
```

Again, we aren't interested in appending `etc` from the source path to the path for the `SYSCONF` type (this has already been provided by including `GNUInstallDirs`) because we would end up putting the files in `/etc/etc`. Additionally, we must specify two permission rules:

- Subdirectories should only be editable and listable by the owner.
- Files ending with `nested.conf` should only be editable by the owner.

Installing directories handles a lot of different use cases, but for really advanced installation scenarios (such as post-install configuration), we may need to involve external tools. How would we do that?

Invoking scripts during installation

If you have ever installed a shared library on a Unix-like system, you may remember that before you can use it, you'll likely need to tell the dynamic linker to scan trusted directories and build its cache by calling `ldconfig` (see the *Further reading* section for references). If you'd like to make your installation fully automatic, CMake offers the `install(SCRIPT|CODE)` command to support such cases. Here's the full command's signature:

```
install([[SCRIPT <file>] [CODE <code>]]
        [ALL_COMPONENTS | COMPONENT <component>]
        [EXCLUDE_FROM_ALL] [...])
```

You should pick `SCRIPT` or `CODE` mode and provide the appropriate arguments – either a path to the CMake script to run or a CMake snippet to execute during the installation. To see how this works, we'll modify the `02-install-targets` example to build a shared library:

chapter-11/05-install-code/src/CMakeLists.txt

```
add_library(calc SHARED calc.cpp)
target_include_directories(calc INTERFACE include)
set_target_properties(calc PROPERTIES
    PUBLIC_HEADER src/include/calc/calc.h
)
```

We need to change the artifact type from ARCHIVE to LIBRARY in the installation script to copy the files. Then, we can just add the logic to run `ldconfig` after:

chapter-11/05-install-code/CMakeLists.txt (fragment)

```
...
install(TARGETS calc LIBRARY
  PUBLIC_HEADER
  DESTINATION ${CMAKE_INSTALL_INCLUDEDIR}/calc
)
if (UNIX)
  install(CODE "execute_process(COMMAND ldconfig)")
endif()
```

The `if()` condition checks if the command matches the operating system (it wouldn't be correct to execute `ldconfig` on Windows or macOS). Of course, the provided code must have valid CMake syntax to work (however, it won't be checked during the initial build; any failures will surface during installation).

After running an installation command, we can confirm that it worked by printing the cached libraries:

```
# cmake -S <source-tree> -B <build-tree>
# cmake --build <build-tree>
# cmake --install <build-tree>
-- Install configuration: ""
-- Installing: /usr/local/lib/libcalc.so
-- Installing: /usr/local/include/calc/calc.h
# ldconfig -p | grep libcalc
        libcalc.so (libc6,x86-64) => /usr/local/lib/libcalc.so
```

Both modes support generator expressions, should you need them. As such, this command is as versatile as CMake itself and can be used for all sorts of things: printing messages for users, verifying that the installation was successful, extensive configuration, file signing – you name it.

Now that we know all the different ways we can install a set of files on the system, let's learn how to turn them into a natively available package for other CMake projects.

Creating reusable packages

We have used `find_package()` extensively in previous chapters. We saw how convenient it is and how it simplifies the whole process. To make our project accessible through this command, we need to complete a few steps so that CMake can treat our project as a coherent package:

- Make our targets relocatable.
- Install the target export file to a standard location.
- Create a config-files and *version file* for the package.

Let's start from the beginning: why do targets need to be relocatable and how can we do this?

Understanding the issues with relocatable targets

Installation solves many problems but unfortunately, it also introduces some complexity: not only is `CMAKE_INSTALL_PREFIX` platform-specific but it can also be set by the user at the installation stage with the `--prefix` option. However, target export files are generated before the installation, during the build stage, at which point we don't know where the installed artifacts will go. Take a look at the following code:

chapter-11/01-export/src/CMakeLists.txt

```
add_library(calc STATIC calc.cpp)
target_include_directories(calc INTERFACE include)
```

In this example, we specifically add the *include directory* to the *include directories* of `calc`. Since this is a relative path, CMake's exported target generation will implicitly prepend this path with the contents of the `CMAKE_CURRENT_SOURCE_DIR` variable, which points to the directory where this listfile is located.

However, that's not going to cut it. The installed project shouldn't need files from the source or build tree anymore. Everything (including library headers) is copied to a shared location, such as `/usr/lib/calc/` on Linux. We cannot use the target that's been defined in this snippet in another project since the target's *include directory* path still points to its source tree.

CMake solves this with two generator expressions that will filter out the expression, depending on the context:

- `$<BUILD_INTERFACE>`: This includes the content for regular builds but excludes it for installation.
- `$<INSTALL_INTERFACE>`: This includes the content for installation but excludes it for regular builds.

The following code shows how you can use them in practice:

chapter-11/06-install-export/src/CMakeLists.txt

```
add_library(calc STATIC calc.cpp)
target_include_directories(calc INTERFACE
    "$<BUILD_INTERFACE:${CMAKE_CURRENT_SOURCE_DIR}/include>"
    "$<INSTALL_INTERFACE:${CMAKE_INSTALL_INCLUDEDIR}>"
)
set_target_properties(calc PROPERTIES
    PUBLIC_HEADER src/include/calc/calc.h
)
```

For regular builds, the value of the `calc` target property, `INTERFACE_INCLUDE_DIRECTORIES`, will be expanded, like so:

```
"/root/examples/chapter-11/05-package/src/include" ""
```

Empty double quotes mean that the value provided in `INSTALL_INTERFACE` was excluded and evaluated as an empty string. On the other hand, when we install, the value will get expanded like so:

```
"" "/usr/lib/calc/include"
```

This time, the value that was provided in the `BUILD_INTERFACE` generator expression was evaluated as an empty string, and we're left with the value from the other generator expression.

One more word about `CMAKE_INSTALL_PREFIX`: this variable shouldn't be used as a component in paths specified in targets. It would be evaluated during the build stage, making the path absolute and not necessarily the same as the one that was provided in the installation stage (as users may use the `--prefix` option). Instead, use the `$<INSTALL_PREFIX>` generator expression:

```
target_include_directories(my_target PUBLIC
    $<INSTALL_INTERFACE:$<INSTALL_PREFIX>/include/MyTarget>
)
```

Or, even better, you can use relative paths (they will get prepended with the correct installation prefix):

```
target_include_directories(my_target PUBLIC
    $<INSTALL_INTERFACE:include/MyTarget>
)
```

Please take a look at the official documentation for more examples and information (a link to this can be found in the *Further reading* section).

Now that our targets are "installation-compatible," we can safely generate and install their target export files.

Installing target export files

We discussed target export files a little bit in the *Exporting without installation* section. Target export files that are intended for installation are quite similar, as is the signature of the command for creating them:

```
install(EXPORT <export-name> DESTINATION <dir>
        [NAMESPACE <namespace>] [[FILE <name>.cmake] |
        [PERMISSIONS permissions...]
        [CONFIGURATIONS [Debug|Release|...]]
        [EXPORT_LINK_INTERFACE_LIBRARIES]
        [COMPONENT <component>]
        [EXCLUDE_FROM_ALL])
```

It's a combination of "plain" `export(EXPORT)` and other `install()` commands (its options work the same way). Just remember that it will create and install a target export file for a named export that must be defined with the `install(TARGETS)` command. The major difference to be aware of here is that the generated export file will contain the target paths that were evaluated in the `INSTALL_INTERFACE` generator expression and not `BUILD_INTERFACE` like `export(EXPORT)` did.

In this example, we'll generate and install the target export file for the target from `chapter-11/06-install-export/src/CMakeLists.txt`. To do so, we must call `install(EXPORT)` in our top listfile:

chapter-11/06-install-export/CMakeLists.txt

```
cmake_minimum_required(VERSION 3.20.0)
project(InstallExport CXX)
include(GNUInstallDirs) # so it's available in ./src/
add_subdirectory(src bin)

install(TARGETS calc EXPORT CalcTargets ARCHIVE
  PUBLIC_HEADER DESTINATION
    ${CMAKE_INSTALL_INCLUDEDIR}/calc
)
install(EXPORT CalcTargets
  DESTINATION ${CMAKE_INSTALL_LIBDIR}/calc/cmake
  NAMESPACE Calc::
)
```

Again, note how we're referencing the `CalcTargets` export name in `install(EXPORT)`.

Running `cmake --install` in the build tree will result in the export file being generated in the specified destination:

```
...
-- Installing: /usr/local/lib/calc/cmake/CalcTargets.cmake
-- Installing: /usr/local/lib/calc/cmake/CalcTargets-noconfig.cmake
```

If, for some reason, the override default name for the target export file (`<export name>.cmake`) doesn't work for you, you can add the `FILE new-name.cmake` argument to change it (the filename must end with `.cmake`).

Don't get confused by this – the target export file isn't a config file, so you can't use `find_package()` to consume installed targets just yet. However, it's possible to `include()` export files directly if needed. So, how do we define the package that can be consumed by other projects? Let's find out!

Writing basic config-files

A complete package definition consists of the target export files, the package's *config file*, and the package's *version file*, but technically, all that's needed for `find_package()` to work is a config-file. It's considered a package definition and it's responsible for providing any package functions and macros, checking requirements, finding dependencies, and including target export files.

As we mentioned earlier, users can install your package anywhere on their system by using the following command:

```
cmake --install <build tree> --prefix=<installation path>
```

This prefix determines where the installed files will be copied. To support this, you must at least ensure the following:

- The paths on the target properties can be relocated (as described in the *Understanding the issues with relocatable targets* section).
- The paths that are used in your config-file are relative to it.

To use such packages that have been installed in non-default locations, the consuming projects need to provide `<installation path>` through the `CMAKE_PREFIX_PATH` variable during the configuration stage. We can do this with the following command:

```
cmake -B <build tree> -DCMAKE_PREFIX_PATH=<installation path>
```

The `find_package()` command will scan the list of paths that are outlined in the documentation (link in the *Further reading* section) in a platform-specific way. One of the patterns that's checked on Windows and Unix-like systems is as follows:

```
<prefix>/<name>*/(lib/<arch>|lib*|share)/<name>*/(cmake|CMake)
```

This tells us that installing the config-file in a path such as `lib/calc/cmake` should work just fine. Also, it's important to highlight that config-files must be named `<PackageName>-config.cmake` or `<PackageName>Config.cmake` to be found.

Let's add the installation of the config-file to the `06-install-export` example:

chapter-11/07-config-file/CMakeLists.txt (fragment)

```
...
install(EXPORT CalcTargets
  DESTINATION ${CMAKE_INSTALL_LIBDIR}/calc/cmake
  NAMESPACE Calc::
)
install(FILES "CalcConfig.cmake"
  DESTINATION ${CMAKE_INSTALL_LIBDIR}/calc/cmake
)
```

This command will install `CalcConfig.cmake` from the same source directory (`CMAKE_INSTALL_LIBDIR` will be evaluated to the correct `lib` path for the platform).

The most basic config-file we can provide consists of a single line that includes the target export file:

chapter-11/07-config-file/CalcConfig.cmake

```
include("${CMAKE_CURRENT_LIST_DIR}/CalcTargets.cmake")
```

The `CMAKE_CURRENT_LIST_DIR` variable refers to the directory that the config-file lives in. Because `CalcConfig.cmake` and `CalcTargets.cmake` are installed in the same directory in our example (as set by `install(EXPORT)`), the target export file will be included correctly.

To make sure that our package is usable, we'll create a simple project consisting of just one listfile:

chapter-11/08-find-package/CMakeLists.txt

```
cmake_minimum_required(VERSION 3.20.0)
project(FindCalcPackage CXX)

find_package(Calc REQUIRED)
```

```
include(CMakePrintHelpers)
message("CMAKE_PREFIX_PATH: ${CMAKE_PREFIX_PATH}")
message("CALC_FOUND: ${Calc_FOUND}")
cmake_print_properties(TARGETS "Calc::calc" PROPERTIES
  IMPORTED_CONFIGURATIONS
  INTERFACE_INCLUDE_DIRECTORIES
)
```

To test this in practice, we can build and install the `07-config-file` example to one directory, and then build `08-find-package` while referencing it with the `DCMAKE_PREFIX_PATH` argument, like so:

```
# cmake -S <source-tree-of-07> -B <build-tree-of-07>
# cmake --build <build-tree-of-07>
# cmake --install <build-tree-of-07>
# cmake -S <source-tree-of-08> -B <build-tree-of-08>
    -DCMAKE_PREFIX_PATH=<build-tree-of-07>
```

This will produce the following output (all the `<_tree-of_>` placeholders will be replaced with real paths):

```
CMAKE_PREFIX_PATH: <build-tree-of-07>
CALC_FOUND: 1
--
  Properties for TARGET Calc::calc:
    Calc::calc.IMPORTED_CONFIGURATIONS = "NOCONFIG"
    Calc::calc.INTERFACE_INCLUDE_DIRECTORIES = "<build-tree-of-07>/include"

-- Configuring done
-- Generating done
-- Build files have been written to: <build-tree-of-08>
```

The `CalcTargets.cmake` file was found and included correctly, and the path to the *include directory* was set to follow the chosen prefix. This solves packaging for a very basic case. Now, let's learn how to handle more advanced scenarios.

Creating advanced config-files

If you have more things to manage than a single target export file, it might be useful to include a few macros in your config-file. The CMakePackageConfigHelpers utility module gives us access to the configure_package_config_file() command. To use it, we need to supply a template file that will be interpolated with CMake variables to generate a config-file with two embedded macro definitions:

- set_and_check(<variable> <path>): This works like set(), but it checks that <path> actually exists and fails with FATAL_ERROR otherwise. It is recommended to use this in your config-files to detect incorrect paths early.
- check_required_components(<PackageName>): This is added to the end of the config-file and will verify whether all the components in our package, which are required by the user in find_package(<package> REQUIRED <component>), have been found. This is done by checking that the <package>_<component>_FOUND variables are true.

Paths for more convoluted directory trees can be prepared for the installation stage while you're generating the config-file. Take a look at the following signature:

```
configure_package_config_file(<template> <output>
  INSTALL_DESTINATION <path>
  [PATH_VARS <var1> <var2> ... <varN>]
  [NO_SET_AND_CHECK_MACRO]
  [NO_CHECK_REQUIRED_COMPONENTS_MACRO]
  [INSTALL_PREFIX <path>]
)
```

The file that's been provided as <template> will be interpolated with variables and stored in the <output> path. Here, the path that's required after INSTALL_DESTINATION will be used to transform the paths stored in the variables listed in PATH_VARS so that they are relative to the install destination. We can also indicate that INSTALL_DESTINATION is relative to INSTALL_PREFIX by providing it as its base path.

NO_SET_AND_CHECK_MACRO and NO_CHECK_REQUIRED_COMPONENTS_MACRO tell CMake not to add these macro definitions to the generated config-file. Let's see this generation in practice. Again, we'll extend the 06-install-export example:

chapter-11/09-advanced-config/CMakeLists.txt (fragment)

```
...
install(EXPORT CalcTargets
    DESTINATION ${CMAKE_INSTALL_LIBDIR}/calc/cmake
    NAMESPACE Calc::
)

include(CMakePackageConfigHelpers)
set(LIB_INSTALL_DIR ${CMAKE_INSTALL_LIBDIR}/calc)
configure_package_config_file(
    ${CMAKE_CURRENT_SOURCE_DIR}/CalcConfig.cmake.in
    "${CMAKE_CURRENT_BINARY_DIR}/CalcConfig.cmake"
    INSTALL_DESTINATION ${CMAKE_INSTALL_LIBDIR}/calc/cmake
    PATH_VARS LIB_INSTALL_DIR
)

install(FILES "${CMAKE_CURRENT_BINARY_DIR}/CalcConfig.cmake"
    DESTINATION ${CMAKE_INSTALL_LIBDIR}/calc/cmake
)
```

Let's take a look at what we must do in the preceding code:

1. include() the utility module with helpers.
2. set() a variable that will be used to make a relocatable path.
3. Generate the CalcConfig.cmake config-file for the build tree using the CalcConfig.cmake.in template located in the source tree. Finally, provide LIB_INSTALL_DIR as a variable name to be computed as relative to INSTALL_DESTINATION or ${CMAKE_INSTALL_LIBDIR}/calc/cmake.
4. Pass the config-file that was generated for the build tree to install(FILE).

Note that DESTINATION in install(FILE) and INSTALL_DESTINATION in install(FILES) are the same so that the relative paths can be computed correctly.

Finally, we'll need a config file template (their names are usually suffixed with `.in`):

chapter-11/09-advanced-config/CalcConfig.cmake.in

```
@PACKAGE_INIT@

set_and_check(CALC_LIB_DIR "@PACKAGE_LIB_INSTALL_DIR@")
include("${CALC_LIB_DIR}/cmake/CalcTargets.cmake")

check_required_components(Calc)
```

It should start with a `@PACKAGE_INIT@` placeholder. The generator will fill it with the definitions of the `set_and_check` and `check_required_components` commands so that they can consume the project. You may recognize these `@PLACEHOLDERS@` from our plain `configure_file()` – they work the same as they do in C++ files.

Next, we'll set (`CALC_LIB_DIR`) to the path that's passed in the `@PACKAGE_LIB_INSTALL_DIR@` placeholder. It will contain the path of `$LIB_INSTALL_DIR` that's provided in the listfile, but it will be calculated relative to the installation path. Then, we'll use it to include the target export files.

Finally, `check_required_components()` verifies if all the components that are required by the package consumer have been found. Adding this command is recommended, even if the package doesn't have any components, to verify that the user has not accidentally added unsupported requirements.

The `CalcConfig.cmake` config-file, when generated this way, looks like this:

```
#### Expanded from @PACKAGE_INIT@ by
    configure_package_config_file() #######
#### Any changes to this file will be overwritten by the
    next CMake run ####
#### The input file was CalcConfig.cmake.in   #####
get_filename_component(PACKAGE_PREFIX_DIR
    "${CMAKE_CURRENT_LIST_DIR}/../../../" ABSOLUTE)
macro(set_and_check _var _file) # ... removed for brevity
macro(check_required_components _NAME) # ... removed for
    brevity
###############################################################
###########
```

```
set_and_check(CALC_LIB_DIR
    "${PACKAGE_PREFIX_DIR}/lib/calc")
include("${CALC_LIB_DIR}/cmake/CalcTargets.cmake")
check_required_components(Calc)
```

The following diagram, which shows how the various package files are related to each other, puts this into perspective:

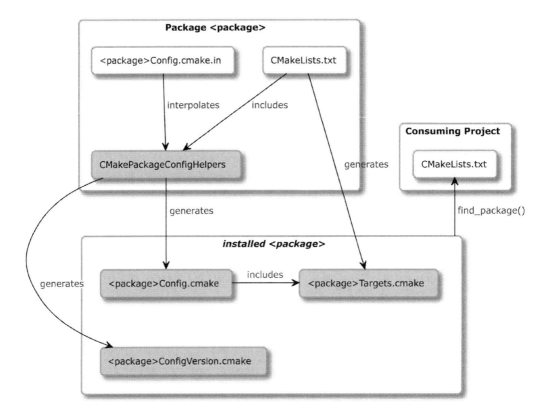

Figure 11.1 – The file structure for advanced packages

All the required sub-dependencies of a package must also be found in the package config file. This can be done by calling the `find_dependency()` macro from the `CMakeFindDependencyMacro` helper. We learned how to use it in *Chapter 7, Managing Dependencies with CMake*.

If you decide to expose any macros or functions to the consuming project, it is recommended that you put their definitions in a separate file that you can `include()` from the package's config-file.

Interestingly, `CMakePackageConfigHelpers` also provides a helper command to generate package's version files. Let's take a look.

Generating package version files

As your package grows, it will slowly gain new features, old ones will be marked as deprecated, and eventually be removed. It's important to keep track of these modifications in a changelog that's available to developers that use your package. When a specific feature is needed, a developer can find the lowest version that supports it and use it as an argument to `find_package()`, like so:

```
find_package(Calc 1.2.3 REQUIRED)
```

CMake will then search the config-file for `Calc` and check if a *version file* named `<config-file>-version.cmake` or `<config-file>Version.cmake` is present in the same directory, that is, `CalcConfigVersion.cmake`. Next, this file will be read for its version information and the compatibility it provides with other versions. For example, you may not have version `1.2.3` installed as required, but you may have `1.3.5`, which is marked as "compatible" with any older versions. CMake will gladly accept such a package as it knows that the package vendor provides backward compatibility.

You can use the `CMakePackageConfigHelpers` utility module to generate package's *version files* by calling `write_basic_package_version_file()`:

```
write_basic_package_version_file(<filename> [VERSION <ver>]
   COMPATIBILITY <AnyNewerVersion | SameMajorVersion |
                  SameMinorVersion | ExactVersion>
   [ARCH_INDEPENDENT]
)
```

First, we need to provide the `<filename>` property of the artifact we want to create; it must follow the rules we outlined earlier. Other than that, keep in mind that we should store all the generated files in the build tree.

Optionally, we can pass an explicit `VERSION` (the usual format, `major.minor.patch`, is supported here). If we don't do this, the version that's provided in the `project()` command will be used instead (expect an error if your project doesn't specify one).

The `COMPATIBILITY` keyword is self-explanatory:

- `ExactVersion` must match all three components of the version and won't support ranged versions: `find_package(<package> 1.2.8...1.3.4)`.
- `SameMinorVersion` matches if the first two components are the same (ignores `patch`).
- `SameMajorVersion` matches if the first component is the same (ignores `minor` and `patch`).
- `AnyNewerVersion` seems to have a reversed name: it will match any older version. In other words, `<package>` on version `1.4.2` will be a good match for `find_package(<package> 1.2.8)`.

Normally, all packages must be built for the same architecture as the consuming project to match (an exact check is performed). However, for packages that don't compile anything (header-only libraries, macro packages, and so on), you can specify the `ARCH_INDEPENDENT` keyword to skip this check.

Now, it's time for a practical example. The following code shows how to provide the *version file* for the project that we started in the `06-install-export` example:

chapter-11/10-version-file/CMakeLists.txt (fragment)

```cmake
cmake_minimum_required(VERSION 3.20.0)
project(VersionFile VERSION 1.2.3 LANGUAGES CXX)
...
include(CMakePackageConfigHelpers)
write_basic_package_version_file(
    "${CMAKE_CURRENT_BINARY_DIR}/CalcConfigVersion.cmake"
    COMPATIBILITY AnyNewerVersion
)

install(FILES "CalcConfig.cmake"
    "${CMAKE_CURRENT_BINARY_DIR}/CalcConfigVersion.cmake"
    DESTINATION ${CMAKE_INSTALL_LIBDIR}/calc/cmake
)
```

For convenience, we configure the version of the package at the top of the file, in the `project()` command. This requires us to switch from the short `project(<name> <languages>)` syntax to an explicit, full syntax by adding the `LANGUAGE` keyword.

After including the helper utility module, we call the generation command and write the file to a build tree with a name conforming to the pattern that's required by `find_package()`. Here, we deliberately skip the `VERSION` keyword to have the version read from the `PROJECT_VERSION` variable. We're also marking our package as fully backward compatible with `COMPATIBILITY AnyNewerVersion`. After that, we install the package *version file* to the same destination as `CalcConfig.cmake`. And that's it – our package is fully configured.

In the next section, we'll learn what components are and how to use them with packages.

Defining components

We'll start talking about package components by clearing up some possible confusion around the term **component**. Look at the full signature for `find_package()`:

```
find_package(<PackageName> [version] [EXACT] [QUIET]
[MODULE]
    [REQUIRED] [[COMPONENTS] [components...]]
               [OPTIONAL_COMPONENTS components...]
               [NO_POLICY_SCOPE])
```

The components that are mentioned here shouldn't be conflated with the `COMPONENT` keyword that's used in the `install()` command. They are different concepts that must be understood separately, despite sharing the same name. We'll look at this in more detail in the following subsections.

How to use components in find_package()

When we call `find_package()` with a list of `COMPONENTS` or `OPTIONAL_COMPONENTS`, we tell CMake that we're only interested in packages that provide them. However, it's important to realize that it's up to the package to verify this requirement, and if the package vendor doesn't add the necessary checks to the config-file mentioned in the *Creating advanced config-file* section, then nothing happens.

Requested components are passed to the config-file in the `<package>_FIND_COMPONENTS` variable (both optional and not). Additionally, for every non-optional component, a `<package>_FIND_REQUIRED_<component>` will be set. As package authors, we could write a macro to scan this list and check if we have provided all the required components. But we don't need to – this is exactly what `check_required_components()` does. To use it, the config-file should set the `<Package>_<Component>_FOUND` variable when the necessary component is found. The macro at the end of the file will check if all the required variables were set.

How to use components in the install() command

Some produced artifacts may not need to be installed for all scenarios. For example, a project may install static libraries and public headers for developing purposes, but by default, it can just install a shared library for the runtime. To make this duality of behavior possible, we can group artifacts under a common name by using the `COMPONENT` keyword, which is available in all the `install()` commands. Users that are interested in limiting installation to a specific component can request this explicitly by running the following command (the component names are case-sensitive):

```
cmake --install <build tree> --component=<component name>
```

Marking an artifact with the `COMPONENT` keyword doesn't mean that it won't be installed by default. To prevent this from happening, we must add the `EXCLUDE_FROM_ALL` keyword.

Let's explore these components using a code example:

chapter-11/11-components/CMakeLists.txt (fragment)

```
...
install(TARGETS calc EXPORT CalcTargets
  ARCHIVE
    COMPONENT lib
  PUBLIC_HEADER
    DESTINATION ${CMAKE_INSTALL_INCLUDEDIR}/calc
    COMPONENT headers
)

install(EXPORT CalcTargets
  DESTINATION ${CMAKE_INSTALL_LIBDIR}/calc/cmake
```

```
    NAMESPACE Calc::
    COMPONENT lib
)

install(CODE "MESSAGE(\"Installing 'extra' component\")"
    COMPONENT extra
    EXCLUDE_FROM_ALL
)
...
```

These install commands define the following components:

- `lib`: This contains the static library and target export files. It's installed by default.
- `headers`: This contains public header files. It is installed by default.
- `extra`: This executes a piece of code by printing a message. It's not installed by default.

Let's reiterate this:

- `cmake --install` without the `--component` argument will install both the `lib` and `headers` components.
- `cmake --install --component headers` will only install public headers.
- `cmake --install --component extra` will print a message that's inaccessible otherwise (because of the `EXCLUDE_FROM_ALL` keyword).

If no COMPONENT keyword is specified for the installed artifact, it will get a default value of `Unspecified` from the CMAKE_INSTALL_DEFAULT_COMPONENT_NAME variable.

> **Note**
> Since there's no easy way to list all the components that are available from the `cmake` command line, users of your package will benefit from exhaustive documentation listing your package's components. Perhaps the `INSTALL` file would be a good place to mention it.

If `cmake` is called with the `--component` argument for a component that doesn't exist, then the command will succeed without any warnings or errors. It just won't install anything.

Partitioning our installation into components enables users to cherry-pick what they want to install. We have mostly discussed grouping installed files into components, but there are also are procedural steps such as `install(SCRIPT|CODE)` or creating symlinks for shared libraries.

Managing symbolic links for versioned shared libraries

The target platform for your installation may use symbolic links to help linkers discover the currently installed version of a shared library. After creating a `lib<name>.so` symlink to the `lib<name>.so.1` file, it's possible to link this library by passing the `-l<name>` argument to the linker. The creation of such symlinks is handled by CMake's `install(TARGETS <target> LIBRARY)` block when needed.

However, we may decide to move that step into another `install()` command by adding `NAMELINK_SKIP` to this block:

```
install(TARGETS <target> LIBRARY COMPONENT cmp
    NAMELINK_SKIP)
```

To assign symlinking to another component (instead of disabling it altogether), we can repeat the `install()` command for the same target and specify a different component, followed by the `NAMELINK_ONLY` keyword:

```
install(TARGETS <target> LIBRARY COMPONENT lnk
    NAMELINK_ONLY)
```

The same can be achieved with the `NAMELINK_COMPONENT` keyword:

```
install(TARGETS <target> LIBRARY
    COMPONENT cmp NAMELINK_COMPONENT lnk)
```

Now that we have configured automatic installation, we can provide pre-built artifacts for our users using the CPack tool, which is included with CMake.

Packaging with CPack

Building projects from a source has its benefits, but it can take a long time and introduce a lot of complexity. This isn't the best experience for end users who just want to use the package, especially if they aren't developers themselves. A much more convenient form of software distribution is to use binary packages that contain compiled artifacts and other static files that are needed by the runtime. CMake supports generating multiple kinds of such packages through a command-line tool called `cpack`.

The following table lists the available package generators:

Name	File Types	Platform
Archive	7Z – 7zip – (.7z)	Cross-platform
	TBZ2 (.tar.bz2)	
	TGZ (.tar.gz)	
	TXZ (.tar.xz)	
	TZ (.tar.Z)	
	TZST (.tar.zst)	
	ZIP (.zip)	
Bundle	Bundle (.bundle)	macOS
DEB	DEB (.deb)	Linux
DragNDrop	DMG (.dmg)	macOS
External	JSON (.json)	Integration with external packaging tools
FreeBSD	PKG (pkg)	*BSD, Linux, OSX
IFW	Binary	Linux, Windows, macOS
NSIS	Binary (.exe)	Windows
NuGet	NuGet (.nupkg)	Windows
productbuild	PKG (.pkg)	macOS
RPM	RPM (.rpm)	Linux
WIX	MSI (.msi)	Windows

Most of these generators have extensive configurations. It is beyond the scope of this book to delve into all their details, so be sure to check out the full documentation, which can be found in the *Further reading* section. Instead, we'll focus on the general use case.

> **Note**
> Package generators shouldn't be confused with buildsystem generators (Unix Makefiles, Visual Studio, and so on).

To use CPack, we'll need to correctly configure the installation of our project with the necessary `install()` commands and build our project. The resulting `cmake_install.cmake` that's generated in our build tree will be used by `cpack` to prepare binary packages based on the configuration file (`CPackConfig.cmake`). While it's possible to create this file manually, it's easier to use `include(CPack)` to include the utility module in our project's listfile. It will generate the configuration in the project's build tree and supply all the default values where needed.

Let's see how we can extend the example `11-components` so that it can work with CPack:

chapter-11/12-cpack/CMakeLists.txt (fragment)

```
cmake_minimum_required(VERSION 3.20.0)
project(CPackPackage VERSION 1.2.3 LANGUAGES CXX)
include(GNUInstallDirs)
add_subdirectory(src bin)

install(...)
install(...)
install(...)

set(CPACK_PACKAGE_VENDOR "Rafal Swidzinski")
set(CPACK_PACKAGE_CONTACT "email@example.com")
set(CPACK_PACKAGE_DESCRIPTION "Simple Calculator")
include(CPack)
```

The code is pretty self-explanatory, so we won't dwell on it too much (please refer to the module documentation, which can be found in the *Further reading* section). One thing worth noting here is the fact that the CPack module will infer a few values from the `project()` command:

- CPACK_PACKAGE_NAME
- CPACK_PACKAGE_VERSION
- CPACK_PACKAGE_FILE_NAME

The last value will be used to produce the output package. Its structure is as follows:

```
$CPACK_PACKAGE_NAME-$CPACK_PACKAGE_VERSION-$CPACK_SYSTEM_NAME
```

Here, `CPACK_SYSTEM_NAME` is the name of the target OS; for example, `Linux` or `win32`. For example, by executing a ZIP generator on Debian, CPack will generate a file named `CPackPackage-1.2.3-Linux.zip`.

After building our project, we can generate actual packages by running the `cpack` binary in the build tree:

```
cpack [<options>]
```

Technically speaking, CPack is capable of reading all its options from the configuration file that's been placed in the current working directory, but you may choose to override these settings from the command line:

- `-G <generators>`: This is a semicolon-separated list of package generators to use. The default value can be specified in the `CPackConfig.cmake` in the `CPACK_GENERATOR` variable.
- `-C <configs>`: This is a semicolon-separated list of build configurations (debug, release) to generate packages for (required for multi-configuration buildsystem generators).
- `-D <var>=<value>`: This overrides a `<var>` variable that's set in the `CPackConfig.cmake` file with `<value>`.
- `--config <config-file>`: This is the config-file you should use instead of the default `CPackConfig.cmake`.
- `--verbose`, `-V`: Provides verbose output.
- `-P <packageName>`: Overrides the package name.
- `-R <packageVersion>`: Overrides the package version.
- `--vendor <vendorName>`: Overrides the package vendor.
- `-B <packageDirectory>`: Specifies the output directory for `cpack` (by default, this will be the current working directory).

Let's try generating packages for our `12-cpack` output. We're going to use ZIP, 7Z, and the Debian package generator:

```
cpack -G "ZIP;7Z;DEB" -B packages
```

The following packages should be generated:

- `CPackPackage-1.2.3-Linux.7z`
- `CPackPackage-1.2.3-Linux.deb`
- `CPackPackage-1.2.3-Linux.zip`

In this format, binary packages are ready to be published on the website of our project, in a GitHub release, or sent to a package repository for end users to enjoy.

Summary

Writing installation scripts in a cross-platform way is an incredibly complex task without a tool such as CMake. While it still requires a little bit of work to set up, it's a much more streamlined process that ties closely to all the other concepts and techniques we've used so far in this book.

First, we learned how to export CMake targets from projects so that they can be consumed in other projects without installing them. Then, we learned how to install projects that had already been configured for this purpose.

After that, we started exploring the basics of installation by starting with the most important subject: installing CMake targets. We now know how CMake handles different destinations for various artifact types and how to deal with public headers that are somewhat special. To manage these installation steps at lower levels, we discussed other modes of the `install()` command, including installing files, programs, and directories and invoking scripts during the installation.

After explaining how to codify the installation steps, we learned about CMake's reusable packages. Specifically, we learned how to make targets in our projects relocatable so that the packages can be installed wherever the user wants. Then, we focused on forming a fully-defined package that can be consumed by other projects with `find_package()`, which required preparing target export files, config-files, and *version files*.

Recognizing that different users may need different parts of our package, we discovered how to group artifacts and actions in installation components, as well as how they differ from the components of CMake packages.

Finally, we touched on CPack and learned how to prepare basic binary packages that can be used to distribute our software in a pre-compiled form.

There's still a long way to go to fully grasp all the details and complexities of installation and packaging, but this chapter has given us a solid foundation to handle the most common scenarios and explore them further with confidence.

In the next chapter, we will put everything we've learned so far into practice by creating a coherent, professional project.

Further reading

To learn more about the topics that were covered in this chapter, take a look at the following resources:

- *GNU Coding Standards for Destinations*: https://www.gnu.org/prep/standards/html_node/Directory-Variables.html
- *Discussion on new public header management with the* `FILE_SET` *keyword*: https://gitlab.kitware.com/cmake/cmake/-/issues/22468#note_991860
- *How to install a shared library*: https://tldp.org/HOWTO/Program-Library-HOWTO/shared-libraries.html
- *Creating relocatable packages*: https://cmake.org/cmake/help/latest/guide/importing-exporting/index.html#creating-relocatable-packages
- *List of paths scanned by* `find_package()` *to find the config file*: https://cmake.org/cmake/help/latest/command/find_package.html#config-mode-search-procedure
- *Full documentation of* `CMakePackageConfigHelpers`: https://cmake.org/cmake/help/latest/module/CMakePackageConfigHelpers.html
- *CPack package generators*: https://cmake.org/cmake/help/latest/manual/cpack-generators.7.html
- *On preferred package generators for different platforms*: https://stackoverflow.com/a/46013099
- *CPack utility module documentation*: https://cmake.org/cmake/help/latest/module/CPack.html

12
Creating Your Professional Project

We gathered all the required knowledge to build professional projects; we learned about structuring, building, dependency management, testing, analyzing, installing, and packaging. It's time to put these acquired skills into practice by creating a coherent, professional project.

The important thing to understand is that even trivial programs will benefit from automated quality checks and a streamlined end-to-end process that turns raw code into a fully fledged solution. It's true that this is often a considerable investment, as many steps need to be taken in order to prepare everything right – even more so if we're trying to add these mechanisms to already existing code bases (usually, they're already large and convoluted).

That's the very reason to use CMake from the get-go and set all the piping upfront; not only it will be easier to configure but, more importantly, it's also much more efficient to do it early, as all the quality controls and build automation have to be added to long-term projects at some point anyway.

This is exactly what we'll do in this chapter – we'll write a new solution that is as small and as simple as possible. It will perform just a single (almost) practical function – adding two numbers together. Limiting the functionality of the business code will allow us to focus on every other aspect of the project that we learned about in the previous chapters.

To have a more involved problem to solve, this project will build both a library and an executable. The library will provide the internal business logic and will also be available for other projects to consume as a CMake package. The executable will be meant for end users only and will implement a user interface that shows the functionality of the underlying library.

In this chapter, we're going to cover the following main topics:

- Planning our work
- Project layout
- Building and managing dependencies
- Testing and program analysis
- Installing and packaging
- Providing the documentation

Technical requirements

You can find the code files present in this chapter at GitHub:

https://github.com/PacktPublishing/Modern-CMake-for-Cpp/tree/main/examples/chapter12

To build examples provided in this book always use recommended commands:

```
cmake -B <build tree> -S <source tree>
cmake --build <build tree>
```

Be sure to replace placeholders `<build tree>` and `<source tree>` with appropriate paths. As a reminder: **build tree** is the path to target/output directory, **source tree** is the path at which your source code is located.

Planning our work

The software we'll be building in this chapter isn't meant to be extremely complex – we'll create a simple calculator that adds two numbers together (*Figure 12.1*). It will be released as a console application with a text user interface and a library to perform mathematical operations, which can potentially be used in another project. While there isn't much use for such a project in real life, as C++ offers plenty of support for calculations in its standard library, its banality will be perfect to explore how all techniques discussed in this book work together in practice:

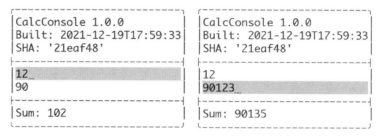

Figure 12.1 – The two states of a console calculator's user interface

Usually, projects either produce a user-facing executable or a library for developers. Projects that do both are a bit rarer but not totally uncommon – some applications offer standalone SDKs or libraries supporting the creation of plugins. Another case may be a library that offers examples of its usage. The project we'll build in this chapter somewhat fits into the last category.

We will start planning by reviewing the list of chapters, recalling their content, and selecting the techniques and tools described therein that we will use to build our computing application:

Chapter 1, First Steps with CMake:

The first chapter gave us basic information on CMake – how to install it and use its command line to build prepared projects. Information on project files provided here will be key: the responsibilities of different files, conventionally used names, and some quirks. In this chapter, we also discussed preset files for generators, but we'll skip these in this project.

Chapter 2, The CMake Language:

Here, we introduced tools necessary to write correct listfiles and scripts. We shared fundamental information on code: comments, command invocations, and arguments. We also thoroughly explained variables, lists, and control structures and presented a few very useful commands. This knowledge will be applied throughout the project.

Chapter 3, Setting Up Your First CMake Project:

Topics covered in the third chapter will have a critical impact on the project:

- Specifying a minimal CMake version decides which CMake policies will apply; naming, versioning, and configuring a project's language affects the basic behavior of the build.
- Insights into project partitioning and structuring that shape the layout of directories and files.
- System discovery variables to help us decide how to handle different environments, specifically for this project – for example, do we need to run `ldconfig`?
- Toolchain configuration allows the requirement of a particular version of C++ and a standard supported by the compiler.

This chapter also tells us that it's often a good idea to disable in-source builds, so we'll do that.

Chapter 4, Working with Targets:

Here, we highlighted how every modern CMake project makes extensive use of targets. Ours will too, for the following reasons:

- Defining a few libraries and executables (both for test and production) will keep the project organized and *DRY*.
- Target properties and transitive usage requirements (propagated properties) keep configuration close to target definitions.
- Generator expressions are going to appear throughout the solution, but we'll keep them as simple as possible.

In this project, we'll use custom commands to generate files for Valgrind and coverage reports, and we'll use target hooks (`PRE_BUILD`) to clean the `.gcda` files produced by coverage instrumentation.

Chapter 5, Compiling C++ Sources with CMake:

There's no C++ project without compilation. The basics are quite simple, but CMake allows us to tweak this process in so many ways: extend the sources of a target, configure the optimizer, and provide debugging information. For this project, the default compilation flags will do just fine, but we'll go ahead and play a bit with the preprocessor:

- We'll store build metadata (the project version, build time, and the Git commit SHA) in the compiled executable and show it to the user.
- We'll enable the precompilation of headers. It's not really a necessity in such a small project, but it will help us practice this concept.

Unity builds won't be necessary – the project won't be big enough to make adding them worthwhile.

Chapter 6, Linking with CMake:

The sixth chapter provides us with general information on linking (useful in any project), most of which comes in handy by default. But since this project also provides a library, we'll explicitly refer to some building instructions on the following:

- Static libraries for testing and development
- Shared libraries for release

This chapter outlines how to separate `main()` for testing, which we'll do as well.

Chapter 7, Managing Dependencies with CMake:

To make the project more interesting, we'll bring an external dependency: a text UI library. We described a few dependency management methods in this chapter. Picking the right one isn't too difficult: the `FetchContent` utility module is usually recommended and most convenient (unless we are solving a specific corner case described in the chapter).

Chapter 8, Testing Frameworks:

Proper automated tests are imperative to assure that quality of our solution doesn't degrade over time. We'll add the support for CTest and properly structure our project for testing (we'll apply the `main()` separation mentioned earlier).

Also, in this chapter, we discussed two testing frameworks: Catch2 and GTest with gMock; for this project, we'll use the latter. To get clear information on our coverage, we'll generate HTML reports with LCOV

Chapter 9, Program Analysis Tools:

To perform static analysis, we can choose from a variety of tools: Clang-Tidy, Cpplint, Cppcheck, include-what-you-use, and link what you use. In this case, we'll go with Cppcheck , as Clang-Tidy doesn't work very well with precompiled headers built with GCC. The dynamic analysis will be done with Valgrind's Memcheck tool, and we'll use the Memcheck-cover wrapper to generate HTML reports. Our source will be also automatically formatted during the build with ClangFormat.

Chapter 10, Generating Documentation:

Since we'll be providing a library as part of this project, it's key to provide at least some documentation to go with it. As we already know, CMake allows us to automate the generation of it with Doxygen. We'll do that in a refreshed design by adding the doxygen-awesome-css look to it.

Chapter 11, Installing and Packaging:

Finally, we'll configure the installation and packaging of our solution. We'll prepare files to form the package as described, along with target definitions. We'll install that and the artifacts from build targets to appropriate directories by including the `GNUInstallDirs` module. We will additionally configure a few components to modularize the solution and prepare it for use with CPack.

Professional projects also come with a few text files: `README`, `LICENSE`, `INSTALL`, and so on. We'll touch on this briefly at the end.

> **Note**
> To make things simpler, we won't implement logic that checks whether all the required utilities and dependencies are available. We'll rely on CMake here to show its diagnostics and tell users what's missing. If projects that you publish after reading this book get significant traction, you might want to consider adding these mechanisms to improve the user experience.

Having formed a clear plan, let's discuss how to actually structure the project, both in terms of logical targets and directory structure.

Project layout

To build any project, we should start with a clear understanding of what logical targets are going to be created in it. In this case, we'll follow the structure shown in *Figure 12.2*:

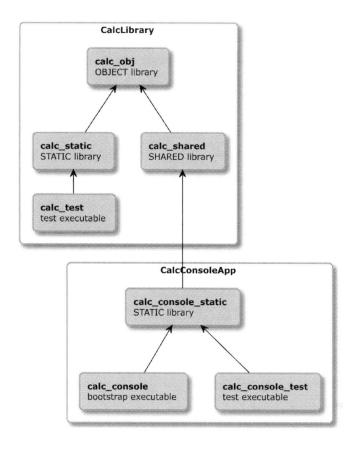

Figure 12.2 – A structure of logical targets

Let's explore the structure by following the build order. First, we'll compile `calc_obj`, which is an **object library**. We did mention *object libraries* a few times in the book, but we didn't actually introduce them as a concept. Let's do this now.

Object libraries

Object libraries are used to group multiple source files under a single logical target and are compiled into the (.o) *object files* during a build. To create an *object library*, we use the same method as with other libraries with the OBJECT keyword:

```
add_library(<target> OBJECT <sources>)
```

Object files produced during the build can be added as compiled elements to other targets with the $<TARGET_OBJECTS:objlib> generator expression:

```
add_library(... $<TARGET_OBJECTS:objlib> ...)
add_executable(... $<TARGET_OBJECTS:objlib> ...)
```

Alternatively, you can add them as dependencies with the target_link_libraries() command.

In our Calc library, *object libraries* will be useful to avoid repeating the compilation of library sources for the static and shared versions of the library. We'll just need to remember to explicitly compile the *object files* with POSITION_INDEPENDENT_CODE, as this is a requirement for a shared library.

With this out of the way, let's get back to the targets of this project: calc_obj will provide compiled *object files*, which then will be used for both the calc_static and calc_shared libraries. What are the practical differences between them and why provide two libraries at all?

Shared libraries versus static libraries

We briefly introduced both types of libraries in *Chapter 6*, *Linking with CMake*. We then mentioned that overall memory usage can be better for multiple programs using the same shared library and that it's likely that a user already has the most popular libraries or knows how to quickly install them. More importantly, shared libraries are delivered in separate files that must be installed in specific paths for the dynamic linker to find them, while static libraries are merged as part of the executable file. In that form, they are slightly faster to use, as no additional lookups are required to find the location of code in memory.

As library authors, we can decide whether we're providing a static or shared version of the library, or we can simply ship both versions and leave this decision to the programmer using our library. We're opting for the latter here (just to see how it's done).

A static library will be consumed by the `calc_test` target, which will contain unit tests that guarantee that the provided business functionality of the library works as expected. As mentioned, we're building both versions from the same set of compiled *object files*. In this scenario, it's perfectly fine to test either version, as there really should be no practical difference in their behavior.

The console app provided with `calc_console_static` target will use the shared library. This target will also link against an external dependency: the **Functional Terminal (X) User Interface** (**FTXUI**) library by Arthur Sonzogni (there is a link to the GitHub project in the *Further reading section*). It provides a dependence-free, cross-platform framework for text user interfaces.

The last two targets are `calc_console` and `calc_console_test`. The `calc_console` target is just a bootstrap `main()` wrapper around `calc_console_static`. Its only purpose is to extract the entry point from the business code. This allows us to write the unit tests (which need to provide their own entry point) and run them from `calc_console_test`.

We now know what targets need to be built and how they relate to each other. Let's figure out how to structure the project with files and directories.

Project file structure

The project consists of two primary targets, the `calc` library and the `calc_console` executable, each of which will reside in directory trees under `src` and `test` to separate production code from tests (shown in *Figure 12.3*). Additionally, we'll have our files in two other directories:

- The *root directory* containing top-level configuration and key project documentation files

- The cmake directory for all the utility modules and helper files used by CMake to build and install the project:

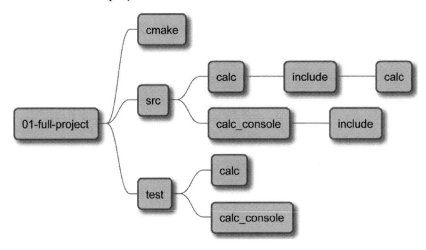

Figure 12.3 – The directory structure of the project

Here's the full list of files in each of the four main directories:

./	./test
CHANGELOG	CMakeLists.txt
CMakeLists.txt	calc/CMakeLists.txt
CalcConfig.cmake	calc/calc_test.cpp
INSTALL	calc_console/CMakeLists.txt
LICENSE	calc_console/tui_test.cpp
README.md	
./src	./cmake
CMakeLists.txt	buildinfo.h.in
calc/CMakeLists.txt	BuildInfo.cmake
calc/calc.cpp	Coverage.cmake
calc/include/calc/calc.h	CppCheck.cmake
calc_console/CMakeLists.txt	Doxygen.cmake
calc_console/bootstrap.cpp	Format.cmake
calc_console/include/tui.h	GetFTXUI.cmake
calc_console/tui.cpp	Install.cmake
	Memcheck.cmake
	NoInSourceBuilds.cmake
	Testing.cmake

Initially, the cmake directory is busier than the business code, but this will quickly change as the project grows in functionality. The effort to start a clean project is significant, but don't worry – it will pay off very soon.

We'll go through all files and see in detail what they do and what role they play in the project. This will happen in four steps: building, testing, installing and providing documentation.

Building and managing dependencies

All build processes work the same way. We start from the top-level listfile and navigate downward into the project source tree. *Figure 12.4* shows which project files partake in building. Numbers in parentheses indicate the order of the CMake script execution:

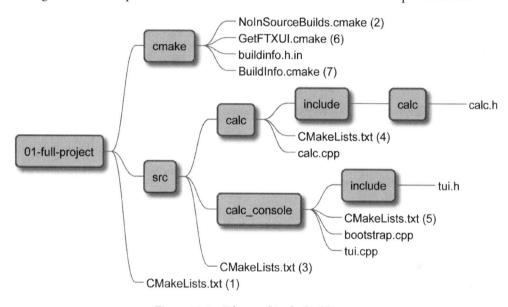

Figure 12.4 – Files used in the build stage

Our top-level listfile will configure the project and load nested elements:

chapter-12/01-full-project/CMakeLists.txt

```
cmake_minimum_required(VERSION 3.20.0)
project(Calc VERSION 1.0.0 LANGUAGES CXX)
list(APPEND CMAKE_MODULE_PATH "${CMAKE_SOURCE_DIR}/cmake")

include(NoInSourceBuilds)
```

```
add_subdirectory(src bin)
add_subdirectory(test)

include(Install)
```

We start by providing key project details and adding a path to the CMake utility modules (the `cmake` directory in our project). We then disable in-source builds (through a custom module) and include two key directories:

- `src`, containing the project source (to be named `bin` in the build tree)
- `test`, containing all the testing utilities

Finally, we include another module that will set up the installation of the project. This will be discussed in another section. Meanwhile, let's take a look at the `NoInSourceBuilds` module to understand how it works:

chapter-12/01-full-project/cmake/NoInSourceBuilds.cmake

```
if(PROJECT_SOURCE_DIR STREQUAL PROJECT_BINARY_DIR)
  message(FATAL_ERROR
    "\n"
    "In-source builds are not allowed.\n"
    "Instead, provide a path to build tree like so:\n"
    "cmake -B <destination>\n"
    "\n"
    "To remove files you accidentally created execute:\n"
    "rm -rf CMakeFiles CMakeCache.txt\n"
  )
endif()
```

No surprises here – we simply check whether the user provided a destination directory as an argument to the `cmake` command to store generated files. It has to be a different path than the project source tree. If that's not the case, we inform the user how to provide it and how to clean the repository after the mistake.

Our top-level listfile then includes the `src` subdirectory, instructing CMake to read the listfile in it:

chapter-12/01-full-project/src/CMakeLists.txt

```
add_subdirectory(calc)
add_subdirectory(calc_console)
```

This file is very subtle – it simply steps into the nested directories, executing the listfiles in them. Let's follow the listfile of the `calc` library – it's a bit involved, so we'll discuss it in parts.

Building the Calc library

The list file for `calc` contains bits of testing configuration, but we'll focus on the building for now; the remainder will be discussed in the *Testing and program analysis* section:

chapter-12/01-full-project/src/calc/CMakeLists.txt (fragment)

```
add_library(calc_obj OBJECT calc.cpp)
target_include_directories(calc_obj INTERFACE
    "$<BUILD_INTERFACE:${CMAKE_CURRENT_SOURCE_DIR}/include>"
    "$<INSTALL_INTERFACE:${CMAKE_INSTALL_INCLUDEDIR}>"
)
set_target_properties(calc_obj PROPERTIES
    PUBLIC_HEADER src/calc/include/calc/calc.h
    POSITION_INDEPENDENT_CODE 1
)
add_library(calc_shared SHARED)
target_link_libraries(calc_shared calc_obj)
add_library(calc_static STATIC)
target_link_libraries(calc_static calc_obj)

# ... testing and program analysis modules
# ... documentation generation
```

We declare three targets:

- `calc_obj`, an *object library* compiling a `calc.cpp` implementation file. It also references the `calc.h` header file through the `PUBLIC_HEADER` property, which can be found in the configured *include directory* (thanks to generator expressions providing appropriate paths for a specific mode – build or install). By using this library, we avoid repeated compilation of other targets, but we also need to enable `POSITION_INDEPENDENT_CODE` so that generated *object files* are usable by the shared library.
- `calc_shared`, a shared library depending on `calc_obj`.
- `calc_static`, a static library depending on `calc_obj`.

For completeness, we'll add a listing of the `calc` library's C++ code:

chapter-12/01-full-project/src/calc/include/calc/calc.h

```cpp
#pragma once

namespace Calc {
int Sum(int a, int b);
int Multiply(int a, int b);
} // namespace Calc
```

This code is quite basic: it declares two global functions enclosed in a `Calc` namespace (C++ namespaces are extremely useful in libraries, helping to avoid name collisions).

The implementation file is also very straightforward:

chapter-12/01-full-project/src/calc/calc.cpp

```cpp
namespace Calc {
int Sum(int a, int b) {
    return a + b;
}

int Multiply(int a, int b) {
    return a * b;
}
} // namespace Calc
```

This wraps up the explanation of files in the `src/calc` directory. Next up is the `src/calc_console` and building the executable of the console calculator using this library.

Building the Calc Console executable

The source directory of `calc_console` contains several files: a listfile, two implementation files (business code and a bootstrap), and a header file. The listfile looks as follows:

chapter-12/01-full-project/src/calc_console/CMakeLists.txt (fragment)

```
include(GetFTXUI)
add_library(calc_console_static STATIC tui.cpp)
target_include_directories(calc_console_static PUBLIC
include)
target_precompile_headers(calc_console_static PUBLIC
<string>)
target_link_libraries(calc_console_static PUBLIC
calc_shared
   ftxui::screen ftxui::dom ftxui::component)
include(BuildInfo)
BuildInfo(calc_console_static)
# ... testing and program analysis modules
# ... documentation generation

add_executable(calc_console bootstrap.cpp)
target_link_libraries(calc_console calc_console_static)
```

The listfile seem very busy, but now, as experienced CMake users, we can easily untangle what's happening inside:

1. Include CMake module to fetch FTXUI dependency.
2. Declare the `calc_console_static` target, which contains the business code, but not the `main()` function, to allow GTest to define its own entry point.
3. Add a header precompilation – we're just adding a standard `string` header to prove a point, but for larger projects, we could add many more (including headers belonging to the project).
4. Link the business code with the shared `calc_shared` library and the FTXUI library.

5. Add all the actions to be taken on this target: the generation of build information, testing, program analysis, and documentation.
6. Add and link the `calc_console` bootstrap executable, which provides the entry point.

Again, we'll defer discussing testing and documentation to appropriate sections in this chapter. Let's take a look at dependency management and build info generation instead.

Note that we're preferring the utility module over find-module to bring in the FTXUI. This is because it isn't very likely that this dependency is already present in the system. Rather than hoping to find it, we'll fetch and install it:

chapter-12/01-full-project/cmake/GetFTXUI.cmake

```
include(FetchContent)

FetchContent_Declare(
  FTXTUI
  GIT_REPOSITORY https://github.com/ArthurSonzogni/FTXUI.git
  GIT_TAG        v0.11
)
option(FTXUI_ENABLE_INSTALL "" OFF)
option(FTXUI_BUILD_EXAMPLES "" OFF)
option(FTXUI_BUILD_DOCS "" OFF)
FetchContent_MakeAvailable(FTXTUI)
```

We're using the recommended `FetchContent` method, described in detail in *Chapter 7, Managing Dependencies with CMake*. The only unusual addition is the calls of the `option()` command. They allow us to skip lengthy steps of the FTXUI build and disengage its installation configuration from the installation of this project. The same will be necessary for GTest dependency. The `option()` command is referenced in the *Further reading* section.

The listfile for `calc_command` includes one more custom utility module that is build-related: `BuildInfo`. We'll use it to record three values that can be surfaced in the executable:

- SHA of the current Git commit
- The timestamp of the build
- The project version specified in the top-level listfile

You might remember from *Chapter 5, Compiling C++ Sources with CMake*, that we can use CMake to capture some build-time values and provide them to C++ code through template files – for example, with a handy C++ struct:

chapter-12/01-full-project/cmake/buildinfo.h.in

```
struct BuildInfo {
  static inline const std::string CommitSHA =
    "@COMMIT_SHA@";
  static inline const std::string Timestamp =
    "@TIMESTAMP@";
  static inline const
  std::string Version = "@PROJECT_VERSION@";
};
```

To fill that structure during the configuration stage, we'll use the following code:

chapter-12/01-full-project/cmake/BuildInfo.cmake

```
set(BUILDINFO_TEMPLATE_DIR ${CMAKE_CURRENT_LIST_DIR})
set(DESTINATION "${CMAKE_CURRENT_BINARY_DIR}/buildinfo")

string(TIMESTAMP TIMESTAMP)
find_program(GIT_PATH git REQUIRED)
execute_process(COMMAND
  ${GIT_PATH} log --pretty=format:'%h' -n 1
  OUTPUT_VARIABLE COMMIT_SHA)

configure_file(
  "${BUILDINFO_TEMPLATE_DIR}/buildinfo.h.in"
  "${DESTINATION}/buildinfo.h" @ONLY
)

function(BuildInfo target)
  target_include_directories(${target} PRIVATE
    ${DESTINATION})
endfunction()
```

Including the module will set variables containing information we're after and then we'll call `configure_file()` to generate `buildinfo.h`. All that's left is to call the `BuildInfo` function and add the directory of the produced file to *include directories* of the desired target. The file can be then shared with multiple different consumers if needed. In such a case, you'll probably want to add `include_guard(GLOBAL)` at the top of the listfile to avoid running the `git` command for every target.

Before delving into the implementation of the console calculator, I'd like to underline that you shouldn't worry too much about the complexity of the `tui.cpp` file. To fully understand it, you'll require some knowledge of the FXTUI library – we don't want to get in too deep here. Instead, let's focus on the highlighted lines:

chapter-12/01-full-project/src/calc_console/tui.cpp

```cpp
#include "tui.h"
#include <ftxui/dom/elements.hpp>
#include "buildinfo.h"
#include "calc/calc.h"

using namespace ftxui;
using namespace std;

string a{"12"}, b{"90"};
auto input_a = Input(&a, "");
auto input_b = Input(&b, "");
auto component = Container::Vertical({input_a, input_b});

Component getTui() {
  return Renderer(component, [&] {
    auto sum = Calc::Sum(stoi(a), stoi(b));
    return vbox({
      text("CalcConsole " + BuildInfo::Version),
      text("Built: " + BuildInfo::Timestamp),
      text("SHA: " + BuildInfo::CommitSHA),
      separator(),
      input_a->Render(),
      input_b->Render(),
      separator(),
```

```
            text("Sum: " + to_string(sum)),
    }) |
    border;
});
}
```

This piece of code provides a `getTui()` function, which returns a `ftxui::Component`, an object that encapsulates an interactive UI element with labels, text fields, separators, and a border. If you're interested in how it works in detail, you'll find suitable references in the *Further reading* section.

More importantly, look at the include directives: they refer to the headers we provided earlier with the `calc_obj` target and the `BuildInfo` module. The first line of the lambda function provided to the constructor of the `Renderer` class will call the library's `Calc::Sum` method and use the resulting value to print a label with sum (by calling the `text()` function below).

Similarly, the labels are used to present the user with the `BuildInfo::` values collected at build time in three consecutive calls to `text()`.

This method has its declaration in the related header file:

chapter-12/01-full-project/src/calc_console/include/tui.h

```
#include <ftxui/component/component.hpp>
ftxui::Component getTui();
```

This is then used by the bootstrap from the `calc_console` target:

chapter-12/01-full-project/src/calc_console/bootstrap.cpp

```
#include <ftxui/component/screen_interactive.hpp>
#include "tui.h"

int main(int argc, char** argv) {
    ftxui::ScreenInteractive::FitComponent().Loop(getTui());
}
```

This short piece of code utilizes `ftxui` to create an interactive console screen that takes the `Component` object returned by `getTui()`, makes it visible to the user, and collects keyboard events in a loop, creating an interface, as shown in *Figure 12.1*. Again, understanding this in full isn't really crucial, as the main purpose of `ftxui` is to provide us with an external dependency that we can use to practice CMake techniques.

We've covered all the files in the `src` directory. Let's move on to the aforementioned topic of testing and analyzing the program.

Testing and program analysis

Program analysis and testing go hand in hand to assure the quality of our solutions. For example, running Valgrind becomes more consistent when test code is used. For this reason, we'll configure those two things together. *Figure 12.5* illustrates the execution flow and files needed to set them up (a few snippets will be added to the `src` directory):

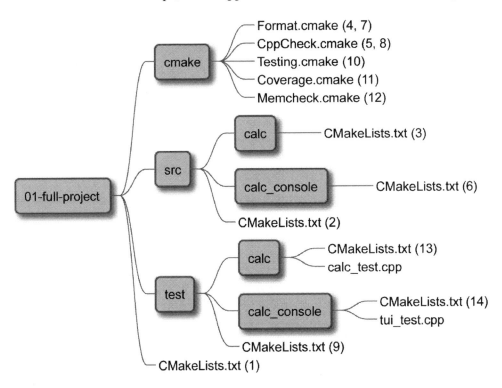

Figure 12.5 – Files used to enable testing and program analysis

As we already know, tests live in the `test` directory, and their listfile gets executed from the top-level listfile with the `add_subdirectory()` command. Let's see what's inside:

chapter-12/01-full-project/test/CMakeLists.txt

```
include(Testing)
add_subdirectory(calc)
add_subdirectory(calc_console)
```

Testing utilities defined in the `Testing` module are included at this level to allow both target groups (from the `calc` and the `calc_console` directories) to use them:

chapter-12/01-full-project/cmake/Testing.cmake (fragment)

```
enable_testing()

include(FetchContent)
FetchContent_Declare(
  googletest
  GIT_REPOSITORY https://github.com/google/googletest.git
  GIT_TAG release-1.11.0
)
# For Windows: Prevent overriding the parent project's
# compiler/linker settings
set(gtest_force_shared_crt ON CACHE BOOL "" FORCE)
option(INSTALL_GMOCK "Install GMock" OFF)
option(INSTALL_GTEST "Install GTest" OFF)
FetchContent_MakeAvailable(googletest)
...
```

We enabled testing and included the `FetchContent` module to get GTest and GMock. We're not really using GMock in this project, but these two frameworks are bundled in a single repository, so we need to configure GMock as well. The highlighted part of this configuration disengages the installation of both frameworks from the installation of our project (by setting the appropriate `option()` to `OFF`).

Next, we need to create a function that enables the thorough testing of business targets. We'll keep it in the same file:

chapter-12/01-full-project/cmake/Testing.cmake (continued)

```
...
include(GoogleTest)
include(Coverage)
include(Memcheck)

macro(AddTests target)
    target_link_libraries(${target} PRIVATE gtest_main gmock)
    gtest_discover_tests(${target})
    AddCoverage(${target})
    AddMemcheck(${target})
endmacro()
```

Here, we first include the necessary modules: `GoogleTest` is bundled with CMake, but `Coverage` and `Memcheck` will be written by us. We then provide an `AddTests` macro, which will prepare a target for testing, instrument coverage, and memory checking. Let's see how it works in detail.

Preparing the coverage module

Adding coverage to multiple targets is a little bit tricky, as it consists of a few steps. We start by introducing two functions that enable coverage tracking and clean stale tracking files between builds:

chapter-12/01-full-project/cmake/Coverage.cmake (fragment)

```
function(EnableCoverage target)
    if (CMAKE_BUILD_TYPE STREQUAL Debug)
        target_compile_options(${target} PRIVATE --coverage
            -fno-inline)
        target_link_options(${target} PUBLIC --coverage)
    endif()
endfunction()

function(CleanCoverage target)
```

```
    add_custom_command(TARGET ${target} PRE_BUILD COMMAND
      find ${CMAKE_BINARY_DIR} -type f
      -name '*.gcda' -exec rm {} +)
endfunction()
```

The preceding functions will be used later, when we get to individual target configurations (`calc_...` and `calc_console_...`). The `Coverage` module will also provide a function that generates the custom coverage target:

chapter-12/01-full-project/cmake/Coverage.cmake (continued)

```
function(AddCoverage target)
  find_program(LCOV_PATH lcov REQUIRED)
  find_program(GENHTML_PATH genhtml REQUIRED)
  add_custom_target(coverage-${target}
    COMMAND ${LCOV_PATH} -d . --zerocounters
    COMMAND $<TARGET_FILE:${target}>
    COMMAND ${LCOV_PATH} -d . --capture -o coverage.info
    COMMAND ${LCOV_PATH} -r coverage.info '/usr/include/*'
      -o filtered.info
    COMMAND ${GENHTML_PATH} -o coverage-${target}
      filtered.info --legend
    COMMAND rm -rf coverage.info filtered.info
    WORKING_DIRECTORY ${CMAKE_BINARY_DIR}
  )
endfunction()
```

`AddCoverage()` is called in the `AddTests()` function in the `Testing` module. It differs slightly from the one introduced in *Chapter 8, Testing Frameworks*, as it takes the name of the target into account and adds it to the output path to avoid any collisions.

To generate reports for both test targets, we simply need to run two `cmake` commands (after configuring the project with the `Debug` build type):

```
cmake --build <build-tree> -t coverage-calc_test
cmake --build <build-tree> -t coverage-calc_console_test
```

It's now time to modify the Memcheck module that we created earlier (in *Chapter 9, Program Analysis Tools*) to handle multiple targets.

Preparing the Memcheck module

Generation of the Valgrind memory management report is called by `AddTests()`. We'll start this module with the general setup:

chapter-12/01-full-project/cmake/Memcheck.cmake (fragment)

```cmake
include(FetchContent)
FetchContent_Declare(
  memcheck-cover
  GIT_REPOSITORY https://github.com/Farigh/memcheck-cover.git
  GIT_TAG        release-1.2
)
FetchContent_MakeAvailable(memcheck-cover)
```

We're familiar with this code already; let's look at the function that'll create appropriate targets for report generation:

chapter-12/01-full-project/cmake/Memcheck.cmake (continued)

```cmake
function(AddMemcheck target)
  set(MEMCHECK_PATH ${memcheck-cover_SOURCE_DIR}/bin)
  set(REPORT_PATH "${CMAKE_BINARY_DIR}/valgrind-${target}")

  add_custom_target(memcheck-${target}
    COMMAND ${MEMCHECK_PATH}/memcheck_runner.sh -o
      "${REPORT_PATH}/report"
      -- $<TARGET_FILE:${target}>
    COMMAND ${MEMCHECK_PATH}/generate_html_report.sh
      -i ${REPORT_PATH}
      -o ${REPORT_PATH}
    WORKING_DIRECTORY ${CMAKE_BINARY_DIR}
  )
endfunction()
```

To handle multiple targets, the `REPORT_PATH` variable is set to store the path to a target-specific report. This variable is then used in subsequent commands.

Generation of Memcheck reports can be achieved with following commands (this works better in the `Debug` build type):

```
cmake --build <build-tree> -t memcheck-calc_test
cmake --build <build-tree> -t memcheck-calc_console_test
```

These are all modules used by the `Testing` module. Let's see how it is used.

Applying testing scenarios

A few things have to happen for the testing to work:

1. We need to create nested listfiles and define test targets for both directories.
2. Unit tests need to be written and prepared as executable targets.
3. These targets need to have `AddTests()` called on them.
4. **Software Under Test (SUT)** needs to be instrumented to enable coverage collection.
5. Collected coverage should be cleaned between the builds to avoid segmentation faults.

As implied in `test/CMakeLists.txt`, we'll create two nested listfiles that configure our tests. Once more, we'll provide one for the library:

chapter-12/01-full-project/test/calc/CMakeLists.txt (fragment)

```
add_executable(calc_test calc_test.cpp)
target_link_libraries(calc_test PRIVATE calc_static)
AddTests(calc_test)
EnableCoverage(calc_obj)
```

We'll also provide one for the executable:

chapter-12/01-full-project/test/calc_console/CMakeLists.txt (fragment)

```
add_executable(calc_console_test tui_test.cpp)
target_link_libraries(calc_console_test
   PRIVATE calc_console_static)
AddTests(calc_console_test)
EnableCoverage(calc_console_static)
```

To keep things brief, we'll provide as simple unit tests as possible. One file will cover the library:

chapter-12/01-full-project/test/calc/calc_test.cpp

```cpp
#include "calc/calc.h"
#include <gtest/gtest.h>

TEST(CalcTest, SumAddsTwoInts) {
    EXPECT_EQ(4, Calc::Sum(2, 2));
}
TEST(CalcTest, MultiplyMultipliesTwoInts) {
    EXPECT_EQ(12, Calc::Multiply(3, 4));
}
```

And we'll have a second file to test the business code. For this purpose, we'll use the FXTUI library. Again, there's no expectation that you will understand this source code in every detail. Test listings are provided in this chapter merely for completeness:

chapter-12/01-full-project/test/calc_console/tui_test.cpp

```cpp
#include "tui.h"
#include <gmock/gmock.h>
#include <gtest/gtest.h>
#include <ftxui/screen/screen.hpp>
using namespace ::ftxui;

TEST(ConsoleCalcTest, RunWorksWithDefaultValues) {
    auto component = getTui();
    auto document = component->Render();
    auto screen = Screen::Create(Dimension::Fit(document));
    Render(screen, document);
    auto output = screen.ToString();
    ASSERT_THAT(output, testing::HasSubstr("Sum: 102"));
}
```

This test code simply renders the textual UI in a default state to a static screen object, which then gets stored in a string. In order for the test to pass, the output needs to contain a substring with the default sum.

Now, we'll need to complete the remaining steps: after we have created test targets and prepared their source code, it's time to register them in CPack with the `AddTests()` function from the `Testing` module.

We do this for the library:

chapter-12/01-full-project/test/calc/CMakeLists.txt (continued)

```
# ... calc_test target definition
AddTests(calc_test)
EnableCoverage(calc_obj)
```

We then do it for the executable:

chapter-12/01-full-project/test/calc_console/CMakeLists.txt (continued)

```
# ... calc_console_test target definition
AddTests(calc_console_test)
EnableCoverage(calc_console_static)
```

Subsequently, we instruct the SUT to enable coverage instrumentation with `EnableCoverage()`. Note that in the case of the library, we had to add instrumentation to the *object library* rather than the static one. This is because the `--coverage` flag has to be added to the compilation step, which happens when `calc_obj` is being built.

Unfortunately, we can't add cleaning of the coverage files here, as CMake requires `add_custom_command` hooks to be called in the same directory as the target definition. This brings us back to the `src/calc` and `src/calc_console` listfiles that we didn't complete previously. We'll need to add `CleanCoverage(calc_static)` and `CleanCoverage(calc_console_static)` respectively (we have to include the `Coverage` module first). What else needs to be added to these files? Instructions to enable static analysis!

Adding static analysis tools

We postponed the continuation of business code listfiles until now so that we can discuss added modules in the appropriate context. We can add a `CleanCoverage` function call and a few other things to the library listfile:

chapter-12/01-full-project/src/calc/CMakeLists.txt (continued)

```
# ... calc_static target definition
include(Coverage)
CleanCoverage(calc_static)
include(Format)
Format(calc_static .)
include(CppCheck)
AddCppCheck(calc_obj)
# ... documentation generation
```

We can also add them to the executable:

chapter-12/01-full-project/src/calc_console/CMakeLists.cmake (continued)

```
# ... calc_console_static target definition
include(BuildInfo)
BuildInfo(calc_console_static)
include(Coverage)
CleanCoverage(calc_console_static)
include(Format)
Format(calc_console_static .)
include(CppCheck)
AddCppCheck(calc_console_static)
# ... documentation generation
# ... calc_console bootstrap target definition
```

These files are almost complete now (as the second comment suggests, we still need to add the documentation code, which will happen in the *Automatic documentation generation* section).

Two new modules appear in the listings: `Format` and `CppCheck`. Let's dive into the first one:

chapter-12/01-full-project/cmake/Format.cmake

```
function(Format target directory)
  find_program(CLANG-FORMAT_PATH clang-format REQUIRED)
  set(EXPRESSION h hpp hh c cc cxx cpp)
  list(TRANSFORM EXPRESSION PREPEND "${directory}/*.")
  file(GLOB_RECURSE SOURCE_FILES FOLLOW_SYMLINKS
    LIST_DIRECTORIES false ${EXPRESSION}
  )
  add_custom_command(TARGET ${target} PRE_BUILD COMMAND
    ${CLANG-FORMAT_PATH} -i --style=file ${SOURCE_FILES}
  )
endfunction()
```

The `Format()` function is an exact copy of the formatting function described in *Chapter 9, Program Analysis Tools*; we're simply reusing it here.

Next up is a completely new `CppCheck` module:

chapter-12/01-full-project/cmake/CppCheck.cmake

```
function(AddCppCheck target)
  find_program(CPPCHECK_PATH cppcheck REQUIRED)
  set_target_properties(${target}
    PROPERTIES CXX_CPPCHECK
    "${CPPCHECK_PATH};--enable=warning;--error-exitcode=10"
  )
endfunction()
```

This is simple and convenient. You may see some resemblance to the Clang-Tidy module (from *Chapter 9, Program Analysis Tools*); this is CMake's strength – many concepts working the same way. Note the arguments passed to `cppcheck`:

- `--enable=warning` – This specifies that we'd like to get warning messages. You can enable additional checks – refer to the Cppcheck manual for more details (the link can be found in the *Further reading section*).

- `--error-exitcode=10` – This specifies that we'd like to get an error code when `cppcheck` detects an issue. This can be any number from `1` to `255` (as `0` indicates success), although some numbers can be reserved by the system.

Usage is very convenient – calling `AddCppCheck` will inform CMake that it needs to run the checks automatically on the specified target.

We have virtually created all files in the `src` and `test` subdirectories. Now, our solution builds and can be fully tested. It's finally time to move to installation and packaging.

Installing and packaging

We're circling back to the subject discussed in the previous chapter and starting with a quick overview of the files needed to set up installation and packaging:

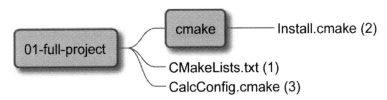

Figure 12.6 – Files configuring installation and packaging

Only files are needed here – most of the work is already done in previous sections. As you may remember, the top-level listfile includes a CMake module that's going to handle this process:

chapter-12/01-full-project/CMakeLists.txt (fragment)

```
...
include(Install)
```

We're interested in installing two items:

- The Calc library artifacts: the static library, the shared library, and header files along with their target export file
- The Calc console executable

The package definition config-file will only introduce library targets, as potential consuming projects won't depend on the executable.

After configuring the installation steps, we'll move on to the CPack configuration. The high-level overview of the `Install` module looks like this:

chapter-12/01-full-project/cmake/Install.cmake (overview)

```
# Includes
# Installation of Calc library
# Installation of Calc Console executable
# Configuration of CPack
```

Everything is planned, so it's time to write an installation module for the library.

Installation of the library

To install the library, it's best to start by configuring logical targets and specifying the destination for their artifacts. To avoid providing paths manually, we'll be using default values provided by the `GNUInstallDirs` module. For modularity, we'll group the artifacts into components. The default installation will install all files, but you may choose to only install the `runtime` component and skip the `development` artifacts:

chapter-12/01-full-project/cmake/Install.cmake (fragment)

```
include(GNUInstallDirs)
# Calc library
install(TARGETS calc_obj calc_shared calc_static
    EXPORT CalcLibrary
    ARCHIVE COMPONENT development
    LIBRARY COMPONENT runtime
    PUBLIC_HEADER DESTINATION
        ${CMAKE_INSTALL_INCLUDEDIR}/calc
        COMPONENT runtime
)
```

During the installation, we'd like to register the shared library we copied with `ldconfig`:

chapter-12/01-full-project/cmake/Install.cmake (continued)

```
if (UNIX)
    install(CODE "execute_process(COMMAND ldconfig)"
        COMPONENT runtime
```

```
    )
endif()
```

Having those steps prepared, we can make the library visible to other CMake projects by wrapping it in a reusable CMake package. We'll need to generate and install the target export file and the config-file that includes it:

chapter-12/01-full-project/cmake/Install.cmake (continued)

```
install(EXPORT CalcLibrary
    DESTINATION ${CMAKE_INSTALL_LIBDIR}/calc/cmake
    NAMESPACE Calc::
    COMPONENT runtime
)

install(FILES "CalcConfig.cmake"
    DESTINATION ${CMAKE_INSTALL_LIBDIR}/calc/cmake
)
```

As we already know, for very simple packages, the config-file can be really minimal:

chapter-12/01-full-project/CalcConfig.cmake

```
include("${CMAKE_CURRENT_LIST_DIR}/CalcLibrary.cmake")
```

That's it. The library will now be installed when you run cmake in --install mode after building the solution. All that remains to be installed is the executable.

Installation of the executable

The installation of binary executables is the simplest step of all. We just need to use a single command:

chapter-12/01-full-project/cmake/Install.cmake (continued)

```
# CalcConsole runtime
install(TARGETS calc_console
    RUNTIME COMPONENT runtime
)
```

And it's done! Let's move on to the last part of the configuration – packing.

Packaging with CPack

We can go wild and configure a vast multitude of supported package types; for this project, however, a basic configuration will be enough:

chapter-12/01-full-project/cmake/Install.cmake (continued)

```
# CPack configuration
set(CPACK_PACKAGE_VENDOR "Rafal Swidzinski")
set(CPACK_PACKAGE_CONTACT "email@example.com")
set(CPACK_PACKAGE_DESCRIPTION "Simple Calculator")
include(CPack)
```

Such a minimal setup works well for standard archives, such as ZIP files. We can test the whole installation and packaging with a single command (the project has to be built beforehand):

```
# cpack -G TGZ -B packages
CPack: Create package using TGZ
CPack: Install projects
CPack: - Run preinstall target for: Calc
CPack: - Install project: Calc []
CPack: Create package
CPack: - package: /tmp/b/packages/Calc-1.0.0-Linux.tar.gz generated.
```

This concludes the installation and packaging; the next order of business is documentation.

Providing the documentation

The final element of a professional project is, of course, the documentation. It comes in two categories:

- Technical documentation (interfaces, designs, classes, and files)
- General documentation (all other not-as-technical documents)

As we saw in *Chapter 10, Generating Documentation*, a lot of technical documentation can be generated automatically with CMake by using Doxygen.

Automatic documentation generation

A thing to mention: some projects generate documentation during the build stage and package it with the rest of the project. It's a matter of preference. For this project, we have decided not to do so. You might have a good reason to choose otherwise (such as hosting the documentation online).

Figure 12.7 shows the overview of the execution flow that is used in this process:

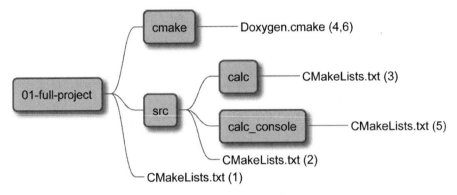

Figure 12.7 – Files used to generate documentation

To generate documentation for our targets, we'll create another CMake utility module, Doxygen. We'll start by using the Doxygen find-module and downloading the doxygen-awesome-css project for themes:

chapter-12/01-full-project/cmake/Doxygen.cmake (fragment)

```
find_package(Doxygen REQUIRED)

include(FetchContent)
FetchContent_Declare(doxygen-awesome-css
  GIT_REPOSITORY
    https://github.com/jothepro/doxygen-awesome-css.git
  GIT_TAG
    v1.6.0
)
FetchContent_MakeAvailable(doxygen-awesome-css)
```

Then, we'll need a function to create targets that generate documentation. We'll draw closely from code introduced in *Chapter 10, Generating Documentation*, and modify it to support many targets:

chapter-12/01-full-project/cmake/Doxygen.cmake (continued)

```cmake
function(Doxygen target input)
  set(NAME "doxygen-${target}")
  set(DOXYGEN_HTML_OUTPUT
    ${PROJECT_BINARY_DIR}/${NAME})
  set(DOXYGEN_GENERATE_HTML        YES)
  set(DOXYGEN_GENERATE_TREEVIEW    YES)
  set(DOXYGEN_HAVE_DOT             YES)
  set(DOXYGEN_DOT_IMAGE_FORMAT     svg)
  set(DOXYGEN_DOT_TRANSPARENT      YES)
  set(DOXYGEN_HTML_EXTRA_STYLESHEET
      ${doxygen-awesome-css_SOURCE_DIR}/doxygen-
        awesome.css)

  doxygen_add_docs(${NAME}
    ${PROJECT_SOURCE_DIR}/${input}
      COMMENT "Generate HTML documentation"
  )
endfunction()
```

Now, we need to use this function by calling it for the library target:

chapter-12/01-full-project/src/calc/CMakeLists.txt (continued)

```cmake
# ... calc_static target definition
# ... testing and program analysis modules
include(Doxygen)
Doxygen(calc src/calc)
```

And we call it for the console executable:

chapter-12/01-full-project/src/calc_console/CMakeLists.txt (continued)

```
# ... calc_static target definition
# ... testing and program analysis modules
include(Doxygen)
Doxygen(calc_console src/calc_console)

add_executable(calc_console bootstrap.cpp)
target_link_libraries(calc_console calc_console_static)
```

Two new targets are added to the project: `doxygen-calc` and `doxygen-calc_console`, and technical documentation can be generated on demand.

What other documents should we provide?

Not-as-technical documents of professional project

Professional projects should always include at least two documents that are stored in a top-level directory:

- `README` – generally describes the project
- `LICENSE` – specifies the legal characteristics of the project

You might also consider adding these:

- `INSTALL` – describes the steps required for installation
- `CHANGELOG` – lists important changes that happened in different versions
- `AUTHORS` – contains credits and contact information if a project has multiple contributors
- `BUGS` – informs about known bugs and instructs how to report new ones

CMake as such doesn't play any role when it comes to these files – there's no automated behavior or scripts to use. However, these files are an essential part of C++ projects and should be covered for completeness. For reference, we'll provide a minimal set of exemplary files, starting with a short README file:

chapter-12/01-full-project/README.md

```
# Calc Console

Calc Console is a calculator that adds two numbers in a
terminal. It does all the math by using a **Calc** library.
This library is also available in this package.

This application is written in C++ and built with CMake.

## More information
- Installation instructions are in the INSTALL file
- License is in the LICENSE file
```

This is short and maybe a little silly. Note the .md extension – it stands for *Markdown*, which is a text-based formatting language that is easily readable. Websites such as GitHub and many text editors will render these files with rich formatting.

Our INSTALL file will look like this:

chapter-12/01-full-project/INSTALL

```
To install this software you'll need to provide the following:

- C++ compiler supporting C++17
- CMake >= 3.20
- GIT
- Doxygen + Graphviz
- CPPCheck
- Valgrind

This project also depends on GTest, GMock and FXTUI. This
software is automatically pulled from external repositories
during the installation.
```

To configure the project type:

```
cmake -B <temporary-directory>
```

Then you can build the project:

```
cmake --build <temporary-directory>
```

And finally install it:

```
cmake --install <temporary-directory>
```

To generate the documentation run:

```
cmake --build <temporary-directory> -t doxygen-calc
cmake --build <temporary-directory> -t doxygen-calc_console
```

This file turned out to be a bit longer, but it covers the most important requirements, steps, and commands, and it will work just fine for our needs.

The `LICENSE` file is a bit tricky, as it requires some expertise in copyright law (and otherwise). Instead of writing all clauses by ourselves, we can do what many other projects do and use a readily available software license. For this project, we'll go with the MIT License, which is extremely permissive. You might want to choose something else, depending on the needs of a specific project – check the *Further reading* section for some useful references:

chapter-12/01-full-project/LICENSE

```
Copyright 2022 Rafal Swidzinski

Permission is hereby granted, free of charge, to any person
obtaining a copy of this software and associated documentation
files (the "Software"), to deal in the Software without
restriction, including without limitation the rights to use,
copy, modify, merge, publish, distribute, sublicense, and/
or sell copies of the Software, and to permit persons to whom
the Software is furnished to do so, subject to the following
conditions:
```

```
The above copyright notice and this permission notice shall be
included in all copies or substantial portions of the Software.
```

```
THE SOFTWARE IS PROVIDED "AS IS", WITHOUT WARRANTY OF ANY
KIND, EXPRESS OR IMPLIED, INCLUDING BUT NOT LIMITED TO THE
WARRANTIES OF MERCHANTABILITY, FITNESS FOR A PARTICULAR PURPOSE
AND NONINFRINGEMENT. IN NO EVENT SHALL THE AUTHORS OR COPYRIGHT
HOLDERS BE LIABLE FOR ANY CLAIM, DAMAGES OR OTHER LIABILITY,
WHETHER IN AN ACTION OF CONTRACT, TORT OR OTHERWISE, ARISING
FROM, OUT OF OR IN CONNECTION WITH THE SOFTWARE OR THE USE OR
OTHER DEALINGS IN THE SOFTWARE.
```

Lastly, we have the CHANGELOG. As suggested earlier, it's good to keep track of changes in a file so that developers using your project can easily find out which version supports the features they need. For example, it might be useful to say that a multiplication feature was added to the library in version 0.8.2. Something as simple as the following is already helpful:

chapter-12/01-full-project/CHANGELOG

```
1.0.0 Public version with installer
0.8.2 Multiplication added to the Calc Library
0.5.1 Introducing the Calc Console application
0.2.0 Basic Calc library with Sum function
```

Our professional project is now complete – we can build it, test it, generate packages, upload all sources to a repository, and release artifacts. Of course, it would be easier if this could happen automatically, perhaps with a CI/CD pipeline. But that's a story for another book.

Summary

This chapter wraps up our long journey through CMake. Now you fully understand what problems CMake aims to solve and which steps are necessary to automate these solutions.

In the first three chapters, we explored all the basics: what CMake is and how users leverage it to bring raw source code to life, what the key components of CMake are, and what purpose different project files have. We explained the syntax of CMake: comments, command invocation, arguments, variables, and control structures. We've discovered how modules and subprojects work, what the correct project structure is, and how to work with various platforms and toolchains.

The second part of the book taught us about building with CMake: how to use targets, custom commands, build types, and generator expressions. We dove deep into the technicalities of compilation, and the configuration of a preprocessor and an optimizer. We discussed linking and introduced different library types. Then, we investigated how CMake helps to manage the dependencies of a project with the `FetchContent` and `ExternalProject` modules. We also researched Git submodules as a possible alternative. Most importantly, we studied how to find installed packages with `find_package()` and `FindPkgConfig`. If these weren't enough, we looked into writing our own find-modules.

The last part told us how to go about the automation of testing, analysis, documentation, installing, and packaging. We looked into CTest and testing frameworks: Catch2, GoogleTest, and GoogleMock. Coverage reporting was covered too. *Chapter 9, Program Analysis Tools*, gave us an understanding of different analysis tools: a formatter and static checkers (Clang-Tidy, Cppcheck, and so on), and explained how to add the Memcheck memory analyzer from the Valgrind suite. Next, we briefly described how to generate documentation with Doxygen and how to make it presentable. Lastly, we demonstrated how to install projects on the system, create reusable CMake packages, and configure and use CPack to generate binary packages.

The last chapter drew on all this knowledge to showcase a completely professional project.

Congratulations on completing this book. We've covered everything necessary to develop, test, and package high-quality C++ software. The best way to make progress from here is to put what you have learned into practice and create great software for your users. Good luck!

R.

Further reading

For more information, you can refer to the following links:

- *Building both a static library and a shared library*: https://stackoverflow.com/q/2152077
- *A FXTUI library project*: https://github.com/ArthurSonzogni/FTXUI
- *The documentation of the option() command*: https://cmake.org/cmake/help/latest/command/option.html
- *Preparing for Release (of open source software) by Google*: https://opensource.google/docs/releasing/preparing/

- *Why we can't use Clang-Tidy for GCC-precompiled headers*: https://gitlab.kitware.com/cmake/cmake/-/issues/22081#note_943104
- *Cppcheck manual*: https://cppcheck.sourceforge.io/manual.pdf
- *How to write a README*: https://www.freecodecamp.org/news/how-to-write-a-good-readme-file/
- *Creative Commons Licenses for GitHub Projects*: https://github.com/santisoler/cc-licenses
- *Commonly used project licenses recognized by GitHub*: https://docs.github.com/en/repositories/managing-your-repositorys-settings-and-features/customizing-your-repository/licensing-a-repository

Appendix
Miscellaneous Commands

Every language has utility commands that come in handy on a myriad of occasions. CMake is no different in that matter: it provides tools for simple arithmetic, bitwise operations, string manipulations, and operations on lists and on files. Interestingly enough, the occasions when they are necessary are relatively rare (thanks to all the enhancements and modules written over the years), but can still be required in more automated projects.

Hence this appendix, which is a short summary of miscellaneous commands and their multiple modes. Treat this as a handy offline reference or a simplified version of the official documentation. If you need more information, visit the provided links.

In this chapter, we're going to cover the following main topics:

- The `string()` command
- The `list()` command
- The `file()` command
- The `math()` command

The string() command

The `string()` command is used to manipulate strings. It comes with a variety of modes that perform different actions on the string: search and replace, manipulation, comparison, hashing, generation, and JSON operations (the last one available since CMake 3.19).

Full details can be found in the online documentation: https://cmake.org/cmake/help/latest/command/string.html.

`string()` modes that accept the `<input>` argument will accept multiple `<input>` values and concatenate them before the execution of the command:

```
string(PREPEND myVariable "a" "b" "c")
```

This is the equivalent of the following:

```
string(PREPEND myVariable "abc")
```

Let's explore all available `string()` modes.

Search and replace

The following modes are available:

- `string(FIND <haystack> <pattern> <out> [REVERSE])` searches for `<pattern>` in the `<haystack>` string and writes the position found as an integer to the `<out>` variable. If the REVERSE flag was used, it searches from the end of the string to the beginning. This works only for ASCII strings (multibyte support isn't provided).

- `string(REPLACE <pattern> <replace> <out> <input>)` replaces all occurrences of `<pattern>` in `<input>` with `<replace>` and stores them in the `<out>` variable.

- `string(REGEX MATCH <pattern> <out> <input>)` regex-matches the first occurrence of `<pattern>` in `<input>` with `<replace>` and stores it in the `<out>` variable.

- `string(REGEX MATCHALL <pattern> <out> <input>)` regex-matches all occurrences of `<pattern>` in `<input>` with `<replace>` and stores them in the `<out>` variable as a comma-separated list.

- `string(REGEX REPLACE <pattern> <replace> <out> <input>)` regex-replaces all occurrences of `<pattern>` in `<input>` with the `<replace>` expression and stores them in the `<out>` variable.

Regular expression operations follow C++ syntax as defined in the standard library in the `<regex>` header. You can use capturing groups to add matches to the `<replace>` expression with numeric placeholders: \\1, \\2... (double backslashes are required so arguments are parsed correctly).

Manipulation

The following modes are available:

- `string(APPEND <out> <input>)` mutates strings stored in `<out>` by appending the `<input>` string.

- `string(PREPEND <out> <input>)` mutates strings stored in `<out>` by prepending the `<input>` string.

- `string(CONCAT <out> <input>)` concatenates all provided `<input>` strings and stores them in the `<out>` variable.

- `string(JOIN <glue> <out> <input>)` interleaves all provided `<input>` strings with a `<glue>` value and stores them as a concatenated string in the `<out>` variable (don't use this mode for list variables).

- `string(TOLOWER <string> <out>)` converts `<string>` to lowercase and stores it in the `<out>` variable.

- `string(TOUPPER <string> <out>)` converts `<string>` to uppercase and stores it in the `<out>` variable.

- `string(LENGTH <string> <out>)` counts the bytes of `<string>` and stores the result in the `<out>` variable.

- `string(SUBSTRING <string> <begin> <length> <out>)` extracts a substring of `<string>` of `<length>` bytes starting at the `<begin>` byte, and stores it in the `<out>` variable. Providing `-1` as the length is understood as "till the end of the string."

- `string(STRIP <string> <out>)` removes trailing and leading whitespace from `<string>` and stores the result in the `<out>` variable.

- `string(GENEX_STRIP <string> <out>)` removes all generator expressions used in `<string>` and stores the result in the `<out>` variable.

- `string(REPEAT <string> <count> <out>)` generates a string containing `<count>` repetitions of `<string>` and stores it in the `<out>` variable.

Comparison

A comparison of strings takes the following form:

```
string(COMPARE <operation> <stringA> <stringB> <out>)
```

The `<operation>` argument is one of the following: `LESS`, `GREATER`, `EQUAL`, `NOTEQUAL`, `LESS_EQUAL`, or `GREATER_EQUAL`. It will be used to compare `<stringA>` with `<stringB>` and the result (`true` or `false`) will be stored in the `<out>` variable.

Hashing

The hashing mode has the following signature:

```
string(<algorithm> <out> <string>)
```

It hashes `<string>` with `<algorithm>` and stores the result in the `<out>` variable. The following algorithms are supported:

- `MD5`: Message-Digest Algorithm 5, RFC 1321
- `SHA1`: US Secure Hash Algorithm 1, RFC 3174
- `SHA224`: US Secure Hash Algorithms, RFC 4634
- `SHA256`: US Secure Hash Algorithms, RFC 4634
- `SHA384`: US Secure Hash Algorithms, RFC 4634
- `SHA512`: US Secure Hash Algorithms, RFC 4634
- `SHA3_224`: Keccak SHA-3
- `SHA3_256`: Keccak SHA-3
- `SHA3_384`: Keccak SHA-3
- `SHA3_512`: Keccak SHA-3

Generation

The following modes are available:

- `string(ASCII <number>... <out>)` stores ASCII characters of given `<number>` in the `<out>` variable.
- `string(HEX <string> <out>)` converts `<string>` to its hexadecimal representation and stores it in the `<out>` variable (since CMake 3.18).

- `string(CONFIGURE <string> <out> [@ONLY] [ESCAPE_QUOTES])` works exactly like `configure_file()` but for strings. The result is stored in the `<out>` variable.

- `string(MAKE_C_IDENTIFIER <string> <out>)` converts non-alphanumeric characters in `<string>` to underscores and stores the result in the `<out>` variable.

- `string(RANDOM [LENGTH <len>] [ALPHABET <alphabet>] [RANDOM_SEED <seed>] <out>)` generates a random string of `<len>` characters (default 5) using the optional `<alphabet>` from the random seed, `<seed>`, and stores the result in the `<out>` variable.

- `string(TIMESTAMP <out> [<format>] [UTC])` generates a string representing the current date and time and stores it in the `<out>` variable.

- `string(UUID <out> ...)` generates a universally unique identifier. This mode is a bit involved to use.

JSON

Operations on JSON-formatted strings use the following signature:

```
string(JSON <out> [ERROR_VARIABLE <error>] <operation + args>)
```

Several operations are available. They all store their results in the `<out>` variable, and errors in the `<error>` variable. Operations and their arguments are as follows:

- GET `<json>` `<member|index>`... returns the value of one or more elements from a `<json>` string using the `<member>` path or `<index>`.

- TYPE `<json>` `<member|index>`... returns the type of one or more elements from a `<json>` string using the `<member>` path or `<index>`.

- MEMBER `<json>` `<member|index>`... `<array-index>` returns the member name of one or more array-typed elements on the `<array-index>` position from the `<json>` string using the `<member>` path or `<index>`.

- LENGTH `<json>` `<member|index>`... returns the element count of one or more array-typed elements from the `<json>` string using the `<member>` path or `<index>`.

- `REMOVE <json> <member|index>...` returns the result of removal of one or more elements from the `<json>` string using the `<member>` path or `<index>`.
- `SET <json> <member|index>... <value>` returns the result of upsertion of `<value>` to one or more elements from a `<json>` string using the `<member>` path or `<index>`.
- `EQUAL <jsonA> <jsonB>` evaluates whether `<jsonA>` and `<jsonB>` are equal.

The list() command

This command provides basic operations on lists: reading, searching, modification, and ordering. Some modes will change list (mutate the original value). Be sure to copy the original value if you'll need it later.

Full details can be found in the online documentation:

`https://cmake.org/cmake/help/latest/command/list.html`

Reading

The following modes are available:

- `list(LENGTH <list> <out>)` counts the elements in the `<list>` variable and stores the result in the `<out>` variable.
- `list(GET <list> <index>... <out>)` copies the `<list>` elements specified with the list of `<index>` indexes to the `<out>` variable.
- `list(JOIN <list> <glue> <out>)` interleaves `<list>` elements with the `<glue>` delimiter and stores the resulting string in the `<out>` variable.
- `list(SUBLIST <list> <begin> <length> <out>)` works like the `GET` mode, but operates on range instead of explicit indexes. If `<length>` is `-1`, elements from `<begin>` index to the end of the list provided in the `<list>` variable will be returned.

Searching

This mode simply finds the index of the `<needle>` element in the `<list>` variable and stores the result in the `<out>` variable (or `-1` if the element wasn't found):

```
list(FIND <list> <needle> <out>)
```

Modification

The following modes are available:

- `list(APPEND <list> <element>...)` adds one or more `<element>` value to the end of the `<list>` variable.

- `list(PREPEND <list> [<element>...])` works like `APPEND`, but adds elements to the beginning of the `<list>` variable.

- `list(FILTER <list> {INCLUDE | EXCLUDE} REGEX <pattern>)` filters the `<list>` variable to `INCLUDE` or `EXCLUDE` the elements matching the `<pattern>` value.

- `list(INSERT <list> <index> [<element>...])` adds one or more `<element>` values to the `<list>` variable at the given `<index>`.

- `list(POP_BACK <list> [<out>...])` removes an element from the end of the `<list>` variable and stores it in the optional `<out>` variable. If multiple `<out>` variables were provided, more elements will be removed to fill them.

- `list(POP_FRONT <list> [<out>...])` works like `POP_BACK` but removes an element from the beginning of the `<list>` variable.

- `list(REMOVE_ITEM <list> <value>...)` shorthand for `FILTER EXCLUDE`, but without the support of regular expressions.

- `list(REMOVE_AT <list> <index>...)` removes elements from `<list>` at a specific `<index>`.

- `list(REMOVE_DUPLICATES <list>)` removes duplicates from `<list>`.

- `list(TRANSFORM <list> <action> [<selector>] [OUTPUT_VARIABLE <out>])` applies a specific transformation to the `<list>` elements. By default, the action is applied to all elements, but we may limit the effect by adding a `<selector>`. Provided list will be mutated (changed in place) unless the `OUTPUT_VARIABLE` keyword was provided, in which case, the result is stored in the `<out>` variable.

    The following selectors are available: `AT <index>`, `FOR <start> <stop> [<step>]`, and `REGEX <pattern>`.

    Actions include `APPEND <string>`, `PREPEND <string>`, `TOLOWER`, `TOUPPER`, `STRIP`, `GENEX_STRIP`, and `REPLACE <pattern> <expression>`. They work exactly like the `string()` modes with the same name.

Ordering

The following modes are available:

- `list(REVERSE <list>)` simply reverses the order of `<list>`.
- `list(SORT <list>)` sorts the list alphabetically. Refer to the online manual for more advanced options.

The file() command

This command provides all kinds of operations related to files: reading, transferring, locking, and archiving. It also provides modes to inspect the filesystem and operations on strings representing paths.

Full details can be found in the online documentation:

`https://cmake.org/cmake/help/latest/command/file.html`

Reading

The following modes are available:

- `file(READ <filename> <out> [OFFSET <o>] [LIMIT <max>] [HEX])` reads the file from `<filename>` to the `<out>` variable. The read optionally starts at offset `<o>` and follows the optional limit of `<max>` bytes. The `HEX flag` specifies that output should be converted to hexadecimal representation.
- `file(STRINGS <filename> <out>)` reads strings from the file at `<filename>` to the `<out>` variable.
- `file(<algorithm> <filename> <out>)` computes the `<algorithm>` hash from the file at `<filename>` and stores the result in the `<out>` variable. Available algorithms are the same as for the `string()` hashing function.
- `file(TIMESTAMP <filename> <out> [<format>])` generates a string representation of a timestamp of the file at `<filename>` and stores it in the `<out>` variable. Optionally accepts a `<format>` string.
- `file(GET_RUNTIME_DEPENDENCIES [...])` gets runtime dependencies for specified files. This is an advanced command to be used only in `install(CODE)` or `install(SCRIPT)` scenarios.

Writing

The following modes are available:

- `file({WRITE | APPEND} <filename> <content>...)` writes or appends all `<content>` arguments to the file at `<filename>`. If the provided system path doesn't exist, it will be recursively created.

- `file({TOUCH | TOUCH_NOCREATE} [<filename>...])` updates the timestamp of the `<filename>`. If the file doesn't exist, it will only be created in the TOUCH mode.

- `file(GENERATE OUTPUT <output-file> [...])` is an advanced mode that generates an output file for each build configuration of the current CMake Generator.

- `file(CONFIGURE OUTPUT <output-file> CONTENT <content> [...])` works like GENERATE_OUTPUT, but also configures the generated files by substituting variable placeholders with values.

Filesystem

The following modes are available:

- `file({GLOB | GLOB_RECURSE} <out> [...] [<globbing-expression>...])` generates a list of files matching `<globbing-expression>` and stores it in the `<out>` variable. GLOB_RECURSE mode will also scan nested directories.

- `file(RENAME <oldname> <newname>)` moves a file from `<oldname>` to `<newname>`.

- `file({REMOVE | REMOVE_RECURSE } [<files>...])` deletes `<files>`. REMOVE_RECURSE will also remove directories.

- `file(MAKE_DIRECTORY [<dir>...])` creates a directory.

- `file(COPY <file>... DESTINATION <dir> [...])` copies `files` to the `<dir>` destination. Offers options for filtering, setting permissions, symlink chain following, and more.

- `file(SIZE <filename> <out>)` reads the size of `<filename>` in bytes and stores it in the `<out>` variable.

- `file(READ_SYMLINK <linkname> <out>)` reads the destination path of the `<linkname>` symlink and stores it in the `<out>` variable.

- `file(CREATE_LINK <original> <linkname> [...])` creates a symlink to `<original>` at `<linkname>`.
- `file({CHMOD|CHMOD_RECURSE} <files>... <directories>... PERMISSIONS <permissions>... [...])` sets permissions on files and directories.

Path conversion

The following modes are available:

- `file(REAL_PATH <path> <out> [BASE_DIRECTORY <dir>])` computes the absolute path from the relative path and stores it in the `<out>` variable. Optionally accepts the `<dir>` base directory. It's been available since CMake 3.19.
- `file(RELATIVE_PATH <out> <directory> <file>)` computes the `<file>` path relative to `<directory>` and stores it in the `<out>` variable.
- `file({TO_CMAKE_PATH | TO_NATIVE_PATH} <path> <out>)` converts `<path>` to a CMake path (directories separated with a forward slash) to the native path of the platform and back. The result is stored in the `<out>` variable.

Transfer

The following modes are available:

- `file(DOWNLOAD <url> [<path>] [...])` downloads a file from `<url>` and stores it in path.
- `file(UPLOAD <file> <url> [...])` uploads `<file>` to an URL.

Locking

Locking mode places an advisory lock on the `<path>` resource:

```
file(LOCK <path> [DIRECTORY] [RELEASE]
     [GUARD <FUNCTION|FILE|PROCESS>]
     [RESULT_VARIABLE <out>]
     [TIMEOUT <seconds>])
```

This lock can be optionally scoped to `FUNCTION`, `FILE`, or `PROCESS` and limited with a timeout of `<seconds>`. To release the lock, provide the `RELEASE` keyword. The result will be stored in the `<out>` variable.

Archiving

The creation of archives is provided with the following signature:

```
file(ARCHIVE_CREATE OUTPUT <destination> PATHS <source>...
  [FORMAT <format>]
  [COMPRESSION <type> [COMPRESSION_LEVEL <level>]]
  [MTIME <mtime>] [VERBOSE])
```

It creates an archive at the `<destination>` path comprising `<source>` files in one of the supported formats: `7zip`, `gnutar`, `pax`, `paxr`, `raw`, or `zip` (`paxr` is the default). If the chosen format supports the compression level, it can be provided as a single-digit integer `0-9`, with `0` being the default.

The extraction mode has the following signature:

```
file(ARCHIVE_EXTRACT INPUT <archive> [DESTINATION <dir>]
  [PATTERNS <patterns>...] [LIST_ONLY] [VERBOSE])
```

It extracts files matching optional `<patterns>` values from `<archive>` to the destination `<dir>`. If the `LIST_ONLY` keyword is provided, files won't be extracted, but only listed instead.

The math() command

CMake also supports some simple arithmetical operations. See the online documentation for full details:

`https://cmake.org/cmake/help/latest/command/math.html`

To evaluate a mathematical expression and store it in the `<out>` variable as the string in an optional `<format>` (`HEXADECIMAL` or `DECIMAL`), use the following signature:

```
math(EXPR <out> "<expression>" [OUTPUT_FORMAT <format>])
```

The `<expression>` value is a string that supports operators present in C code (they have the same meaning here):

- Arithmetical: `+`, `-`, `*`, `/`, `%` modulo division
- Bitwise: `|` or, `&` and, `^` xor, `~` not, `<<` shift left, `>>` shift right
- Parenthesis (...)

Constant values can be provided in decimal or hexadecimal format.

Index

Symbols

7-bit ASCII text files 45

A

abbreviated variables 100
AddClangTidy function 299
add_custom_target() command 118
advanced config files
  creating 353-356
alias targets 129
AppleClang 156
architecture
  32-bit 102
  64-bit 102
  big-endian 103
  little-endian 103
automated tests
  limitations 246, 247

B

basic config files
  writing 350-352
behavior-driven development (BDD) 267
binary tree 30

bracket arguments 49, 50
break() loop 68
build
  debugging 178
  individual stages, debugging 178, 179
build-and-test mode 250, 251
builder
  issues, debugging with header
    file inclusion 180
build root 30
buildsystem 8
build targets 130, 131
build tool 8
build tree 7, 30, 31
Byte Order Markers (BOM) 45

C

C++20 modules 175
C++ program
  creating 153
  running 153
C++ source code
  compilation 5
C++ standard
  setting 103, 104

Cachegrind 303
cache variables
　using 57, 58
Calc Console executable
　building 383-388
Calc library
　building 381-383
Callgrind 303
Catch2
　about 204, 267-270
　URL 267
ccmake 14
CCMake 29
CDash
　URL 249
CI/CD pipeline 92
Clang 156
Clang-Format 293
Clang-Tidy
　about 301
　reference link 298
CLion 92
cmake 14
CMake
　about 6, 10
　building, from source 14
　building stage 8-10
　configuration stage 7
　features 6, 7
　generation stage 8
　installing, on Docker 11
　installing, on Linux 13
　installing, on macOS 13
　installing, on Windows 12
　operation modes 15
　reference link 236
　reference link, for documentation 10

　stages 8, 9
　URL 10
　working 7
CMakeCache.txt 33, 34
CMake-GUI
　accessing 28
cmake-gui utility 8, 14
cmake_install.cmake file 35
CMake Language syntax 45
CMakeLists.txt 32
cmake_minimum_required() 85
CMakePresets.json file 35-37
CMakeUserPresets.json file 35-38
code coverage report 282-286
code formatting
　enforcing 292-297
command arguments
　about 47-49
　bracket arguments 49, 50
　quoted arguments 50, 51
　unquoted arguments 51-53
command definitions 70
command invocations 47, 48
command-line tool
　running 26
commands, for scripts
　execute_process() 79
　file() 79
　include() 78, 79
　include_guard() 79
　message() 76-78
comments
　about 45
　avoiding 47
　good comments, guidelines 46
　multiline comments 46
　single-line comments 45
comparison operations 66

compilation
    basics 152
    process, managing 171
    working 153
compilation time
    reducing 171
compiled version
    tracking, with git commit 161, 162
compiler features
    checking 106
components
    defining 359
    using, in find_package() 359
    using, in install() command 360, 361
Concurrent Versions System (CVS) 228
conditional blocks 63
conditional commands
    syntax 64
conditional expressions
    about 137
    versus evaluation of BOOL
        operator 146, 147
config-file 209
Config-files 34
conflicting propagated properties
    managing 126-128
continue() loop 68
continuous integration/continuous
        deployment (CI/CD) 248
control structures 63
coverage module
    preparing 390, 391
cpack 14
CPack
    about 27
    using, for packaging 362-365, 401
CPackConfig.cmake file 35
CPP-Check 298

cppchecker
    reference link 298
Cpplint 301
cross-compilation
    about 100
    reference link 100
ctest 14
CTest
    about 27
    basic unit test, creating 257-262
    commands 48
    using, to standardize testing 248
CTestTestfile.cmake file 35
custom commands
    using, as generator 132, 133
    using, as target hook 134
    writing 131
custom find-module
    writing 219-223
custom targets 118
CXX_STANDARD property 104

D

debugger
    information, providing for 181, 182
dependencies
    installed packages, finding 209-214
    visualizing 121, 122
dependency graph 118-120
dependency injection (DI) 275
destination path
    for platforms 334
directory scope 59
disassembler 181
Docker
    CMake, installing on 11
    URL 11

documentation
  modern design, generating 321, 322
Doxygen
  adding, to project 314
  documentation formats 314
  documentation, generating 315-321
  reference link 314
dynamically linked duplicated symbols 197-199
Dynamically Linked Libraries (DLL) 141
dynamic analysis
  with Valgrind 303

E

endianness
  of system 103
environment
  scoping 99
environment variables
  using 55, 56
errors
  configuring 177
evaluation of BOOL operator
  versus conditional expression 146, 147
evaluation to Boolean, generator expressions
  logical operators 138
  string comparison 138
  variable queries 139, 140
evaluation to string, generator expressions
  escaping 142
  output-related expressions 143
  string transformations 142, 143
  target-dependent queries 141, 142
  variable queries 140
executable
  directory structure 95

Executable and Linkable Format (ELF) 153
execute_process() command 79
ExternalProject module
  about 229
  dependencies, downloading from CVS 233
  dependencies, downloading from Git 232
  dependencies, downloading from Mercurial 233
  dependencies, downloading from Subversion 233
  dependencies, downloading from URL 231, 232
  features 230
  patch step options 234
  reference link 234
  step options, downloading 231
  step options, updating 233
  using 230-236
external projects 92

F

fake 274
FakeIt
  URL 271
FetchContent module
  about 229, 236
  using 236-240
file() command
  about 79, 418
  archiving mode 421
  extraction mode 421
  filesystem modes 419
  locking mode 420
  path conversion modes 420

Index   427

reading modes 418
reference link 418
transfer modes 420
writing modes 419
files
  ignoring, in Git 39
file sets
  installing, with
      install(FILES|PROGRAMS) 337-339
filesystem
  examining 67, 68
FindCURL module 42
Find-module 34, 41
find modules 209
find_package()
  about 42, 209
  components, using 359
  reference link 214
FindPkgConfig
  legacy packages, discovering
      with 215-218
  reference link 218
foreach() loop 68, 70
Functional Terminal (X) User
      Interface (FTXUI) 377
function() command 70
function inlining 167, 168
functions 72, 73
function scope 59

G

generator
  custom command, using as 132, 133
generator expressions
  about 8, 135
  build configurations 144

interface libraries, with
    compiler-specific flags 145
nested generator expressions 145, 146
system-specific one-liners 144
generator expressions, evaluation
  about 137
  to Boolean 138
  to string 140
generator expressions, general syntax
  about 136
  conditional expressions 137
  nesting 136, 137
Git
  files, ignoring 39
git commit
  using, to track compiled
      version 161, 162
Git repositories
  automatic Git submodule
      initialization 227, 228
  external libraries, providing through
      Git submodules 224-226
  Git-cloning dependencies 228, 229
  working with 224
Git submodules 224
Global Offset Table (GOT) 194
GMock
  about 274
  using 275-280
GNU 156
GNU Compiler Collection (GCC) 282
GNU Coverage Data 287
GNU Coverage Notes 287
GoogleTest 204
Graphviz
  URL 121

GTest
  about 267, 271
  URL 267
  using 271-274

H

headers
  configuring 162, 163
  precompilation 171-173
Helgrind 303
hello.cpp application 5
helper tool 216
help mode
  syntax 26
Hippomocks
  URL 271
host system 100
host system information 101, 102

I

imported targets 128
include() command 78, 79
included files
  paths, providing to 158
include_guard() command 79
include-what-you-use
  about 302
  URL 298
initial configuration 155
in-source builds
  about 31
  disabling 108, 109
install() command
  components, using 360, 361
install(FILES|PROGRAMS)
  used, for installing file sets 337-339

integrated development
    environment (IDE) 92, 248
Intel 156
interface libraries 129, 130
interprocedural optimization 105

J

jumbo build 173, 174

K

Kitware 109

L

languages
  defining 86, 87
LCOV 282
legacy packages
  discovering, with
      FindPkgConfig 215-218
library
  directory structure 96
library types
  building 191
linking
  basics 186-188
  order 200, 201
link-what-you-use 302
Linux
  CMake, installing on 13
list() command
  about 416
  modification modes 417
  ordering modes 418
  reading modes 416

reference link 416
searching modes 416
listfiles 31
lists
  using 61-63
logical operators 64
logical targets
  installing 332, 333
loops
  about 68
  foreach() 68-70
  while() 68
loop unrolling 168, 169
loop vectorization 170
low-level installation 336

M

macOS
  CMake, installing on 13
macro() command 70
macros 71, 72
main() function
  using 203, 204
makefiles 92
Massif 303
math() command
  about 421
  reference link 421
Memcheck 303-307
Memcheck-cover 308-310
Memcheck module
  preparing 392, 393
memory management unit (MMU) 193
message() command
  about 76
  example 77, 78
  modes 76

metadata
  defining 86, 87
miscellaneous commands
  file() command 418
  list() command 416
  math() command 421
  string() command 412
mock 275
modules, CMake
  reference link 210
MSVC 156
multiline comments 46

N

naming conventions 75
nested generator expressions 145, 146
nested projects 92
nesting 136, 137

O

object file
  about 154
  creating, stages 154, 155
  structure 187-190
object library 376
One Definition Rule (ODR)
  about 194
  issues, solving 195, 196
operating system
  discovering 99
optimizer
  configuring 164, 165
  general level 165, 166
out-of-source builds 31

P

package generators 363
package version files
  generating 357-359
PkgConfig
  reference link 215
position-independent code (PIC) 193, 194
POSIX regex matching 67
preprocessor configuration 158
preprocessor definitions 159, 160
presets 35
procedural paradigm 74, 75
professional projects
  dependencies, building 379-381
  dependencies, managing 379-381
  documentation, providing 401
  file structure 377-379
  installation and packaging 398, 399
  layout 375
  object library 376
  program analysis 388-390
  shared libraries, versus static
    libraries 376, 377
  techniques and tools, for
    planning work 371-374
  testing 388-390
  work, planning 371
professional projects, dependencies
  Calc Console executable,
    building 383-388
  Calc library, building 381-383
professional projects, documentation
  automatic documentation
    generation 402-404
  not-so-technical documents 404-407

professional projects, installation
    and packaging
  binary executables, installing 400
  library, installing 399, 400
  with CPack 401
professional projects, testing
    and program analysis
  coverage module, preparing 390, 391
  Memcheck module, preparing 392, 393
  static analysis tools, adding 396-398
  testing scenarios, applying 393-395
project
  about 83
  building 21
  characteristics 93
  debugging, options 23
  installing, on system 330, 331
  multi-configuration generators,
    options 23
  parallel builds, options 22
  partitioning 87-89
  structuring, for testing 263-266
  structure 93-98
  targets, options 22
project buildsystem
  caching, options 18, 19
  debugging, options 19
  examples 16
  generating 15
  generators, options 16
  presets, options 20
  tracing, options 20
project() command 86
project commands 48
project files
  navigating 30

Index 431

project, installing
  about 24
  components, options 24
  debugging, options 25
  installation directory, options 25
  multi-configuration generators,
      options 24
  permissions, options 24
project root 30
propagation keywords 124, 126
Protobuf
  about 132
  reference link 209
pseudo targets
  about 128
  alias targets 129
  imported targets 128
public headers
  managing 335, 336

Q

quoted arguments 50, 51

R

relocatable targets
  issues 346-348
relocation 188
reusable packages
  creating 346

S

scoped subdirectories 90, 91
script
  about 40

invoking, during installation 344, 345
  running 25
scripting commands 48
SEGFAULT gotcha
  avoiding 287
segment 190
separation of concerns (SoC) 87
separation of stages, CMake GUI
  reference link 42
shared libraries
  about 192
  building 193
  versus static libraries 376, 377
shared modules
  building 193
single-configuration generators
  reference link 42
Single Instruction Multiple
    Data (SIMD) 170
single-line comments 45
Software Under Test (SUT) 393
sources
  managing, for targets 156, 157
source tree 7, 30
stages, to create object files
  assembly 154
  code emission 155
  linguistic analysis 154
  optimization 155
  preprocessing 154
static analysis tools
  adding 396-398
static checkers
  about 301
  Clang-Tidy 301
  cppcheck 301
  Cpplint 301
  include-what-you-use 302

link-what-you-use 302
 using 297-300
static compilation 153
static libraries
 about 191, 192
 building 192
string
 evaluation 64, 65
string() command
 about 412
 comparison mode 414
 generation modes 414
 hashing mode 414
 JSON-formatted string operations 415
 manipulation modes 413
 reference link 412
 search and replace modes 412
stub 274
Subversion (SVN) 228
SunPro 156
symbolic links
 managing, for versioned
  shared libraries 362
system
 endianness 103
system under test (SUT) 248

T

target export files
 about 327
 installing 348-350
target hook
 custom command, using as 134
targets
 about 8, 116
 build targets 130, 131
 creating, commands 117

exporting, without installation 326-329
 properties 122, 123
 pseudo targets 128
 sources, managing for 156, 157
target system 100
test coverage reports
 generating 281
test doubles 274
test file
 compiling 106-108
testing
 projects, structuring for 263-266
testing scenarios
 applying 393-395
test mode 251
tests
 failures, handling 254
 filtering 252
 miscellaneous options 256, 257
 output, controlling 256
 querying 252
 repeating 255
 shuffling 253
toolchain
 configuring 103
trace mode 20
transitive usage requirements 123-126
Trompeloeil
 URL 271

U

undefined symbols
 resolving 201
unified build 173
unit test
 creating, for CTest 257-262

unit-testing frameworks
  about 267
  Catch2 267-270
  GTest 267-271
unit-testing private class fields
  gotchas 160, 161
unit under test (UUT) 264
unity builds
  about 173, 174
  enabling 174
unquoted arguments 51-53
user namespaces 199
UTF-8 45
UTF-16 45
utility modules 41

V

Valgrind
  about 303
  Memcheck 303-307
  Memcheck-cover 308-310
  tools 303
  URL 303
  used, for dynamic analysis 303
values
  comparing 66
variable references 54
variables
  about 53
  evaluation 64, 65
  facts 53
  setting 53, 54
  unsetting 54
variable scope
  using 59-61
vendor-specific extensions 105
Version Control Systems (VCS) 15

versioned shared libraries
  symbolic links, managing for 362
Visual Studio
  URL 13

W

warnings
  configuring 177
while() loop 68
whole directories
  working with 339-343
Windows
  CMake, installing on 12

Y

YAGNI (you aren't gonna need it) 98
yaml-cpp
  reference link 224

Packt.com

Subscribe to our online digital library for full access to over 7,000 books and videos, as well as industry leading tools to help you plan your personal development and advance your career. For more information, please visit our website.

Why subscribe?

- Spend less time learning and more time coding with practical eBooks and Videos from over 4,000 industry professionals
- Improve your learning with Skill Plans built especially for you
- Get a free eBook or video every month
- Fully searchable for easy access to vital information
- Copy and paste, print, and bookmark content

Did you know that Packt offers eBook versions of every book published, with PDF and ePub files available? You can upgrade to the eBook version at packt.com and as a print book customer, you are entitled to a discount on the eBook copy. Get in touch with us at customercare@packtpub.com for more details.

At www.packt.com, you can also read a collection of free technical articles, sign up for a range of free newsletters, and receive exclusive discounts and offers on Packt books and eBooks.

Other Books You May Enjoy

If you enjoyed this book, you may be interested in these other books by Packt:

CMake Cookbook

Radovan Bast, Roberto Di Remigio

ISBN: 978-1-78847-071-1

- Configure, build, test, and install code projects using CMake
- Detect operating systems, processors, libraries, files, and programs for conditional compilation
- Increase the portability of your code
- Refactor a large codebase into modules with the help of CMake
- Build multi-language projects
- Know where and how to tweak CMake configuration files written by somebody else
- Package projects for distribution
- Port projects to CMake

The Art of Writing Efficient Programs

Fedor G. Pikus

ISBN: 978-1-80020-811-7

- Discover how to use the hardware computing resources in your programs effectively
- Understand the relationship between memory order and memory barriers
- Familiarize yourself with the performance implications of different data structures and organizations
- Assess the performance impact of concurrent memory accessed and how to minimize it
- Discover when to use and when not to use lock-free programming techniques
- Explore different ways to improve the effectiveness of compiler optimizations
- Design APIs for concurrent data structures and high-performance data structures to avoid inefficiencies

Packt is searching for authors like you

If you're interested in becoming an author for Packt, please visit `authors.packtpub.com` and apply today. We have worked with thousands of developers and tech professionals, just like you, to help them share their insight with the global tech community. You can make a general application, apply for a specific hot topic that we are recruiting an author for, or submit your own idea.

Share Your Thoughts

Now you've finished *Modern CMake for C++*, we'd love to hear your thoughts! Scan the QR code below to go straight to the Amazon review page for this book and share your feedback or leave a review on the site that you purchased it from.

`https://packt.link/r/1801070059`

Your review is important to us and the tech community and will help us make sure we're delivering excellent quality content.

Printed in Great Britain
by Amazon